CORTINA/GROSSET

BASIC ITALIAN DICTIONARY

ENGLISH-ITALIAN / ITALIAN-ENGLISH

by
Dilaver Berberi, Ph.D.
Assoc. Professor of Linguistics and Languages
St. Mary's College, Notre Dame, Indiana

•

SERIES GENERAL EDITORS
Dilaver Berberi, Ph.D.
Edel A. Winje, Ed.D.

•

Under the Editoral Direction of
R. D. Cortina Co., Inc., New York

A GD/PERIGEE BOOK

OTHER BOOKS IN THIS SERIES:

Basic French Dictionary
Basic Spanish Dictionary
Basic German Dictionary

Perigee Books
are published by
The Putnam Publishing Group
200 Madison Avenue
New York, NY 10016

Published simultaneously in Canada by
General Publishing Co. Limited, Toronto

Library of Congress catalog card number: 73-18524
ISBN 0-399-51297-7

First Perigee Printing 1986
Printed in the United States of America
1 2 3 4 5 6 7 8 9 10

Contents

How to Use This Dictionary — v
Key to Italian Pronunciation — vii
Abbreviations — x
English to Italian — 1
Italian To English — 169
Phrases for Use Abroad — 327
Menu Reader — 337
A Concise Italian Grammar — 343

How to Use This Dictionary

This handy Dictionary was created especially for your needs as a traveler planning to spend a day, a month, or a year in Italy. It can be used equally well by beginners and by readers who already have a knowledge of Italian.

The entries number over 10,000 (5000-plus in the English-Italian section, 5000-plus in the Italian-English). In choosing English entries, the needs and concerns of a traveler have been carefully considered: what situations is he most likely to encounter, and what words and phrases is he most likely to need? Italian entries were selected from words that occur most frequently in the course of everyday life in Italy. Thus you will find here the words you are actually hearing and seeing most often during your stay.

Special Features of This Dictionary

In addition to the entries themselves, this Dictionary includes the following extra features to enable you to actually use the Italian language during your travels.

Guide to Pronunciation. The pronunciation of each Italian entry is given in simple English transcriptions. Thus the user can pronounce a new word immediately, just by following the simple guide which appears with each entry. The "Key to Italian Pronunciation," found on page vii, explains Italian sounds and gives examples of each one, and shows how they compare with English.

Concise Italian Grammar. For the user who wishes a quick overview of Italian grammar or an explanation of how verbs are conjugated or noun plurals formed, this Grammar is an invaluable aid. It is divided into sections treating nouns, verbs, adjectives, adverbs, and so on for easy reference and use.

Helpful Notes for the Reader

1. *All verbs* are marked *v.*, and irregular verbs are marked *irreg.* Tables of irregular verbs showing their conjugation appear at the end of the "Concise Grammar," which explains the conjugation of regular verbs.

2. *Reflexive verbs* are those that have the suffix *-si*. These are always used with the reflexive pronoun. See the "Concise Grammar" for an explanation of the use of these verbs.

3. *All Italian nouns* have a designated gender. Regularly, nouns ending in *-o* are masculine, and those ending in *-a* are feminine. Exceptions, and all other nouns, are marked *m.* or *f.* in the Dictionary. The formation of plurals of regular nouns is explained in the "Concise Grammar." Irregular plurals are given in the Dictionary along with the singular form.

4. *Adjectives* must agree in gender and number with the nouns they modify. "Gender" adjectives regularly have four forms for masculine and feminine, singular and plural, ending in *-o*, *-a*, *-i*, and *-e*. "Neuter" adjectives, ending in *-e* (singular) and *-i* (plural), are the same for both masculine and feminine.

5. *Parts of speech* of entries (except verbs) are not marked unless the translation does not indicate the part of speech or if the word appears more than once as different parts of speech.

6. *Many common or idiomatic expressions* are included in the Dictionary, along with their pronunciation, so that the reader can use them correctly.

Using this Dictionary before and during your trip is sure to make your contact with the Italian people and their language much more pleasurable and satisfying.

Key to Italian Pronunciation

Vowels

Unlike English vowels, Italian vowels are always pronounced the same no matter where they occur in a word. They will be transcribed, however, according to their English pronunciation. There are five vowel sounds in Italian: *i*, *e*, *u*, *o*, *a*. The following is an approximate English pronunciation of Italian vowels:

Italian spelling	*Phonetic symbol*	*Sound description & examples*
i	ee	as *i* in mach*i*ne, or as *ee* in p*ee*l, or *ea* in m*ea*t. *Ex.*: **cabina** [*kah-bee'-nah*] cabin
e	eh	as *e* in n*e*ver, in b*e*t, as the *e* (without *y*) in fate. *Ex.*: **mela** [*meh'-lah*] apple; **fedele** [*feh-deh'-leh*] faithful
u	oo	as *u* in p*u*t or as *oo* in f*oo*t. *Ex.*: **sucursale** [*soo-koor-sah'-leh*] branch
o	oh	as *o* in n*o*rth or z*o*ne. *Ex.*: **poco** [*poh'-koh*] little, few; **solo** [*soh'-loh*] alone
a	ah	as *a* in f*a*ther, b*a*rter, c*a*rbon. *Ex.*: **casa** [*kah'-zah*] house; **cassa** [*kahs'-sah*] case, box

Diphthongs

For diphthongs or two adjacent vowels, each vowel will be transcribed with its phonetic symbol:

ieri [*ee-eh'-ree*] yesterday
maiale [*mah-ee-ah'-leh*] pig
sei [*seh'-ee*] six; you (sing.) are
lui [*loo'-ee*] he
suoi [*soo-oh'-ee*] his, hers, yours (sing.) [polite form]

Consonants

Italian consonants *p*, *b*, *t*, *d*, *g*, *f*, *v*, *m*, and *n* are pronounced approximately like their English counterparts.

Italian spelling	*Phonetic symbol*	*Sound description & examples*
h		is never pronounced in Italian. *Ex.*: **ho** [*oh*] I have; **hanno** [*ahn'-noh*] they have; **laghi** [*lah'-gee*] lakes
l	l	is always pronounced like the first *l* in *l*ittle, never as the second one. *Ex.*: **la luna** [*lah loo'-nah*] the moon
r	r	is pronounced with the tip of the tongue touching the upper teeth quickly and vibrating. *Ex.*: **caro** [*kah'*-roh] dear; **rame** [*rah'-meh*] copper; **Roma** [*roh'-mah*] Rome
c	ch	before vowels *i* and *e* as *ch* in *ch*ip or *ch*eat. *Ex.*: **cima** [*chee'-mah*] peak; **cena** [*cheh'-nah*] dinner
c	k	as *k* before consonants (including *h*) and before vowels *a*, *o*, *u*. *Ex.*: **carta** [*kahr'-tah*] paper; **crema** [*kreh'-mah*] cream; **pochi** [*poh'-kee*] few
g		before vowels *i* and *e* as *j* in *j*ello and *j*ust. *Ex.*: **giorno** [*jee-ohr'-noh*] day; **gesso** [*jehs'-soh*] chalk; **giacca** [*jee-ahk'-kah*] jacket
g	g	as *g* in *g*o before a consonant (including *h*) and before vowels *a*, *o*, *u*. *Ex.*: **gara** [*gah'-rah*] race; **grazie** [*grah'-tsee-eh*] thank you; **ghiotto** [*gee-oht'-toh*] greedy
gn	ny	as *ny* in ca*ny*on. *Ex.*: **agnello** [*ah-nyeh'-loh*] lamb; **signore** [*see-nyoh'-reh*] sir
gl	ly	as *lli* in mi*lli*on. *Ex.*: **maglia** [*mah'-lyah*] blouse; **egli** [*eh'-lyee*] he. EXCEPTIONS: **negligenza** [*nehg-lee-jehn'-tsah*] negli-

		gence; **glicerina** [*glee-cheh-ree'-nah*] glycerine
s	s	as in *s*in at the beginning of a word and with a voiceless consonant *p*, *t*, *k*, and *f*. *Ex.*: **sete** [*seh'-teh*] thirst; **sperare** [*speh-rah'-reh*] hope; **psicologia** [*psee-koh-loh-jee'-ah*] psychology
s	z	as in *z*ebra or *z*one between two vowels and before a voiced consonant *b*, *d*, *g*, *v*, *l*, *r*, *m*, *n*. *Ex.*: **casa** [*kah'-zah*] house; **mese** [*meh'-zeh*] month; **sbaglio** [*zbah'-lyoh*] mistake
sc	sh	as in *sh*ip or *sh*ot before vowels *i* and *e*. *Ex.*: **scena** [*sheh'-nah*] scene; **scimmia** [*sheem'-mee-ah*] monkey
sc	sk	as in *sk*irt or *sk*ull before vowels *a*, *o*, *u* and before a consonant. *Ex.*: **scarpa** [*skahr'-pah*] shoe; **scritto** [*skreet'-toh*] written
z	ts	as in ca*ts*. *Ex.*: **lezione** [*leh-tsee-oh'-neh*] lesson; **pezzo** [*pehts'-tsoh*] piece
z	dz	as in be*ds*. *Ex.*: **zio** [*dzee'-oh*] uncle; **mezzo** [*mehdz'-dzoh*] half
qu	koo	as in *qu*est. *Ex.*: **quando** [*koo-ahn'-doh*] when; **quindi** [*koo-een'-dee*] then

Double Consonants

Double consonants are pronounced like single consonants but longer and stronger. The following are contrasts between single and double consonants:

caro [*kah'-roh*] dear	**carro** [*kahr'-roh*] cart
sete [*seh'-teh*] thirsty	**sette** [*seht'-teh*] seven
sano [*sah'-noh*] healthy	**sanno** [*sahn'-noh*] they know
bruto [*broo'-toh*] brute	**brutto** [*broot'-toh*] ugly

Accent or Stress

Accent or stress in Italian words usually falls on the next to the last syllable. Sometimes, however, it falls on the third from the last or on the last syllable. When the stress falls on the last syllable, the vowel is stressed also in Italian spelling with a grave accent: **città,** city; **gioventù,** youth; **finì,** he finished

Accent in this Dictionary is marked in the transcription of the word with a primary stress symbol on the stressed syllable:

matematica [*mah-teh-mah'-tee-kah*] mathematics
prendere [*prehn'-deh-reh*] take
mangiare [*mahn-jee-ah'-reh*] eat

Abbreviations Used in This Dictionary

adj.	adjective	*interr*	interrogative
adv.	adverb	*invar.*	invariable
anat.	anatomy	*irreg.*	irregular
arch.	architecture	*m.*	masculine
art.	article	*naut.*	nautical
Aux.	auxiliary verb	*n.*	noun
bot.	botanical	*obj.*	object
conj.	conjunction	*pers.*	person, personal
dem.	demonstrative	*pl.*	plural
eccl.	ecclesiastic	*prep.*	preposition
Ex.	example	*pron.*	pronoun
f.	feminine	*rel.*	relative
geog.	geographic	*sing.*	singular
indecl.	indeclinable	*subj.*	subject
interj.	interjection	*v.*	verb

English / Italian

A

a, un, uno, una, un' [*oon, oo'-noh, oo'-nah, oon*]
abandon *v.*, abbandonare [*ahb-bahn-doh-nah'-reh*]
abbey, abbazia, badia [*ahb-bah-tsee'-ah, bah-dee'-ah*]
abbreviation, abbreviazione (f) [*ahb-breh-vee-ah-tsee-oh'-neh*]
abdomen, addome (m) [*ahd-doh'-meh*]
ability, abilità, capacità (f, indecl) [*ah-bee-lee-tah', kah-pah-chee-tah'*]
able *adj.*, abile, capace [*ah'-bee-leh, kah-pah'-cheh*]
  be able [can, may] *v.*, potere (irreg) [*poh-teh'-reh*]
aboard *adv.* & *prep.*, a bordo, a bordo di [*ah bohr'-doh, ah bohr'-doh dee*]
abolish *v.*, abolire [*ah-boh-lee'-reh*]
about [approximately] *adv.*, circa, verso [*cheer'-kah, vehr'-soh*]
about [around] *adv.*, intorno [*een-tohr'-noh*]
above *prep.*, su, sopra [*soo, soh'-prah*]
  above all, soprattutto [*soh-praht-toot'-toh*]
above-mentioned *adj.*, suddetto [*soo-deht'-toh*]
abroad *adv.*, all'estero [*ahl-lehs'-teh-roh*]
absence, assenza [*ahs-sehn'-tsah*]
absent *adj.*, assente [*ahs-sehn'-teh*]
absent-minded, distratto [*dees-traht'-toh*]
absolute *adj.*, assoluto [*ahs-soh-loo'-toh*]
absolutely, assolutamente [*ahs-soh-loo-tah-mehn'-teh*]
absorb *v.*, assorbire [*ahs-sohr-bee'-reh*]
abstract *adj.*, astratto [*ahs-traht'-toh*]
absurd, assurdo [*ahs-soor'-doh*]
abundance, abbondanza [*ahb-bohn-dahn'-tsah*]
abundant, abbondante [*ahb-bohn-dahn'-teh*]
abuse *v.*, abusare [*ah-boo-zah'-reh*]
academy, accademia [*ahk-kah-deh'-mee-ah*]
accelerate *v.*, accelerare [*ahch-cheh-leh-rah'-reh*]
accelerator, acceleratore (m) [*ahch-cheh-leh-rah-toh'-reh*]

accent *n.*, accento [*ahch-chehn'-toh*]
accept *v.*, accettare [*ahch-cheht-tah'-reh*]
acceptable, accettabile [*ahch-cheht-tah'-bee-leh*]
access, accesso [*ahch-chehs'-soh*]
accessible, accessibile [*ahch-chehs-see'-bee-leh*]
accident [auto, etc.], incidente (m) [*een-chee-dehn'-teh*]
accidental, accidentale [*ahch-chee-dehn-tah'-leh*]
accommodation, accomodamento [*ahk-koh-moh-dah-mehn'-toh*]
accompany *v.*, accompagnare [*ahk-kohm-pah-nyah'-reh*]
accomplish *v.*, compiere, realizzare [*kohm'-pee-eh-reh, reh-ah-leedz-dzah'-reh*]
accomplishment, compimento [*kohm-pee-mehn'-toh*]
accord *n.*, accordo [*ahk-kohr'-doh*]
accordingly, in/di conseguenza [*een/dee kohn-seh-goo-ehn'-tsah*]
according to, secondo a [*seh-kohn'-doh ah*]
account *n.*, conto, conteggio [*kohn'-toh, kohn-tehj'-jee-oh*]
  bank account, conto in banca [*kohn'-toh een bahn'-kah*]
  on account of, a causa di [*ah kah'-oo-sah dee*]
  settle an account *v.*, regolare un conto [*reh-goh-lah'-reh oon kohn'-toh*]
  statement of account, estratto conto [*ehs-traht'-toh kohn'-toh*]
  withdraw from an account, prelevare da un conto [*preh-leh-vah'-reh dah oon kohn'-toh*]
accountant, contabile (m), ragioniere (m) [*kohn-tah'-bee-leh, rah-jee-oh-nee-eh'-reh*]
accuracy, accuratezza, esattezza [*ahk-koo-rah-tehts'-tsah, eh-zaht-tehts'-tsah*]
accurate, esatto, giusto [*eh-saht'-toh, jee-oos'-toh*]
accusation, accusa [*ahk-koo'-zah*]
accuse *v.*, accusare [*ahk-koo-zah'-reh*]
accustom [oneself] *v.*, abituarsi [*ah-bee-too-ahr'-see*]
  be accustomed to, essere abituato [*ehs'-seh-reh ah-bee-too-ah'-toh*]
ace [card], asso [*ahs'-soh*]
ace [fig.], campione (m) [*kahm-pee-oh'-neh*]

ache *n.*, dolore (m), male (m) [*doh-loh'-reh, mah'-leh*]
headache, mal di testa [*mahl dee tehs'-tah*]
ache *v.*, far male [*fahr mah'-leh*]
achieve *v.*, compiere [*kohm'-pee-eh-reh*]
acid *n. & adj.*, acido [*ah'-chee-doh*]
acknowledge *v.*, riconoscere, ammettere [*ree-koh-noh'-sheh-reh, ah-meht'-teh-reh*]
acquaint *v.*, informare, far sapere a [*een-fohr-mah'-reh, fahr sah-peh'-reh ah*]
acquaintance, conoscenza [*koh-noh-shehn'-tsah*]
acquire *v.*, acquistare [*ahk-koo-ees-tah'-reh*]
acquisition, acquisizione (f) [*ahk-koo-ee-zee-tsee-oh'-neh*]
acquit *v.*, assolvere [*ahs-sohl'-veh-reh*]
acre *n.*, acro [*ahk'-roh*]
across *adv. & prep.*, attraverso [*aht-trah-vehr'-soh*]
act *n.*, atto [*aht'-toh*]
action, azione (f) [*ahts-ee-oh'-neh*]
act [do] *v.*, agire, fare [*ah-jee'-reh, fah'-reh*]
act [represent] *v.*, recitare [*reh-chee-tah'-reh*]
active, attivo [*aht-tee'-voh*]
activity, attività (f, indecl) [*aht-tee-vee-tah'*]
actor, actress, attore (m), attrice (f) [*aht-toh'-reh, aht-tree'-cheh*]
actual, attuale, reale [*aht-too-ah'-leh, reh-ah'-leh*]
actually, attualmente [*aht-too-ahl-mehn'-teh*]
adapt *v.*, adattare [*ah-daht-tah'-reh*]
add *v.*, aggiungere [*ahj-jee-oon'-jeh-reh*]
add up [arith.], addizionare, sommare [*ahd-dee-tsee-oh-nah'-reh, sohm-mah'-reh*]
addition, addizione (f) [*ahd-dee-tsee-oh'-neh*]
additional *adj.*, supplementare [*soop-pleh-mehn-tah'-reh*]
address [place] *n.*, indirizzo [*een-dee-reets'-tsoh*]
address [speech] *n.*, discorso [*dees-kohr'-soh*]
address [a letter] *v.*, indirizzare [*een-dee-reets-tsah'-reh*]
address [speak] *v.*, rivolgere la parola a [*ree-vohl'-jeh-reh lah pah-roh'-lah ah*]
adept *adj.*, esperto [*ehs-pehr'-toh*]
adequate, adeguato [*ah-deh-goo-ah'-toh*]

adhesive *adj.* & *n.*, adesivo [*ah-deh-see'-voh*]
adjacent, adiacente [*ah-dee-ah-chehn'-teh*]
adjective, aggettivo [*ahj-jeht-tee'-voh*]
adjoining, attiguo, contiguo [*aht-tee'-goo-oh, kohn-tee'-goo-oh*]
adjust *v.*, aggiustare [*ahj-jee-oos-tah'-reh*]
adjustment, adattamento [*ah-daht-tah-mehn'-toh*]
administer *v.*, amministrare [*ahm-mee-nees-trah'-reh*]
administration, amministrazione (f) [*ahm-mee-nees-trah-tsee-oh'-neh*]
admirable, ammirabile [*ahm-mee-rah'-bee-leh*]
admiral, ammiraglio [*ahm-mee-rah'-lyoh*]
admiration, ammirazione (f) [*ahm-mee-rah-tsee-oh'-neh*]
admire *v.*, ammirare [*ahm-mee-rah'-reh*]
admirer, ammiratore (m) [*ahm-mee-rah-toh'-reh*]
admission [entry], ammissione (f) [*ahm-mees-see-oh'-neh*]
admit *v.*, ammettere [*ahm-meht'-teh-reh*]
admittance, ammissione (f), ingresso [*ahm-mees-see-oh'-neh, een-grehs'-soh*]
  no admittance, vietato l'ingresso [*vee-eh-tah'-toh leen-grehs'-soh*]
adopt *v.*, adottare [*ah-doht-tah'-reh*]
adoption, adozione (f) [*ah-doh-tsee-oh'-neh*]
adorable, adorabile [*ah-doh-rah'-bee-leh*]
adore *v.*, adorare, venerare [*ah-doh-rah'-reh, veh-neh-rah'-reh*]
adorn *v.*, adornare [*ah-dohr-nah'-reh*]
adult, adulto [*ah-dool'-toh*]
advance [motion] *n.*, avanzamento [*ah-vahn-tsah-mehn'-toh*]
  in advance, in anticipo [*een ahn-tee'-chee-poh*]
advance *v.*, avanzare, progredire [*ah-vahn-tsah'-reh, proh-greh-dee'-reh*]
advantage, vantaggio, beneficio [*vahn-tahj'-jee-oh, beh-neh-fee'-chee-oh*]
adverse, contrario, ostile [*kohn-trah'-ree-oh, ohs-tee'-leh*]
adventure, avventura [*ahv-vehn-too'-rah*]
adverb, avverbio [*ahv-vehr'-bee-oh*]
adversary, avversario [*ahv-vehr-sah'-ree-oh*]

advertise *v.*, reclamizzare, fare pubblicità [*rehk-klah-meedz-dzah'-reh, fah'-reh poob-blee-chee-tah'*]
advertisement, pubblicità (f, indecl), reclame (f) [*poob-blee-chee-tah', reh'-klah-meh*]
advice, consiglio [*kohn-see'-lyoh*]
advise *v.*, consigliare [*kohn-see-lyah'-reh*]
affair, affare (m), faccenda [*ahf-fah'-reh, fahch-chehn'-dah*]
affect *v.*, influenzare, riguardare [*een-floo-ehn-tsah'-reh, ree-goo-ahr-dah'-reh*]
affection, affezione (f), amore (m) [*ahf-feh-tsee-oh'-neh, ah-moh'-reh*]
affectionate, affettuoso [*ahf-feht-too-oh'-zoh*]
affectionately [close of letter], affettuosamente [*ahf-feht-too-oh-zah-mehn'-teh*]
affirm *v.*, affermare [*ahf-fehr-mah'-reh*]
affirmative *adj.*, affermativo [*ahf-fehr-mah-tee'-voh*]
afflict *v.*, affliggere [*ahf-fleej'-jeh-reh*]
affliction, afflizione (f) [*ahf-flee-tsee-oh'-neh*]
afloat *adv.*, a galla [*ah gahl'-lah*]
afford to *v.*, potere permettersi [*poh-teh'-reh pehr-meht-tehr'-see*]
I can't afford to drink, Non posso permettermi di bere [*nohn pohs'-soh pehr-meht'-tehr-mee dee beh'-reh*]
afraid, impaurito, spaventato [*eem-pah-oo-ree'-toh, spah-vehn-tah'-toh*]
be afraid *v.*, avere paura [*ah-veh'-reh pah-oo'-rah*]
Africa, Africa [*ah'-free-kah*]
African, africano [*ah-free-kah'-noh*]
after *adv.*, dopo, poi [*doh'-poh, poh'-ee*]
after *prep.*, dopo, in seguito a [*doh'-poh, een seh'-goo-ee-toh ah*]
after all, dopotutto [*doh-poh-toot'-toh*]
afternoon, pomeriggio [*poh-meh-reej'-jee-oh*]
Good afternoon, Buon giorno [*boo-ohn' jee-ohr'-noh*]
afterwards, in seguito, dopo, poi [*een seh'-goo-ee-toh, doh'-poh, poh'-ee*]
again *adv.*, ancora, di nuovo [*ahn-koh'-rah, dee noo-oh'-voh*]
never again, mai più [*mah'-ee pee-oo'*]

once again, ancora una volta [*ahn-koh'-rah oo'-nah vohl'-tah*]
against *prep.*, contro [*kohn'-troh*]
age [era] *n.*, epoca, era [*eh'-poh-kah, eh'-rah*]
age [of a person] *n.*, età (f, indecl) [*eh-tah'*]
of age, maggiorenne [*mahj-jee-oh-rehn'-neh*]
under age, minorenne [*mee-noh-rehn'-neh*]
age *v.*, invecchiare [*een-vehk-kee-ah'-reh*]
agency, agenzia [*ah-jehn-tsee'-ah*]
travel agency, agenzia di viaggi [*ah-jehn-tsee'-ah dee vee-ahj'-jee*]
agent, agente (m) [*ah-jehn'-teh*]
aggressive, aggressivo [*ahg-grehs-see'-voh*]
ago *adv.*, fa, or sono [*fah, ohr soh'-noh*]
How long ago? Quanto tempo fa? [*koo-ahn'-toh tehm'-poh fah*]
long ago, molto tempo fa [*mohl'-toh tehm'-poh fah*]
two weeks ago, due settimane fa [*doo'-eh seht-tee-mah'-neh fah*]
agree *v.*, essere d'accordo [*ehs'-seh-reh dahk-kohr'-doh*]
agreeable, gradevole, piacevole [*grah-deh'-voh-leh, pee-ah-cheh'-voh-leh*]
agreement, accordo [*ahk-kohr'-doh*]
agriculture, agricoltura [*ah-gree-kohl-too'-rah*]
ahead, avanti [*ah-vahn'-tee*]
get ahead *v.*, farsi avanti, farsi strada [*fahr'-see ah-vahn'-tee, fahr'-see strah'-dah*]
aid *n.*, aiuto, soccorso [*ah-ee-oo'-toh, sohk-kohr'-soh*]
first aid, pronto soccorso [*prohn'-toh sohk-kohr'-soh*]
aid *v.*, aiutare [*ah-ee-oo-tah'-reh*]
aim [goal] *n.*, scopo [*skoh'-poh*]
aim (at) *v.*, mirare (a), aspirare (a) [*mee-rah'-reh (ah), ahs-pee-rah'-reh (ah)*]
air, aria [*ah'-ree-ah*]
air conditioning, aria condizionata [*ah'-ree-ah kohn-dee-tsee-oh-nah'-tah*]
airline, linea aerea [*lee'-neh-ah ah-eh'-reh-ah*]
airmail, posta aerea, via aerea [*poh'-stah ah-eh'-reh-ah,*

vee'-ah ah-eh'-reh-ah]
airplane, aereo, aeroplano [*ah-eh'-reh-oh, ah-eh-roh-plah'-noh*]
airport, aeroporto [*ah-eh-roh-pohr'-toh*]
airsickness, mal (m) d'aria [*mahl dah'-ree-ah*]
aisle, navata [*nah-vah'-tah*]
alarm *n.*, allarme (m) [*ahl-lahr'-meh*]
alarm clock, sveglia [*zveh'-lyah*]
Albania, Albania [*ahl-bah-nee'-ah*]
Albanian, albanese [*ahl-bah-neh'-zeh*]
alcohol, alcool (m) [*ahl'-koh-ohl*]
alert *adj.*, sveglio, vigile [*zveh'-lyoh, vee'-jee-leh*]
alike, simile [*see'-mee-leh*]
alive, vivo, vivente [*vee'-voh, vee-vehn'-teh*]
all, tutto [*toot'-toh*]
  all alone, da solo, da se [*dah soh'-loh, dah seh*]
  All right! Va bene! [*vah beh'-neh*]
  not at all, niente affatto [*nee-ehn'-teh ahf-faht'-toh*]
  That's all! Ecco tutto! [*ehk'-koh toot'-toh*]
alley, vicolo [*vee'-koh-loh*]
allow *v.*, permettere [*pehr-meht'-teh-reh*]
  Allow me to . . . , Mi permetta di . . . [*mee pehr-meht'-tah dee*]
almost, quasi [*koo-ah'-zee*]
alone *adj.*, solo [*soh'-loh*]
alone *adv.*, da solo, da se [*dah soh'-loh, dah seh*]
along, lungo [*loon'-goh*]
  get along [together] *v.*, andare d'accordo [*ahn-dah'-reh dahk-kohr'-doh*]
  along with, con [*kohn*]
alongside of, accanto a [*ahk-kahn'-toh ah*]
aloud, ad alta voce [*ahd ahl'-tah voh'-cheh*]
alphabet, alfabeto [*ahl-fah-beh'-toh*]
Alps, (le) Alpi [(*leh*) *ahl'-pee*]
already, già [*jee-ah'*]
also, anche, pure [*ahn'-keh, poo'-reh*]
altar, altare (m) [*ahl-tah'-reh*]
alter *v.*, cambiare, modificare [*kahm-bee-ah'-reh, moh-dee-*

fee-kah'-reh]

alteration [clothing], modifica, ritocco [*moh-dee'-fee-kah, ree-tohk'-koh*]

although, benchè, sebbene [*behn-keh', sehb-beh'-neh*]

altitude, altitudine (f) [*ahl-tee-too'-dee-neh*]

altogether, nell'insieme, in tutto [*nehl-leen-see-eh'-meh, een toot'-toh*]

always, sempre [*sehm'-preh*]

am: I am, (Io) sono [(*ee'-oh*) *soh'-noh*]

I am happy, Sono felice [*soh'-noh feh-lee'-cheh*]

I am sick, Sto male [*stoh mah'-leh*]

amazement, meraviglia, stupore (m) [*meh-rah-vee'-lyah, stoo-poh'-reh*]

ambassador, ambasciatore (m), ambasciatrice (f) [*ahm-bah-shee-ah-toh'-reh, ahm-bah-shee-ah-tree'-cheh*]

ambiguity, ambiguità (f, indecl) [*ahm-bee-goo-ee-tah'*]

ambition, ambizione (f) [*ahm-bee-tsee-oh'-neh*]

ambitious, ambizioso [*ahm-bee-tsee-oh'-zoh*]

ambulance, ambulanza [*ahm-boo-lahn'-tsah*]

America, America [*ah-meh'-ree-kah*]

North America, America del Nord [*ah-meh'-ree-kah dehl nohrd*]

South America, America del Sud [*ah-meh'-ree-kah dehl sood*]

American, americano [*ah-meh-ree-kah'-noh*]

among, fra, tra [*frah, trah*]

amount *n.*, quantità (f, indecl) [*koo-ahn-tee-tah'*]

amuse *v.*, divertire [*dee-vehr-tee'-reh*]

amuse oneself, divertirsi [*dee-vehr-teer'-see*]

amusement, divertimento, passatempo [*dee-vehr-tee-mehn'-toh, pahs-sah-tehm'-poh*]

amusing, divertente [*dee-vehr-tehn'-teh*]

an, un, uno, una, un' [*oon, oo'-noh, oo'-nah, oon*]

analysis, analisi (f, pl) [*ah-nah'-lee-zee*]

analyze *v.*, analizzare [*ah-nah-leedz-dzah'-reh*]

anarchy, anarchia [*ah-nahr-kee'-ah*]

ancestor, antenato [*ahn-teh-nah'-toh*]

anchor *n.*, ancora [*ahn'-koh-rah*]

ancient, antico [*ahn-tee'-koh*]
and, e, ed [*eh*, *ehd*]
anecdote, aneddoto [*ah-nehd'-doh-toh*]
angel, angelo [*ahn'-jeh-loh*]
anger *n.*, rabbia, furia [*rahb'-bee-ah*, *foo'-ree-ah*]
angle, angolo [*ahn'-goh-loh*]
angry, arrabbiato [*ahr-rahb-bee-ah'-toh*]
get angry *v.*, arrabbiarsi [*ahr-rahb-bee-ahr'-see*]
anguish, angoscia, tormento [*ahn-goh'-shee-ah*, *tohr-mehn'-toh*]
animal, animale (m) [*ah-nee-mah'-leh*]
ankle, caviglia [*kah-vee'-lyah*]
anniversary, anniversario [*ahn-nee-vehr-sah'-ree-oh*]
announce *v.*, annunciare [*ahn-noon-chee-ah'-reh*]
announcement, annuncio, avviso [*ahn-noon'-chee-oh*, *ahv-vee'-zoh*]
annoy *v.*, dar fastidio, disturbare [*dahr fahs-tee'-dee-oh*, *dees-toor-bah'-reh*]
annoying, fastidioso, seccante [*fahs-tee-dee-oh'-zoh*, *sehk-kahn'-teh*]
annual, annuale [*ahn-noo-ah'-leh*]
anonymous, anonimo [*ah-noh'-nee-moh*]
another, un altro [*oon ahl'-troh*]
answer [reply] *n.*, risposta [*rees-pohs'-tah*]
answer *v.*, rispondere [*rees-pohn'-deh-reh*]
ant, formica [*fohr-mee'-kah*]
anticipate [pay in advance] *v.*, anticipare [*ahn-tee-chee-pah'-reh*]
anticipate [foresee] *v.*, prevedere [*preh-veh-deh'-reh*]
antidote, antidoto [*ahn-tee'-doh-toh*]
antique *adj.*, antico [*ahn-tee'-koh*]
antique *n.*, antichità (f, indecl) [*ahn-tee-kee-tah'*]
antique dealer, antiquario [*ahn-tee-koo-ah'-ree-oh*]
anxious, ansioso, inquieto [*ahn-see-oh'-zoh*, *een-koo-ee-eh'-toh*]
any, alcuno, qualche [*ahl-koo'-noh*, *koo-ahl'-keh*]
anybody, chiunque, qualcuno [*kee-oon'-koo-eh*, *koo-ahl-koo'-noh*]

anyhow, comunque, ad ogni modo [*koh-moon'-koo-eh, ahd oh'-nyee moh'-doh*]
anything, qualunque cosa, qualsiasi cosa [*koo-ah-loon'-koo-eh koh'-zah, koo-ahl-see'-ah-see koh'-zah*]
anyway, ad ogni modo [*ahd oh'-nyee moh'-doh*]
anywhere, dovunque, ovunque [*doh-voon'-koo-eh, oh-voon'-koo-eh*]
apart, separatamente, da parte [*seh-pah-rah-tah-mehn'-teh, dah pahr'-teh*]
apartment, appartamento [*ahp-pahr-tah-mehn'-toh*]
apiece, a testa, al pezzo [*ah tehs'-tah, ahl pehts'-tsoh*]
apologize *v.*, scusarsi, chiedere scusa [*skoo-zahr'-see, kee-eh'-deh-reh skoo'-zah*]
apology, scusa [*skoo'-zah*]
apparatus, apparecchio [*ahp-pah-rehk'-kee-oh*]
apparent, apparente, evidente, manifesto [*ahp-pah-rehn'-teh, eh-vee-dehn'-teh, mah-nee-fehs'-toh*]
appeal *n.*, appello, ricorso [*ahp-pehl'-loh, ree-kohr'-soh*]
appeal *v.*, fare appello, ricorrere [*fah'-reh ahp-pehl'-loh, ree-kohr'-reh-reh*]
appear [show oneself] *v.*, apparire, presentarsi [*ahp-pah-ree'-reh, preh-zehn-tahr'-see*]
appear [seem] *v.*, parere, sembrare [*pah-reh'-reh, sehm-brah'-reh*]
appearance [look] *n.*, aspetto [*ahs-peht'-toh*]
appearance [presence] *n.*, apparizione (f), apparenza [*ahp-pah-ree-tsee-oh'-neh, ahp-pah-rehn'-tsah*]
appendicitis, appendicite (f) [*ahp-pehn-dee-chee'-teh*]
appendix [anat.], appendice (f) [*ahp-pehn-dee'-cheh*]
appetite, appetito [*ahp-peh-tee'-toh*]
appetizer [drink], aperitivo [*ah-peh-ree-tee'-voh*]
appetizer [food], antipasto [*ahn-tee-pahs'-toh*]
applaud *v.*, applaudire [*ahp-plah-oo-dee'-reh*]
applause, applauso [*ahp-plah'-oo-zoh*]
apple, mela [*meh'-lah*]
apple pie, torta di mele [*tohr'-tah dee meh'-leh*]
application, domanda, richiesta [*doh-mahn'-dah, ree-kee-ehs'-tah*]

apply [inquire of] *v.*, rivolgersi [*ree-vohl'-jehr-see*]
apply for, fare la richiesta [*fah'-reh lah ree-kee-ehs'-tah*]
apply to [concern], applicare a [*ahp-plee-kah'-reh ah*]
appoint *v.*, nominare [*noh-mee-nah'-reh*]
appointment [meeting], appuntamento [*ahp-poon-tah-mehn'-toh*]
appreciate *v.*, apprezzare [*ahp-prehts-tsah'-reh*]
apprentice, apprendista [*ahp-prehn-dees'-tah*]
approach *v.*, avvicinare [*ahv-vee-chee-nah'-reh*]
appropriate *adj.*, adatto, proprio, appropriato [*ah-daht'-toh, proh'-pree-oh, ahp-proh-pree-ah'-toh*]
approval, approvazione (f) [*ahp-proh-vah-tsee-oh'-neh*]
approve *v.*, approvare [*ahp-proh-vah'-reh*]
approximately, approssimativamente [*ahp-prohs-see-mah-tee-vah-mehn'-teh*]
April, aprile (m) [*ah-pree'-leh*]
apron, grembiule (m) [*grehm-bee-oo'-leh*]
Arab *n.* & *adj.*, arabo [*ah'-rah-boh*]
Arabia, Arabia [*ah-rah'-bee-ah*]
arbitrary, arbitrario [*ahr-bee-trah'-ree-oh*]
arch *n.*, arco [*ahr'-koh*]
archbishop, arcivescovo [*ahr-chee-vehs'-koh-voh*]
architect, architetto [*ahr-kee-teht'-toh*]
architecture, architettura [*ahr-kee-teht-too'-rah*]
are: you are, we are, they are, sei (sing), siete (pl), siamo, sono [*seh'-ee, see-eh'-teh, see-ah'-moh, soh'-noh*]
How are you? [polite form], Come sta (Lei)? [*koh'-meh stah (leh'-ee)*]
I am fine, thanks, Sto bene, grazie [*stoh beh'-neh, grah'-tsee-eh*]
I'm not well, Sto male, Non mi sento bene [*stoh mah'-leh, nohn mee sehn'-toh beh'-neh*]
there is, there are, c'è, ci sono [*cheh', chee soh'-noh*]
area [measure], area [*ah'-reh-ah*]
Argentina, Argentina [*ahr-jehn-tee'-nah*]
Argentine, argentino [*ahr-jehn-tee'-noh*]
argue *v.*, disputare [*dees-poo-tah'-reh*]
argument, disputa, lite (f) [*dees-poo'-tah, lee'-teh*]

arise *v.*, sorgere, alzarsi [*sohr'-jeh-reh, ahl-tsahr'-see*]
aristocracy, aristocrazia [*ah-rees-toh-krah-tsee'-ah*]
aristocratic, aristocratico [*ah-rees-toh-krah'-tee-koh*]
arithmetic, aritmetica [*ah-reet-meh'-tee-kah*]
arm [anat.] *n.*, braccio (m), le braccia (pl) [*brahch'-chee-oh, leh brahch'-chee-ah*]
arms [weapon] *n.*, (l') arma, (le) armi (pl) [(*l*)*ahr'-mah*, (*leh*) *ahr'-mee*]
armchair, poltrona [*pohl-troh'-nah*]
army, esercito, armata [*eh-zehr'-chee-toh, ahr-mah'-tah*]
around *adv.*, intorno [*een-tohr'-noh*]
around *prep.*, intorno a [*een-tohr'-noh ah*]
arrange *v.*, sistemare, ordinare [*sees-teh-mah'-reh, ohr-dee-nah'-reh*]
arrangement, sistemazione (f), disposizione (f) [*sees-teh-mah-tsee-oh'-neh, dees-poh-zee-tsee-oh'-neh*]
arrest [legal] *n.*, arresto, fermo di polizia [*ahr-rehs'-toh, fehr'-moh dee poh-lee-tsee'-ah*]
arrest *v.*, arrestare [*ahr-rehs-tah'-reh*]
arrival, arrivo [*ahr-ree'-voh*]
arrive *v.*, arrivare, giungere [*ahr-ree-vah'-reh, jee-oon'-jeh-reh*]
arrogance, arroganza [*ahr-roh-gahn'-tsah*]
art, arte (f) [*ahr'-teh*]
artery [anat.], arteria [*ahr-teh'-ree-ah*]
artichoke, carciofo [*kahr-chee-oh'-foh*]
article, articolo [*ahr-tee'-koh-loh*]
artificial, artificiale [*ahr-tee-fee-chee-ah'-leh*]
artist, artista (m, f) [*ahr-tees'-tah*]
artistic, artistico [*ahr-tees'-tee-koh*]
as *adv.*, come [*koh'-meh*]
as [because, while] *conj.*, siccome, mentre [*seek-koh'-meh, mehn'-treh*]
  as . . . as, as much as, tanto . . . quanto [*tahn'-toh, koo-ahn'-toh*]
  as for, in quanto a [*een koo-ahn'-toh ah*]
  as long as, as far as *prep.*, fino a [*fee'-noh ah*]
  as long as *conj.*, finché [*feen-keh'*]

as well, anche, pure [*ahn'-keh, poo'-reh*]
as yet, finora [*fee-noh'-rah*]
ascend *v.*, ascendere, salire [*ah-shehn'-deh-reh, sah-lee'-reh*]
ash, cenere (f) [*cheh'-neh-reh*]
ashamed, vergognoso [*vehr-goh-nyoh'-zoh*]
ashore, a terra [*ah tehr'-rah*]
ashtray, portacenere (m) [*pohr-tah-cheh'-neh-reh*]
Asia, Asia [*ah'-zee-ah*]
Asiatic, asiatico [*ah-zee-ah'-tee-koh*]
aside, da parte [*dah pahr'-teh*]
ask (for) *v.*, chiedere [*kee-eh'-deh-reh*]
ask a question, domandare [*doh-mahn-dah'-reh*]
ask [oneself], domandarsi [*doh-mahn-dahr'-see*]
asleep, addormentato [*ahd-dohr-mehn-tah'-toh*]
fall asleep *v.*, addormentarsi [*ahd-dohr-mehn-tahr'-see*]
asparagus, asparago [*ah-spah'-rah-goh*]
aspirin, aspirina [*ahs-pee-ree'-nah*]
assault *n.*, assalto [*ahs-sahl'-toh*]
assault *v.*, assalire [*ahs-sah-lee'-reh*]
assemble [gather] *v.*, radunare, riunire [*rah-doo-nah'-reh, ree-oo-nee'-reh*]
assemble [put together] *v.*, montare [*mohn-tah'-reh*]
assembly, assemblea [*ahs-sehm-bleh'-ah*]
assign *v.*, assegnare [*ahs-seh-nyah'-reh*]
assist *v.*, assistere, aiutare [*ahs-sees'-teh-reh, ah-ee-oo-tah'-reh*]
assistance, aiuto, assistenza [*ah-ee-oo'-toh, ahs-sees-tehn'-zah*]
assistant, assistente (m) [*ahs-sees-tehn'-teh*]
associate *n.*, socio, collega [*soh'-chee-oh, kohl-leh'-gah*]
associate *v.*, associare [*ahs-soh-chee-ah'-reh*]
association, associazione (f) [*ahs-soh-chee-ah-tsee-oh'-neh*]
assortment, assortimento [*ahs-sohr-tee-mehn'-toh*]
assume *v.*, assumere [*ahs-soo'-meh-reh*]
assumption, supposizione (f) [*soop-poh-zee-tsee-oh'-neh*]
assurance, assicurazione (f) [*ahs-see-koo-rah-tsee-oh'-neh*]
assure *v.*, assicurare [*ahs-see-koo-rah'-reh*]
astonish *v.*, meravigliare [*meh-rah-vee-lyah'-reh*]

be astonished, meravigliarsi [*meh-rah-vee-lyahr'-see*]
astronomy, astronomia [*ahs-troh-noh-mee'-ah*]
at, a, ad (before vowel), da, di, in [*ah, ahd, dah, dee, een*]
at all, affatto [*ahf-faht'-toh*]
at first, al principio [*ahl preen-chee'-pee-oh*]
at last, alla fine [*ahl'-lah fee'-neh*]
at once, subito [*soo'-bee-toh*]
at six o'clock, alle sei [*ahl'-leh seh'-ee*]
at the hotel, all'albergo [*ahl-lahl-behr'-goh*]
at the same time, allo stresso tempo [*ahl'-loh stehs'-soh tehm'-poh*]
not at all, niente affatto [*nee-ehn'-teh ahf-faht'-toh*]
athlete, atleta (m, f) [*aht-leh'-tah*]
athletics, atletica [*aht-leh'-tee-kah*]
Atlantic, Atlantico [*aht-lahn'-tee-koh*]
atmosphere, atmosfera [*aht-mohs-feh'-rah*]
attach *v.*, attaccare, legare [*aht-tahk-kah'-reh, leh-gah'-reh*]
attack *n.*, attacco, assalto [*aht-tahk'-koh, ahs-sahl'-toh*]
attack *v.*, attaccare, assalire [*aht-tahk-kah'-reh, ahs-sah-lee'-reh*]
attempt *n.*, tentativo [*tehn-tah-tee'-voh*]
attempt *v.*, tentare, provare [*tehn-tah'-reh, proh-vah'-reh*]
attend *v.*, attendere, intervenire a [*aht-tehn'-deh-reh, een-tehr-veh-nee'-reh ah*]
attend to, occuparsi, assistere [*ohk-koo-pahr'-see, ahs-sees'-teh-reh*]
attention, attenzione (f) [*aht-tehn-tsee-oh'-neh*]
attire *n.*, abbigliamento, abiti [*ahb-bee-lyah-mehn'-toh, ah'-bee-tee*]
attitude, atteggiamento [*aht-tehj-jee-ah-mehn'-toh*]
attorney, avvocato [*ahv-voh-kah'-toh*]
attract *v.*, attrarre (irreg) [*aht-trahr'-reh*]
attraction, attrazione (f) [*aht-trah-tsee-oh'-neh*]
attractive, attraente, piacevole [*aht-trah-ehn'-teh, pee-ah-cheh'-voh-leh*]
auction, asta [*ahs'-tah*]
audience, pubblico, udienza [*poob'-blee-koh, oo-dee-ehn'-tsah*]

August, agosto [*ah-gohs'-toh*]
aunt, zia [*dzee'-ah*]
Australia, Australia [*ah-oos-trah'-lee-ah*]
Australian, australiano [*ah-oos-trah-lee-ah'-noh*]
Austria, Austria [*ah'-oos-tree-ah*]
Austrian, austriaco [*ah-oos-tree'-ah-koh*]
authentic, autentico [*ah-oo-tehn'-tee-koh*]
author, autore (m), autrice (f) [*ah-oo-toh'-reh, ah-oo-tree'-cheh*]
authority, autorità (f, indecl) [*ah-oo-toh-ree-tah'*]
authorize *v.*, autorizzare [*ah-oo-toh-reedz-dzah'-reh*]
automatic, automatico [*ah-oo-toh-mah'-tee-koh*]
automobile, automobile (f), macchina [*ah-oo-toh-moh'-bee-leh, mahk'-kee-nah*]
autonomy, autonomia [*ah-oo-toh-noh-mee'-ah*]
autumn, autunno [*ah-oo-toon'-noh*]
available, disponibile [*dees-poh-nee'-bee-leh*]
avalanche, valanga [*vah-lahn'-gah*]
avenue, viale (m) [*vee-ah'-leh*]
average *n.*, media [*meh'-dee-ah*]
on the average, in media [*een meh'-dee-ah*]
avoid *v.*, evitare [*eh-vee-tah'-reh*]
awake *adj.*, sveglio [*zveh'-lyoh*]
awake *v.*, svegliare [*zveh-lyah'-reh*]
award *n.*, premio [*preh'-mee-oh*]
aware, conscio, consapevole [*kohn'-shee-oh, kohn-sah-peh'-voh-leh*]
away, via, lontano [*vee'-ah, lohn-tah'-noh*]
Go away! Vada via! [*vah'-dah vee'-ah*]
awful, terribile [*tehr-ree'-bee-leh*]
awkward, scomodo [*skoh'-moh-doh*]
ax, ascia [*ah'-shee-ah*]
axle, asse (m) [*ahs'-seh*]

B

baby, bimbo, bambino [*beem'-boh, bahm-bee'-noh*]
babysitter, bambinaia [*bahm-bee-nah'-ee-ah*]
bachelor, scapolo, celibe (m) [*skah'-poh-loh, cheh'-lee-beh*]
back [anat.] *n.*, schiena, dorso [*skee-eh'-nah, dohr'-soh*]
back [of a seat] *n.*, spalliera [*spahl-lee-eh'-rah*]
back [support] *v.*, appoggiare, sostenere [*ahp-pohj-jee-ah'-reh, sohs-teh-neh'-reh*]
back *adj.*, posteriore [*pohs-teh-ree-oh'-reh*]
back *adv.*, indietro [*een-dee-eh'-troh*]
  come back *v.*, ritornare [*ree-tohr-nah'-reh*]
  in back of, dietro a [*dee-eh'-troh ah*]
background, sfondo [*sfohn'-doh*]
backward *adv.*, indietro [*een-dee-eh'-troh*]
bad, cattivo [*kaht-tee'-voh*]
  Too bad! Che peccato! [*keh pehk-kah'-toh*]
badge, distintivo, insegna [*dees-teen-tee'-voh, een-seh'-nyah*]
badly, male, malamente [*mah'-leh, mah-lah-mehn'-teh*]
bad-tempered, di cattivo carattere, di malumore [*dee kaht-tee'-voh kah-raht'-teh-reh, dee mahl-oo-moh'-reh*]
bag, borsa, sacco [*bohr'-sah, sahk'-koh*]
baggage, bagaglio [*bah-gah'-lyoh*]
bake *v.*, cuocere [*koo-oh'-cheh-reh*]
bakery, panificio, forno [*pah-nee-fee'-chee-oh, fohr'-noh*]
balance *n.*, equilibrio [*eh-koo-ee-leeb'-ree-oh*]
balance *v.*, bilanciare, equilibrare [*bee-lahn-chee-ah'-reh, eh-koo-ee-lee-brah'-reh*]
balcony, balcone (m) [*bahl-koh'-neh*]
bald, calvo, pelato [*kahl'-voh, peh-lah'-toh*]
ball [dance], ballo [*bahl'-loh*]
ball [sports], palla, pallone (m) [*pahl'-lah, pahl-loh'-neh*]
ballet, balletto [*bahl-leht'-toh*]
band [music], banda [*bahn'-dah*]

bandage *n.*, benda, fascia [*behn'-dah, fah'-shee-ah*]
bank [finance], banca [*bahn'-kah*]
bank [of river], riva, ripa [*ree'-vah, ree'-pah*]
banker, banchiere (m) [*bahn-kee-eh'-reh*]
banknote, banconota [*bahn-koh-noh'-tah*]
baptism, battesimo [*baht-teh'-zee-moh*]
bar [barrier], sbarra [*zbahr'-rah*]
bar [for drinks], bar (m), taverna [*bahr, tah-vehr'-nah*]
barber, barbiere (m) [*bahr-bee-eh'-reh*]
bare *adj.*, nudo [*noo'-doh*]
barefoot, scalzo [*skahl'-tsoh*]
barely [scarcely], appena [*ahp-peh'-nah*]
bargain [merchandise] *n.*, buon affare (m) [*boo'-ohn ahf-fah'-reh*]
bark *v.*, abbaiare [*ahb-bah-ee-ah'-reh*]
barrel, barile (m) [*bah-ree'-leh*]
base *n.*, base (f) [*bah'-zeh*]
basement, seminterrato [*seh-meen-tehr-rah'-toh*]
basic, fondamentale [*fohn-dah-mehn-tah'-leh*]
basket, cesta, cestino [*chehs'-tah, chehs-tee'-noh*]
basketball, pallacanestro [*pahl-lah-kah-nehs'-troh*]
bath, bagno [*bah'-nyoh*]
  take a bath *v.*, fare il bagno [*fah'-reh eel bah'-nyoh*]
bathe, bagnare, fare il bagno [*bah-nyah'-reh, fah'-reh eel bah'-nyoh*]
bathing suit, costume da bagno (m) [*kohs-too'-meh dah bah'-nyoh*]
bathrobe, accappatoio [*ahk-kahp-pah-toh'-ee-oh*]
bathroom, stanza da bagno [*stahn'-tsah dah bah'-nyoh*]
bathtub, vasca da bagno [*vahs'-kah da bah'-nyoh*]
battery, batteria [*baht-teh-ree'-ah*]
battle, battaglia [*baht-tah'-lyah*]
bay [geog.], baia [*bah'-ee-ah*]
be *v.*, essere (irreg), stare [*ehs'-seh-reh, stah'-reh*]
  How are you? come sta? [*koh'-meh stah*]
  I am fine, thank you, Sto bene, grazie [*stoh beh'-neh, grah'-tsee-eh*]
  I don't feel well, I am sick, Non sto bene, sono malato

[*nohn stoh beh'-neh, soh'-noh mah-lah'-toh*]
be afraid, avere paura [*ah-veh'-reh pah-oo'-rah*]
be ashamed, avere vergogna [*ah-veh'-reh vehr-goh'-nyah*]
be cold, avere freddo [*ah-veh'-reh frehd'-doh*]
be hungry, avere fame [*ah-veh'-reh fah'-meh*]
be right, avere ragione [*ah-veh'-reh rah-jee-oh'-neh*]
be sleepy, avere sonno [*ah-veh'-reh sohn'-noh*]
be thirsty, avere sete [*ah-veh'-reh seh'-teh*]
be warm, avere caldo [*ah-veh'-reh kahl'-doh*]
be wrong, avere torto [*ah-veh'-reh tohr'-toh*]
beach, spiaggia [*spee-ahj'-jee-ah*]
bean, faggiolo [*fahj-jee-oh'-loh*]
bear [endure] *v.*, sopportare [*sohp-pohr-tah'-reh*]
bear [produce] *v.*, produrre [*proh-door'-reh*]
beard, barba [*bahr'-bah*]
beat [strike] *v.*, battere (irreg) [*baht'-teh-reh*]
beat [win] *v.*, vincere (irreg) [*veen'-cheh-reh*]
beautiful, bello [*behl'-loh*]
beauty, bellezza [*behl-lehts'-tsah*]
beauty parlor, salone (m) di bellezza [*sah-loh'-neh dee behl-lehts'-tsah*]
because, perchè [*pehr-keh'*]
because of, a causa di [*ah kah'-oo-zah dee*]
become *v.*, diventare, divenire (irreg) [*dee-vehn-tah'-reh, dee-veh-nee'-reh*]
bed, letto [*leht'-toh*]
bedroom, camera da letto [*kah'-meh-rah dah leht'-toh*]
bedsheet, lenzuolo, (le) lenzuola (pl) [*lehn-tsoo-oh'-loh, (leh) lehn-tsoo-oh'-lah*]
beef, manzo [*mahn'-tsoh*]
beefsteak, bistecca [*bees-tehk'-kah*]
beer, birra [*beer'-rah*]
before [place] *adv. & prep.*, davanti [*dah-vahn'-tee*]
before [time] *adv. & prep.*, prima (di) [*pree'-mah (dee)*]
before four o'clock, prima delle quattro [*pree'-mah dehl'-leh koo-aht'-troh*]
before *conj.*, prima che [*pree'-mah keh*]
beforehand, in anticipo [*een ahn-tee'-chee-poh*]

beg *v.*, pregare [*preh-gah'-reh*]
begin *v.*, cominciare, iniziare [*koh-meen-chee-ah'-reh, ee-nee-tsee-ah'-reh*]
behave *v.*, comportarsi [*kohm-pohr-tahr'-see*]
Behave yourself! Comportati bene! [*kohm-pohr'-tah-tee beh'-neh*]
behavior, condotta, comportamento [*kohn-doht'-tah, kohm-pohr-tah-mehn'-toh*]
behind *adv. & prep.*, dietro (a) [*dee-eh'-troh (ah)*]
being *n.*, essere (m) [*ehs'-seh-reh*]
Belgian, belga (m & f) [*behl'-gah*]
Belgium, Belgio [*behl'-jee-oh*]
belief, credenza, fede (f) [*kreh-dehn'-tsah, feh'-deh*]
believe *v.*, credere [*kreh'-deh-reh*]
bell, campana [*kahm-pah'-nah*]
bellboy, facchino, fattorino [*fahk-kee'-noh, faht-toh-ree'-noh*]
belong (to) *v.*, appartenere [*ahp-pahr-teh-neh'-reh*]
belongings [personal], effetti personali [*ehf-feht'-tee pehr-soh-nah'-lee*]
below *adv.*, (di) sotto, giù [*(dee) soht'-toh, jee-oo'*]
below *prep.*, sotto (a) [*soht'-toh (ah)*]
belt, cintura [*cheen-too'-rah*]
bench, banco [*bahn'-koh*]
bend *v.*, piegare [*pee-eh-gah'-reh*]
bend down, chinarsi [*kee-nahr'-see*]
benefit *n.*, vantaggio [*vahn-tahj'-jee-oh*]
beside *prep.*, accanto a, al lato di [*ahk-kahn'-toh ah, ahl lah'-toh dee*]
besides *adv.*, inoltre [*ee-nohl'-treh*]
besides *prep.*, oltre a [*ohl'-treh ah*]
best *adj.*, (il, la) migliore [*(eel, lah) mee-lyoh'-reh*]
best *adv.*, meglio [*meh'-lyoh*]
bet *n.*, scommessa [*skohm-mehs'-sah*]
betray *v.*, tradire [*trah-dee'-reh*]
better *adj.*, migliore, meglio [*mee-lyoh'-reh, meh'-lyoh*]
between, fra, tra [*frah, trah*]
beware [watch out] *v.*, (fare) attenzione [*(fah'-reh) aht-tehn-*

tsee-oh'-neh]

Beware! Guai! [*goo-ah'-ee*]

beyond, al di là, oltre [*ahl dee lah', ohl'-treh*]

Bible, bibbia [*beeb'-bee-ah*]

bicycle, bicicletta [*bee-chee-kleht'-tah*]

big, grande [*grahn'-deh*]

very big, grandissimo [*grahn-dees'-see-moh*]

bigger, più grande [*pee-oo' grahn'-deh*]

biggest, (il, la) più grande [(*eel, lah*) *pee-oo' grahn'-deh*]

bill, conto [*kohn'-toh*]

bill of fare, lista delle vivande [*lees'-tah dehl'-leh vee-vahn'-deh*]

bind *v.*, legare [*leh-gah'-reh*]

bird, uccello [*ooch-chehl'-loh*]

birth, nascita [*nah'-shee-tah*]

childbirth, parto [*pahr'-toh*]

birthday, compleanno [*kohm-pleh-ahn'-noh*]

Happy birthday! Buon compleanno! [*boo-ohn' kohm-pleh-ahn'-noh*]

bit, little bit, pezzetto, poco [*pehts-tseht'-toh, poh'-koh*]

bite *n.*, morso [*mohr'-soh*]

bite *v.*, mordere (irreg) [*mohr'-deh-reh*]

bitter, amaro [*ah-mah'-roh*]

black, nero [*neh'-roh*]

blame *n.*, colpa [*kohl'-pah*]

blame *v.*, dare la colpa (a) [*dah'-reh lah kohl'-pah* (*ah*)]

blank *adj.*, in bianco [*een bee-ahn'-koh*]

blanket, coperta [*koh-pehr'-tah*]

bless *v.*, benedire [*beh-neh-dee'-reh*]

blessing, benedizione (f) [*beh-neh-dee-tsee-oh'-neh*]

blind, cieco [*chee-eh'-koh*]

blister, bolla [*bohl'-lah*]

blonde, biondo [*bee-ohn'-doh*]

blood, sangue (m) [*sahn'-goo-eh*]

blossom *n.*, fioritura [*fee-oh-ree-too'-rah*]

blouse, blusa, camicetta [*bloo'-za, kah-mee-cheht'-tah*]

blow *n.*, colpo [*kohl'-poh*]

blow *v.*, soffiare [*sohf-fee-ah'-reh*]

blue, azzurro, blu [*ahdz-dzoor'-roh, bloo'*]
blush *v.*, arrossire [*ahr-rohs-see'-reh*]
board [lumber] *n.*, asse (f), tavola [*ahs'-seh, tah'-voh-lah*]
board [ship, train] *v.*, salire su [*sah-lee'-reh soo*]
boardinghouse, pensione (f) [*pehn-see-oh'-neh*]
boarding school, collegio, convitto [*kohl-leh'-jee-oh, kohn-veet'-toh*]
boat, barca, battello [*bahr'-kah, baht-teh'-loh*]
body, corpo [*kohr'-poh*]
boil *v.*, bollire [*bohl-lee'-reh*]
bold, coraggioso [*koh-rahj-jee-oh'-zoh*]
bomb *n.*, bomba [*bohm'-bah*]
bone, osso, le ossa (pl) [*ohs'-soh, leh ohs'-sah*]
book *n.*, libro [*lee'-broh*]
bookkeeper, contabile (m, f), ragioniere (m) [*kohn-tah'-bee-leh, rah-gee-oh-nee-eh'-reh*]
bookstore, libreria [*lee-breh-ree'-ah*]
boot, stivale (m) [*stee-vah'-leh*]
booth, cabina, [*kah-bee'-nah*]
border *n.*, confine (m), frontiera [*kohn-fee'-neh, frohn-tee-eh'-rah*]
bore *v.*, annoiare [*ahn-noh-ee-ah'-reh*]
boring, seccante, noioso [*sehk-kahn'-teh, noh-ee-oh'-zoh*]
born: be born, nascere (irreg) [*nah'-sheh-reh*]
borrow *v.*, prendere in prestito [*prehn'-deh-reh een prehs'-tee-toh*]
bosom, petto, seno [*peht'-toh, seh'-noh*]
boss *n.*, capo, padrone (m) [*kah'-poh, pah-droh'-neh*]
both, ambedue, entrambi [*ahm-beh-doo'-eh, ehn-trahm'-bee*]
both . . . and, sia . . . sia [*see'-ah . . . see'-ah*]
bother *v.*, infastidire, seccare [*een-fahs-tee-dee'-reh, sehk-kah'-reh*]
Don't bother! Non si preoccupi! [*nohn see preh-ohk'-koo-pee*]
Don't bother me! Non mi disturbi [*nohn mee dees-toor'-bee*]
bottle, bottiglia [*boht-tee'-lyah*]
bottle opener, cavatappi (m) [*kah-vah-tahp'-pee*]

bottom, fondo [*fohn'-doh*]
boundary, limite (m) [*lee'-mee-teh*]
bow [salutation] *n.*, inchino [*een-kee'-noh*]
bow [of ship] *n.*, prora [*proh'-rah*]
bowels, intestini, visceri (m, pl) [*een-tehs-tee'-nee, vee'-sheh-ree*]
bowl, scodella [*skoh-dehl'-lah*]
box, scatola [*skah'-toh-lah*]
boxing [sport], pugilato [*poo-jee-lah'-toh*]
box office, biglietteria, botteghino [*bee-lyeht-teh-ree'-ah, boht-teh-gee'-noh*]
boy, ragazzo [*rah-gahts'-tsoh*]
bracelet, braccialetto [*brahch-chee-ah-leht'-toh*]
brag *v.*, vantarsi [*vahn-tahr'-see*]
brain, cervello [*chehr-vehl'-loh*]
brake *n.*, freno [*freh'-noh*]
brand [trade name] *n.*, marca [*mahr'-kah*]
brand-new, nuovo fiammante [*noo-oh'-voh fee-ahm-man'-teh*]
brandy, cognac, brandy [*koh'-nyahk, brahn'-dee*]
brass, ottone (m) [*oht-toh'-neh*]
brassiere, reggiseno [*rehj-jee-seh'-noh*]
brave, coraggioso [*koh-rahj-jee-oh'-zoh*]
Brazil, Brasile (m) [*brah-zee'-leh*]
Brazilian, brasiliano [*brah-zee-lee-ah'-noh*]
bread, pane (m) [*pah'-neh*]
break *v.*, rompere [*rohm'-peh-reh*]
breakfast, prima colazione [*pree'-mah koh-lah-tsee-oh'-neh*]
breast, petto [*peht'-toh*]
breath, respiro, fiato [*rehs-pee'-roh, fee-ah'-toh*]
breathe *v.*, respirare [*rehs-pee-rah'-reh*]
breathing, respirazione (f) [*rehs-pee-rah-tsee-oh'-neh*]
breeze, brezza [*brehts'-tsah*]
bribe *v.*, corrompere [*kohr-rohm'-peh-reh*]
brick, mattone (m) [*maht-toh'-neh*]
bride, sposa [*spoh'-zah*]
bridegroom, sposo [*spoh'-zoh*]
bridesmaid, damigella d'onore [*dah-mee-jehl'-lah doh-noh'-reh*]

bridge [structure], ponte (m) [*pohn'-teh*]
brief *adj.*, breve [*breh'-veh*]
bright, luminoso, chiaro [*loo-mee-noh'-zoh, kee-ah'-roh*]
bring *v.*, portare [*pohr-tah'-reh*]
bring in, introdurre (irreg) [*een-troh-door'-reh*]
bring together, riunire (irreg) [*ree-oo-nee'-reh*]
bring up [rear], educare [*eh-doo-kah'-reh*]
British, britannico, inglese [*bree-tahn'-nee-koh, een-gleh'-zeh*]
broad, largo [*lahr'-goh*]
broadcast *n.*, trasmissione (f) [*trahz-mees-see-oh'-neh*]
broadcast *v.*, trasmettere [*traz-meht'-teh-reh*]
broken *adj.*, rotto, guasto [*roht'-toh, goo-ahs'-toh*]
broil *v.*, arrostire [*ahr-rohs-tee'-reh*]
bronze, bronzo [*brohn'-tsoh*]
broom, scopa [*skoh'-pah*]
broth, brodo [*broh'-doh*]
brother, fratello [*frah-tehl'-loh*]
brother-in-law, cognato [*koh-nyah'-toh*]
brown, marrone, bruno [*mahr-roh'-neh, broo'-noh*]
bruise *n.*, contusione (f) [*kohn-too-zee-oh'-neh*]
brunette, brunetta [*broo-neht'-tah*]
brush *n.*, spazzola [*spahts'-tsoh-lah*]
clothes brush, spazzola per abiti [*spahts'-tsoh-lah pehr ah'-bee-tee*]
paintbrush, pennello [*pehn-nehl'-loh*]
toothbrush, spazzolino da denti [*spahts-tsoh-lee'-noh dah dehn'-tee*]
brush *v.*, spazzolare [*spahts-tsoh-lah'-reh*]
brutal, brutale [*broo-tah'-leh*]
bucket, secchia, secchio [*sehk'-kee-ah, sehk'-kee-oh*]
budget *n.*, bilancio [*bee-lahn'-chee-oh*]
bug, insetto [*een-seht'-toh*]
bulb [light], lampadina [*lahm-pah-dee'-nah*]
build *v.*, costruire [*kohs-troo-ee'-reh*]
building, edificio [*eh-dee-fee'-chee-oh*]
Bulgaria, Bulgaria [*bool-gah-ree'-ah*]
Bulgarian, bulgaro [*bool'-gah-roh*]

bulky, voluminoso [*voh-loo-mee-noh'-zoh*]
bull, toro [*toh'-roh*]
bulletin, bollettino [*bohl-leht-tee'-noh*]
bundle *n.*, fascio, pacco [*fah'-shee-oh*, *pahk'-koh*]
burden *n.*, carico, peso [*kah'-ree-koh*, *peh'-zoh*]
bureau [office], ufficio [*oof-fee'-chee-oh*]
burglar, ladro, scassinatore [*lah'-droh*, *skahs-see-nah-toh'-reh*]
burial, sepoltura [*seh-pohl-too'-rah*]
burn *n.*, bruciatura [*broo-chee-ah-too'-rah*]
burn *v.*, bruciare [*broo-chee-ah'-reh*]
bury *v.*, seppellire [*sehp-pehl-lee'-reh*]
bus, autobus (m) [*ah'-oo-toh-boos*]
bus line, autolinea [*ah-oo-toh-lee'-neh-ah*]
bush, cespuglio [*chehs-poo'-lyoh*]
business, affare (m), commercio [*ahf-fah'-reh*, *kohm-mehr'-chee-oh*]
businessman, uomo d'affari, commerciante (m, f) [*oo-oh'-moh dahf-fah'-ree*, *kohm-mehr-chee-ahn'-teh*]
busy, occupato [*ohk-koo-pah'-toh*]
but, ma, peró [*mah*, *peh-roh'*]
butcher, macellaio [*mah-chehl-lah'-ee-oh*]
butcher shop, macelleria [*mah-chehl-leh-ree'-ah*]
butter, burro [*boor'-roh*]
button, bottone (m) [*boht-toh'-neh*]
buy *v.*, comprare [*kohm-prah'-reh*]
by *prep.*, da, con, per, vicino [*dah*, *kohn*, *pehr*, *vee-chee'-noh*]
  by chance, per caso [*pehr kah'-zoh*]
  by hand, a mano [*ah mah'-noh*]
  by the way, a proposito [*ah proh-poh'-zee-toh*]

C

cab, tassì (m), taxi (m) [*tahs-see'*, *tahk'-see*]
cabin, cabina, capanna [*kah-bee'-nah*, *kah-pahn'-nah*]

cabinet [government], gabinetto [*gah-bee-neht'-toh*]
cable *v.*, mandare un cablogramma [*mahn-dah'-reh oon kahb-loh-grahm'-mah*]
cablegram, cablogramma (m) [*kah-bloh-grahm'-mah*]
café, caffè (m) [*kahf-feh'*]
cage, gabbia [*gahb'-bee-ah*]
cake, dolce (m), torta [*dohl'-cheh, tohr'-tah*]
calendar, calendario [*kah-lehn-dah'-ree-oh*]
call *n.*, chiamata [*kee-ah-mah'-tah*]
  telephone call, chiamata telefonica, telefonata [*kee-ah-mah'-tah teh-leh-foh'-nee-kah, teh-leh-foh-nah'-tah*]
call *v.*, chiamare [*kee-ah-mah'-reh*]
  call off, sospendere [*sohs-pehn'-deh-reh*]
  call on, fare una visita [*fah'-reh oo'-nah vee'-zee-tah*]
  call out, gridare [*gree-dah'-reh*]
  call up, call together, convocare [*kohn-voh-kah'-reh*]
calm *adj.*, calmo, tranquillo [*kahl'-moh, trahn-koo-eel'-loh*]
calm *v.*, calmare [*kahl-mah'-reh*]
  Calm down! Si calmi! [*see kahl'-mee*]
camera, macchina fotografica [*mahk'-kee-nah foh-toh-grah'-fee-kah*]
camp *n.*, campo, campeggio [*kahm'-poh, kahm-pehj'-jee-oh*]
can *n.*, scatola [*skah'-toh-lah*]
can [be able] *v.*, potere (irreg) [*poh-teh'-reh*]
Canada, (il) Canada [(*eel*) *kah'-nah-dah*]
Canadian *n.* & *adj.*, canadese [*kah-nah-deh'-zeh*]
canal, canale (m) [*kah-nah'-leh*]
cancel *v.*, cancellare [*kahn-chehl-lah'-reh*]
candle, candela [*kahn-deh'-lah*]
candy, caramella [*kah-rah-mehl'-lah*]
cane, bastone (m) [*bahs-toh'-neh*]
can opener, apriscatole (m) [*ah-pree-skah'-toh-leh*]
cap *n.*, berretto [*behr-reht'-toh*]
capable, capace [*kah-pah'-cheh*]
capacity, capacità (f, indecl) [*kah-pah-chee-tah'*]
capital [city], capitale (f) [*kah-pee-tah'-leh*]
capital [money], capitale (m) [*kah-pee-tah'-leh*]
car, automobile (f), macchina [*ah-oo-toh-moh'-bee-leh,*

mahk'-kee-nah]
streetcar, tram (m) [*trahm*]
carbon paper, carta carbone [*kahr'-tah kahr-boh'-neh*]
card, carta, cartolina, tessera [*kahr'-tah, kahr-toh-lee'-nah, tehs'-seh-rah*]
calling card, biglietto da visita [*bee-lyeht'-toh dah vee'-zee-tah*]
Christmas card, cartolina di natale [*kahr-toh-lee'-nah dee nah-tah'-leh*]
playing card, carta da gioco [*kahr'-tah dah jee-oh'-koh*]
postcard, cartolina postale [*kahr-toh-lee'-nah pohs-tah'-leh*]
care *v.*, curarsi, importare [*koo-rahr'-see, eem-pohr-tah'-reh*]
care for, interessarsi [*een-teh-rehs-sahr'-see*]
I don't care, Non m'importa [*nohn meem-pohr'-tah*]
in care of, presso [*prehs'-soh*]
take care of, preoccuparsi, curare [*preh-ohk-koo-pahr'-see, koor-ah'-reh*]
career, carriera [*kahr-ree-eh'-rah*]
careful, attento, prudente [*aht-tehn'-toh, proo-dehn'-teh*]
Be careful! (Faccia) Attenzione! [(*fahch'-chee-ah*) *aht-tehn-tsee-oh'-neh*]
carefully, attentamente [*aht-tehn-tah-mehn'-teh*]
careless, imprudente, trascurato [*eem-proo-dehn'-teh, trah-skoo-rah'-toh*]
cargo, carico [*kah'-ree-koh*]
carnival, carnevale (m) [*kahr-neh-vah'-leh*]
carpenter, carpentiere (m), falegname (m) [*kahr-pehn-tee-eh'-reh, fah-leh-nyah'-meh*]
carpet, tappeto [*tahp-peh'-toh*]
carriage, carrozza, vettura [*kahr-rohts'-tsah, veht-too'-rah*]
carry *v.*, portare [*pohr-tah'-reh*]
carve *v.*, scolpire, intagliare [*skohl-pee'-reh, een-tah-lyah'-reh*]
case [situation], caso [*kah'-zoh*]
in any case, ad ogni modo [*ahd oh'-nyee moh'-doh*]
in that case, in tal caso [*een tahl kah'-zoh*]
cash *n.*, denaro, contanti (pl) [*deh-nah'-roh, kohn-tahn'-tee*]

pay cash *v.*, pagare in contanti [*pah-gah'-reh een kohn-tahn'-tee*]
cashier, cassiere (m) [*kahs-see-eh'-reh*]
castle, castello [*kahs-tehl'-loh*]
casually, casualmente, per caso [*kah-zoo-ahl-mehn'-teh, pehr kah'-zoh*]
cat, gatto [*gaht'-toh*]
catalog, catalogo [*kah-tah'-loh-goh*]
catch *v.*, afferrare, prendere [*ahf-fehr-rah'-reh, prehn'-deh-reh*]
catch cold, prendere un raffreddore [*prehn'-deh-reh oon rahf-frehd-doh'-reh*]
catch up, raggiungere [*raj-jee-oon'-jeh-reh*]
cathedral, cattedrale (f) [*kaht-teh-drah'-leh*]
Catholic, cattolico [*kaht-toh'-lee-koh*]
cause *n.*, causa [*kah'-oo-zah*]
cause *v.*, causare [*kah-oo-zah'-reh*]
caution, cauzione (f), prudenza [*kah-oo-tsee-oh'-neh, proo-dehn'-tsah*]
Caution! Attenzione! [*aht-tehn-tsee-oh'-neh*]
cave, caverna, grotta [*kah-vehr'-nah, groht'-tah*]
cease *v.*, cessare, fermarsi [*ches-sah'-reh, fehr-mahr'-see*]
celebrate *v.*, celebrare, festeggiare [*cheh-leh-brah'-reh, fehs-tehj-jee-ah'-reh*]
cellar, cantina [*kahn-tee'-nah*]
cement *n.*, cemento [*cheh-mehn'-toh*]
cemetery, cimitero [*chee-mee-teh'-roh*]
censorship, censura [*chehn-soo'-rah*]
cent, centesimo [*chehn-teh'-zee-moh*]
center, centro [*chehn'-troh*]
century, secolo [*seh'-koh-loh*]
cereal, cereale (m) [*cheh-reh-ah'-leh*]
ceremony, cerimonia [*cheh-ree-moh'-nee-ah*]
certain, certo, sicuro [*chehr'-toh, see-koo'-roh*]
certainly, certamente, sicuramente [*chehr-tah-mehn'-teh, see-koo-rah-mehn'-teh*]
certificate, certificato [*chehr-tee-fee-kah'-toh*]
certify *v.*, certificare, attestare [*chehr-tee-fee-kah'-reh, aht-*

tehs-tah'-reh]
chain, catena [*kah-teh'-nah*]
chair, sedia [*seh'-dee-ah*]
chairman, presidente (m) [*preh-see-dehn'-teh*]
challenge *n.*, sfida [*sfee'-dah*]
champagne, sciampagna [*shee-ahm-pah'-nyah*]
champion, campione (m) [*kahm-pee-oh'-neh*]
chance *n.*, caso [*kah'-zoh*]
by chance, per caso, forse [*pehr kah'-zoh, fohr'-seh*]
take a chance *v.*, rischiare [*rees-kee-ah'-reh*]
change [money] *n.*, resto [*rehs'-toh*]
Keep the change, Tenga il resto [*tehn'-gah eel rehs'-toh*]
change *v.*, cambiare [*kahm-bee-ah'-reh*]
chapel, cappella [*kahp-pehl'-lah*]
chapter, capitolo [*kah-pee'-toh-loh*]
character, carattere (m) [*kah-raht'-teh-reh*]
characteristic, caratteristico [*kah-raht-teh-rees'-tee-koh*]
charge *n.*, accusa, carica [*ahk-koo'-zah, kah'-ree-kah*]
charge [a battery] *v.*, caricare [*kah-ree-kah'-reh*]
charge [a customer] *v.*, addebitare [*ahd-deh-bee-tah'-reh*]
charity, beneficenza [*beh-neh-fee-chehn'-tsah*]
charming, affascinante, attraente [*ahf-fah-shee-nahn'-teh, aht-trah-ehn'-teh*]
chart *n.*, carta, cartella [*kahr'-tah, kahr-tehl'-lah*]
charter [lease] *v.*, noleggiare [*noh-lehj-jee-ah'-reh*]
chase *v.*, cacciare [*kahch-chee-ah'-reh*]
chauffeur, autista [*ah-oo-tees'-tah*]
cheap, a buon mercato [*ah boo-ohn' mehr-kah'-toh*]
cheat *v.*, truffare [*troof-fah'-reh*]
check [bill] *n.*, conto [*kohn'-toh*]
check [receipt] *n.*, scontrino [*skohn-tree'-noh*]
check [bank] *n.*, assegno [*ahs-seh'-nyoh*]
check *v.*, controllare, verificare [*kohn-troh-lah'-reh, veh-ree-fee-kah'-reh*]
checking account, conto corrente [*kohn'-toh kohr-rehn'-teh*]
checkroom, guardaroba [*goo-ahr-dah-roh'-bah*]
cheek, guancia [*goo-ahn'-chee-ah*]
cheer *v.*, incoraggiare [*een-koh-rahj-jee-ah'-reh*]

cheerful, allegro [*ahl-leh'-groh*]
cheese, formaggio [*fohr-mahj'-jee-oh*]
cherry, ciliegia [*chee-lee-eh'-jee-ah*]
chest [anat.], torace (m), petto [*toh-rah'-cheh*, *peht'-toh*]
chest of drawers, cassettone (m) [*kahs-seht-toh'-neh*]
chew *v.*, masticare [*mahs-tee-kah'-reh*]
chicken, pollo [*pohl'-loh*]
chief *n. & adj.*, principale, capo [*preen-chee-pah'-leh*, *kah'-poh*]
chiefly, principalmente [*preen-chee-pahl-mehn'-teh*]
child, bambino [*bahm-bee'-noh*]
Chile, Cile [*chee'-leh*]
Chilean *n. & adj.*, cileno [*chee-leh'-noh*]
chilly, freddo, fresco [*frehd'-doh*, *frehs'-koh*]
chin, mento [*mehn'-toh*]
China, Cina [*chee'-nah*]
chinaware, stoviglie (f, pl) di porcellana [*stoh-vee'-lyeh dee pohr-chehl-lah'-nah*]
Chinese *n. & adj.*, cinese [*chee-neh'-zeh*]
chocolate, cioccolata [*chee-oh-koh-lah'-tah*]
choice, scelta [*shehl'-tah*]
choose *v.*, scegliere [*sheh'-lyeh-reh*]
chop [cut of meat] *n.*, costoletta [*kohs-toh-leht'-tah*]
  lamb chop, costoletta d'agnello [*kohs-toh-leht'-tah dah-nyehl'-loh*]
  porkchop, costoletta di maiale [*kohs-toh-leht'-tah dee mah-ee-ah'-leh*]
Christian, cristiano [*krees-tee-ah'-noh*]
Christmas, Natale (m) [*nah-tah'-leh*]
  Merry Christmas! Buon Natale! [*boo-ohn' nah-tah'-leh*]
church, chiesa [*kee-eh'-zah*]
cigar, sigaro [*see'-gah-roh*]
cigarette, sigaretta [*see-gah-reht'-tah*]
circle *n.*, circolo [*cheer'-koh-loh*]
circulation, circolazione (f) [*cheer-koh-lah-tsee-oh'-neh*]
circumstance, circostanza [*cheer-kohs-tahn'-tsah*]
circus, circo [*cheer'-koh*]
citizen, cittadino [*cheet-tah-dee'-noh*]

citizenship, cittadinanza [*cheet-tah-dee-nahn'-tsah*]
city, città (f, indecl) [*cheet-tah'*]
city hall, palazzo del municipio [*pah-lats'-tsoh dehl moo-nee-chee'-pee-oh*]
civilian, borghese [*bohr-geh'-zeh*]
civilization, civilizzazione (f) [*chee-vee-leedz-dza-tsee-oh'-neh*]
claim *n.*, pretesa [*preh-teh'-zah*]
claim *v.*, reclamare [*reh-klah-mah'-reh*]
class, classe (f) [*klahs'-seh*]
classic *n. & adj.*, classico [*klahs'-see-koh*]
classmate, compagno di scuola [*kohm-pah'-nyoh dee skoo-oh'-lah*]
classroom, aula [*ah'-oo-lah*]
clean *adj.*, pulito [*poo-lee'-toh*]
clean *v.*, pulire [*poo-lee'-reh*]
cleaner's (shop), lavanderia a secco, tintoria [*lah-vahn-deh-ree'-ah ah sehk'-koh, teen-toh-ree'-ah*]
cleaning *n.*, pulizia [*poo-lee-tsee'-ah*]
cleaning woman, donna di servizio [*dohn'-nah dee sehr-vee'-tsee-oh*]
clear *adj.*, chiaro [*kee-ah'-roh*]
clergy, clero [*kleh'-roh*]
clerk, impiegato [*eem-pee-eh-gah'-toh*]
clever, abile, astuto [*ah'-bee-leh, ahs-too'-toh*]
client, cliente (m) [*klee-ehn'-teh*]
climate, clima (m) [*klee'-mah*]
climb *v.*, scalare [*skah-lah'-reh*]
clock, orologio [*oh-roh-loh'-jee-oh*]
  at seven o'clock, alle sette [*ahl'-leh seht'-teh*]
  It is three o'clock, Sono le tre [*soh'-noh leh treh*]
close [near] *adj.*, vicino [*vee-chee'-noh*]
close *v.*, chiudere [*kee-oo'-deh-reh*]
closed *adj.*, chiuso [*kee-oo'-zoh*]
closet, armadio [*ahr-mah'-dee-oh*]
cloth, panno [*pahn'-noh*]
clothes, vestiti, abiti [*vehs-tee'-tee, ah'-bee-tee*]
  put on clothes *v.*, vestirsi [*vehs-teer'-see*]
  take off clothes *v.*, spogliarsi [*spoh-lyahr'-see*]

cloud, nuvola [*noo'-voh-lah*]
cloudy, nuvoloso [*noo-voh-loh'-zoh*]
club [association] *n.*, circolo, club (m) [*cheer'-koh-loh, cloob*]
coarse, rude, ruvido [*roo'-deh, roo'-vee-doh*]
coast, costa [*kohs'-tah*]
coat, giacca, giacche (pl) [*jee-ahk'-kah, jee-ahk'-keh*]
  overcoat, cappotto [*kahp-poht'-toh*]
coffee, caffè (m) [*kahf-feh'*]
coffeehouse, caffè (m) [*kahf-feh'*]
coin *n.*, moneta [*moh-neh'-tah*]
coincidence, coincidenza [*koh-een-chee-dehn'-tsah*]
cold, freddo [*frehd'-doh*]
  be cold *v.*, avere freddo [*ah-veh'-reh frehd'-doh*]
  catch a cold *v.*, raffreddarsi [*rahf-frehd-dahr'-see*]
  Are you cold? Ha freddo? [*ah frehd'-doh*]
collar, colletto [*kohl-leht'-toh*]
colleague, collega (m, f) [*kohl-leh'-gah*]
collect *v.*, raccogliere [*rahk-koh'-lyeh-reh*]
collection, raccolta [*rahk-kohl'-tah*]
college, università (f, indecl) [*oo-nee-vehr-see-tah'*]
collide *v.*, urtare [*oor-tah'-reh*]
colloquial, lingua popolare [*leen'-goo-ah poh-poh-lah'-reh*]
color, colore (m) [*koh-loh'-reh*]
Colosseum, Colosseo [*koh-lohs-seh'-oh*]
column, colonna [*koh-lohn'-nah*]
comb *n.*, pettine (m) [*peht'-tee-neh*]
combination, combinazione (f) [*kohm-bee-nah-tsee-oh'-neh*]
combustible, combustibile [*kohm-boos-tee'-bee-leh*]
come *v.*, venire (irreg) [*veh-nee'-reh*]
  come about, accadere [*ahk-kah-deh'-reh*]
  come after, seguire [*seh-goo-ee'-reh*]
  come again, come back, ritornare [*ree-tohr-nah'-reh*]
  come by, passare [*pahs-sah'-reh*]
  come down, discendere [*dee-shehn'-deh-reh*]
  come forward, presentarsi [*preh-zehn-tahr'-see*]
  come in, entrare [*ehn-trah'-reh*]
  Come in! Avanti! [*ah-vahn'-tee*]
  Come on! Via!, Andiamo! [*vee'-ah ahn-dee-ah'-moh*]

comfort, comodità (f, indecl) [*koh-moh-dee-tah'*]
comfortable, comodo [*koh'-moh-doh*]
Are you comfortable? Sta comodo? [*stah koh'-moh-doh*]
command *n.*, ordine (m) [*ohr'-dee-neh*]
command *v.*, comandare, controllare [*koh-mahn-dah'-reh, kohn-troh-lah'-reh*]
comment *n.*, commento [*kohm-mehn'-toh*]
commentary, commentario [*kohm-mehn-tah'-ree-oh*]
commercial, commerciale [*kohm-mehr-chee-ah'-leh*]
commission, commissione (f) [*kohm-mees-see-oh'-neh*]
commit *v.*, commettere [*kohm-meht'-teh-reh*]
common, comune [*koh-moo'-neh*]
commotion, commozione (f) [*kohm-moh-tsee-oh'-neh*]
communicate *v.*, comunicare [*koh-moo-nee-kah'-reh*]
communication, comunicazione (f) [*koh-moo-nee-kah-tsee-oh'-neh*]
communist, comunista (m, f) [*koh-moo-nees'-tah*]
community, comunità (undecl) [*koh-moo-nee-tah'*]
companion, compagno [*kohm-pah'-nyoh*]
compare *v.*, comparare, paragonare [*kohm-pah-rah'-reh, pah-rah-goh-nah'-reh*]
comparison, comparazione (f), paragone (m) [*kohm-pah-rah-tsee-oh'-neh, pah-rah-goh'-neh*]
compartment, scompartimento [*skohm-pahr-tee-mehn'-toh*]
compass, bussola [*boos'-soh-lah*]
compassion, compassione (f) [*kohm-pahs-see-oh'-neh*]
compel *v.*, costringere [*kohs-treen'-jeh-reh*]
compensation, compensazione (f) [*kohm-pehn-sah-tsee-oh'-neh*]
competent, competente [*kohm-peh-tehn'-teh*]
competition, concorrenza, competizione (f) [*kohn-kohr-rehn'-tsah, kohm-peh-tee-tsee-oh'-neh*]
compile *v.*, compilare [*kohm-pee-lah'-reh*]
complain *v.*, lagnarsi [*lah-nyahr'-see*]
complaint, protesto, lagnanza [*proh-tehs'-toh, lah-nyahn'-tsah*]
complete, completo [*kohm-pleh'-toh*]
completely, completamente [*kohm-pleh-tah-mehn'-teh*]

complex, complesso [*kohm-plehs'-soh*]
complexion [of skin], carnagione (f) [*kahr-nah-jee-oh'-neh*]
complicated, complicato [*kohm-plee-kah'-toh*]
compliment, complimento [*kohm-plee-mehn'-toh*]
compose *v.*, comporre (irreg) [*kohm-pohr'-reh*]
composer, compositore (m) [*kohm-poh-zee-toh'-reh*]
composure, compostezza [*kohm-pohs-tehts'-tsa*]
comprehend *v.*, comprendere [*kohm-prehn'-deh-reh*]
compromise, compromesso [*kohm-proh-mehs'-soh*]
conceal *v.*, nascondere [*nahs-kohn'-deh-reh*]
conceited, vanitoso [*vah-nee-toh'-zoh*]
conceive *v.*, concepire [*kohn-cheh-pee'-reh*]
concentrate *v.*, concentrare [*kohn-chehn-trah'-reh*]
concept, concetto [*kohn-cheht'-toh*]
concerning, riguardo a [*ree-goo-ahr'-doh ah*]
concert, concerto [*kohn-chehr'-toh*]
concise, conciso [*kohn-chee'-zoh*]
conclusion, conclusione (f) [*kohn-kloo-zee-oh'-neh*]
condemn *v.*, condannare [*kohn-dahn-nah'-reh*]
condense *v.*, condensare [*kohn-dehn-sah'-reh*]
condition, condizione (f) [*kohn-dee-tsee-oh'-neh*]
  in good condition, in buono stato [*een boo-oh'-noh stah'-toh*]
conduct *n.*, condotta [*kohn-doht'-tah*]
conduct *v.*, condurre (irreg) [*kohn-door'-reh*]
conductor [of orchestra], direttore (m) [*dee-reht-toh'-reh*]
conductor [of train], conduttore (m) [*kohn-doot-toh'-reh*]
conference, conferenza [*kohn-feh-rehn'-tsah*]
confess *v.*, confessare [*kohn-fehs-sah'-reh*]
confession, confessione (f) [*kohn-fehs-see-oh'-neh*]
confident, fiducioso [*fee-doo-chee-oh'-zoh*]
confidential, confidenziale [*kohn-fee-dehn-tsee-ah'-leh*]
confirm *v.*, confermare [*kohn-fehr-mah'-reh*]
conflict *n.*, conflitto [*kohn-fleet'-toh*]
conflict *v.*, contrastare [*kohn-trahs-tah'-reh*]
confusion, confusione (f) [*kohn-foo-zee-oh'-neh*]
congratulate *v.*, congratularsi [*kohn-grah-too-lahr'-see*]
  Congratulations! Congratulazioni! [*kohn-grah-too-lah-*

tsee-oh'-nee]
connection, connessione (f) [*kohn-nehs-see-oh'-neh*]
conquer *v.*, conquistare [*kohn-koo-ees-tah'-reh*]
conscientious, coscienzioso [*kohn-shee-ehn-tsee-oh'-zoh*]
conscious, conscio [*kohn'-shee-oh*]
consecutive, consecutivo [*kohn-seh-koo-tee'-voh*]
consent *n.*, consenso [*kohn-sehn'-soh*]
consent *v.*, acconsentire [*ahk-kohn-sehn-tee'-reh*]
consequence, conseguenza [*kohn-seh-goo-ehn'-tsah*]
conservative, conservativo [*kohn-sehr-vah-tee'-voh*]
consider *v.*, considerare [*kohn-see-deh-rah'-reh*]
consideration, considerazione (f) [*kohn-see-deh-rah-tsee-oh'-neh*]
consist *v.*, consistere [*kohn-sees'-teh-reh*]
consistent, compatibile [*kohm-pah-tee'-bee-leh*]
constant, costante [*kohs-tahn'-teh*]
constitute *v.*, costituire [*kohs-tee-too-ee'-reh*]
constitution, costituzione (f) [*kohs-tee-too-tsee-oh'-neh*]
construction, costruzione (f) [*kohs-troo-tsee-oh'-neh*]
consul, console (m) [*kohn'-soh-leh*]
consulate, consolato [*kohn-soh-lah'-toh*]
consult *v.*, consultare [*kohn-sool-tah'-reh*]
consume *v.*, consumare [*kohn-soo-mah'-reh*]
consumer, consumatore (m) [*kohn-soo-mah-toh'-reh*]
contagious, contagioso [*kohn-tah-jee-oh'-zoh*]
contain *v.*, contenere [*kohn-teh-neh'-reh*]
container, recipiente (m) [*reh-chee-pee-ehn'-teh*]
contemporary, contemporaneo [*kohn-tehm-poh-rah'-neh-oh*]
contempt, disprezzo [*dees-prehts'-tsoh*]
content *adj.*, contento [*kohn-tehn'-toh*]
contents, contenuto [*kohn-teh-noo'-toh*]
contest *n.*, concorso [*kohn-kohr'-soh*]
continent, continente (m) [*kohn-tee-nehn'-teh*]
continuation, continuazione (f) [*kohn-tee-noo-ah-tsee-oh'-neh*]
continue *v.*, continuare [*kohn-tee-noo-ah'-reh*]
contract *n.*, contratto [*kohn-traht'-toh*]
contradiction, contradizione (f) [*kohn-trah-dee-tsee-oh'-neh*]

contrary, contrario [*kohn-trah'-ree-oh*]
on the contrary, al contrario [*ahl kohn-trah'-ree-oh*]
contrast *n.*, contrasto [*kohn-trahs'-toh*]
contribute *v.*, contribuire [*kohn-tree-boo-ee'-reh*]
contribution, contribuzione (f) [*kohn-tree-boo-tsee-oh'-neh*]
control *n.*, controllo [*kohn-trohl'-loh*]
control *v.*, controllare [*kohn-trohl-lah'-reh*]
controversy, controversia, disputa [*kohn-troh-vehr'-see-ah, dees'-poo-tah*]
convenient, conveniente [*kohn-veh-nee-ehn'-teh*]
convent, convento [*kohn-vehn'-toh*]
conversation, conversazione (f) [*kohn-vehr-sah-tsee-oh'-neh*]
convert *v.*, convertire [*kohn-vehr-tee'-reh*]
convict *n.*, condannato [*kohn-dah-nah'-toh*]
convince *v.*, convincere [*kohn-veen'-cheh-reh*]
cook *n.*, cuoco [*koo-oh'-koh*]
cook *v.*, cucinare [*koo-chee-nah'-reh*]
cool *adj.*, fresco [*frehs'-koh*]
cool *v.*, raffreddare [*rahf-frehd-dah'-reh*]
cooperation, cooperazione (f) [*koh-oh-peh-rah-tsee-oh'-neh*]
copper *n.*, rame (m) [*rah'-meh*]
copy *n.*, copia [*koh'-pee-ah*]
copy *v.*, copiare [*koh-pee-ah'-reh*]
cord, corda [*kohr'-dah*]
cordial, cordiale [*kohr-dee-ah'-leh*]
cork, tappo [*tahp'-poh*]
corkscrew, cavatappi (m, sing) [*kah-vah-tahp'-pee*]
corn, granoturco [*grah-noh-toor'-koh*]
corner, angolo [*ahn'-goh-loh*]
corporation, corporazione (f) [*kohr-poh-rah-tsee-oh'-neh*]
correct *adj.*, corretto [*kohr-reht'-toh*]
correction, correzione (f) [*kohr-reh-tsee-oh'-neh*]
correspondence, corrispondenza [*kohr-rees-pohn-dehn'-tsah*]
corridor, corridoio [*kohr-ree-doh'-ee-oh*]
corrupt *adj.*, corrotto [*kohr-roht'-toh*]
cosmetics, cosmetici [*kohz-meh'-tee-chee*]
cost *n.*, costo, spesa [*kohs'-toh, speh'-zah*]
cost of living, costo della vita [*kohs'-toh dehl'-lah vee'-tah*]

cost *v.*, costare [*kohs-tah'-reh*]
How much does this cost? Quanto costa questo? [*koo-ahn'-toh kohs'-tah koo-ehs'-toh*]
cot, branda [*brahn'-dah*]
cottage, casa di campagna [*kah'-zah dee kahm-pah'-nyah*]
cotton, cotone (m) [*koh-toh'-neh*]
couch, divano [*dee-vah'-noh*]
cough *n.*, tosse (f) [*tohs'-seh*]
cough *v.*, tossire [*tohs-see'-reh*]
counsel *v.*, concigliare [*kohn-chee-lyah'-reh*]
count *v.*, contare [*kohn-tah'-reh*]
count on, contare su [*kohn-tah'-reh soo*]
country, nazione (f), paese (m) [*nah-tsee-oh'-neh, pah-eh'-zeh*]
country house, casa di campagna [*kah'-zah dee kahm-pah'-nyah*]
countryman, compatriota [*kohm-pah-tree-oh'-tah*]
countryside, campagna [*kahm-pah'-nyah*]
couple *n.*, coppia [*kohp'-pee-ah*]
coupon, scontrino [*skohn-tree'-noh*]
courage, coraggio [*koh-rahj'-jee-oh*]
courageous, coraggioso [*koh-rahj-jee-oh'-zoh*]
course [way], corso [*kohr'-soh*]
of course, naturalmente [*nah-too-rahl-mehn'-teh*]
a matter of course, una cosa ovvia [*oo'-nah koh'-zah ohv'-vee-ah*]
course [of a meal], portata [*pohr-tah'-tah*]
court, corte (f), tribunale (m) [*kohr'-teh, tree-boo-nah'-leh*]
courteous, cortese [*kohr-teh'-zeh*]
courtyard, cortile (m) [*kohr-tee'-leh*]
cousin [female], cugina [*koo-jee'-nah*]
cousin [male], cugino [*koo-jee'-noh*]
cover *n.*, copertura [*koh-pehr-too'-rah*]
cover *v.*, coprire [*koh-pree'-reh*]
coward, vigliacco [*vee-lyahk'-koh*]
cracker, biscotto [*bees-koht'-toh*]
cradle, culla [*kool'-lah*]
craftsman, artigiano [*ahr-tee-jee-ah'-noh*]

crash *n.*, fracasso [*frah-kahs'-soh*]
crawl *v.*, strisciarsi [*stree-shee-ahr'-see*]
crazy, pazzo [*pahts'-tsoh*]
cream, crema [*kreh'-mah*]
create *v.*, creare [*kreh-ah'-reh*]
creation, creazione (f) [*kreh-ah-tsee-oh'-neh*]
creature, creatura [*kreh-ah-too'-rah*]
credit *n.*, credito [*kreh'-dee-toh*]
creditor, creditore (m) [*kreh-dee-toh'-reh*]
crew, equipaggio [*eh-koo-ee-pahj'-jee-oh*]
crib, letto da bambino [*leht'-toh dah bahm-bee'-noh*]
crime, crimine (m) [*kree'-mee-neh*]
criminal, criminale [*kree-mee-nah'-leh*]
crisis, crisi (f) [*kree'-zee*]
critical, critico [*kree'-tee-koh*]
criticize *v.*, criticare [*kree-tee-kah'-reh*]
crook [cheat], imbroglione (m) [*eem-broh-lyoh'-neh*]
crop *n.*, raccolto [*rahk-kohl'-toh*]
cross *n.*, croce (f) [*kroh'-cheh*]
cross *v.*, attraversare [*aht-trah-vehr-sah'-reh*]
crossing, traversata [*trah-vehr-sah'-tah*]
crossroad, incrocio [*een-kroh'-chee-oh*]
crowd, folla [*fohl'-lah*]
crowded, affollato [*ahf-fohl-lah'-toh*]
crown *n.*, corona [*koh-roh'-nah*]
cruel, crudele [*kroo-deh'-leh*]
cruelty, crudeltà (f, indecl) [*kroo-dehl-tah'*]
cruise *n.*, crociera [*kroh-chee-eh'-rah*]
crumb, briciola [*bree'-chee-oh-lah*]
crush *v.*, schiacciare [*skee-ahch-chee-ah'-reh*]
cry *n.*, grido [*gree'-doh*]
cry [weep] *v.*, piangere [*pee-ahn'-jeh-reh*]
cry [shout] *v.*, gridare [*gree-dah'-reh*]
crystal, cristallo [*krees-tahl'-loh*]
cube, cubo [*koo'-boh*]
culture [intellectual], cultura [*kool-too'-rah*]
cunning, astuto [*ahs-too'-toh*]
cup, tazza [*tahts'-tsah*]

cupboard, credenza [*kreh-dehn'-tsah*]
cure *v.*, curare [*koo-rah'-reh*]
curiosity, curiosità (f, indecl) [*koo-ree-oh-zee-tah'*]
curious, curioso [*koo-ree-oh'-zoh*]
currency, moneta corrente [*moh-neh'-tah kohr-rehn'-teh*]
current *n.* & *adj.*, corrente (f) [*kohr-rehn'-teh*]
curse *n.*, maledizione (f) [*mah-leh-dee-tsee-oh'-nèh*]
curtain, tenda, cortina [*tehn'-dah, kohr-tee'-nah*]
curve, curva [*koor'-vah*]
dangerous curve, curva pericolosa [*koor'-vah peh-ree-koh-loh'-zah*]
cushion, cuscino [*koo-shee'-noh*]
custody, custodia [*koos-toh'-dee-ah*]
custom, costume (m), usanza [*kohs-too'-meh, oo-zahn'-tsah*]
customary, abituale [*ah-bee-too-ah'-leh*]
customer, cliente (m) [*klee-ehn'-teh*]
customs, customshouse, dogana [*doh-gah'-nah*]
customs duty, dazio di dogana [*dah'-tsee-oh dee doh-gah'-nah*]
customs officer, agente di dogana [*ah-jehn'-teh dee doh-gah'-nah*]
cut [wound] *n.*, ferita [*feh-ree'-tah*]
cut [pattern] *n.*, taglio [*tah'-lyoh*]
cut *v.*, tagliare [*tah-lyah'-reh*]
cylinder, cilindro [*chee-leen'-droh*]
Czechoslovak *n.* & *adj.*, ceco-slovacco [*cheh-koh-sloh-vahk'-koh*]
Czechoslovakia, Ceco-slovacchia [*cheh-kohs-loh-vahk-kee'-ah*]

D

dad, daddy, papà, babbo [*pah-pah', bahb'-boh*]
daily, quotidiano, giornalmente [*koo-oh-tee-dee-ah'-noh, jee-ohr-nahl-mehn'-teh*]

dairy, latteria [*laht-teh-ree'-ah*]
dam *n.*, diga [*dee'-gah*]
damage *v.*, danneggiare [*dahn-nehj-jee-ah'-reh*]
damaged, danneggiato [*dahn-nej-jee-ah'-toh*]
damp, umido [*oo'-mee-doh*]
dance *n.*, danza [*dahn'-tsah*]
dance *v.*, ballare [*bahl-lah'-reh*]
dancer, ballerino, ballerina [*bahl-leh-ree'-noh, bahl-leh-ree'-nah*]
danger, pericolo [*peh-ree'-koh-loh*]
dangerous, pericoloso [*peh-ree-koh-loh'-zoh*]
dare [attempt] *v.*, osare [*oh-zah'-reh*]
daring, intrepido [*een-treh'-pee-doh*]
dark, buio [*boo'-ee-oh*]
  dark complexion, bruno [*broo'-noh*]
darkness, oscurità (f, indecl) [*ohs-koo-ree-tah'*]
darling *adj.*, caro [*kah'-roh*]
date [day] *n.*, dàta [*dah'-tah*]
date [appointment] *n.*, appuntamento [*ahp-poon-tah-mehn'-toh*]
daughter, figlia [*fee'-lyah*]
daughter-in-law, nuora [*noo-oh'-rah*]
dawn, alba, aurora [*ahl'-bah, ah-oo-roh'-rah*]
day, giorno [*jee-ohr'-noh*]
  all day, tutto il giorno [*toot'-toh eel jee-ohr'-noh*]
  day after tomorrow, dopodomani [*doh-poh-doh-mah'-nee*]
  day before yesterday, l'altro ieri [*lahl-troh ee-eh'-ree*]
  every day, ogni giorno [*oh'-nyee jee-ohr'-noh*]
  the next day, il giorno prossimo [*eel jee-ohr'-noh prohs'-see-moh*]
  twice a day, due volte al giorno [*doo'-eh vohl'-teh ahl jee-ohr'-noh*]
daydream, sogno ad occhi aperti [*soh'-nyoh ahd ohk'-kee ah-pehr'-tee*]
dead, morto [*mohr'-toh*]
deadly, mortale [*mohr-tah'-leh*]
deaf, sordo [*sohr'-doh*]
deal *n.*, affare (m) [*ahf-fah'-reh*]

a great deal, molto [*mohl'-toh*]
deal *v.*, trattare [*traht-tah'-reh*]
dealer, negoziante (m) [*neh-goh-tsee-ahn'-teh*]
dear *adj.*, caro [*kah'-roh*]
dearly, caramente [*kah-rah-mehn'-teh*]
death, morte (f) [*mohr'-teh*]
debt, debito [*deh'-bee-toh*]
decade, decennio [*deh-chehn'-nee-oh*]
decay *n.*, decadenza, rovina [*deh-kah-dehn'-tsah, roh-vee'-nah*]
deceased, defunto [*deh-foon'-toh*]
deceit, inganno [*een-gahn'-noh*]
deceive *v.*, ingannare [*een-gahn-nah'-reh*]
December, dicembre (m) [*dee-chehm'-breh*]
decency, correttezza [*kohr-reht-tehts'-tsah*]
decent, decente [*deh-chehn'-teh*]
deception, illusione (f) [*eel-loo-zee-oh'-neh*]
deck [of ship], ponte (m) [*pohn'-teh*]
deck [of cards], mazzo [*mahts'-tsoh*]
decide *v.*, decidere [*deh-chee'-deh-reh*]
decision, decisione (f) [*deh-chee-zee-oh'-neh*]
declare *v.*, dichiarare [*dee-kee-ah-rah'-reh*]
decline [refuse] *v.*, declinare [*deh-klee-nah'-reh*]
decorate *v.*, decorare [*deh-koh-rah'-reh*]
decoration, decorazione (f) [*deh-koh-rah-tsee-oh'-neh*]
decrease *v.*, diminuire [*dee-mee-noo-ee'-reh*]
decree, decreto [*deh-kreh'-toh*]
dedicate *v.*, consacrare, dedicare [*kohn-sah-krah'-reh, deh-dee-kah'-reh*]
deed [act], fatto, azione (f) [*faht'-toh, ah-tsee-oh'-neh*]
deep, profondo [*proh-fohn'-doh*]
defeat *n.*, sconfitta [*skohn-feet'-tah*]
defeat *v.*, sconfiggere [*skohn-feej'-jeh-reh*]
defective, difettoso [*dee-feht-toh'-zoh*]
defend *v.*, difendere [*dee-fehn'-deh-reh*]
deficient, deficiente [*deh-fee-chee-ehn'-teh*]
define *v.*, definire [*deh-fee-nee'-reh*]
definite, definito [*deh-fee-nee'-toh*]

definition, definizione (f) [*deh-fee-nee-tsee-oh'-neh*]
degree, grado, laurea [*grah'-doh, lah'-oo-reh-ah*]
delay *v.*, ritardare [*ree-tahr-dah'-reh*]
deliberate *v.*, deliberare [*deh-lee-beh-rah'-reh*]
delicate, delicato [*deh-lee-kah'-toh*]
delicious, delizioso [*deh-lee-tsee-oh'-zoh*]
delight *n.*, diletto [*dee-leht'-toh*]
delight *v.*, dilettare [*dee-leht-tah'-reh*]
deliver *v.*, consegnare [*kohn-seh-nyah'-reh*]
demand *n.*, richiesta [*ree-kee-ehs'-tah*]
demand *v.*, richiedere [*ree-kee-eh'-deh-reh*]
democracy, democrazia [*deh-moh-krah-tsee'-ah*]
demonstrate *v.*, dimostrare [*dee-mohs-trah'-reh*]
demonstration, dimostrazione (f) [*dee-mohs-trah-tsee-oh'-neh*]
denial, rifiuto [*ree-fee-oo'-toh*]
dentist, dentista (m) [*dehn-tees'-tah*]
deny *v.*, negare [*neh-gah'-reh*]
depart *v.*, partire [*pahr-tee'-reh*]
department, dipartimento [*dee-pahr-tee-mehn'-toh*]
departure, partenza [*pahr-tehn'-tsah*]
depend on *v.*, dipendere da [*dee-pehn'-deh-reh dah*]
That depends, Dipende [*dee-pehn'-deh*]
dependent, dipendente [*dee-pehn-dehn'-teh*]
deposit *v.*, depositare [*deh-poh-zee-tah'-reh*]
depot, magazzino [*mah-gahdz-dzee'-noh*]
deprive *v.*, privare [*pree-vah'-reh*]
depth, profondità (f, indecl) [*proh-fohn-dee-tah'*]
deputy, deputato [*deh-poo-tah'-toh*]
descend *v.*, discendere [*dee-shehn'-deh-reh*]
describe *v.*, descrivere [*dehs-kree'-veh-reh*]
description, descrizione (f) [*dehs-kree-tsee-oh'-neh*]
desert *n.*, deserto [*deh-zehr'-toh*]
desert *v.*, disertare [*dee-zehr-tah'-reh*]
deserve *v.*, meritare [*meh-ree-tah'-reh*]
design *n.*, disegno [*dee-zeh'-nyoh*]
desirable, desiderabile [*deh-zee-deh-rah'-bee-leh*]
desire *n.*, desiderio [*deh-zee-deh'-ree-oh*]
desire *v.*, desiderare [*deh-zee-deh-rah'-reh*]

desk, scrivania [*skree-vah-nee'-ah*]
despair *n.*, disperazione (f) [*dees-peh-rah-tsee-oh'-neh*]
desperate, disperato [*dees-peh-rah'-toh*]
despite, malgrado [*mahl-grah'-doh*]
dessert, dolce [*dohl'-cheh*]
destiny, destino [*dehs-tee'-noh*]
destroy *v.*, distruggere [*dees-trooj'-jeh-reh*]
destruction, distruzione (f) [*dees-troo-tsee-oh'-neh*]
detail, dettaglio [*deht-tah'-lyoh*]
detain *v.*, trattenere [*traht-teh-neh'-reh*]
detective, agente (investigativo) (m) [*ah-jehn'-teh* (*een-vehs-tee-gah-tee'-voh*)]
determine *v.*, determinare [*deh-tehr-mee-nah'-reh*]
detour *n.*, deviazione (f) [*deh-vee-ah-tsee-oh'-neh*]
develop *v.*, sviluppare [*zvee-loop-pah'-reh*]
development, sviluppo [*zvee-loop'-poh*]
device, meccanismo [*mehk-kah-neez'-moh*]
devil, diavolo [*dee-ah'-voh-loh*]
devoted, devoto [*deh-voh'-toh*]
devotion, devozione (f) [*deh-voh-tsee-oh'-neh*]
diagnosis, diagnosi (f, sing) [*dee-ahg-noh'-zee*]
dialect, dialetto [*dee-ah-leht'-toh*]
dialogue, dialogo [*dee-ah'-loh-goh*]
diameter, diametro [*dee-ah'-meh-troh*]
diamond, diamante (m) [*dee-ah-mahn'-teh*]
diary, diario [*dee-ah'-ree-oh*]
dice [gambling] *n. pl.*, dadi (pl) [*dah'-dee*]
dictate *v.*, dettare [*deht-tah'-reh*]
dictation, dettato [*deht-tah'-toh*]
dictionary, dizionario [*dee-tsee-oh-nah'-ree-oh*]
die *v.*, morire (irreg) [*moh-ree'-reh*]
diet *n.*, dieta [*dee-eh'-tah*]
difference, differenza [*deef-feh-rehn'-tsah*]
It does not make any difference, È la stessa cosa [*eh' lah stehs'-sah koh'-zah*]
What difference does it make? Che importa? [*keh eem-pohr'-tah*]
different, differente [*deef-feh-rehn'-teh*]

difficult, difficile [*deef-fee'-chee-leh*]
difficulty, difficoltà (f, indecl) [*deef-fee-kohl-tah'*]
dig *v.*, scavare [*skah-vah'-reh*]
digestion, digestione (f) [*dee-jehs-tee-oh'-neh*]
dignity, dignità (f, indecl) [*dee-nyee-tah'*]
dim *adj.*, oscuro [*ohs-koo'-roh*]
diminish *v.*, diminuire [*dee-mee-noo-ee'-reh*]
dine *v.*, cenare [*cheh-nah'-reh*]
dining car, vagone ristorante (m) [*vah-goh'-neh rees-toh-rahn'-teh*]
dining room, sala da pranzo [*sah'-lah dah prahn'-tsoh*]
dinner, cena [*cheh'-nah*]
  Dinner is ready! La cena è pronto! [*lah cheh'-nah eh' prohn'-toh*]
diploma, diploma (m) [*dee-ploh'-mah*]
diplomat, **diplomatic**, diplomatico [*dee-ploh-mah'-tee-koh*]
direct *adj.*, diretto [*dee-reht'-toh*]
direct *v.*, dirigere [*dee-ree'-jeh-reh*]
direction, direzione (f) [*dee-reh-tsee-oh'-neh*]
director, direttore (m), direttrice (f) [*dee-reht-toh'-reh, dee-reht-tree'-cheh*]
dirt, sporcizia [*spohr-chee'-tsee-ah*]
dirty, sporco [*spohr'-koh*]
disability, incapacità (f, indecl) [*een-kah-pah-chee-tah'*]
disabled, incapace [*een-kah-pah'-cheh*]
disadvantage, svantaggio [*zvahn-tahj'-jee-oh*]
disagree *v.*, non essere d'accordo [*nohn ehs'-seh-reh dahk-kohr'-doh*]
disagreeable, sgradevole [*zgrah-deh'-voh-leh*]
disagreement, disaccordo [*deez-ahk-kohr'-doh*]
disappear *v.*, scomparire [*skohm-pah-ree'-reh*]
disappoint *v.*, deludere [*deh-loo'-deh-reh*]
disappointed, deluso [*deh-loo'-zoh*]
disapprove *v.*, disapprovare [*deez-ahp-proh-vah'-reh*]
disaster, disastro [*dee-zahs'-troh*]
discharge [an employee] *v.*, congedare [*kohn-jeh-dah'-reh*]
discipline *n.*, disciplina [*dee-shee-plee'-nah*]
disclose *v.*, rivelare [*ree-veh-lah'-reh*]

discomfort, disagio [*dee-zah'-jee-oh*]
disconnect *v.*, staccare [*stahk-kah'-reh*]
discontinue *v.*, interrompere [*een-tehr-rohm'-peh-reh*]
discount *n.*, sconto [*skohn'-toh*]
discourage *v.*, scoraggiare [*skoh-rahj-jee-ah'-reh*]
discouraged, demoralizzato [*deh-moh-rah-leedz-dzah'-toh*]
discouraging, demoralizzante [*deh-moh-rah-leedz-dzahn'-teh*]
discover *v.*, scoprire [*skoh-pree'-reh*]
discovery, scoperta [*skoh-pehr'-tah*]
discuss *v.*, discutere [*dees-koo'-teh-reh*]
discussion, discussione (f) [*dees-koos-see-oh'-neh*]
disease, malattia [*mah-laht-tee'-ah*]
disgrace *n.*, disgrazia, disonore (m) [*deez-grah'-tsee-ah, deez-oh-noh'-reh*]
disguise *n.*, travestimento [*trah-vehs-tee-mehn'-toh*]
disgusted, disgustato [*deez-goos-tah'-toh*]
dish, piatto [*pee-aht'-toh*]
dishonest, disonesto [*deez-oh-nehs'-toh*]
dislike *v.*, non amare [*nohn ah-mah'-reh*]
I dislike it, Non mi piace [*nohn mee pee-ah'-cheh*]
dismiss *v.*, congedare [*kohn-jeh-dah'-reh*]
disobey *v.*, disobbedire [*deez-ohb-beh-dee'-reh*]
disorder, disordine (m) [*deez-ohr'-dee-neh*]
display *v.*, esporre (irreg) [*ehs-pohr'-reh*]
dispose *v.*, disporre (irreg) [*dees-pohr'-reh*]
dispute *n.*, disputa [*dees'-poo-tah*]
dissolve *v.*, dissolvere [*dees-sohl'-veh-reh*]
distance, distanza [*dees-tahn'-tsah*]
distant, distante [*dees-tahn'-teh*]
distinct, distinto [*dees-teen'-toh*]
distinguish *v.*, distinguere [*dees-teen'-goo-eh-reh*]
distinguished, distinto, illustre [*dees-teen'-toh, eel-loos'-treh*]
distress *n.*, difficoltà, pena [*deef-fee-kohl-tah', peh'-nah*]
distress *v.*, affliggere [*ahf-fleej'-jeh-reh*]
distribute *v.*, distribuire [*dees-tree-boo-ee'-reh*]
district, distretto [*dees-treht'-toh*]
distrust *v.*, diffidare [*deef-fee-dah'-reh*]
disturb *v.*, disturbare [*dees-toor-bah'-reh*]

disturbance, disturbo [*dees-toor'-boh*]
ditch *n.*, fossa [*fohs'-sah*]
dive *v.*, tuffarsi (refl) [*toof-fahr'-see*]
divide *v.*, dividere [*dee-vee'-deh-reh*]
divine *adj.*, divino [*dee-vee'-noh*]
division, divisione (f) [*dee-vee-zee-oh'-neh*]
divorce *n.*, divorzio [*dee-vohr'-tsee-oh*]
dizzy, stordito [*stohr-dee'-toh*]
  feel dizzy *v.*, avere le vertigini [*ah-veh'-reh leh vehr-tee'-jee-nee*]
do *v.*, fare (irreg) [*fah'-reh*]
  Do you like it? Vi piace? [*vee pee-ah'-cheh*]
  Don't leave, Non partire [*nohn pahr-tee'-reh*]
  Do me a favor, Mi faccia un favore [*mee fahch'-chee-ah oon fah-voh'-reh*]
  do without, fare a meno di [*fah'-reh ah meh'-noh dee*]
  How do you do? Come sta? [*koh'-meh stah*]
  I do not know her, Non la conosco [*nohn lah koh-nohs'-koh*]
  What can I do for you? Cosa posso servirla? [*koh'-zah pohs'-soh sehr-veer'-lah*]
dock *n.*, molo [*moh'-loh*]
doctor, dottore (m), dottoressa (f) [*doht-toh'-reh, doht-toh-rehs'-sah*]
document, documento [*doh-koo-mehn'-toh*]
dog, cane (m) [*kah'-neh*]
doll, bambola [*bahm'-boh-lah*]
dollar, dollaro [*dohl'-lah-roh*]
domestic, domestico [*doh-mehs'-tee-koh*]
door, porta [*pohr'-tah*]
  Close the door! Chiuda la porta! [*kee-oo'-dah lah pohr'-tah*]
  Open the door! [Apra la porta! [*ah'-prah lah pohr'-tah*]
dormitory, dormitorio [*dohr-mee-toh'-ree-oh*]
double, doppio [*dohp'-pee-oh*]
doubt, dubbio [*doob'-bee-oh*]
doubt *v.*, dubitare [*doo-bee-tah'-reh*]
doubtful, dubbioso [*doob-bee-oh'-zoh*]

doubtless, senza dubbi [*sehn'-tsah doob'-bee*]
down, giù, in basso [*jee-oo', een bahs'-soh*]
  Down with . . . ! Abbasso con . . . ! [*ahb-bahs'-soh kohn*]
  fall down *v.*, cadere [*kah-deh'-reh*]
  go down *v.*, scendere [*shehn'-deh-reh*]
  lie down *v.*, sdraiarsi [*zdrah-ee-ahr'-see*]
  sit down *v.*, sedersi [*seh-dehr'-see*]
  take down *v.*, annotare, demolire [*ahn-noh-tah'-reh, deh-moh-lee'-reh*]
downfall, caduta [*kah-doo'-tah*]
downstairs, al piano inferiore [*ahl pee-ah'-noh een-feh-ree-oh'-reh*]
doze *v.*, sonnecchiare [*sohn-nehk-kee-ah'-reh*]
dozen, dozzina [*dohdz-dzee'-nah*]
draft [bank], tratta di pagamento [*traht'-tah dee pah-gah-mehn'-toh*]
draft [air], corrente (f) d'aria [*kohr-rehn'-teh dahr'-ee-ah*]
drag *v.*, trascinare [*trah-shee-nah'-reh*]
drain, fogna [*foh'-nyah*]
drama, dramma (m) [*drahm'-mah*]
dramatic, drammatico [*drahm-mah'-tee-koh*]
draw [picture], disegnare [*dee-zeh-nyah'-reh*]
drawer, cassetto [*kahs-seht'-toh*]
dreadful, spaventoso [*spah-vehn-toh'-zoh*]
dream *n.*, sogno [*soh'-nyoh*]
dream *v.*, sognare [*soh-nyah'-reh*]
dress *n.*, abito [*ah'-bee-toh*]
  evening dress, abito da sera [*ah'-bee-toh dah seh'-rah*]
dress *v.*, vestire [*vehs-tee'-reh*]
  get dressed, vestirsi (refl) [*vehs-teer'-see*]
dresser, guardarobiere (m) [*goo-ahr-dah-roh-bee-eh'-reh*]
dressing table, toletta [*toh-leht'-tah*]
dressmaker, sarta [*sahr'-tah*]
drink *n.*, bevanda [*beh-vahn'-dah*]
drink *v.*, bere (irreg) [*beh'-reh*]
drive [a car] *v.*, guidare [*goo-ee-dah'-reh*]
driver, autista (m) [*ah-oo-tees'-tah*]
driving license, patente automobilistica (f) [*pah-tehn'-teh*

ah-oo-toh-moh-bee-lees'-tee-kah]
drop *v.*, lasciar cadere [*lah-shee-ahr' kah-deh'-reh*]
drown *v.*, annegarsi [*ahn-neh-gahr'-see*]
drug, droga, narcotico [*droh'-gah, nahr-koh'-tee-koh*]
drugstore, farmacia [*fahr-mah-chee'-ah*]
drum, tamburo [*tahm-boo'-roh*]
drunk, ubriaco [*oo-bree-ah'-koh*]
dry *adj.*, asciutto [*ah-shee-oot'-toh*]
dry *v.*, asciugare [*ah-shee-oo-gah'-reh*]
dry-clean *v.*, pulire a secco [*poo-lee'-reh ah sehk'-koh*]
due (to), a causa di [*ah kah'-oo-zah dee*]
dues *n., pl.*, tributo, debito [*tree-boo'-to, deh'-bee-toh*]
dull, noioso [*noh-ee-oh'-zoh*]
dumb, muto [*moo'-toh*]
durable, durevole [*doo-reh'-voh-leh*]
during, durante [*doo-rahn'-teh*]
dusk, crepuscolo [*kreh-poos'-koh-loh*]
dust *n.*, polvere (f) [*pohl'-veh-reh*]
dusty, polveroso [*pohl-veh-roh'-zoh*]
Dutch *n. & adj.*, olandese [*oh-lahn-deh'-zeh*]
duty, dovere (m) [*doh-veh'-reh*]
be on duty *v.*, essere di servizio [*ehs'-seh-reh dee sehr-vee'-tsee-oh*]
duty-free, esente da tassa [*eh-zehn'-teh dah tahs'-sah*]
dwell *v.*, abitare [*ah-bee-tah'-reh*]
dye *n.*, tinta, tintura [*teen'-tah, teen-too'-rah*]
dye *v.*, tingere [*teen'-jeh-reh*]
dysentery, dissenteria [*dees-sehn-teh-ree'-ah*]

E

each, ogni, ciascuno [*oh'-nyee, chee-ahs-koo'-noh*]
each one, ciascuno [*chee-ahs-koo'-noh*]
each other, l'un l'altro, a vicenda [*loon lahl'-troh, ah vee-chehn'-dah*]

each time, ogni volta [*oh'-nyee vohl'-tah*]
eager, avido [*ah'-vee-doh*]
ear, orecchio, le orecchie (pl) [*oh-rehk'-kee-oh, leh oh-rehk'-kee-eh*]
earring, orecchino [*oh-rehk-kee'-noh*]
early, presto, di buon'ora [*prehs'-toh, dee boo-ohn-oh'-rah*]
earn *v.*, guadagnare [*goo-ah-dah-nyah'-reh*]
earth, terra [*tehr'-rah*]
earthquake, terremoto [*tehr-reh-moh'-toh*]
ease, facilità (f, indecl) [*fah-chee-lee-tah'*]
easily, facilmente [*fah-cheel-mehn'-teh*]
east, est (m) [*ehst*]
Far East, Oriente (m) [*oh-ree-ehn'-teh*]
Middle East, Medio Oriente [*meh'-dee-oh oh-ree-ehn'-teh*]
Near East, Levante (m) [*leh-vahn'-teh*]
easy, facile [*fah'-chee-leh*]
Take it easy! Con calma! [*kohn kahl'-mah*]
eat *v.*, mangiare [*mahn-jee-ah'-reh*]
echo, eco [*eh'-koh*]
economical, economico [*eh-koh-noh'-mee-koh*]
edge, orlo [*ohr'-loh*]
edition, edizione (f) [*eh-dee-tsee-oh'-neh*]
editor, redattore [*reh-daht-toh'-reh*]
education, istruzione (f) [*ees-troo-tsee-oh'-neh*]
effective, effettivo [*ehf-feht-tee'-voh*]
efficient, efficiente [*ehf-fee-chee-ehn'-teh*]
effort, sforzo [*sfohr'-tsoh*]
egg, uovo, le uova (pl) [*oo-oh'-voh, leh oo-oh'-vah*]
fried eggs, uova fritte [*oo-oh'-vah freet'-teh*]
hard-boiled eggs, uova sode [*oo-oh'-vah soh'-deh*]
scrambled eggs, uova strapazzate [*oo-oh'-vah strah-pahts-tsah'-teh*]
soft-boiled eggs, uova a la coque [*oo-oh'-vah ah lah kohk*]
Egypt, Egitto [*eh-jeet'-toh*]
Egyptian *n. & adj.*, egiziano [*eh-jee-tsee-ah'-noh*]
eight, otto [*oht'-toh*]
eighteen, diciotto [*dee-chee-oht'-toh*]
eighth, ottavo [*oht-tah'-voh*]

eighty, ottanta [*oht-tahn'-tah*]
either, l'uno o l'altro [*loo'-noh oh lahl'-troh*]
elaborate, accurato [*ahk-koo-rah'-toh*]
elastic *n. & adj.*, elastico [*eh-lahs'-tee-koh*]
elbow, gomito [*goh'-mee-toh*]
elderly, anziano [*ahn-tsee-ah'-noh*]
election, elezione (f) [*eh-leh-tsee-oh'-neh*]
electricity, elettricità (f, indecl) [*eh-leht-tree-chee-tah'*]
elegant, elegante [*eh-leh-gahn'-teh*]
elementary, elementare [*eh-leh-mehn-tah'-reh*]
elevator, ascensore (m) [*ah-shehn-soh'-reh*]
eleven, undici [*oon'-dee-chee*]
eliminate *v.*, eliminare [*eh-lee-mee-nah'-reh*]
else, altro [*ahl'-troh*]
  Anything else? Qualche altra cosa? [*koo-al'-keh ahl'-trah koh'-zah*]
  nobody else, nessun altro [*nehs-soon' ahl'-troh*]
  Nothing else? Nient' altro? [*nee-ehnt-ahl'-troh*]
  somebody else, qualcun altro [*koo-ahl-koon' ahl'-troh*]
  someone else, un altra persona [*oon ahl'-trah pehr-soh'-nah*]
  somewhere else, in un altro posto [*een oon ahl'-troh pohs'-toh*]
embarrassed, imbarazzato [*eem-bah-rahts-tsah'-toh*]
embassy, ambasciata [*ahm-bah-shee-ah'-tah*]
embrace *v.*, abbracciare [*ahb-brahch-chee-ah'-reh*]
emerald, smeraldo [*smeh-rahl'-doh*]
emergency, emergenza [*eh-mehr-jehn'-tsah*]
  in case of emergency, in caso di emergenza [*een kah'-zoh dee eh-mehr-jehn'-tsah*]
emigrant, emigrante [*eh-mee-grahn'-teh*]
emotion, emozione (f) [*eh-moh-tsee-oh'-neh*]
emotional, emotivo [*eh-moh-tee'-voh*]
emperor, imperatore (m) [*eem-peh-rah-toh'-reh*]
emphasize *v.*, mettere in rilievo [*meht'-teh-reh een ree-lee-eh'-voh*]
employ *v.*, impiegare [*eem-pee-eh-gah'-reh*]
employee, impiegato [*eem-pee-eh-gah'-toh*]

employer, datore di lavoro [*dah-toh'-reh dee lah-voh'-roh*]
employment, impiego [*eem-pee-eh'-goh*]
employment agency, agenzia di collocamento [*ah-jehn-tsee'-ah dee kohl-loh-kah-mehn'-toh*]
empty, vuoto [*voo-oh'-toh*]
enclose [surround] *v.*, rinchiudere [*reen-kee-oo'-deh-reh*]
encounter *v.*, incontrare [*een-kohn-trah'-reh*]
encourage *v.*, incoraggiare [*een-koh-rahj-jee-ah'-reh*]
encouragement, incoraggiamento [*een-koh-rahj-jee-ah-mehn'-toh*]
end, ending *n.*, fine (f) [*fee'-neh*]
end *v.*, finire [*fee-nee'-reh*]
endless, infinito [*een-fee-nee'-toh*]
endorse *v.*, girare [*jee-rah'-reh*]
endure *v.*, sopportare [*sohp-pohr-tah'-reh*]
enemy, nemico [*neh-mee'-koh*]
energy, energia [*eh-nehr-jee'-ah*]
engaged, fidanzato [*fee-dahn-tsah'-toh*]
engagement [betrothal], fidanzamento [*fee-dahn-tsah-mehn'-toh*]
engagement [appointment], appuntamento [*ahp-poon-tah-mehn'-toh*]
engine, motore (m), macchina [*moh-toh'-reh, mahk'-kee-nah*]
engineer, ingegnere (m) [*een-jeh-nyeh'-reh*]
England, Inghilterra [*een-geel-tehr'-rah*]
English, inglese [*een-gleh'-zeh*]
enjoy *v.*, godere [*goh-deh'-reh*]
  enjoy life, godere la vita [*goh-deh'-reh lah vee'-tah*]
enjoy (oneself), divertirsi [*dee-vehr-teer'-see*]
  Enjoy yourself! Si diverta! [*see dee-vehr'-tah*]
enjoyment, piacere (m), gioia [*pee-ah-cheh'-reh, jee-oh'-ee-ah*]
enormous, enorme [*eh-nohr'-meh*]
enough, abbastanza [*ahb-bahs-tahn'-tsah*]
  more than enough, più che abbastanza [*pee-oo' keh ahb-bahs-tahn'-tsah*]
  That's enough! Basta! [*bahs'-tah*]
enroll *v.*, arruolare [*ahr-roo-oh-lah'-reh*]

enter *v.*, entrare [*ehn-trah'-reh*]
Do not enter! Non entri! [*nohn ehn'-tree*]
enterprise, impresa [*eem-preh'-zah*]
entertain *v.*, intrattenere [*een-traht-teh-neh'-reh*]
entertaining, divertente [*dee-vehr-tehn'-teh*]
entertainment, divertimento [*dee-vehr-tee-mehn'-toh*]
enthusiasm, entusiasmo [*ehn-too-zee-ahz'-moh*]
entire, intero [*een-teh'-roh*]
entirely, interamente [*een-teh-rah-mehn'-teh*]
entrance, entrata, ingresso [*ehn-trah'-tah, een-grehs'-soh*]
envelope, busta [*boos'-tah*]
environment, ambiente (m) [*ahm-bee-ehn'-teh*]
envy *n.*, invidia [*een-vee'-dee-ah*]
envy *v.*, invidiare [*een-vee-dee-ah'-reh*]
equal *adj.*, uguale [*oo-goo-ah'-leh*]
equality, uguaglianza [*oo-goo-ah-lyahn'-tsah*]
equipment, equipaggiamento [*eh-koo-ee-pahj-jee-ah-mehn'-toh*]
equivalent, equivalente [*eh-koo-ee-vah-lehn'-teh*]
erase *v.*, cancellare [*kahn-chehl-lah'-reh*]
eraser, gomma da cancellare [*gohm'-mah dah kahn-chehl-lah'-reh*]
err *v.*, sbagliare [*zbah-lyah'-reh*]
errand, commissione (f) [*kohm-mees-see-oh'-neh*]
error, errore (m) [*ehr-roh'-reh*]
escape *v.*, scappare [*skahp-pah'-reh*]
especially, specialmente [*speh-chee-ahl-mehn'-teh*]
essential, essenziale [*ehs-sehn-tsee-ah'-leh*]
establish *v.*, stabilire, fondare [*stah-bee-lee'-reh, fohn-dah'-reh*]
establishment, fondazione, istituto [*fohn-dah-tsee-oh'-neh, ees-tee-too'-toh*]
estate, proprietà (f, indecl) immobiliare [*proh-pree-eh-tah' eem-moh-bee-lee-ah'-reh*]
esteem *v.*, stimare [*stee-mah'-reh*]
estimate *n.*, valutazione (f) [*vah-loo-tah-tsee-oh'-neh*]
estimate *v.*, valutare [*vah-loo-tah'-reh*]
eternal, eterno [*eh-tehr'-noh*]

Europe, Europa [*eh-oo-roh'-pah*]
European *n. & adj.*, europeo [*eh-oo-roh-peh'-oh*]
eve, vigilia [*vee-jee'-lee-ah*]
Christmas Eve, Vigilia di Natale [*vee-jee'-lee-ah dee nah-tah'-leh*]
even *adv.*, anche [*ahn'-keh*]
even him, anche lui [*ahn'-keh loo'-ee*]
even so, eppure, ció nonostante [*ehp-poo'-reh, chee-oh' noh-nohs-tahn'-teh*]
even then, anche allora [*ahn'-keh ahl-loh'-rah*]
even though, anche se [*ahn'-keh seh*]
not even, neppure, nemmeno [*nehp-poo'-reh, nehm-meh'-noh*]
even *adj.*, pari, uguale, liscio [*pah'-ree, oo-goo-ah'-leh, lee'-shee-oh*]
even number, numero pari [*noo'-meh-roh pah'-ree*]
evening, sera [*seh'-rah*]
Good evening! Buona sera! [*boo-oh'-nah seh'-rah*]
in the evening, durante la sera [*doo-rahn'-teh lah seh'-rah*]
tomorrow evening, domani sera [*doh-mah'-nee seh'-rah*]
yesterday evening, ieri sera [*ee-eh'-ree seh'-rah*]
event, avvenimento [*ahv-veh-nee-mehn'-toh*]
in the event of, nel caso che [*nehl kah'-zoh keh*]
eventually, eventualmente [*eh-vehn-too-ahl-mehn'-teh*]
ever, qualche volta, mai [*koo-ahl'-keh vohl'-ta, mah'-ee*]
as ever, come sempre [*koh'-meh sehm'-preh*]
every, ogni, ciascuno [*oh'-nyee, chee-ahs-koo'-noh*]
every day, ogni giorno [*oh'-nyee jee-ohr'-noh*]
every other day, ogni altro giorno [*oh'-nyee ahl'-troh jee-ohr'-noh*]
every time, ogni volta [*oh'-nyee vohl'-tah*]
everybody, ognuno [*oh-nyoo'-noh*]
everyone, ciascuno [*chee-ahs-koo'-noh*]
everything, ogni cosa [*oh-nyee koh'-zah*]
everywhere, ovunque [*oh-voon'-koo-eh*]
evidence, evidenza [*eh-vee-dehn'-tsah*]
evidently, evidentemente [*eh-vee-dehn-teh-mehn'-teh*]
evil, male, maligno, cattivo [*mah'-leh, mah-lee'-nyoh, kaht-*

tee'-voh]
exact, esatto [*eh-zaht'-toh*]
exactly, esattamente [*eh-zaht-tah-mehn'-teh*]
exaggerate *v.*, esagerare [*eh-zah-jeh-rah'-reh*]
examination, esame (m) [*eh-zah'-meh*]
examine *v.*, esaminare [*eh-zah-mee-nah'-reh*]
example, esempio [*eh-zehm'-pee-oh*]
exceed *v.*, eccedere [*ehch-cheh'-deh-reh*]
excellent, eccellente [*ehch-chehl-lehn'-teh*]
except, eccetto [*ehch-cheht'-toh*]
exception, eccezione (f) [*ehch-cheh-tsee-oh'-neh*]
exceptional, eccezionale [*ehch-cheh-tsee-oh-nah'-leh*]
excess, eccesso [*ehch-chehs'-soh*]
exchange *n.*, cambio [*kahm'-bee-oh*]
in exchange for, in cambio di [*een kahm'-bee-oh dee*]
exchange *v.*, scambiare [*skahm-bee-ah'-reh*]
excited, eccitato, agitato [*ehch-chee-tah'-toh, ah-jee-tah'-toh*]
Don't get excited! Non si agiti! [*nohn see ah'-jee-tee*]
exclusive, esclusivo [*ehs-kloo-zee'-voh*]
excursion, escursione (f) [*ehs-koor-see-oh'-neh*]
excuse *n.*, scusa [*skoo'-zah*]
excuse *v.*, scusare [*skoo-zah'-reh*]
Excuse me! Mi scusi! [*mee skoo'-zee*]
exercise *n.*, esercizio [*eh-zehr-chee'-tsee-oh*]
exercise *v.*, esercitare [*eh-zehr-chee-tah'-reh*]
exhausted, esaurito [*eh-zah-oo-ree'-toh*]
exhibit *v.*, esibire [*eh-zee-bee'-reh*]
exhibition, esibizione (f) [*eh-zee-bee-tsee-oh'-neh*]
exist *v.*, esistere [*eh-zees'-teh-reh*]
existence, esistenza [*eh-zees-tehn'-tsah*]
exit, uscita [*oo-shee'-tah*]
expect *v.*, aspettare [*ahs-peht-tah'-reh*]
expedition, spedizione (f) [*speh-dee-tsee-oh'-neh*]
expense, spesa [*speh'-zah*]
expensive, caro [*kah'-roh*]
experience *n.*, esperienza [*ehs-peh-ree-ehn'-tsah*]
experiment *n.*, esperimento [*ehs-peh-ree-mehn'-toh*]
expert *adj.*, esperto [*ehs-pehr'-toh*]

explain *v.*, spiegare [*spee-eh-gah'-reh*]
explanation, spiegazione (f) [*spee-eh-gah-tsee-oh'-neh*]
explore *v.*, esplorare [*ehs-ploh-rah'-reh*]
explosion, esplosione (f) [*ehs-ploh-zee-oh'-neh*]
export *n.*, esportazione (f) [*ehs-pohr-tah-tsee-oh'-neh*]
export *v.*, esportare [*ehs-pohr-tah'-reh*]
express *adj.*, espresso [*ehs-prehs'-soh*]
express *v.*, esprimere [*ehs-pree'-meh-reh*]
exquisite, squisito [*skoo-ee-zee'-toh*]
extend *v.*, estendere [*ehs-tehn'-deh-reh*]
extent, extension, estensione (f) [*ehs-tehn-see-oh'-neh*]
to a certain extent, sino ad un certo punto [*see'-noh ahd oon chehr'-to poon'-toh*]
exterior, esteriore [*ehs-teh-ree-oh'-reh*]
external, esterno [*ehs-tehr'-noh*]
extinguish *v.*, estinguere [*ehs-teen'-goo-eh-reh*]
extra *adj.*, supplementare, straordinario [*soop-pleh-mehn-tah'-reh, strah-ohr-dee-nah'-ree-oh*]
extravagant, stravagante [*strah-vah-gahn'-teh*]
extrarodinary, straordinario [*strah-ohr-dee-nah'-ree-oh*]
extreme, estremo [*ehs-treh'-moh*]
extremely, estremamente [*ehs-treh-mah-mehn'-teh*]
eye, occhio, occhi (pl) [*ohk'-kee-oh, ohk'-kee*]
eyeball, bulbo [*bool'-boh*]
eyebrow, sopracciglio [*soh-prah-chee'-lyoh*]
eye doctor, oculista (m) [*oh-koo-lees'-tah*]
eyeglasses, occhiali (m, pl) [*ohk-kee-ah'-lee*]
eyelashes, ciglia (f, pl) [*chee'-lyah*]
eyelid, palpebra [*pahl'-peh-brah*]
eyesight, vista [*vees'-tah*]
eyewitness, testimone oculare (m) [*tehs-tee-moh'-neh oh-koo-lah'-reh*]

F

fabric, tessuto, stoffa [*tehs-soo'-toh, stohf'-fah*]
face *n.*, faccia, viso [*fahch'-chee-ah, vee'-zoh*]
face *v.*, affrontare [*ahf-frohn-tah'-reh*]
fact, fatto [*faht'-toh*]
  in fact, infatti [*een-faht'-tee*]
factory, fabbrica [*fahb'-bree-kah*]
faculty, facoltà (f, indecl) [*fah-kohl-tah'*]
fad, mania [*mah-nee'-ah*]
fade *v.*, svanire [*zvah-nee'-reh*]
fail *v.*, fallire [*fahl-lee'-reh*]
failure, fallimento [*fahl-lee-mehn'-toh*]
faint *v.*, svenire [*zveh-nee'-reh*]
fairness, giustezza [*jee-oos-tehts'-tsah*]
faith, fede (f) [*feh'-deh*]
faithful, fedele [*feh-deh'-leh*]
fall [descent] *n.*, caduta [*kah-doo'-tah*]
fall [season] *n.*, autunno [*ah-oo-toon'-noh*]
fall *v.*, cadere [*kah-deh'-reh*]
  fall asleep, addormentarsi [*ahd-dohr-mehn-tahr'-see*]
  fall back, retrocedere [*reh-troh-cheh'-deh-reh*]
  fall in love, innamorarsi [*een-nah-moh-rahr'-see*]
fallen, caduto, degradato [*kah-doo'-toh, deh-grah-dah'-toh*]
false, falso [*fahl'-soh*]
fame, fama [*fah'-mah*]
familiar, familiare [*fah-mee-lee-ah'-reh*]
family, famiglia [*fah-mee'-lyah*]
famous, famoso [*fah-moh'-zoh*]
fan [mechanical] *n.*, ventilatore (m) [*vehn-tee-lah-toh'-reh*]
fan [hand] *n.*, ventaglio [*vehn-tah'-lyoh*]
fan [enthusiast] *n.*, ammiratore (m), tifoso [*ahm-mee-rah-toh'-reh, tee-foh'-zoh*]
fancy *n.*, fantasia, capriccio [*fahn-tah-zee'-ah, kah-preech'-*

chee-oh]
fantastic, fantastico [*fahn-tahs'-tee-koh*]
far, lontano, distante [*lohn-tah'-noh, dees-tahn'-teh*]
far away, molto lontano [*mohl'-toh lohn-tah'-noh*]
How far? Quanto lontano? [*koo-ahn'-toh lohn-tah'-noh*]
fare [transportation] *n.*, prezzo del viaggio [*prehts'-tsoh dehl vee-ahj'-jee-oh*]
bill of fare, lista delle vivande, menù (m) [*lees'-tah dehl'-leh vee-vahn'-deh, meh'-noo*]
farewell *n.*, addio [*ahd-dee'-oh*]
farm *n.*, fattoria [*faht-toh-ree'-ah*]
farther, più lontano [*pee-oo' lohn-tah'-noh*]
fascinating, affascinante [*ahf-fah-shee-nahn'-teh*]
fashion, moda [*moh'-dah*]
fashionable, di moda, elegante [*dee moh'-dah, eh-leh-gahn'-teh*]
fast *adj.*, rapido, veloce [*rah'-pee-doh, veh-loh'-cheh*]
fast *v.*, digiunare [*dee-jee-oo-nah'-reh*]
fasten *v.*, fissare, stringere [*fees-sah'-reh, streen'-jeh-reh*]
fat, grasso [*grahs'-soh*]
fatal, fatale [*fah-tah'-leh*]
fate, destino [*dehs-tee'-noh*]
father, padre (m) [*pah'-dreh*]
father-in-law, suocero [*soo-oh'-cheh-roh*]
fatigue *n.*, fatica, stanchezza [*fah-tee'-kah, stahn-kehts'-tsah*]
faucet, rubinetto [*roo-bee-neht'-toh*]
fault *n.*, colpa [*kohl'-pah*]
It's my fault, È colpa mia [*eh' kohl'-pah mee'-ah*]
favor *n.*, favore (m), piacere (m) [*fah-voh'-reh, pee-ah-cheh'-reh*]
favorite, preferito [*preh-feh-ree'-toh*]
fear *n.*, paura [*pah-oo'-rah*]
fear *v.*, temere [*teh-meh'-reh*]
fearless, intrepido [*een-treh'-pee-doh*]
feast *n.*, festa [*fehs'-tah*]
feather, piuma [*pee-oo'-mah*]
features, lineamenti (m, pl) [*lee-neh-ah-mehn'-tee*]

February, febbraio [*fehb-brah'-ee-oh*]
federal, federale [*feh-deh-rah'-leh*]
fee, onorario [*oh-noh-rah'-ree-oh*]
feed *v.*, nutrire [*noo-tree'-reh*]
feel *v.*, sentire [*sehn-tee'-reh*]
feeling, sentimento [*sehn-tee-mehn'-toh*]
female, femmina [*fehm'-mee-nah*]
feminine, femminile [*fehm-mee-nee'-leh*]
fence, recinto [*reh-cheen'-toh*]
fencing, scherma [*skehr'-mah*]
fender [of car], paracarro [*pah-rah-kahr'-roh*]
ferryboat, nave traghetto [*nah'-veh trah-geht'-toh*]
festival, festival [*fehs'-tee-vahl*]
fever, febbre (f) [*fehb'-breh*]
feverish, febbrile [*fehb-bree'-leh*]
few, pochi (m), poche (f) [*poh'-kee, poh'-keh*]
fewer, di meno [*dee meh'-noh*]
fiancé, fidanzato [*fee-dahn-tsah'-toh*]
fiancée, fidanzata [*fee-dahn-tsah'-tah*]
fiction, narrativa [*nahr-rah-tee'-vah*]
field, campo [*kahm'-poh*]
field glasses, cannocchiali [*kahn-nohk-kee-ah'-lee*]
fifteen, quindici [*koo-een'-dee-chee*]
fifth, quinto [*koo-een'-toh*]
fifty, cinquanta [*cheen-koo-ahn'-tah*]
fight *n.*, lotta [*loht'-tah*]
fight *v.*, lottare [*loht-tah'-reh*]
fill *v.*, riempire [*ree-ehm-pee'-reh*]
filling [tooth], otturazione (f) [*oht-too-rah-tsee-oh'-neh*]
film *n.*, pellicola, film [*pehl-lee'-koh-lah, feelm*]
filter *n.*, filtro [*feel'-troh*]
final, finale [*fee-nah'-leh*]
finally, finalmente [*fee-nahl-mehn'-teh*]
financial, finanziario [*fee-nahn-tsee-ah'-ree-oh*]
find *v.*, trovare [*troh-vah'-reh*]
fine [penalty] *n.*, multa [*mool'-tah*]
fine *adj.*, fine, eccellente [*fee'-neh, ehch-chehl-lehn'-teh*]
finger, dito, le dita (pl) [*dee'-toh, leh dee'-tah*]

fingerprint, impronta digitale [*eem-prohn'-tah dee-jee-tah'-leh*]
finish *v.*, finire [*fee-nee'-reh*]
fire, fuoco [*foo-oh'-koh*]
fireman, pompiere (m) [*pohm-pee-eh'-reh*]
fireplace, focolare (m) [*foh-koh-lah'-reh*]
fireproof, incombustibile [*een-kohm-boos-tee'-bee-leh*]
firm *adj.*, fermo [*fehr'-moh*]
first, primo [*pree'-moh*]
first aid, pronto soccorso [*prohn'-toh sohk-kohr'-soh*]
first class, prima classe [*pree'-mah klahs'-seh*]
first name, nome [*noh'-meh*]
fish *n.*, pesce (m) [*peh'-sheh*]
fish *v.*, pescare [*pehs-kah'-reh*]
fisherman, pescatore (m) [*pehs-kah-toh'-reh*]
fishing, pesca [*pehs'-kah*]
fishing boat, barca da pesca [*bahr'-kah dah pehs'-kah*]
fist, pugno [*poo'-nyoh*]
fit [try on] *v.*, provare [*proh-vah'-reh*]
fit [adjust] *v.*, adattare [*ah-daht-tah'-reh*]
five, cinque [*cheen'-koo-eh*]
fix [fasten] *v.*, fissare [*fees-sah'-reh*]
fix [repair] *v.*, riparare [*ree-pah-rah'-reh*]
fixed price, prezzo fisso [*prehts'-tsoh fees'-soh*]
flag *n.*, bandiera [*bahn-dee-eh'-rah*]
flame, fiamma [*fee-ahm'-mah*]
flannel, flanella [*flah-nehl'-lah*]
flash *n.*, lampo [*lahm'-poh*]
flask, fiaschetta [*fee-ahs-keht'-tah*]
flat *adj.*, piatto [*pee-aht'-toh*]
flatter *v.*, lusingare, adulare [*loo-zeen-gah'-reh, ah-doo-lah'-reh*]
flavor *n.*, sapore (m), aroma [*sah-poh'-reh, ah-roh'-mah*]
flee *v.*, fuggire [*fooj-jee'-reh*]
fleet *n.*, flotta [*floht'-tah*]
flesh, carne (f) [*kahr'-neh*]
flexible, flessibile [*flehs-see'-bee-leh*]
flight [escape], fuga [*foo'-gah*]

flight [flying], volo [*voh'-loh*]
float *v.*, galleggiare [*gahl-lehj-jee-ah'-reh*]
flood *n.*, inondazione (f) [*ee-nohn-dah-tsee-oh'-neh*]
floor, pavimento, piano [*pah-vee-mehn'-toh, pee-ah'-noh*]
Florence, Firenze [*fee-rehn'-tseh*]
flour, farina [*fah-ree'-nah*]
flow *v.*, scorrere [*skohr-reh'-reh*]
flower, fiore (m) [*fee-oh'-reh*]
flower shop, fioraio [*fee-oh-rah'-ee-oh*]
fluent, fluente [*floo-ehn'-teh*]
fluid *n. & adj.*, fluido [*floo'-ee-doh*]
flute, flauto [*flah'-oo-toh*]
fly *n.*, mosca [*mohs'-kah*]
fly *v.*, volare [*voh-lah'-reh*]
foggy, nebbioso [*nehb-bee-oh'-zoh*]
fold *v.*, piegare [*pee-eh-gah'-reh*]
follow *v.*, seguire [*seh-goo-ee'-reh*]
following, seguito [*seh'-goo-ee-toh*]
fond, appassionato, amante di [*ahp-pahs-see-oh-nah'-toh, ah-mahn'-teh dee*]
food, cibo [*chee'-boh*]
fool *n.*, stupido [*stoo'-pee-doh*]
foolish, sciocco [*shee-ohk'-koh*]
foot, piede [*pee-eh'-deh*]
football, (gioco del) calcio [(*jee-oh'-koh dehl*) *kahl'-chee-oh*]
for, per [*pehr*]
  for example, per esempio [*pehr eh-zehm'-pee-oh*]
  for us, for them, per noi, per loro [*pehr noh'-ee, pehr loh'-roh*]
  What for? Perchè? [*pehr-keh'*]
forbid *v.*, proibire [*proh-ee-bee'-reh*]
forbidden, proibito [*proh-ee-bee'-toh*]
forehead, fronte (f) [*frohn'-teh*]
foreign, straniero [*strah-nee-eh'-roh*]
foreigner, straniero [*strah-nee-eh'-roh*]
foreign minister, ministro degli esteri [*mee-nees'-troh deh'-lyee ehs'-teh-ree*]
foreign office, ministero degli affari esteri [*mee-nees-teh'-*

roh deh'-lyee ahf-fah'-ree ehs'-teh-ree]
foreign policy, politica straniera [*poh-lee'-tee-kah strah-nee-eh'-rah*]
foreign trade, commercio con l'estero [*kohm-mehr'-chee-oh kohn lehs'-teh-roh*]
forest, foresta [*foh-rehs'-tah*]
forever, per sempre [*pehr sehm'-preh*]
forget *v.*, dimenticare [*dee-mehn-tee-kah'-reh*]
forgive *v.*, perdonare [*pehr-doh-nah'-reh*]
fork, forchetta [*fohr-keht'-tah*]
formal, formale [*fohr-mah'-leh*]
formality, formalità (f, indecl) [*fohr-mah-lee-tah'*]
former *pron.*, primo [*pree'-moh*]
fortunate, fortunato [*fohr-too-nah'-toh*]
fortunately, fortunatamente [*fohr-too-nah-tah-mehn'-teh*]
fortune, fortuna [*fohr-too'-nah*]
forty, quaranta [*koo-ah-rahn'-tah*]
forward *adv.*, in avanti [*een ah-vahn'-tee*]
foundation, fondazione (f) [*fohn-dah-tsee-oh'-neh*]
fountain, fontana [*fohn-tah'-nah*]
fountain pen, penna stilografica [*pehn'-nah stee-loh-grah'-fee-kah*]
four, quattro [*koo-aht'-troh*]
fourteen, quattordici [*koo-aht-tohr'-dee-chee*]
fourth, quarto [*koo-ahr'-toh*]
fracture *n.*, rottura, frattura [*roht-too'-rah, fraht-too'-rah*]
fragile, fragile [*frah'-jee-leh*]
fragrance, fragranza [*frah-grahn'-tsah*]
frail, fragile [*frah'-jee-leh*]
frame *n.*, forma, struttura [*fohr'-mah, stroot-too'-rah*]
France, Francia [*frahn'-chee-ah*]
frank, franco [*frahn'-koh*]
frantic, frenetico [*freh-neh'-tee-koh*]
fraud, frode (f) [*froh'-deh*]
free [not bound] *adj.*, libero [*lee'-beh-roh*]
free [at no cost] *adj.*, gratuito [*grah-too'-ee-toh*]
free *v.*, liberare [*lee-beh-rah'-reh*]
freedom, libertà (f, indecl) [*lee-behr-tah'*]

freeze *v.*, congelare [*kohn-jeh-lah'-reh*]
freight, carico, trasporto [*kah'-ree-koh, trah-spohr'-toh*]
French *adj.*, francese [*frahn-cheh'-zeh*]
Frenchman, -woman *n.*, francese (m, f) [*frahn-cheh'-zeh*]
frequently, frequentemente [*freh-koo-ehn-teh-mehn'-teh*]
fresh, fresco [*frehs'-koh*]
Friday, venerdì [*veh-nehr-dee'*]
fried, fritto [*freet'-toh*]
friend, amico, amici (pl) [*ah-mee'-koh, ah-mee'-chee*]
frighten *v.*, spaventare [*spah-vehn-tah'-reh*]
from, da, per [*dah, pehr*]
  come from *v.*, venire da [*veh-nee'-reh dah*]
  Where do you come from? Da dove viene? [*dah doh'-veh vee-eh'-neh*]
  from far, da lontano [*dah lohn-tah'-noh*]
  from now on, da ora in poi [*dah oh'-rah een poh'-ee*]
front, fronte (m) [*frohn'-teh*]
  in front of, davanti a [*dah-vahn'-tee ah*]
frozen, gelato [*jeh-lah'-toh*]
fruit, frutta [*froot'-tah*]
fruit salad, insalata di frutta [*een-sah-lah'-tah dee froot'-tah*]
fruit store, fruttivendolo [*froot-tee-vehn'-doh-loh*]
fry *v.*, friggere [*freej'-jeh-reh*]
frying pan, padella [*pah-dehl'-lah*]
fuel *n.*, combustibile [*kohm-boos-tee'-bee-leh*]
full, pieno [*pee-eh'-noh*]
fun, divertimento [*dee-vehr-tee-mehn'-toh*]
function *n.*, funzione (f) [*foon-tsee-oh'-neh*]
funds, fondi (m, pl) [*fohn'-dee*]
funeral, funerale (m) [*foo-neh-rah'-leh*]
fur, pellicia [*pehl-lee'-chee-ah*]
funny, comico, scherzoso [*koh'-mee-koh, skehrts-tsoh'-zoh*]
furious, furioso [*foo-ree-oh'-zoh*]
furnish [provide] *v.*, fornire [*fohr-nee'-reh*]
furnish [put furniture into] *v.*, mobiliare [*moh-bee-lee-ah'-reh*]
furnished room, camera da affittare [*kah'-meh-rah dah ahf-fee-tah'-reh*]

furniture, mobili (m, pl) [*moh'-bee-lee*]
further *adj.*, ulteriore [*ool-teh-ree-oh'-reh*]
furthermore, inoltre [*een-ohl'-treh*]
future *n.*, futuro, avvenire (m) [*foo-too'-roh ahv-veh-nee'-reh*]

G

gadget, meccanismo [*mehk-kah-neez'-moh*]
gaiety, allegria [*ahl-leh-gree'-ah*]
gain *v.*, guadagnare [*goo-ah-dah-nyah'-reh*]
gallon, gallone (m) [*gahl-loh'-neh*]
gamble *v.*, giocare d'azzardo [*jee-oh-kah'-reh dahdz-dzahr'-doh*]
game, gioco, partita [*jee-oh'-koh, pahr-tee'-tah*]
garage, autorimessa [*ah-oo-toh-ree-mehs'-sah*]
garbage, immondizia, rifiuti (m, pl) [*eem-mohn-dee'-tsee-ah, ree-fee-oo'-tee*]
garden, giardino [*jee-ahr-dee'-noh*]
gardener, giardiniere (m) [*jee-ahr-dee-nee-eh'-reh*]
garlic, aglio [*ah'-lyoh*]
garment, indumento [*een-doo-mehn'-toh*]
garret, soffitta [*sohf-feet'-tah*]
gasoline, benzina [*behn-dzee'-nah*]
gasoline station, pompa di benzina [*pohm'-pah dee behn-dzee'-nah*]
gate, cancello, porta [*kahn-chehl'-loh, pohr'-tah*]
gather *v.*, raccogliere [*rahk-koh'-lyeh-reh*]
gauge, indicatore (m) [*een-dee-kah-toh'-reh*]
gear [auto] *n.*, ingranaggio [*een-grah-nahj'-jee-oh*]
gem, gemma [*jehm'-mah*]
gender, genere (m) [*jeh'-neh-reh*]
general *n. & adj.*, generale [*jeh-neh-rah'-leh*]
  in general, in generale [*een jeh-neh-rah'-leh*]
general delivery, fermo posta [*fer'-moh pohs'-tah*]
generally, generalmente [*jeh-neh-rahl-mehn'-teh*]

generation, generazione (f) [*jeh-neh-rah-tsee-oh'-neh*]
generator, generatore (m) [*jeh-neh-rah-toh'-reh*]
generous, generoso [*jeh-neh-roh'-zoh*]
genius, genio [*jeh'-nee-oh*]
Genoa, Genova [*jeh'-noh-vah*]
gentle, soave, dolce [*soh-ah'-veh, dohl'-cheh*]
genuine, genuino [*jeh-noo-ee'-noh*]
germ, germe (m) [*jehr'-meh*]
German *n. & adj.*, tedesco [*teh-dehs'-koh*]
Germany, Germania [*jehr-mah'-nee-ah*]
get [obtain] *v.*, ottenere [*oht-teh-neh'-reh*]
get [receive] *v.*, ricevere [*ree-cheh'-veh-reh*]
get [become] *v.*, divenire [*dee-veh-nee'-reh*]
  get back, ritornare [*ree-tohr-nah'-reh*]
  get down, scendere [*shehn'-deh-reh*]
  get in, entrare [*ehn-trah'-reh*]
  get married, sposarsi [*spoh-zahr'-see*]
  get off, scendere [*shehn'-deh-reh*]
  get on, salire [*sah-lee'-reh*]
  get up, alzarsi [*ahl-tsahr'-see*]
gift, regalo [*reh-gah'-loh*]
gifted, dotato [*doh-tah'-toh*]
gin, liquore di ginepro [*lee-koo-oh'-reh dee jee-neh'-proh*]
girdle, reggicalze (f, pl) [*rehj-jee-kahl'-tseh*]
girl, ragazza [*rah-gahts'-tsah*]
give *v.*, dare (irreg) [*dah'-reh*]
  give him, give her, gli dia, le dia [*lyee dee'-ah, leh dee'-ah*]
  give me, mi dia [*mee dee'-ah*]
  give them, dia loro [*dee'-ah loh'-roh*]
  give us, ci dia [*chee dee'-ah*]
  give back, restituire [*rehs-tee-too-ee'-reh*]
  give in, cedere [*cheh'-deh-reh*]
  give up, rinunciare, arrendersi [*ree-noon-chee-ah'-reh, ahr-rehn'-dehr-see*]
glad, contento [*kohn-tehn'-toh*]
glance *n.*, occhiata [*ohk-kee-ah'-tah*]
glance *v.*, dare un'occhiata [*dah'-reh oon-ohk-kee-ah'-tah*]
gland, glandola [*glahn'-doh-lah*]

glare *v.*, splendere [*splehn'-deh-reh*]
glass [container], bicchiere (m) [*beek-kee-eh'-reh*]
glass [material], vetro [*veh'-troh*]
glasses, occhiali (m, pl) [*ohk-kee-ah'-lee*]
glimpse *n.*, sguardo [*zgoo-ahr'-doh*]
gloomy, oscuro, triste [*ohs-koo'-roh, trees'-teh*]
glove, guanto [*goo-ahn'-toh*]
glue *n.*, colla [*kohl'-lah*]
go *v.*, andare (irreg) [*ahn-dah'-reh*]
go across, attraversare, incontrare [*aht-trah-vehr-sah'-reh, een-kohn-trah'-reh*]
go away, andare via [*ahn-dah'-reh vee'-ah*]
Go away! Vada via! [*vah'-dah vee'-ah*]
go back, ritornare [*ree-tohr-nah'-reh*]
go by, passare [*pahs-sah'-reh*]
go down, scendere [*shehn'-deh-reh*]
go in, entrare [*ehn-trah'-reh*]
go on, continuare [*kohn-tee-noo-ah'-reh*]
Go on! Continui! [*kohn-tee'-noo-ee*]
go out, uscire [*oo-shee'-reh*]
go to bed, coricarsi [*koh-ree-kahr'-see*]
go up, salire (irreg) [*sah-lee'-reh*]
goal, meta [*meh'-tah*]
God, Dio [*dee'-oh*]
gold, oro [*oh'-roh*]
golf, golf (m) [*gohlf*]
good, buono [*boo-oh'-noh*]
Good afternoon! Buon pomeriggio! [*boo-ohn' poh-meh-reej'-jee-oh*]
Good-bye! Arrivederla!, Ciao!, Addio! [*ahr-ree-veh-dehr'-lah, chee-ah'-oh, ahd-dee'-oh*]
Good day! Buon giorno! [*boo-ohn' jee-ohr'-noh*]
Good evening! Buona sera! [*boo-oh'-nah seh'-rah*]
Good luck! Buona fortuna! [*boo-oh'-nah fohr-too'-nah*]
Good morning! Buon giorno! [*boo-ohn' jee-ohr'-noh*]
Good night! Buona notte! [*boo-oh'-nah noht'-teh*]
good-looking, bello [*behl'-loh*]
goodness, bontà (f, indecl) [*bohn-tah'*]

goods, merce (f) [*mehr'-cheh*]
gorgeous, splendido [*splehn'-dee-doh*]
gossip [person], pettegolo (m), pettegola (f) [*peht-teh'-goh-loh, peht-teh'-goh-lah*]
govern *v.*, governare [*goh-vehr-nah'-reh*]
government, governo [*goh-vehr'-noh*]
governor, governatore (m) [*goh-vehr-nah-toh'-reh*]
graceful, grazioso [*grah-tsee-oh'-zoh*]
gradually, gradualmente [*grah-doo-ahl-mehn'-teh*]
graduate *n.*, laureato [*lah-oo-reh-ah'-toh*]
graduate *v.*, laurearsi [*lah-oo-reh-ahr'-see*]
grain, grano, chicco [*grah'-noh, keek'-koh*]
grammar, grammatica [*grahm-mah'-tee-kah*]
grandchild, nipotino (m), nipotina (f) [*nee-poh-tee'-noh, nee-poh-tee'-nah*]
grandfather, nonno [*nohn'-noh*]
grandmother, nonna [*nohn'-nah*]
grant *v.*, accordare [*ahk-kohr-dah'-reh*]
 granted that, ammesso che [*ahm-mehs'-soh keh*]
grape, uva [*oo'-vah*]
grass, erba [*ehr'-bah*]
grateful, riconoscente [*ree-koh-noh-shehn'-teh*]
gratitude, gratitudine (f) [*grah-tee-too'-dee-neh*]
grave *adj.*, grave [*grah'-veh*]
grave *n.*, tomba [*tohm'-bah*]
gravity, gravità (f, indecl) [*grah-vee-tah'*]
grease *n.*, grasso, unto [*grahs'-soh, oon'-toh*]
great, grande [*grahn'-deh*]
greatness, grandezza [*grahn-dehts'-tsah*]
Great Britain, Gran Bretagna [*grahn breh-tah'-nyah*]
Greece, Grecia [*greh'-chee-ah*]
greedy, avido [*ah'-vee-doh*]
Greek, greco [*greh'-koh*]
green, verde [*vehr'-deh*]
greet *v.*, salutare [*sah-loo-tah'-reh*]
greetings, saluti (m, pl) [*sah-loo'-tee*]
grey, grigio [*gree'-jee-oh*]
grief, dolore (m) [*doh-loh'-reh*]

grieve *v.*, affliggere [*ahf-fleej'-jeh-reh*]
grin *n.*, smorfia [*zmohr'-fee-ah*]
grind *v.*, macinare [*mah-chee-nah'-reh*]
grip, stretta [*streht'-tah*]
groan *n.*, gemito, lamento [*jeh'-mee-toh, lah-mehn'-toh*]
groan *v.*, gemere [*jeh'-meh-reh*]
grocery, drogheria [*droh-geh-ree'-ah*]
ground, terra, suolo [*tehr'-rah, soo-oh'-loh*]
ground floor, pianterreno [*pee-ahn-tehr-reh'-noh*]
group, gruppo [*groop'-poh*]
grow [cultivate] *v.*, coltivare [*kohl-tee-vah'-reh*]
grow [increase] *v.*, aumentare [*ah-oo-mehn-tah'-reh*]
grow [become] *v.*, diventare [*dee-vehn-tah'-reh*]
grow old *v.*, invecchiare [*een-vehk-kee-ah'-reh*]
guarantee *n.*, garanzia [*gah-rahn-tsee'-ah*]
guarantee *v.*, garantire [*gah-rahn-tee'-reh*]
guard *n.*, guardia [*goo-ahr'-dee-ah*]
guard *v.*, sorvegliare [*sohr-veh-lyah'-reh*]
guardian, guardiano [*goo-ahr-dee-ah'-noh*]
guess *n.*, supposizione (f) [*soop-poh-zee-tsee-oh'-neh*]
guess *v.*, indovinare [*een-doh-vee-nah'-reh*]
guest, ospite (m, f) [*ohs'-pee-teh*]
guide *n.*, guida [*goo-ee'-dah*]
guide *v.*, guidare [*goo-ee-dah'-reh*]
guilt, colpa [*kohl'-pah*]
guilty, colpevole [*kohl-peh'-voh-leh*]
guitar, chitarra [*kee-tahr'-rah*]
gum [teeth], gengiva [*jehn-jee'-vah*]
gum [chewing], gomma americana [*gohm'-mah ah-meh-ree-kah'-nah*]
gun, fucile (m), cannone (m) [*foo-chee'-leh, kahn-noh'-neh*]
gutter, bassifondi (m, pl) [*bahs-see-fohn'-dee*]
gymnasium [sports], palestra [*pah-lehs'-trah*]
gypsy, zingaro [*dzeen'-gah-roh*]

H

habit, abitudine (f) [*ah-bee-too'-dee-neh*]
hair, capello, pelo [*kah-pehl'-loh, peh'-loh*]
hairbrush, spazzola per capelli [*spahts'-tsoh-lah pehr kah-pehl'-lee*]
haircut, taglio di capelli [*tah'-lyoh dee kah-pehl'-lee*]
hairdresser, parrucchiere (m) [*pahr-rook-kee-eh'-reh*]
hair tonic, tonico per capelli [*toh'-nee-koh pehr kah-pehl'-lee*]
half *n.*, metà (f, indecl) [*meh-tah'*]
half *adj.*, mezzo [*mehdz'-dzo*]
  half past two, le due e mezzo [*leh doo'-eh eh mehdz'-dzo*]
halfway, a metà strada [*ah meh-tah' strah'-dah*]
hall, corridoio, vestibolo, sala [*kohr-ree-doh'-ee-oh, vehs-tee'-boh-loh, sah'-lah*]
halt *v.*, fermare [*fehr-mah'-reh*]
Halt! Alt! [*ahlt*]
ham, prosciutto [*proh-shee-oot'-toh*]
hammer, martello [*mahr-tehl'-loh*]
hand, mano, le mani (pl) [*mah'-noh, leh mah'-nee*]
  on the other hand, d'altro canto [*dahl'-troh kahn'-toh*]
handbag, borsa [*bohr'-sah*]
handkerchief, fazzoletto [*fahts-tsoh-leht'-toh*]
handmade, fatto a mano [*faht'-toh ah mah'-noh*]
handsome, bello [*behl'-loh*]
hang [an object] *v.*, appendere [*ahp-pehn'-deh-reh*]
hanger [clothes], attaccapanni (m, pl) [*aht-tahk-kah-pahn'-nee*]
happen *v.*, accadere [*ahk-kah-deh'-reh*]
  What happened? Cosa è successo?, Che è accaduto? [*koh'-zah eh' sooch-chehs'-soh, keh eh' ahk-kah-doo'-toh*]
happiness, felicità (f, indecl) [*feh-lee-chee-tah'*]

happy, felice [*feh-lee'-cheh*]
Happy Birthday! Buon compleanno! [*boo-ohn' kohm-pleh-ahn'-noh*]
Happy New Year! Buon Capodanno! [*boo-ohn' kah-poh-dahn'-noh*]
harbor *n.*, porto [*pohr'-toh*]
hard, duro [*doo'-roh*]
hardhearted, inumano [*een-oo-mah'-noh*]
harm *v.*, nuocere [*noo-oh'-cheh-reh*]
harmful, dannoso [*dahn-noh'-zoh*]
harvest *n.*, raccolta [*rahk-kohl'-tah*]
hat, cappello [*kahp-pehl'-loh*]
hate *n.*, odio [*oh'-dee-oh*]
hate *v.*, odiare [*oh-dee-ah'-reh*]
have *v.*, avere (irreg) [*ah-veh'-reh*]
have to [must], dovere [*doh-veh'-reh*]
Do you have to study so late? Deve studiare cosi tardi? [*deh'-veh stoo-dee-ah'-reh coh-see' tahr'-dee*]
I have to study a lot, Devo studiare molto [*deh'-voh stoo-dee-ah'-reh mohl'-toh*]
he, lui, egli [*loo'-ee, eh'-lyee*]
head [body], testa [*tehs'-tah*]
head [chief], capo [*kah'-poh*]
headache, mal di testa [*mahl dee tehs'-tah*]
headlight, fanale (m) [*fah-nah'-leh*]
heal *v.*, guarire [*goo-ah-ree'-reh*]
health, salute (f) [*sah-loo'-teh*]
To your health! Alla sua salute! [*ahl'-lah soo'-ah sah-loo'-teh*]
in good health, in buona salute [*een boo-oh'-nah sah-loo'-teh*]
healthy, sano [*sah'-noh*]
hear *v.*, sentire, udire (irreg) [*sehn-tee'-reh, oo-dee'-reh*]
heart, cuore (m) [*koo-oh'-reh*]
by heart, a memoria [*ah meh-moh'-ree-ah*]
heart disease, malattia del cuore [*mah-laht-tee'-ah dehl koo-oh'-reh*]
heat *n.*, calore (m), caldo [*kah-loh'-reh, kahl'-doh*]

heat *v.*, riscaldare [*rees-kahl-dah'-reh*]
heaven, cielo [*chee-eh'-loh*]
Heavens! Per l'amor del cielo! [*pehr lah-mohr' dehl chee-eh'-loh*]
heavy, pesante [*peh-zahn'-teh*]
Hebrew, ebreo [*eh-breh'-oh*]
heel [foot], calcagno [*kahl-kah'-nyoh*]
heel [shoe], tacco [*tahk'-koh*]
height, altezza [*ahl-tehts'-tsah*]
heir, heiress, erede [*eh-reh'-deh*]
hell, inferno [*een-fehr'-noh*]
Hello! Ciao!, Salve! [*chee-ah'-oh, sahl'-veh*]
help *n.*, aiuto [*ah-ee-oo'-toh*]
help *v.*, aiutare [*ah-ee-oo-tah'-reh*]
her *pron.*, la, lei [*lah, leh'-ee*]
her *poss. adj.*, suo [*soo'-oh*]
here, quì, quà [*koo-ee', koo-ah'*]
Come here! Venga quì! [*vehn'-gah koo-ee'*]
Here it is Eccolo quì [*ehk'-koh-loh koo-ee'*]
hero, eroe (m) [*eh-roh'-eh*]
hers, il suo, la sua (sing), i suoi, le sue (pl) [*eel soo'-oh, lah soo'-ah, ee soo-oh'-ee, leh soo'-eh*]
herself, lei stessa [*leh'-ee stehs'-sah*]
hide *v.*, nascondere [*nahs-kohn'-deh-reh*]
high, alto, elevato [*ahl'-toh, eh-leh-vah'-toh*]
higher, più alto [*pee-oo' ahl'-toh*]
high school, scuola media [*skoo-oh'-lah meh'-dee-ah*]
highway, autostrada [*ah-oo-toh-strah'-dah*]
hill, collina [*kohl-lee'-nah*]
him *pron.*, lo, lui [*loh, loo'-ee*]
himself, lui stesso [*loo'-ee stehs'-soh*]
hint *n.*, accenno [*ahch-chehn'-noh*]
hip, fianco [*fee-ahn'-koh*]
hire [rent] *v.*, affittare [*ahf-feet-tah'-reh*]
history, storia [*stoh'-ree-ah*]
hit *v.*, colpire [*kohl-pee'-reh*]
hitchhiking, autostop [*ah'-oo-toh-stohp*]
hold *v.*, tenere [*teh-neh'-reh*]

hole, buco, cavità (f, indecl) [*boo'-koh, kah-vee-tah'*]
holiday, festa [*fehs'-tah*]
Holland, Olanda [*oh-lahn'-dah*]
holy, santo [*sahn'-toh*]
home, casa [*kah'-zah*]
at home, a casa [*ah kah'-zah*]
Make yourself at home! Si faccia comodo! [*see fahch'-chee-ah koh'-moh-doh*]
homeland, patria [*pah'-tree-ah*]
homesick, nostalgico [*nohs-tahl'-jee-koh*]
honest, onesto [*oh-nehs'-toh*]
honey, miele (m) [*mee-eh'-leh*]
honeymoon, luna di miele [*loo'-nah dee mee-eh'-leh*]
honor *n.*, onore (m) [*oh-noh'-reh*]
hook, gancio [*gahn'-chee-oh*]
hope *n.*, speranza [*speh-rahn'-tsah*]
hope *v.*, sperare [*speh-rah'-reh*]
hopeful, promettente [*proh-meht-tehn'-teh*]
hopeless, disperato [*dees-peh-rah'-toh*]
horizon, orizzonte (m) [*oh-reedz-dzohn'-teh*]
horn [animal or shape], corno [*kohr'-noh*]
horn [auto], tromba [*trohm'-bah*]
horrible, orribile [*ohr-ree'-bee-leh*]
horse, cavallo [*kah-vahl'-loh*]
hospital, ospedale (m) [*ohs-peh-dah'-leh*]
hospitality, ospitalità (f, indecl) [*ohs-pee-tah-lee-tah'*]
host, ospite (che òspita) [*ohs'-pee-teh*]
hostess, ostessa, hostess [*ohs-tehs'-sah, ohs'-tehs*]
hostile, ostile [*ohs-tee'-leh*]
hot, caldo [*kahl'-doh*]
hotel, albergo [*ahl-behr'-goh*]
hotel room, camera d'albergo [*kah'-meh-rah dahl-behr'-goh*]
hour, ora [*oh'-rah*]
house, casa [*kah'-zah*]
housekeeper, governante di casa [*goh-vehr-nahn'-teh dee kah'-zah*]
housewife, massaia [*mahs-sah'-ee-ah*]
how, come [*koh'-meh*]

How do you do? Come sta? [*koh'-meh stah*]
How far is it? Quanto è lontano? [*koo-ahn'-toh eh' lohn-tah'-noh*]
How long [time]? Per quanto tempo? [*pehr koo-ahn'-toh tehm'-poh*]
How many? Quanti? Quante? [*koo-ahn'-tee, koo-ahn'-teh*]
How much? Quanto? [*koo-ahn'-toh*]
however, comunque [*koh-moon'-koo-eh*]
hug *n.*, abbraccio [*ahb-brach'-chee-oh*]
human, umano [*oo-mah'-noh*]
humanity, umanità (f, indecl) [*oo-mah-nee-tah'*]
humid, umido [*oo'-mee-doh*]
humility, umiltà (f, indecl) [*oo-meel-tah'*]
humorous, umoristico [*oo-moh-rees'-tee-koh*]
hundred, cento (invar.) [*chen'-toh*]
one hundred, cento [*chen'-toh*]
two hundred, due cento [*doo'-eh chehn'-toh*]
Hungarian, ungherese [*oon-geh-reh'-zeh*]
Hungary, Ungheria [*oon-geh-ree'-ah*]
hunger *n.*, fame (f) [*fah'-meh*]
hungry: be hungry, avere fame [*ah-veh'-reh fah'-meh*]
hunt *v.*, cacciare [*kahch-chee-ah'-reh*]
hunting, caccia [*kahch'-chee-ah*]
hurricane, uragano [*oo-rah-gah'-noh*]
hurry *n.*, fretta [*freht'-tah*]
be in a hurry, avere fretta [*ah-veh'-reh freht'-tah*]
Hurry up! Presto, presto! [*prehs'-toh, prehs'-toh*]
hurt [ache] *v.*, sentire dolore [*sehn-tee'-reh doh-loh'-reh*]
hurt [somebody] *v.*, fare male a [*fah'-reh mah'-leh ah*]
hurt one's feelings, offendere [*ohf-fehn'-deh-reh*]
husband, marito [*mah-ree'-toh*]
hypocrisy, ipocrisia [*ee-poh-kree-zee'-ah*]
hysterical, isterico [*ees-teh'-ree-koh*]

I

I, io [*ee'-oh*]
ice, ghiaccio [*gee-ahch'-chee-oh*]
ice cream, gelato [*jeh-lah'-toh*]
idea, idea [*ee-deh'-ah*]
ideal, ideale [*ee-deh-ah'-leh*]
identical, identico [*ee-dehn'-tee-koh*]
identification card, carta d'identità [*kahr'-tah dee-dehn-tee-tah'*]
identify *v.*, identificare [*ee-dehn-tee-fee-kah'-reh*]
identity, identità (f, indecl) [*ee-dehn-tee-tah'*]
idle *adj.*, ozioso [*oh-tsee'-oh-zoh*]
if, se, in caso che [*seh, een kah'-zoh keh*]
  even if, anche se [*ahn'-keh seh*]
ignition, accensione [*ahch-chehn'-see-oh-neh*]
ignorant, ignorante [*ee-nyoh-rahn'-teh*]
ill, ammalato [*ahm-mah-lah'-toh*]
illegal, illegale [*eel-leh-gah'-leh*]
illegible, illegibile [*eel-leh-jee'-bee-leh*]
illiterate *n.*, analfabeta [*ah-nahl-fah-beh'-tah*]
illness, malattia [*mah-laht-tee'-ah*]
image, immagine (f) [*eem-mah'-jee-neh*]
imagination, immaginazione (f) [*eem-mah-jee-nah-tsee-oh'-neh*]
imagine *v.*, immaginare [*eem-mah-jee-nah'-reh*]
  Just imagine! Figurati!, Si figuri! [*fee-goo'-rah-tee, see fee-goo'-ree*]
imitate *v.*, imitare [*ee-mee-tah'-reh*]
imitation, imitazione (f) [*ee-mee-tah-tsee-oh'-neh*]
immaterial, immateriale [*eem-mah-teh-ree-ah'-leh*]
immature, immaturo [*eem-mah-too'-roh*]
immediately, immediatamente [*eem-meh-dee-ah-tah-mehn'-teh*]

immense, immenso [*eem-mehn'-soh*]
immigration, immigrazione (f) [*eem-mee-grah-tsee-oh'-neh*]
immoral, immorale [*eem-moh-rah'-leh*]
immunity, immunità (f, indecl) [*eem-moo-nee-tah'*]
impartial, imparziale [*eem-pah-tsee-ah'-leh*]
impatient, impaziente [*eem-pah-tsee-ehn'-teh*]
imperfect, imperfetto [*eem-pehr-feht'-toh*]
impolite, scortese [*skohr-teh'-zeh*]
import *v.*, importare [*eem-por-tah'-reh*]
importance, importanza [*eem-pohr-tahn'-tsa*]
important, importante [*eem-pohr-tahn'-teh*]
imported, importato [*eem-pohr-tah'-toh*]
impossible, impossibile [*eem-pohs-see'-bee-leh*]
impression, impressione (f) [*eem-prehs-see-oh'-neh*]
impressive, impressionante [*eem-prehs-see-oh-nahn'-teh*]
improbable, improbabile [*eem-proh-bah'-bee-leh*]
improve *v.*, migliorare [*mee-lyoh-rah'-reh*]
improvement, miglioramento [*mee-lyoh-rah-mehn'-toh*]
in, in [*een*]
  in no way, in nessun modo [*een nehs-soon' moh'-doh*]
  in spite of, a dispetto di [*ah dees-peht'-toh dee*]
  in the afternoon, al pomeriggio [*ahl poh-meh-reej'-jee-oh*]
  Is Mr. Cicco in? È in casa il Signor Cicco? [*eh' een kah'-zah eel see-nyohr' cheek'-koh*]
inaccurate, inesatto [*een-eh-zat'-toh*]
inch, pollice (m) [*pohl'-lee-cheh*]
incident, incidente [*een-chee-dehn'-teh*]
incidentally, incidentalmente [*een-chee-dehn-tahl-mehn'-teh*]
inclination, inclinazione (f) [*een-klee-nah-tsee-oh'-neh*]
include *v.*, includere [*een-kloo'-deh-reh*]
included, incluso [*een-kloo'-zoh*]
income, reddito [*rehd'-dee-toh*]
income tax, imposta sul reddito [*eem-pohs'-tah sool rehd'-dee-toh*]
incomparable, incomparabile [*een-kohm-pah-rah'-bee-leh*]
incomplete, incompleto [*een-kohm-pleh'-toh*]
inconvenience, sconvenienza [*skohn-veh-nee-ehn'-tsah*]

incorrect, inesatto [*een-eh-zaht'-toh*]
increase *n.*, aumento [*ah-oo-mehn'-toh*]
increase *v.*, aumentare [*ah-oo-mehn-tah'-reh*]
indeed, in verità [*een veh-ree-tah'*]
Yes, indeed! Davvero! [*dahv-veh'-roh*]
indefinite, indefinito [*een-deh-fee-nee'-toh*]
independent, indipendente [*een-dee-pehn-dehn'-teh*]
India, India [*een'-dee-ah*]
Indian, indiano [*een-dee-ah'-noh*]
indicate *v.*, indicare [*een-dee-kah'-reh*]
indifferent, indifferente [*een-deef-feh-rehn'-teh*]
indigestion, indigestione (f) [*een-dee-jehs-tee-oh'-neh*]
indignant, indignato [*een-dee-nyah'-toh*]
indirect, indiretto [*een-dee-reht'-toh*]
indiscreet, indiscreto [*een-dees-kreh'-toh*]
individual *adj.*, individuale [*een-dee-vee-doo-ah'-leh*]
indoors, dentro [*dehn'-troh*]
industrial, industriale [*een-doos-tree-ah'-leh*]
industry, industria [*een-doos'-tree-ah*]
inefficient, inefficiente [*een-ehf-fee-chee-ehn'-teh*]
inexpensive, economico [*eh-koh-noh'-mee-koh*]
infant, infante (m) [*een-fahn'-teh*]
infection, infezione (f) [*een-feh-tsee-oh'-neh*]
inferior, inferiore [*een-feh-ree-oh'-reh*]
infinite, infinito [*een-fee-nee'-toh*]
infinitive, infinito [*een-fee-nee'-toh*]
influence *n.*, influenza [*een-floo-ehn'-tsah*]
influence *v.*, influenzare [*een-floo-ehn-zah'-reh*]
inform *v.*, informare [*een-fohr-mah'-reh*]
information, informazione (f) [*een-fohr-mah-tsee-oh'-neh*]
infrequent, infrequente [*een-freh-koo-ehn'-teh*]
inhabitant, abitante [*ah-bee-tahn'-teh*]
inherit *v.*, ereditare [*eh-reh-dee-tah'-reh*]
inheritance, eredità (f, indecl) [*eh-reh-dee-tah'*]
initial *n. & adj.*, iniziale (f) [*ee-nee-tsee-ah'-leh*]
injection, iniezione (f) [*ee-nee-eh-tsee-oh'-neh*]
injure *v.*, ferire [*feh-ree'-reh*]
injury, ferita [*feh-ree'-tah*]

injustice, ingiustizia [*een-jee-oos-tee'-tsee-ah*]
ink, inchiostro [*een-kee-ohs'-troh*]
inn, locanda [*loh-kahn'-dah*]
inner, interiore [*een-teh-ree-oh'-reh*]
innkeeper, oste (m) [*ohs'-teh*]
innocent, innocente [*een-noh-chehn'-teh*]
inquire *v.*, informarsi [*een-fohr-mahr'-see*]
insane, pazzo [*pahts'-tsoh*]
insect, insetto [*een-seht'-toh*]
inside, dentro [*dehn'-troh*]
  inside out, rivoltato [*ree-vohl-tah'-toh*]
insight, intuizione (f) [*een-too-ee-tsee-oh'-neh*]
insist *v.*, insistere [*een-sees'-teh-reh*]
inspect *v.*, ispezionare [*ees-peh-tsee-oh-nah'-reh*]
inspection, ispezione (f) [*ees-peh-tsee-oh'-neh*]
inspector, ispettore (m) [*ees-peht-toh'-reh*]
inspiration, ispirazione (f) [*ees-pee-rah-tsee-oh'-neh*]
install *v.*, installare [*een-stahl-lah'-reh*]
instance, istanza [*ees-tahn'-tsah*]
  for instance, per esempio [*pehr eh-zehm'-pee-oh*]
instead, anzichè [*ahn-tsee-keh'*]
  instead of, invece di [*een-veh'-cheh dee*]
instinct, istinto [*ees-teen'-toh*]
institution, istituzione (f) [*ees-tee-too-tsee-oh'-neh*]
instruct *v.*, instruire [*een-stroo-ee'-reh*]
instruction, istruzione (f) [*ees-troo-tsee-oh'-neh*]
instructor, istruttore (m) [*ees-troot-toh'-reh*]
instrument, strumento [*stroo-mehn'-toh*]
insufficient, insufficiente [*een-soof-fee-chee-ehn'-teh*]
insult *n.*, insulto [*een-sool'-toh*]
insult *v.*, insultare [*een-sool-tah'-reh*]
insurance, assicurazione (f) [*ahs-see-koo-rah-tsee-oh'-neh*]
insurance policy, polizza di assicurazione [*poh-leets'-tsah dee ahs-see-koo-rah-tsee-oh'-neh*]
insure *v.*, assicurare [*ahs-see-koo-rah'-reh*]
intact, intatto [*een-taht'-toh*]
intellectual, intellettuale [*een-teh-leht-too-ah'-leh*]
intelligent, intelligente [*een-tehl-lee-jehn'-teh*]

intend *v.*, intendere [*een-tehn'-deh-reh*]
intense, intenso [*een-tehn'-soh*]
intention, intenzione (f) [*een-tehn-tsee-oh'-neh*]
interest [concern] *n.*, interesse (m) [*een-teh-rehs'-seh*]
interest [financial] *n.*, profitto [*proh-feet'-toh*]
interest *v.*, interessare [*een-teh-rehs-sah'-reh*]
be interested in, interessarsi di [*een-teh-rehs-sahr'-see dee*]
interesting, interessante [*een-teh-rehs-sahn'-teh*]
interfere *v.*, interferire [*een-tehr-feh-ree'-reh*]
interior, interiore [*een-teh-ree-oh'-reh*]
intermission, intervallo [*een-tehr-vahl'-loh*]
internal, interno [*een-tehr'-noh*]
international, internazionale [*een-tehr-nah-tsee-oh-nah'-leh*]
interpreter, interprete [*een-tehr'-preh-teh*]
intersection, intersezione (f) [*een-tehr-seh-tsee-oh'-neh*]
interview *n.*, intervista [*een-tehr-vees'-tah*]
intimate *adj.*, intimo [*een'-tee-moh*]
into, nel, nello, nella, nell' [*nehl, nehl'-loh, nehl'-lah, nehl*]
introduce *v.*, presentare, introdurre (irreg) [*preh-zehn-tah'-reh, een-troh-door'-reh*]
introduction, presentazione (f) [*preh-zehn-tah-tsee-oh'-neh*]
intuition, intuizione, intuito [*een-too-ee-tsee-oh'-neh, een-too'-ee-toh*]
invalid, invalido [*een-vah'-lee-doh*]
invaluable, inestimabile [*een-ehs-tee-mah'-bee-leh*]
invasion, invasione (f) [*een-vah-zee-oh'-neh*]
invention, invenzione (f) [*een-vehn-tsee-oh'-neh*]
inventor, inventore (m) [*een-vehn-toh'-reh*]
invest *v.*, investire [*een-vehs-tee'-reh*]
investigate *v.*, investigare [*een-vehs-tee-gah'-reh*]
invisible, invisibile [*een-vee-zee'-bee-leh*]
invitation, invito [*een-vee'-toh*]
invite *v.*, invitare [*een-vee-tah'-reh*]
invoice *n.*, fattura [*faht-too'-rah*]
involuntary, involontario [*een-voh-lohn-tah'-ree-oh*]
Ireland, Irlanda [*eer-lahn'-dah*]
Irish, irlandese [*eer-lahn-deh'-zeh*]
iron [metal] *n.*, ferro [*fehr'-roh*]

iron [for ironing] *n.*, ferro da stiro [*fer'-roh dah stee'-roh*]
iron [clothes] *v.*, stirare [*stee-rah'-reh*]
irrational, illogico [*eel-loh'-jee-koh*]
irregular, irregolare [*eer-reh-goh-lah'-reh*]
irresistible, irresistibile [*eer-reh-zees-tee'-bee-leh*]
irritate *v.*, irritare [*eer-ree-tah'-reh*]
irritation, irritazione (f) [*eer-ree-tah-tsee-oh'-neh*]
is, è, sta [*eh'*, *stah*]
How is he! Come sta?, Com'è? [*koh'-meh stah, koh'-meh*]
island, isola [*ee'-zoh-lah*]
issue [magazine], numero [*noo'-meh-roh*]
it [obj. of verb], lo, la [*loh*, *lah*]
Italian *n. & adj.*, italiano [*ee-tah-lee-ah'-noh*]
Italy, Italia [*ee-tah'-lee-ah*]
itch *v.*, prudere [*proo'-deh-reh*]
item [thing], articolo [*ahr-tee'-koh-loh*]
itinerary, itinerario [*ee-tee-neh-rah'-ree-oh*]
its, suo, sua; suoi, sue (pl) [*soo'-oh*, *soo'-ah*; *soo-oh'-ee*, *soo'-eh*]
itself, stesso [*stehs'-soh*]
ivory, avorio [*ah-voh'-ree-oh*]

J

jack [auto], cric [*kreek*]
jacket, giacca, giacche (pl) [*jee-ahk'-kah*, *jee-ahk'-keh*]
jail, carcere (m, f) [*kahr'-cheh-reh*]
jam, marmellata [*mahr-mehl-lah'-tah*]
janitor, portiere (m) [*pohr-tee-eh'-reh*]
January, gennaio [*jehn-nah'-ee-oh*]
Japan, Giappone (m) [*jee-ahp-poh'-neh*]
Japanese, giapponese [*jee-ahp-poh-neh'-zeh*]
jar [container], giara [*jee-ah'-rah*]
jaw, mascella [*mah-shehl'-lah*]
jazz, giaz [*jee-ahts'*]

jealous, geloso [*jeh-loh'-zoh*]
jelly, gelatina [*jeh-lah-tee'-nah*]
Jew, ebreo [*eh-breh'-oh*]
jewel, gioiello [*jee-oh-ee-ehl'-loh*]
jeweler, gioielliere (m) [*jee-oh-ee-ehl-lee'-eh-reh*]
jeweler's shop, gioielleria [*jee-oh-ee-ehl-leh-ree'-ah*]
Jewish, Giudeo [*jee-oo-deh'-oh*]
job, impiego, lavoro [*eem-pee-eh'-goh*, *lah-voh'-roh*]
join *v.*, unire [*oo-nee'-reh*]
jointly, unitamente [*oo-nee-tah-mehn'-teh*]
joke *n.*, scherzo [*skehr'-tsoh*]
joker, burlone [*boor-loh'-neh*]
journal, giornale (m) [*jee-ohr-nah'-leh*]
journalism, giornalismo [*jee-ohr-nah-leez'-moh*]
journalist, giornalista (m, f) [*jee-ohr-nah-lees'-tah*]
journey *n.*, viaggio, gita [*vee-ahj'-jee-oh*, *jee'-tah*]
jovial, gioviale [*jee-oh-vee-ah'-leh*]
joy, gioia, allegria [*jee-oh'-ee-ah*, *ahl-leh-gree'-ah*]
joyful, gioioso [*jee-oh-ee-oh'-zoh*]
jubilant, giubilante [*jee-oo-bee-lahn'-teh*]
judge *n.*, giudice (m) [*jee-oo'-dee-cheh*]
judge *v.*, giudicare [*jee-oo-dee-kah'-reh*]
judgment, giudizio, sentenza [*jee-oo-dee'-tsee-oh*, *sehn-tehn'-tsah*]
jug, brocca [*brohk'-kah*]
juice, succo [*sook'-koh*]
  fruit juice, succo di frutta, spremuta [*sook'-koh dee froot'-tah*, *spreh-moo'-tah*]
July, luglio [*loo'-lyoh*]
jump *n.*, salto [*sahl'-toh*]
jump *v.*, saltare [*sahl-tah'-reh*]
June, giugno [*jee-oo'-nyoh*]
junior, più giovane [*pee-oo' jee-oh'-vah-neh*]
jurisdiction, giurisdizione (f) [*jee-oo-reez-dee-tsee-oh'-neh*]
jury, giuria [*jee-oo-ree'-ah*]
just *adj.*, giusto, equo [*jee-oos'-toh*, *eh'-koo-oh*]
just *adv.*, proprio, appena [*proh'-pree-oh*, *ahp-peh'-nah*]
  just as, proprio come [*proh'-pree-oh koh'-meh*]

I just arrived, Sono giusto arrivato [*soh'-noh jee-oos'-toh ahr-ree-vah'-toh*]
just now, poco fa [*poh'-koh fah*]
justice, giustizia [*jee-oos-tee'-tsee-ah*]

K

keep *v.*, tenere (irreg) [*teh-neh'-reh*]
keep from, astenersi [*ahs-teh-nehr'-see*]
keep out, tenersi al di fuori [*teh-nehr'-see ahl dee foo-oh'-ree*]
Keep out! Vietato l'ingresso! [*vee-eh-tah'-toh leen-grehs'-soh*]
keep quiet, stare zitto [*stah'-reh dzeet'-toh*]
Keep quiet! Stia zitto! [*stee'-ah dzeet'-toh*]
kettle, pentolino [*pehn-toh-lee'-noh*]
key *n.*, chiave (f) [*kee-ah'-veh*]
kick *n.*, pedata, colpo [*peh-dah'-tah, kohl'-poh*]
kick *v.*, tirar calci a [*tee-rahr' kahl'-chee ah*]
kid [animal] *n.*, capretto [*kah-preht'-toh*]
kid [child] *n.*, ragazzetto [*rah-gahts-tseht'-toh*]
kid *v.*, scherzare [*skehr-tsah'-reh*]
No kidding, Senza scherzi [*sehn'-tsah skehr'-tsee*]
kidnap *v.*, rapire [*rah-pee'-reh*]
kidney [food], rognone (m) [*roh-nyoh'-neh*]
kidney [anat.], rene (m) [*reh'-neh*]
kill *v.*, uccidere [*ooch-chee'-deh-reh*]
kilogram, chilo [*kee'-loh*]
kilometer, chilometro [*kee-loh'-meh-troh*]
kind *n.*, genere (m), specie (f) [*jeh'-neh-reh, speh'-chee-eh*]
kind *adj.*, gentile [*jehn-tee'-leh*]
kindness, gentilezza [*jehn-tee-lehts'-tsah*]
king, re (m) [*reh*]
kiss *n.*, bacio [*bah'-chee-oh*]
kiss *v.*, baciare [*bah-chee-ah'-reh*]

kitchen, cucina [*koo-chee'-nah*]
knee, ginocchio [*jee-nohk'-kee-oh*]
kneel *v.*, inginocchiarsi [*een-jee-nohk-kee-ahr'-see*]
knife, coltello [*kohl-tehl'-loh*]
knock *n.*, colpo, bussata [*kohl'-poh, boos-sah'-tah*]
knock *v.*, bussare, colpire [*boos-sah'-reh, kohl-pee'-reh*]
knot *n.*, nodo [*noh'-doh*]
know [be acquainted with] *v.*, conoscere [*koh-noh'-sheh-reh*]
know [general sense] *v.*, sapere (irreg) [*sah-peh'-reh*]
Do you know? Sa lei? [*sah leh'-ee*]
I don't know, Non so [*nohn soh*]
Who knows? Chi sa? [*kee sah*]
knowledge, sapere (m), conoscenza [*sah-peh'-reh, koh-noh-shehn'-tsa*]

L

label, etichetta [*eh-tee-keht'-tah*]
labor *n.*, lavoro, mano d'opera [*lah-voh'-roh, mah'-noh doh'-peh-rah*]
laboratory, laboratorio [*lah-boh-rah-toh'-ree-oh*]
laborer, operaio [*oh-peh-rah'-ee-oh*]
laces [shoe], lacci (m, pl) [*lahch'-chee*]
lack *n.*, mancanza [*mahn-kahn'-tsah*]
lack: be lacking *v.*, mancare [*mahn-kah'-reh*]
lacking in, privo di [*pree'-voh dee*]
ladder, scala [*skah'-lah*]
ladies' room, per signore (f, pl) [*pehr see-nyoh'-reh*]
lady, signora [*see-nyoh'-rah*]
lake, lago, laghi (pl) [*lah'-goh, lah'-gee*]
lamb, agnello [*ah-nyeh'-loh*]
lame *adj.*, zoppo [*dzohp'-poh*]
lamp, lampada [*lahm'-pah-dah*]
land *n.*, terra [*tehr'-rah*]
land [airplane] *v.*, atterrare [*aht-tehr-rah'-reh*]

land [ship] *v.*, sbarcare [*zbahr-kah'-reh*]
landing [airplane], atterraggio [*aht-tehr-rahj'-jee-oh*]
landing [ship], approdo [*ahp-proh'-doh*]
landlady, padrona di casa [*pah-droh'-nah dee kah'-zah*]
landlord, padrone di casa [*pah-droh'-neh dee kah'-zah*]
landmark, punto di riferimento [*poon'-toh dee ree-feh-ree-mehn'-toh*]
landowner, proprietario di terre [*proh-pree-eh-tah'-ree-oh dee tehr'-reh*]
landscape, paesaggio [*pah-eh-zahj'-jee-oh*]
language, lingua [*leen'-goo-ah*]
large, largo, grande [*lahr'-goh, grahn'-deh*]
last *adj.*, ultimo [*ool'-tee-moh*]
at last, finalmente [*fee-nahl-mehn'-teh*]
last night, la notte scorsa [*lah noht'-teh skohr'-sah*]
last week, la settimana scorsa [*lah seht-tee-mah'-nah skohr'-sah*]
last year, l'ultimo anno [*lool'-tee-moh ahn'-noh*]
last *v.*, durare [*doo-rah'-reh*]
late *adv.*, tardi [*tahr'-dee*]
be late *v.*, essere in ritardo [*ehs'-seh-reh een ree-tahr'-doh*]
lately, recentemente [*reh-chehn-teh-mehn'-teh*]
later, più tardi [*pee-oo' tahr'-dee*]
latest, recentissimo [*reh-chehn-tees'-see-moh*]
Latin, latino [*lah-tee'-noh*]
latter, ultimo, secondo [*ool'-tee-moh, seh-kohn'-doh*]
laugh *n.*, riso [*ree'-zoh*]
laugh *v.*, ridere [*ree'-deh-reh*]
laughter, risata [*ree-zah'-tah*]
laundry, lavanderia [*lah-vahn-deh-ree'-ah*]
law, legge (f) [*lehj'-jeh*]
lawful, legittimo [*leh-jeet'-tee-moh*]
lawn, prato [*prah'-toh*]
lawyer, avvocato [*ahv-voh-kah'-toh*]
lay *v.*, mettere [*meht'-teh-reh*]
lazy, pigro [*pee'-groh*]
lead [metal] *n.*, piombo [*pee-ohm'-boh*]
lead *v.*, guidare [*goo-ee-dah'-reh*]

leader, capo [*kah'-poh*]
lean *v.*, appoggiare [*ahp-pohj-jee-ah'-reh*]
leaning *adj.*, pendente [*pehn-dehn'-teh*]
learn *v.*, imparare [*eem-pah-rah'-reh*]
learned *adj.*, istruito [*ees-troo-ee'-toh*]
lease *n.*, contratto d'affitto [*kohn-traht'-toh dahf-feet'-toh*]
lease *v.*, affittare [*ahf-feet-tah'-reh*]
least, minimo [*mee'-nee-moh*]
at least, al meno [*ahl meh'-noh*]
leather, cuoio [*koo-oh'-ee-oh*]
leave [abandon] *v.*, abbandonare [*ahb-bahn-doh-nah'-reh*]
leave [allow] *v.*, permettere [*pehr-meht'-teh-reh*]
leave [depart] *v.*, partire [*pahr-tee'-reh*]
lecture *n.*, conferenza [*kohn-feh-rehn'-tsah*]
left [direction], sinistro [*see-nees'-troh*]
to the left, a sinistra [*ah see-nees'-trah*]
leg, gamba [*gahm'-bah*]
legal, legale [*leh-gah'-leh*]
legible, leggibile [*lehj-jee'-bee-leh*]
legitimate, legittimo [*leh-jeet'-tee-moh*]
leisure, agio [*ah'-jee-oh*]
lemon, limone (m) [*lee-moh'-neh*]
lemonade, limonata [*lee-moh-nah'-tah*]
lend *v.*, prestare [*prehs-tah'-reh*]
length, lunghezza [*loon-gehts'-tsah*]
lens, lente (f) [*lehn'-teh*]
less, meno [*meh'-noh*]
more or less, più o meno [*pee-oo' oh meh'-noh*]
lesson, lezione (f) [*leh-tsee-oh'-neh*]
let [permit] *v.*, permettere [*pehr-meht'-teh-reh*]
let [rent] *v.*, affittare [*ahf-fee-tah'-reh*]
Room to let, Stanza d'affittare [*stahn'-tsah dahf-feet-tah'-reh*]
let [leave] *v.*, lasciare [*lah-shee-ah'-reh*]
let alone *v.*, lasciar stare [*lah-shee-ahr' stah'-reh*]
Let him go, Lo lasci andare [*loh lah'-shee ahn-dah'-reh*]
letter, lettera [*leht'-teh-rah*]
letter of introduction, lettera di presentazione [*leht'-teh-*

rah dee preh-zehn-tah-tsee-oh'-neh]
letter box, cassetta da lettere [*kahs-seht'-tah dah leht'-teh-reh*]
level *n.*, livello [*lee-vehl'-loh*]
liability, obbligo [*ohb'-blee-goh*]
liar, bugiardo [*boo-jee-ahr'-doh*]
liberal, liberale [*lee-beh-rah'-leh*]
liberty, libertà (f, indecl) [*lee-behr-tah'*]
library, biblioteca [*bee-blee-oh-teh'-kah*]
license *n.*, licenza [*lee-chehn'-tsah*]
lid, coperchio [*koh-pehr'-kee-oh*]
eyelid, palpebra [*pahl'-peh-brah*]
lie [untruth] *n.*, bugia [*boo-jee'-ah*]
lie [tell an untruth] *v.*, mentire [*mehn-tee'-reh*]
lie down, sdraiarsi [*zdrah-ee-ahr'-see*]
life, vita [*vee'-tah*]
lifeboat, scialuppa [*shee-ah-loop'-pah*]
lifeguard, bagnino [*bah-nyee'-noh*]
life insurance, assicurazione sulla vita [*ahs-see-koo-rah-tsee-oh'-neh sool'-lah vee'-tah*]
life jacket, salvagente (m) [*sahl-vah-jehn'-teh*]
lift *v.*, sollevare [*sohl-leh-vah'-reh*]
light *n.*, luce (f) [*loo'-cheh*]
light *v.*, accendere [*ahch-chehn'-deh-reh*]
light *adj.*, leggero, chiaro [*lehj-jeh'-roh, kee-ah'-roh*]
lighter [cigarette] *n.*, accendi-sigaro [*ahch-chehn'-dee-see'-gah-roh*]
lighthouse, faro [*fah'-roh*]
lightning, fulmine (f), lampo [*fool'-mee-neh, lahm'-poh*]
lights [car], fari [*fah'-ree*]
likable, piacevole [*pee-ah-cheh'-voh-leh*]
like *adv. & prep.*, simile, come [*see'-mee-leh, koh'-meh*]
like *v.*, piacere, amare [*pee-ah-cheh'-reh, ah-mah'-reh*]
I don't like it, Non mi piace [*nohn mee pee-ah'-cheh*]
I like it very much, Mi piace moltissimo [*mee pee-ah'-cheh mohl-tees'-see-moh*]
Would you like . . .? Le piacerebbe . . .? [*leh pee-ah-cheh-rehb'-beh*]

limit *n.*, limite (m) [*lee'-mee-teh*]
limit *v.*, limitare [*lee-mee-tah'-reh*]
line, linea [*lee'-neh-ah*]
linen [clothing], biancheria [*bee-ahn-keh-ree'-ah*]
lip, labbro, le labbra (pl) [*lahb'-broh, leh lahb'-brah*]
lipstick, rossetto [*rohs-seht'-toh*]
liquid, liquido [*lee'-koo-ee-doh*]
liquor, liquore (m) [*lee-koo-oh'-reh*]
list *n.*, lista [*lees'-tah*]
listen *v.*, ascoltare, sentire [*ahs-kohl-tah'-reh, sehn-tee'-reh*]
literally, letteralmente [*leht-teh-rahl-mehn'-teh*]
literature, letteratura [*leht-teh-rah-too'-rah*]
little *adj.*, piccolo [*peek'-koh-loh*]
little *adv.*, poco [*poh'-koh*]
  a little bit, proprio un poco [*proh'-pree-oh oon poh'-koh*]
  little by little, poco a poco [*poh'-koh ah poh'-koh*]
live [be alive] *v.*, vivere [*vee'-veh-reh*]
live [reside] *v.*, abitare [*ah-bee-tah'-reh*]
live *adv.*, vivo [*vee'-voh*]
lively, vivace [*vee-vah'-cheh*]
liver, fegato [*feh'-gah-toh*]
living room, stanza soggiorno [*stahn'-tsah sohj-jee-ohr'-noh*]
load *n.*, carico [*kah'-ree-koh*]
load *v.*, caricare [*kah-ree-kah'-reh*]
loaf [of bread], panino [*pah-nee'-noh*]
loan *n.*, prestito [*prehs'-tee-toh*]
lobby, vestibolo [*vehs-tee'-boh-loh*]
local, locale [*loh-kah'-leh*]
locate *v.*, collocare [*kohl-loh-kah'-reh*]
located, situato [*see-too-ah'-toh*]
location, località (f, indecl) [*loh-kah-lee-tah'*]
lock *v.*, chiudere a chiave [*kee-oo'-deh-reh ah kee-ah'-veh*]
lodging, alloggio [*ahl-lohj'-jee-oh*]
logical, logico [*loh'-jee-koh*]
lonely, solitario [*soh-lee-tah'-ree-oh*]
long *adj.*, lungo [*loon'-goh*]
long for *v.*, desiderare [*deh-zee-deh-rah'-reh*]
longer [distance], più lungo [*pee-oo' loon'-goh*]

longer [time], più a lungo [*pee-oo' ah loon'-goh*]
longing, desiderio [*deh-zee-deh'-ree-oh*]
look *n.*, sguardo [*zgoo-ahr'-doh*]
look *v.*, guardare [*goo-ahr-dah'-reh*]
  Look! Guardi! [*goo-ahr'-dee*]
  look for, cercare [*chehr-kah'-reh*]
  Look out! Attenzione! [*aht-tehn-tsee-oh'-neh*]
looks [appearance], aspetto [*ahs-peht'-toh*]
loose, sciolto, libero [*shee-ohl'-toh, lee'-beh-roh*]
loosen *v.*, allentare [*ahl-lehn-tah'-reh*]
lose *v.*, perdere [*pehr'-deh-reh*]
loss, perdita [*pehr'-dee-tah*]
lost, perduto [*pehr-doo'-toh*]
lot [quantity], molto [*mohl'-toh*]
loud, aloud alta voce [*ahl'-tah voh'-cheh*]
loudspeaker, altoparlante [*ahl-toh-pahr-lahn'-teh*]
love *n.*, amore (m) [*ah-moh'-reh*]
love *v.*, amare [*ah-mah'-reh*]
lovely, grazioso [*grah-tsee-oh'-zoh*]
lover, amante (m, f) [*ah-mahn'-teh*]
low *adj.*, basso [*bahs'-soh*]
loyal, leale [*leh-ah'-leh*]
lubricate *v.*, lubrificare [*loo-bree-fee-kah'-reh*]
lubrication, lubrificazione (f) [*loo-bree-fee-kah-tsee-oh'-neh*]
luck, fortuna [*fohr-too'-nah*]
  Good luck! Buona fortuna! [*boo-oh'-nah fohr-too'-nah*]
lucky, fortunato [*fohr-too-nah'-toh*]
luggage, bagaglio [*bah-gah'-lyoh*]
lunch *n.*, pranzo, seconda colazione [*prahn'-tsoh, seh-kohn'-dah koh-lah-tsee-oh'-neh*]
  have lunch *v.*, pranzare [*prahn-tsah'-reh*]
lung, polmone (m) [*pohl-moh'-neh*]
luxurious, lussuoso [*loos-soo-oh'-zoh*]
luxury, lusso [*loos'-soh*]

M

machine, macchina [*mahk'-kee-nah*]
madam, signora [*see-nyoh'-rah*]
made, fatto [*faht'-toh*]
  made of cotton, di cotone [*dee koh-toh'-neh*]
magazine, rivista [*ree-vees'-tah*]
maid, domestica, cameriera [*doh-mehs'-tee-kah, kah-meh-ree-eh'-rah*]
mail *n.*, posta [*pohs'-tah*]
mail *v.*, spedire, imbucare [*speh-dee'-reh, eem-boo-kah'-reh*]
mailbox, cassetta delle lettere [*kahs-seht'-tah dehl'-leh leht'-teh-reh*]
mailman, postino [*pohs-tee'-noh*]
main, principale [*preen-chee-pah'-leh*]
  main office, ufficio centrale [*oof-fee'-chee-oh chehn-trah'-leh*]
  main street, via principale [*vee'-ah preen-chee-pah'-leh*]
mainly, principalmente [*preen-chee-pahl-mehn'-teh*]
majority, maggioranza [*mahj-jee-oh-rahn'-tsah*]
make *v.*, fare (irreg) [*fah'-reh*]
  make a mistake, sbagliarsi (refl) [*zbah-lyahr'-see*]
  make a speech, fare un discorso [*fah'-reh oon dees-kohr'-soh*]
  make fun of, prendere in giro [*prehn'-deh-reh een jee'-roh*]
  make up for, compensare per [*kohm-pehn-sah'-reh pehr*]
male, maschio [*mahs'-kee-oh*]
man, uomo, uomini (pl) [*oo-oh'-mo, oo-oh'-mee-nee*]
  young man, giovanotto [*jee-oh-vah-noht'-toh*]
manage *v.*, amministrare [*ahm-mee-nees-trah'-reh*]
manager, direttore (m), direttrice (f) [*dee-reht-toh'-reh, dee-reht-tree'-chee*]

manicure, manicure (f) [*mah-nee-koo'-reh*]
manner, maniera [*mah-nee-eh'-rah*]
manual, manuale [*mah-noo-ah'-leh*]
manufacture *v.*, fabbricare [*fahb-bree-kah'-reh*]
manufacturer, fabbricante [*fahb-bree-kahn'-teh*]
manuscript, manoscritto [*mah-noh-skreet'-toh*]
many, molti [*mohl'-tee*]
  How many? Quanti? [*koo-ahn'-tee*]
  too many, troppi [*trohp'-pee*]
  very many, moltissimi [*mohl-tees'-see-mee*]
map, carta geografica [*kahr'-tah jeh-oh-grah'-fee-kah*]
  road map, carta stradale [*kahr'-tah strah-dah'-leh*]
mar *v.*, sfigurare [*sfee-goo-rah'-reh*]
marble, marmo [*mahr'-moh*]
March, marzo [*mahr'-tsoh*]
march *n.*, marcia [*mahr'-chee-ah*]
march *v.*, marciare [*mahr-chee-ah'-reh*]
mark *n.*, segno [*seh'-nyoh*]
mark *v.*, segnare [*seh-nyah'-reh*]
market, mercato [*mehr-kah'-toh*]
marriage, matrimonio [*mah-tree-moh'-nee-oh*]
married, sposato [*spoh-zah'-toh*]
  get married *v.*, sposarsi [*spoh-zahr'-see*]
Mass [eccles.], messa [*mehs'-sah*]
mass [quantity], massa [*mahs'-sah*]
mass production, produzione (f) in serie [*proh-doo-tsee-oh'-neh een seh'-ree-eh*]
massage *n.*, massaggio [*mahs-sahj'-jee-oh*]
master *n.*, padrone (m) [*pah-droh'-neh*]
master *v.*, dominare [*doh-mee-nah'-reh*]
masterpiece, capolavoro [*kah-poh-lah-voh'-roh*]
match [for igniting], fiammifero [*fee-ahm-mee'-feh-roh*]
material [matter], materiale (m) [*mah-teh-ree-ah'-leh*]
material [cloth], stoffa [*stohf'-fah*]
maternal, materno [*mah-tehr'-noh*]
maternity, maternità (f, indecl) [*mah-tehr-nee-tah'*]
mathematics, matematica [*mah-teh-mah'-tee-kah*]
matter *n.*, materia, argomento [*mah-teh'-ree-ah, ahr-goh-*

mehn'-toh]
What's the matter? Che cosa c'è? [*keh koh'-zah cheh'*]
matter *v.*, importare [*eem-pohr-tah'-reh*]
It doesn't matter, Non importa [*nohn eem-pohr'-tah*]
matter of fact, positivo [*poh-zee-tee'-voh*]
mattress, materasso [*mah-teh-rahs'-soh*]
mature, maturo [*mah-too'-roh*]
May, maggio [*mahj'-jee-oh*]
may *v.*, posso, puoi, può [*pohs'-soh, poo-oh'-ee, poo-oh'*]
It may be, Può essere, Può darsi [*poo-oh' ehs'-seh-reh, poo-oh' dahr'-see*]
It may be that . . . Può darsi che . . . [*poo-oh' dahr'-see keh*]
maybe, forse [*fohr'-seh*]
mayor, sindaco [*seen'-dah-koh*]
me, me [*meh*]
meal, pasto [*pahs'-toh*]
mean *adj.*, meschino [*mehs-kee'-noh*]
mean *v.*, significare [*see-nyee-fee-kah'-reh*]
What does it mean? Che cosa significa? [*keh koh'-zah see-nyee'-fee-kah*]
What do you mean? Che cosa vuol dire! [*keh koh'-zah voo-ohl' dee'-reh*]
means, mezzi, rendite (pl) [*mehdz'-dzee, rehn'-dee-teh*]
by all means, certamente [*chehr-tah-mehn'-teh*]
by means of, per mezzo di [*pehr mehdz'-dzoh dee*]
by no means, niente affatto [*nee-ehn'-teh ahf-faht'-toh*]
meantime, meanwhile, frattanto, intanto [*fraht-tahn'-toh, een-tahn'-toh*]
measles, morbillo [*mohr-beel'-loh*]
measure *n.*, misura [*mee-zoo'-rah*]
measure *v.*, misurare [*mee-zoo-rah'-reh*]
meat, carne (f) [*kahr'-neh*]
mechanic, mechanical, meccanico [*mehk-kah'-nee-koh*]
medical, medico [*meh'-dee-koh*]
medicine, medicina [*meh-dee-chee'-nah*]
Mediterranean, Mediterraneo [*meh-dee-tehr-rah'-neh-oh*]
medium *adj.*, medio [*meh'-dee-oh*]

meet *v.*, incontrare [*een-kohn-trah'-reh*]
Delighted to meet you! Piacere di conoscerla! [*pee-ah-cheh'-reh dee koh-noh'-shehr-lah*]
I meet him every Sunday, L'incontro ogni domenica [*leen-kohn'-troh oh'-nyee doh-mehn'-ee-kah*]
meeting [group], riunione (f) [*ree-oo-nee-oh'-neh*]
meeting [encounter], incontro [*een-kohn'-troh*]
melon, melone (m) [*meh-loh'-neh*]
melt *v.*, sciogliere [*shee-oh'-lyeh-reh*]
member, membro [*mehm'-broh*]
memory, memoria [*meh-moh'-ree-ah*]
mend *v.*, rammendare [*rahm-mehn-dah'-reh*]
mental, mentale [*mehn-tah'-leh*]
mention *v.*, menzionare [*mehn-tsee-oh-nah'-reh*]
merchandise, merce (f) [*mehr'-cheh*]
merchant, mercante (m) [*mehr-kahn'-teh*]
mercy, misericordia, pietà (f, indecl) [*mee-zeh-ree-kohr'-dee-ah, pee-eh-tah'*]
at the mercy of, alla mercè di [*ahl'-lah mehr-cheh' dee*]
merely, semplicemente [*sehm-plee-cheh-mehn'-teh*]
merit *n.*, merito [*meh'-ree-toh*]
merit *v.*, meritare [*meh-ree-tah'-reh*]
message, messaggio [*mehs-sahj'-jee-oh*]
messenger, messaggero [*mehs-sahj-jeh'-roh*]
metal, metallo [*meh-tahl'-loh*]
meter [measure] *n.*, metro [*meh'-troh*]
meter [counter] *n.*, contatore (m) [*kohn-tah-toh'-reh*]
method, metodo [*meh'-toh-doh*]
metric system, sistema (m) metrico [*sees-teh'-mah meh'-tree-koh*]
Mexican, messicano [*mehs-see-kah'-noh*]
Mexico, Messico [*mehs'-see-koh*]
middle *n.*, mezzo, centro [*mehdz-dzoh, chehn'-troh*]
midnight, mezzanotte (f) [*mehdz-dzah-noht'-teh*]
midway, a metà strada [*ah meh-tah' strah'-dah*]
Milan, Milano [*mee-lah'-noh*]
mild, mite [*mee'-teh*]
mile, miglio, miglia (pl) [*mee'-lyoh, mee'-lyah*]

military, militare [*mee-lee-tah'-reh*]
military service, servizio militare [*sehr-vee'-tsee-oh mee-lee-tah'-reh*]
milk, latte (m) [*laht'-teh*]
million, milione (m) [*mee-lee-oh'-neh*]
two million, due milioni, [*doo'-eh mee-lee-oh'-nee*]
mind *n.*, mente (f) [*mehn'-teh*]
mind *v.*, badare a [*bah-dah'-reh ah*]
Do you mind if I sit here? Le dispiace se mi siedo qui? [*leh dees-pee-ah'-cheh seh mee see-eh'-doh koo-ee'*]
mine *pron.*, mio, mia; miei, mie (pl) [*mee'-oh, mee'-ah; mee-eh'-ee, mee'-eh*]
mine *n.*, miniera [*mee-nee-eh'-rah*]
miner, minatore (m) [*mee-nah-toh'-reh*]
mineral, minerale (m) [*mee-neh-rah'-leh*]
minimum, minimo [*mee'-nee-moh*]
minister [government] *n.*, ministro [*mee-nees'-troh*]
minister [religious] *n.*, sacerdote (m) [*sah-chehr-doh'-teh*]
minister *v.*, somministrare [*sohm-mee-nees-trah'-reh*]
minor [age], minorenne [*mee-noh-rehn'-neh*]
minority, minoranza [*mee-noh-rahn'-tsah*]
minus, meno [*meh'-noh*]
minute, minuto [*mee-noo'-toh*]
Wait a minute! Aspetti un minuto! [*ahs-peht'-tee oon mee-noo'-toh*]
mirror *n.*, specchio [*spehk'-kee-oh*]
mischief, cattiveria [*kaht-tee-veh'-ree-ah*]
miserable, miserabile [*mee-zeh-rah'-bee-leh*]
misery, miseria [*mee-zeh'-ree-ah*]
misfortune, sfortuna [*sfohr-too'-nah*]
Miss, Signorina [*see-nyoh-ree'-na*]
miss [someone] *v.*, sentire la mancanza [*sehn-tee'-reh lah mahn-kahn'-tsah*]
miss [lose, fail] *v.*, perdere [*pehr'-deh-reh*]
I missed the train, Ho perduto il treno [*oh pehr-doo'-toh eel treh'-noh*]
missing, scomparso, sparito [*skohm-pahr'-soh, spah-ree'-toh*]
missionary, missionario [*mees-see-oh-nah'-ree-oh*]

mistake *n.*, errore (m) [*ehr-roh'-reh*]
mistaken, sbagliato [*zbah-lyah'-toh*]
  be mistaken *v.*, sbagliarsi [*zbah-lyahr'-see*]
mistrust *v.*, diffidarsi di [*deef-fee-dahr'-see dee*]
misunderstanding, malinteso [*mahl-een-teh'-zoh*]
mix *v.*, mescolare [*mehs-koh-lah'-reh*]
mixture, mescuglio [*mehs-koo'-lyoh*]
model *n.*, modello [*moh-dehl'-loh*]
modern, moderno [*moh-dehr'-noh*]
modest, modesto [*moh-dehs'-toh*]
modesty, modestia [*moh-dehs'-tee-ah*]
moisture, umidità (f, indecl) [*oo-mee-dee-tah'*]
moment, momento [*moh-mehn'-toh*]
monarchy, monarchia [*moh-nahr-kee'-ah*]
monastery, monastero [*moh-nahs-teh'-roh*]
Monday, lunedì (m) [*loo-neh-dee'*]
money, denaro, soldi, quattrini [*deh-nah'-roh, sohl'-dee, koo-aht-tree'-nee*]
monotonous, monotono [*moh-noh'-toh-noh*]
month, mese (m) [*meh'-zeh*]
monthly, mensile [*mehn-see'-leh*]
monument, monumento [*moh-noo-mehn'-toh*]
mood [feeling], umore (m) [*oo-moh'-reh*]
  be in a bad mood *v.*, essere di malumore [*ehs'-seh-reh dee mahl-oo-moh'-reh*]
  be in a good mood *v.*, essere di buonumore [*ehs'-seh-reh dee boo-ohn-oo-moh'-reh*]
moon, luna [*loo'-nah*]
moonlight, chiaro di luna [*kee-ah'-roh dee loo'-nah*]
moral, morale, morale [*moh-rah'-leh*]
morality, moralità (f, indecl) [*moh-rah-lee-tah'*]
more, più [*pee-oo'*]
  all the more, tanto più [*tahn'-toh pee-oo'*]
  more or less, più o meno [*pee-oo' oh meh'-noh*]
  no more, non più [*nohn pee-oo'*]
  once more, ancora una volta [*ahn-koh'-rah oon'-ah vohl'-tah*]
moreover, inoltre [*een-ohl'-treh*]

morning, mattina [*maht-tee'-nah*]
  Good morning! Buon giorno! [*boo-ohn' jee-ohr'-noh*]
mortgage, ipoteca [*ee-poh'-teh-kah*]
most, il più, la maggior parte [*eel pee-oo'*, *lah mahj-jee-ohr' pahr'-teh*]
mother, madre (f) [*mah'-dreh*]
mother-in-law, suocera [*soo-oh'-cheh-rah*]
motion, movimento [*moh-vee-mehn'-toh*]
motive, motivo [*moh-tee'-voh*]
motor, motore (m) [*moh-toh'-reh*]
motorcycle, motocicletta [*moh-toh-chee-kleht'-tah*]
mountain, montagna [*mohn-tah'-nyah*]
mourning, lutto [*loot'-toh*]
mouth, bocca [*bohk'-kah*]
move [change position of] *v.*, muovere [*moo-oh'-veh-reh*]
move [emotionally] *v.*, commuoversi [*kohm-moo-oh'-vehr-see*]
movies, cinema [*chee'-neh-mah*]
Mr., Sig. (signore) [*see-nyoh'-reh*]
Mrs., Sigra. (signora) [*see-nyoh'-rah*]
much, molto [*mohl'-toh*]
  as much as, tanto quanto [*tahn'-toh koo-ahn'-toh*]
  How much? Quanto? [*koo-ahn'-toh*]
  too much, troppo [*trohp'-poh*]
  very much, moltissimo [*mohl-tees'-see-moh*]
mud, fango [*fahn'-goh*]
murder *v.*, assassinare [*ahs-sahs-see-nah'-reh*]
murderer, assassino [*ahs-sahs-see'-noh*]
muscle, muscolo [*moos'-koh-loh*]
museum, museo [*moo-zeh'-oh*]
music, musica [*moo'-zee-kah*]
musical, musicale [*moo-zee-kah'-leh*]
musician, musicista (m, f) [*moo-zee-chees'-tah*]
must *v.*, dovere (irreg) [*doh-veh'-reh*]
  I must go home, Devo andare a casa [*deh'-voh ahn-dah'-reh ah kah'-zah*]
mustache, baffo [*bahf'-foh*]
mustard, mostarda [*mohs-tahr'-dah*]

mutual, reciproco [*reh-chee'-proh-koh*]
my, mio, mia; miei, mie (pl) [*mee'-oh, mee'-ah; mee-eh'-ee, mee'-eh*]
myself, io stesso [*ee'-oh stehs'-soh*]
mystery, mistero [*mees-teh'-roh*]
mystic, mistico [*mees'-tee-koh*]

N

nail [fingernail], unghia [*oon'-gee-ah*]
nail [carpentry], chiodo [*kee-oh'-doh*]
naive, ingenuo [*een-jeh'-noo-oh*]
naked, nudo [*noo'-doh*]
name *n.*, nome (m) [*noh'-meh*]
  first name, nome [*noh'-meh*]
  last name, cognome (m) [*koh-nyoh'-meh*]
  What is your name? Quale è il suo nome? [*koo-ah'-leh eh' eel soo'-oh noh'-meh*]
  My name is . . ., Mi chiamo . . . [*mee kee-ah'-moh*]
nap, sonnellino [*sohn-nehl-lee'-noh*]
napkin, tovagliolo [*toh-vah-lyoh'-loh*]
  sanitary napkin, tovagliolo igienico [*toh-vah-lyoh'-loh ee-jee-eh'-nee-koh*]
Naples, Napoli [*nah'-poh-lee*]
narrate *v.*, narrare [*nahr-rah'-reh*]
narrative, storia [*stoh'-ree-ah*]
narrow *adj.*, stretto [*streht'-toh*]
nasty, cattivo [*kaht-tee'-voh*]
nation, nazione (f) [*nah-tsee-oh'-neh*]
national, nazionale [*nah-tsee-oh-nah'-leh*]
nationality, nazionalità (f, indecl) [*nah-tsee-oh-nah-lee-tah'*]
native, nativo [*nah-tee'-voh*]
natural, naturale [*nah-too-rah'-leh*]
naturally, naturalmente [*nah-too-rahl-mehn'-teh*]
nature, natura [*nah-too'-rah*]

naughty, birichino [*bee-ree-kee'-noh*]
naval, navale [*nah-vah'-leh*]
navy, marina [*mah-ree'-nah*]
near, nearby, vicino [*vee-chee'-noh*]
nearly, quasi [*koo-ah'-zee*]
neat, lindo [*leen'-doh*]
necessary, necessario [*neh-chehs-sah'-ree-oh*]
neck, collo [*kohl'-loh*]
necklace, collana [*kohl-lah'-nah*]
necktie, cravatta [*krah-vaht'-tah*]
need *n.*, bisogno [*bee-zoh'-nyoh*]
need *v.*, aver bisogno [*ah-vehr' bee-zoh'-nyoh*]
needle, ago, aghi (pl) [*ah'-goh, ah'-gee*]
negative *adj.*, negativo [*neh-gah-tee'-voh*]
negative [film] *n.*, negativa [*neh-gah-tee'-vah*]
neglect *v.*, trascurare [*trahs-koo-rah'-reh*]
Negro, negro [*neh'-groh*]
neighbor, vicino [*vee-chee'-noh*]
neighborhood, quartiere (m) [*koo-ahr-tee-eh'-reh*]
neither, neanche, nessuno [*neh-ahn'-keh, nehs-soo'-noh*]
neither . . . nor, nè . . . nè [*neh' . . . neh'*]
nephew, nipote (m) [*nee-poh'-teh*]
nerves, nervi [*nehr'-vee*]
  What a nerve! Che coraggio! [*keh koh-rahj'-jee-oh*]
nervous, nervoso [*nehr-voh'-zoh*]
net [fishing], rete (f) [*reh'-teh*]
never, mai [*mah'-ee*]
  Never mind! Non fa niente! [*nohn fah nee-ehn'-teh*]
nevermore, mai più [*mah'-ee pee-oo'*]
nevertheless, tuttavia [*toot-tah-vee'-ah*]
new, nuovo [*noo-oh'-voh*]
  What's new? Che c'è di nuovo? [*keh cheh' dee noo-oh'-voh*]
news, notizie (f, pl) [*noh-tee'-tsee-eh*]
newspaper, giornale (m) [*jee-ohr-nah'-leh*]
newsstand, edicola [*eh-dee'-koh-lah*]
next, prossimo [*prohs'-see-moh*]
  next month, il prossimo mese [*eel prohs'-see-moh meh'-zeh*]

next time, la prossima volta [*lah prohs'-see-mah vohl'-tah*]
next week, la settimana prossima [*lah seht-tee-mah'-nah prohs'-see-mah*]
next year, il prossimo anno [*eel prohs'-see-moh ahn'-noh*]
next to, vicino a [*vee-chee'-noh ah*]
nice, buono, simpatico [*boo-oh'-noh, seem-pah'-tee-koh*]
nickname, nomignolo [*noh-mee'-nyoh-loh*]
niece, nipote (f) [*nee-poh'-teh*]
night, notte (f) [*noht'-teh*]
Good night! Buona notte! [*boo-oh'-nah noht'-teh*]
last night, la notte scorsa [*lah noht'-teh skohr'-sah*]
nightclub, locale notturno [*loh-kah'-leh noht-toor'-noh*]
nightfall, sera [*seh'-rah*]
nightgown, camicia da notte [*kah-mee'-chee-ah dah noht'-teh*]
nightmare, incubo [*een'-koo-boh*]
nine, nove [*noh'-veh*]
nineteen, dicianove [*dee-chee-ah-noh'-veh*]
ninety, novanta [*noh-vahn'-tah*]
ninth, nono [*noh'-noh*]
nipple, capezzolo, biberon [*kah-pehts'-tsoh-loh, bee-beh-rohn'*]
no *adv.*, no, non [*noh, nohn*]
No, I'm not going, No, non ci vado [*noh, nohn chee vah'-doh*]
No fooling! Senza scherzi! [*sehn'-tsah skehr'-tsee*]
by no means, in nessun modo, per nessun motivo [*een nehs-soon' moh'-doh, pehr nehs-soon' moh-tee'-voh*]
no longer, non più [*nohn pee-oo'*]
no more, non più [*nohn pee-oo'*]
noble, nobile [*noh'-bee-leh*]
nobody, nessuno [*nehs-soo'-noh*]
noise, chiasso, rumore (m) [*kee-ahs'-soh, roo-moh'-reh*]
noisy, chiassoso, rumoroso [*kee-ahs-soh'-zoh, roo-moh-roh'-zoh*]
none, nessuno, nulla [*nehs-soo'-noh, nool'-lah*]
nonsense, sciocchezza [*shee-ohk-kehts'-tsah*]
noon, mezzogiorno [*mehdz-dzoh-jee-ohr'-noh*]

nor, nè, neppure [*neh', nehp-poo'-reh*]
normal, normale [*nohr-mah'-leh*]
north, nord [*nohrd*]
North America, America del Nord [*ah-meh'-ree-kah dehl nohrd*]
northeast, nord-est [*nohrd-ehst'*]
Northern, settentrionale [*seht-tehn-tree-oh-nah'-leh*]
northwest, nord-ovest [*nohrd-oh'-vehst*]
Norway, Norvegia [*nohr-veh'-jee-ah*]
Norwegian, norvegese [*nohr-veh-jeh'-zeh*]
nose, naso [*nah'-zoh*]
not, non [*nohn*]
  not even, neanche [*neh-ahn'-keh*]
  not once, non una volta [*nohn oo'-nah vohl'-tah*]
note *n.*, nota [*noh'-tah*]
note *v.*, annotare [*ahn-noh-tah'-reh*]
notebook, taccuino [*tahk-koo-ee'-noh*]
nothing, niente, nulla [*nee-ehn'-teh, nool'-lah*]
notice *n.*, avviso, notifica [*ahv-vee'-zoh, noh-tee'-fee-kah*]
notice *v.*, notare [*noh-tah'-reh*]
notify *v.*, notificare [*noh-tee-fee-kah'-reh*]
notion, nozione (f) [*noh-tsee-oh'-neh*]
noun, nome (m) [*noh'-meh*]
novel *n.*, romanzo [*roh-mahn'-tsoh*]
novelist, romanziere (m) [*roh-mahn-tsee-eh'-reh*]
novelty, novità (f, indecl) [*noh-vee-tah'*]
November, novembre (m) [*noh-vehm'-breh*]
now, ora, adesso [*oh'-rah, ah-dehs'-soh*]
  now and then, di quando in quando [*dee koo-ahn'-doh een koo-ahn'-doh*]
  until now, fino ad ora [*fee'-noh ahd oh'-rah*]
nowhere, in nessun posto [*een nehs-soon' pohs'-toh*]
number *n.*, numero [*noo'-meh-roh*]
number *v.*, numerare [*noo-meh-rah'-reh*]
numerous, numeroso [*noo-meh-roh'-zoh*]
nun, monaca [*moh'-nah-kah*]
nurse [for the sick] *n.*, infermiera [*een-fehr-mee-eh'-rah*]
nurse [children] *n.*, bambinaia [*bahm-bee-nah'-ee-ah*]

nurse *v.*, curare [*koo-rah'-reh*]
nut [food] noce (f) [*noh'-cheh*]
nylon, nylon [*nah'-ee-lohn*]

O

oak, quercia [*koo-ehr'-chee-ah*]
oar, remo [*reh'-moh*]
oath, giuramento [*jee-oo-rah-mehn'-toh*]
obedient, ubbidiente [*oob-bee-dee-ehn'-teh*]
obey *v.*, ubbidire [*oob-bee-dee'-reh*]
object *n.*, oggetto [*ohj-jeht'-toh*]
object *v.*, opporsi [*ohp-pohr'-see*]
objection, obiezione (f) [*oh-bee-eh-tsee-oh'-neh*]
obligation, obbligo [*ohb'-blee-goh*]
obscene, osceno [*oh-sheh'-noh*]
obscure *adj.*, oscuro [*ohs-koo'-roh*]
observe *v.*, osservare [*ohs-sehr-vah'-reh*]
obstacle, ostacolo [*ohs-tah'-koh-loh*]
obvious, ovvio [*ohv'-vee-oh*]
occasion, occasione (f) [*ohk-kah-zee-oh'-neh*]
occasionally, di tanto in tanto [*dee tahn'-toh een tahn'-toh*]
occupation, occupazione (f) [*ohk-koo-pah-tsee-oh'-neh*]
occupied, occupato [*ohk-koo-pah'-toh*]
occupy *v.*, occupare [*ohk-koo-pah'-reh*]
occur *v.*, accadere [*ahk-kah-deh'-reh*]
occurrence, avvenimento [*ahv-veh-nee-mehn'-toh*]
ocean, oceano [*oh-cheh'-ah-noh*]
o'clock, l'ora, le ore (pl) [*loh'-rah, leh oh'-reh*]
  one o'clock, l'una, l'ora una [*loo'-nah, loh'-rah oo'-nah*]
  five o'clock, le cinque, le ore cinque [*leh cheen'-koo-eh, leh oh'-reh cheen'-koo-eh*]
October, ottobre [*oht-toh'-breh*]
oculist, oculista (m) [*oh-koo-lees'-tah*]
odd [unusual] strano [*strah'-noh*]

odd [uneven] dispari [*dees'-pah-ree*]
odds probabilità (f, indecl) [*proh-bah-bee-lee-tah'*]
odor, odore (m) [*oh-doh'-reh*]
of, di [*dee*]
  of course, naturalmente [*nah-too-rahl-mehn'-teh*]
off, via, lontano, libero [*vee'-ah, lohn-tah'-noh, lee'-beh-roh*]
offend *v.*, offendere [*ohf-fehn'-deh-reh*]
offer *n.*, offerta [*ohf-fehr'-tah*]
offer *v.*, offrire [*ohf-free'-reh*]
office, ufficio [*oof-fee'-chee-oh*]
officer, ufficiale (m) [*oof-fee-chee-ah'-leh*]
official *adj.*, ufficiale [*oof-fee-chee-ah'-leh*]
often, spesso [*spehs'-soh*]
oil [edible] *n.*, olio [*oh'-lee-oh*]
oil [petroleum] *n.*, petrolio [*peh-troh'-lee-oh*]
oil *v.*, lubrificare [*loo-bree-fee-kah'-reh*]
oil field, campo petrolifero [*kahm'-poh peh-troh-lee'-feh-roh*]
oil painting, pittura ad olio [*peet-too'-rah ahd oh'-lee-oh*]
old, vecchio [*vehk'-kee-oh*]
  How old are you? Quanti anni ha? [*koo-ahn'-tee ahn'-nee ah*]
olive, oliva [*oh-lee'-vah*]
olive oil, olio di oliva [*oh'-lee-oh dee oh-lee'-vah*]
omelet, frittata [*freet-tah'-tah*]
omission, omissione (f) [*oh-mees-see-oh'-neh*]
omit *v.*, omettere [*oh-meht'-teh-reh*]
on, su, sopra [*soo, soh'-prah*]
  and so on, e così via [*eh koh-zee' vee'-ah*]
  on the contrary, al contrario [*ahl kohn-trah'-ree-oh*]
  on duty, di servizio [*dee sehr-vee'-tsee-oh*]
  on foot, a piedi [*ah pee-eh'-dee*]
  on the left, alla sinistra [*ahl'-lah see-nees'-trah*]
  on purpose, di proposito [*dee proh-poh'-zee-toh*]
  on time, a tempo [*ah tehm'-poh*]
once, una volta [*oo'-nah vohl'-tah*]
  at once, subito [*soo'-bee-toh*]
  once more, ancora una volta [*ahn-koh'-rah oo'-nah*

vohl'-tah]
one, un, uno, una [*oon, oo'-noh, oo'-nah*]
one-way street, senso unico [*sehn'-soh oo'-nee-koh*]
onion, cipolla [*chee-pohl'-lah*]
onlooker, spettatore (m) [*speht-tah-toh'-reh*]
only *adv.*, solamente, soltanto [*soh-lah-mehn'-teh, sohl-tahn'-toh*]
only *adj.*, solo, unico [*soh'-loh, oo'-nee-koh*]
open *adj.*, aperto [*ah-pehr'-toh*]
open *v.*, aprire [*ah-pree'-reh*]
opening, apertura [*ah-pehr-too'-rah*]
opera, opera [*oh'-peh-rah*]
operate [a machine] *v.*, maneggiare [*mah-nehj-jee-ah'-reh*]
operate [perform surgery] *v.*, operare [*oh-peh-rah'-reh*]
operation, operazione (f) [*oh-peh-rah-tsee-oh'-neh*]
opinion, opinione (f) [*oh-pee-nee-oh'-neh*]
opportunity, opportunità (f, indecl) [*ohp-pohr-too-nee-tah'*]
oppose *v.*, opporre (irreg) [*ohp-pohr'-reh*]
opposite *n. & adj.*, opposto [*ohp-pohs'-toh*]
optimist, optimistic, ottimista (m & f) [*oht-tee-mees'-tah*]
or, o, oppure [*oh, ohp-poo'-reh*]
oral, orale [*oh-rah'-leh*]
orange, arancia [*ah-rahn'-chee-ah*]
orange juice, succo d'arancia [*sook'-koh dah-rahn'-chee-ah*]
orchard, frutteto [*froot-teh'-toh*]
orchestra, orchestra [*ohr'-kehs-trah*]
order *n.*, ordine (m) [*ohr'-dee-neh*]
order [someone] *v.*, comandare [*koh-mahn-dah'-reh*]
order [something] *v.*, ordinare [*ohr-dee-nah'-reh*]
ordinarily, ordinariamente [*ohr-dee-nah-ree-ah-mehn'-teh*]
ordinary, ordinario [*ohr-dee-nah'-ree-oh*]
organization, organizzazione (f) [*ohr-gah-needz-dzah-tsee-oh'-neh*]
oriental, orientale [*oh-ree-ehn-tah'-leh*]
original, originale [*oh-ree-jee-nah'-leh*]
ornament *n.*, ornamento [*ohr-nah-mehn'-toh*]
other, altro [*ahl'-troh*]
on the other hand, d'altra parte [*dahl'-trah pahr'-teh*]

otherwise, altrimenti [*ahl-tree-mehn'-tee*]
ought *v.*, dovere [*doh-veh'-reh*]
I ought to go, Dovrei andare [*doh-vreh'-ee ahn-dah'-reh*]
You ought to rest, Lei dovrebbe riposare [*leh'-ee doh-vrehb'-beh ree-poh-zah'-reh*]
our, nostro, nostra (sing); nostri, nostre (pl) [*nohs'-troh, nohs'-trah; nohs'-tree, nohs'-treh*]
ours, il nostro, la nostra (sing); i nostri, le nostre (pl) [*eel nohs'-troh, lah nohs'-trah; ee nohs'-tree, leh nohs'-treh*]
out, fuori, via [*foo-oh'-ree, vee'-ah*]
out of order, fuori uso [*foo-oh'-ree oo'-zoh*]
outdoors, all'aperto [*ahl-lah-pehr'-toh*]
outrageous, atroce [*ah-troh'-cheh*]
outside, fuori, esterno [*foo-oh'-ree, ehs-tehr'-noh*]
outstanding, prominente [*proh-mee-nehn'-teh*]
outward, esterno [*ehs-tehr'-noh*]
oven, forno [*fohr'-noh*]
over [finished], finito [*fee-nee'-toh*]
over [above], sopra, su [*soh'-prah, soo*]
overcoat, soprabito [*soh-prah'-bee-toh*]
overcome *v.*, vincere [*veen'-cheh-reh*]
overdo *v.*, esagerare [*eh-zah-jeh-rah'-reh*]
overflow *n.*, eccedenza [*ehch-cheh-dehn'-tsah*]
overhead *n.*, spese generali (pl) [*speh'-zeh jeh-neh-rah'-lee*]
overnight, per una notte [*pehr oo'-nah noht'-teh*]
overseas, oltremare [*ohl-treh-mah'-reh*]
overtime, straordinario [*strah-ohr-dee-nah'-ree-oh*]
overturn *v.*, capovolgere [*kah-poh-vohl'-jeh-reh*]
owe *v.*, dovere [*doh-veh'-reh*]
How much do I owe you? Quanto le devo? [*koo-ahn'-toh leh deh'-voh*]
own *adj.*, proprio [*proh'-pree-oh*]
own *v.*, possedere [*pohs-seh-deh'-reh*]
owner, proprietario [*proh-pree-eh-tah'-ree-oh*]
oxygen, ossigeno [*ohs-see'-jeh-noh*]
oyster, ostrica [*ohs'-tree-kah*]

P

pack *n.*, pacco [*pahk'-koh*]
pack [of cards] *n.*, mazzo di carte [*mahts'-tsoh dee kahr'-teh*]
pack (of cigarettes) *n.*, pacchetto (di sigarette) [*pahk-keht'-toh* (*dee see-gah-reht'-teh*)]
pack *v.*, impaccare [*eem-pahk-kah'-reh*]
package, pacco [*pahk'-koh*]
page *n.*, pagina [*pah'-jee-nah*]
paid, pagato [*pah-gah'-toh*]
pain, dolore (m), pena [*doh-loh'-reh*, *peh'-nah*]
painful, doloroso [*doh-loh-roh'-zoh*]
paint *n.*, pittura, colore (m) [*peet-too'-rah*, *koh-loh'-reh*]
paint *v.*, dipingere [*dee-peen'-jeh-reh*]
painter, pittore (m), pittrice (f) [*peet-toh'-reh*, *peet-tree'-cheh*]
painting, pittura, vernice (f) [*peet-too'-rah*, *vehr-nee'-cheh*]
pair *n.*, paio, paia (pl) [*pah'-ee-oh*, *pah'-ee-ah*]
palace, palazzo [*pah-lahts'-tsoh*]
pale *adj.*, pallido [*pahl'-lee-doh*]
palm, palma [*pahl'-mah*]
pan, padella [*pah-dehl'-lah*]
panic *n.*, panico [*pah'-nee-koh*]
pants, calzoni (pl) [*kahl-tsoh'-nee*]
paper, carta [*kahr'-tah*]
  toilet paper, carta igienica [*kahr'-tah ee-jee-eh'-nee-kah*]
  writing paper, carta da scrivere [*kahr'-tah dah skree'-veh-reh*]
parade *n.*, parata [*pah-rah'-tah*]
paragraph, paragrafo [*pah-rah'-grah-foh*]
paralyzed, paralizzato [*pah-rah-leedz-dzah'-toh*]
pardon *n.*, perdono [*pehr-doh'-noh*]
pardon *v.*, perdonare [*pehr-doh-nah'-reh*]
  Pardon me! Mi scusi! [*mee skoo'-zee*]

parents, genitori [*jeh-nee-toh'-ree*]
park *n.*, parco [*pahr'-koh*]
park *v.*, parcheggiare [*pahr-kehj-jee-ah'-reh*]
parking, parcheggio [*pahr-kehj'-jee-oh*]
No parking! Sosta vietata! [*sohs'-tah vee-eh-tah'-tah*]
parliament, parlamento [*pahr-lah-mehn'-toh*]
parlor, salotto [*sah-loht'-toh*]
part [of whole] *n.*, parte (f) [*pahr'-teh*]
part [of machine] *n.*, pezzo [*pehts'-tsoh*]
participate *v.*, partecipare [*pahr-teh-chee-pah'-reh*]
particular, particolare [*pahr-tee-koh-lah'-reh*]
particularly, particolarmente [*pahr-tee-koh-lahr-mehn'-teh*]
partly, in parte [*een pahr'-teh*]
partner [business], socio [*soh'-chee-oh*]
party [entertainment], ricevimento [*ree-cheh-vee-mehn'-toh*]
party [political], partito [*pahr-tee'-toh*]
pass [permit] *n.*, permesso [*pehr-mehs'-soh*]
pass [mountain] *n.*, passo [*pahs'-soh*]
pass *v.*, passare [*pahs-sah'-reh*]
passage, passaggio [*pahs-sahj'-jee-oh*]
passenger, passeggero [*pahs-sehj-jeh'-roh*]
passenger train, treno passeggeri [*treh'-noh pahs-sehj-jeh'-ree*]
passerby, passante [*pahs-sahn'-teh*]
passionate, appassionato [*ahp-pahs-see-oh-nah'-toh*]
passive, passivo [*pahs-see'-voh*]
passport, passaporto [*pahs-sah-pohr'-toh*]
past, passato [*pahs-sah'-toh*]
paste *n.*, colla, pasta [*kohl'-lah, pahs'-tah*]
pastry, pasta [*pahs'-tah*]
pastry shop, pasticceria [*pahs-tee-cheh-ree'-ah*]
path, sentiero [*sehn-tee-eh'-roh*]
patience, pazienza [*pah-tsee-ehn'-tsah*]
patient *n. & adj.*, paziente [*pah-tsee-ehn'-teh*]
patriotic, patriotico [*pah-tree-oh'-tee-koh*]
pattern *n.*, modello [*moh-dehl'-loh*]
pavement, pavimento [*pah-vee-mehn'-toh*]
pay *v.*, pagare [*pah-gah'-reh*]

pay a compliment, fare un complimento [*fah'-reh oon kohm-plee-mehn'-toh*]
pay a fine, pagare una multa [*pah-gah'-reh oo'-nah mool'-tah*]
pay by installments, pagare mensilmente [*pah-gah'-reh mehn-seel-mehn'-teh*]
pay cash, pagare in contanti [*pah-gah'-reh een kohn-tahn'-tee*]
payment *n.*, pagamento [*pah-gah-mehn'-toh*]
pea, pisello [*pee-zehl'-loh*]
peace, pace (f) [*pah'-cheh*]
peaceful, pacifico [*pah-chee'-fee-koh*]
peach, pesca [*pehs'-kah*]
pear, pera [*peh'-rah*]
pearl, perla [*pehr'-lah*]
peculiar, strano [*strah'-noh*]
pedal *n.*, pedale (m) [*peh-dah'-leh*]
peddler, venditore ambulante (m) [*vehn-dee-toh'-reh ahm-boo-lahn'-teh*]
pedestrian, pedestre [*peh-dehs'-treh*]
peel *v.*, pelare, sbucciare [*peh-lah'-reh, zbooch-chee-ah'-reh*]
pen, penna [*pehn'-nah*]
fountain pen, penna stilografica [*pehn'-nah stee-loh-grah'-fee-kah*]
pen name, pseudonimo [*pseh-oo-doh'-nee-moh*]
penalty, penalità (f, indecl) [*peh-nah-lee-tah'*]
pencil, matita [*mah-tee'-tah*]
people, gente (f), popolo [*jehn'-teh, poh'-poh-loh*]
pepper, pepe (m) [*peh'-peh*]
perceive *v.*, percepire [*pehr-cheh-pee'-reh*]
percent, percento [*pehr-chehn'-toh*]
perfect *adj.*, perfetto [*pehr-feht'-toh*]
performance [showing], esibizione (f) [*eh-zee-bee-tsee-oh'-neh*]
performance [of machine], funzionamento [*foon-tsee-oh-nah-mehn'-toh*]
perfume, profumo [*proh-foo'-moh*]

perhaps, forse [*fohr'-seh*]
period [punctuation], punto fermo [*poon'-toh fehr'-moh*]
period [time], periodo [*peh-ree-oh'-doh*]
permanent *adj.*, permanente [*pehr-mah-nehn'-teh*]
permanent wave, ondulazione permanente [*ohn-doo-lah-tsee-oh'-neh pehr-mah-nehn'-teh*]
permission, permesso [*pehr-mehs'-soh*]
permit *v.*, permettere [*pehr-meht'-teh-reh*]
Persian, persiano [*pehr-see-ah'-noh*]
persist *v.*, persistere [*pehr-sees'-teh-reh*]
person, persona [*pehr-soh'-nah*]
personal, personale [*pehr-soh-nah'-leh*]
personality, personalità (f, indecl) [*pehr-soh-nah-lee-tah'*]
personnel, personale (m) [*pehr-soh-nah'-leh*]
perspiration, sudore (m) [*soo-doh'-reh*]
perspire *v.*, sudare [*soo-dah'-reh*]
persuade *v.*, persuadere [*pehr-soo-ah-deh'-reh*]
pessimist, pessimistic, pessimista [*pehs-see-mees'-tah*]
pet, animale favorito [*ah-nee-mah'-leh fah-voh-ree'-toh*]
pharmacy, farmacia [*fahr-mah-chee'-ah*]
phase, fase (f) [*fah'-zeh*]
philosopher, filosofo [*fee-loh'-zoh-foh*]
philosophy, filosofia [*fee-loh-zoh-fee'-ah*]
phone *n.*, telefono [*teh-leh'-foh-noh*]
by phone, per telefono [*pehr teh-leh'-foh-noh*]
phone *v.*, telefonare [*teh-leh-foh-nah'-reh*]
phonograph, fonografo [*foh-noh'-grah-foh*]
photograph *n.*, fotografia [*foh-toh-grah-fee'-ah*]
photograph *v.*, fotografare [*foh-toh-grah-fah'-reh*]
photographer, fotografo [*foh-toh'-grah-foh*]
physical, fisico [*fee'-zee-koh*]
physician, medico [*meh'-dee-koh*]
pianist, pianista (m, f) [*pee-ah-nees'-tah*]
piano, pianoforte (m) [*pee-ah-noh-fohr'-teh*]
pick *v.*, cogliere [*koh'-lyeh-reh*]
pick up, raccogliere [*rahk-koh'-lyeh-reh*]
pickpocket, borsaiuolo [*bohr-sah-ee-oh'-loh*
picture, quadro [*koo-ah'-droh*]

ciliegia [*chee-lee-eh'-jee-ah*] cherry
cilindro [*chee-leen'-droh*] cylinder
cima [*chee'-mah*] peak, summit
cimitero [*chee-mee-teh'-roh*] cemetery
Cina [*chee'-nah*] China
cinema, cinematografo [*chee'-neh-mah, chee-neh-mah-toh'-grah-foh*] movies
cinese [*chee-neh'-zeh*] Chinese
cinquanta [*cheen-koo-ahn'-tah*] fifty
cinque [*cheen'-koo-eh*] five
cinquecento [*cheen-koo-eh-chehn'-toh*] five hundred
cintura [*cheen-too'-rah*] belt
ciò [*chee-oh'*] that, that which
cioccolata [*chee-oh-koh-lah'-tah*] chocolate
cioè [*chee-oh-eh'*] namely
ciononostante [*chee-oh-noh-nohs-tahn'-teh*] nonetheless
cipolla [*chee-pohl'-lah*] onion
cipria [*chee'-pree-ah*] powder [cosmetic]
circa [*cheer'-kah*] about
circo [*cheer'-koh*] circus
circolazione *f.* [*cheer-koh-lah-tsee-oh'-neh*] circulation
circolo [*cheer'-koh-loh*] circle, club
circondare *v.* [*cheer-kohn-dah'-reh*] surround
circostanza [*cheer-kohs-tahn'-tsah*] circumstance
citare *v.* [*chee-tah'-reh*] quote
citazione *f.* [*chee-tah-tsee-oh'-neh*] quotation, summons
città *f. indecl.* [*cheet-tah'*] city
cittadina [*cheet-tah-dee'-nah*] town
cittadinanza [*cheet-tah-dee-nahn'-tsah*] citizenship
cittadino [*cheet-tah-dee'-noh*] citizen
civile [*chee-vee'-leh*] civilized, civil
civilizzazione *f.*, **civiltà** *f.*, *indecl.* [*chee-vee-leedz-dza-tsee-oh'-neh, chee-veel-tah'*] civilization
classe *f.* [*klahs'-seh*] class
classico [*klahs'-see-koh*] classic
clero [*kleh'-roh*] clergy
cliente *m.* [*klee-ehn'-teh*] customer
clima *m.* [*klee'-mah*] climate
clinica [*klee'-nee-kah*] clinic
coda [*koh'-dah*] tail

cogliere *v.* [*koh'-lyeh-reh*] pick, gather
cognac *m.* [*koh-nyahk'*] brandy
cognata [*koh-nyah'-tah*] sister-in-law
cognato [*koh-nyah'-toh*] brother-in-law
cognome *m.* [*koh-nyoh'-meh*] last name
coincidenza [*koh-een-chee-dehn'-tsah*] coincidence
colazione *f.* [*koh-lah-tsee-oh'-neh*] breakfast
  fare *v.* **colazione** [*fah'-reh koh-lah-tsee-oh'-neh*] have breakfast
  seconda colazione [*seh-kohn'-dah koh-lah-tsee-oh'-neh*] lunch
colla [*kohl'-lah*] glue
collana [*kohl-lah'-nah*] necklace
colle *m.*, **collina** [*cohl'-leh, kohl-lee'-nah*] hill
collega *m., f.* [*kohl-leh'-gah*] colleague
collegamento [*kohl-leh-gah-mehn'-toh*] connection
collegio [*kohl-leh'-jee-oh*] boarding school
colletto [*kohl-leht'-toh*] collar
collo [*kohl'-loh*] neck
collocare *v.* [*kohl-loh-kah'-reh*] place
colmo *n.* [*kohl'-moh*] height, summit
colombo [*koh-lohm'-boh*] pigeon
colonia [*koh-loh'-nee-ah*] colony
colonna [*koh-lohn'-nah*] column
colonnello [*koh-loh-nehl'-loh*] colonel
colorare *v.* [*koh-loh-rah'-reh*] color
colore *m.* [*koh-loh'-reh*] color, paint
Colosseo [*koh-lohs-seh'-oh*] Colosseum
colpa [*kohl'-pah*] guilt, blame, fault
  attribuire *n.* **la colpa** [*aht-tree-boo-ee'-reh lah kohl'-pah*] blame
  É colpa mia [*eh' kohl'-pah mee'-ah*] It's my fault
colpevole [*kohl-peh'-voh-leh*] guilty
colpire [*kohl-pee'-reh*] strike, hit
colpo [*kohl'-poh*] stroke, blow, shot
coltello [*kohl-tehl'-loh*] knife
coltivare [*kohl-tee-vah'-reh*] cultivate
colto [*kohl'-toh*] cultivated, learned
comandare *v.* [*koh-mahn-dah'-reh*] order [someone]
combattere *v.* [*kohm-baht'-teh-reh*] fight

combinazione *f.* [*kohm-bee-nah-tsee-oh'-neh*] combination
combustibile [*kohm-boos-tee'-bee-leh*] fuel
come [*koh'-meh*] as, like, how
Com'è? [*koh-meh'*] What is he (she, it) like?
come lui [*koh'-meh loo'-ee*] like him
Come mai? [*koh'-meh mah'-ee*] How come?, Why?
come questo [*koh'-meh koo-ehs'-toh*] like this
proprio come [*proh'-pree-oh koh'-meh*] just as
Come sta? [*koh'-meh stah*] How do you do?
comico [*koh'-mee-koh*] comedian, funny
cominciare *v.* [*koh-meen-chee-ah'-reh*] begin
comitato [*koh-mee-tah'-toh*] committee
commedia [*kohm-meh'-dee-ah*] comedy
commentare *v.* [*kohm-mehn-tah'-reh*] comment
commentario [*kohm-mehn-tah'-ree-oh*] commentary
commento [*kohm-mehn'-toh*] comment
commerciale [*kohm-mehr-chee-ah'-leh*] commercial
commerciante *m.* [*kohm-mehr-chee-ahn'-teh*] businessman
commercio [*kohm-mehr'-chee-oh*] trade
commesso [*kohm-mehs'-soh*] salesclerk
commestibile [*kohm-mehs-tee'-bee-leh*] edible
commettere *v.* [*kohm-meht'-teh-reh*] commit
commissione *f.* [*kohm-mees-see-oh'-neh*] commission, errand
commovente [*kohm-moh-vehn'-teh*] touching
commozione *f.* [*kohm-moh-tsee-oh'-neh*] commotion
commuoversi *v.*, [*kohm-moo-oh'-vehr-see*] be moved [emotionally]
comodità *f. indecl.* [*koh-moh-dee-tah'*] comfort
comodo [*koh'-moh-doh*] comfortable
Si faccia comodo! [*see fahch'-chee-ah koh'-moh-doh*] Make yourself at home!
compagnia [*kohm-pah-nyee'-ah*] company
compagnia di navigazione [*kohm-pah-nyee'-ah dee nah-vee-gah-tsee-oh'-neh*] steamship line
compagno [*kohm-pah'-nyoh*] companion, pal, mate
compagno di scuola [*kohm-pah'-nyoh dee skoo-oh'-lah*] schoolmate
compagno di giochi [*kohm-pah'-nyoh dee jee-oh'-kee*] playmate
compassione *f.* [*kohm-pahs-see-oh'-neh*] compassion

compatibile [*kohm-pah-tee'-bee-leh*] consistent
compatriota [*kohm-pah-tree-oh'-tah*] countryman
compensazione *f.* [*kohm-pehn-sah-tsee-oh'-neh*] compensation
competente [*kohm-peh-tehn'-teh*] competent
competenza [*kohm-peh-tehn'-tsah*] competence
compiere *v.* [*kohm'-pee-eh-reh*] accomplish, achieve
compilare *v.* [*kohm-pee-lah'-reh*] compile
compimento [*kohm-pee-mehn'-toh*] accomplishment
compito [*kohm'-pee-toh*] task
compleanno [*kohm-pleh-ahn'-noh*] birthday
  Felice compleanno [*feh-lee'-cheh kohm-pleh-ahn'-noh*] Happy birthday
complesso [*kohm-plehs'-soh*] complex
completamente [*kohm-pleh-tah-mehn'-teh*] completely
completare *v.* [*kohm-pleh-tah'-reh*] complete
complicare *v.* [*kohm-plee-kah'-reh*] complicate
complimento [*kohm-plee-mehn'-toh*] compliment
  fare *v.* **un complimento** [*fah'-reh oon kohm-plee-mehn'-toh*] pay a compliment
complotto [*kohm-ploht'-toh*] plot
comporre *v.* [*kohm-pohr'-reh*] compose
comportamento [*kohm-pohr-tah-mehn'-toh*] behavior
comportarsi *v.* [*kohm-pohr-tahr'-see*] behave
  Comportati bene! [*kohm-pohr'-tah-tee beh'-neh*] Behave yourself!
composizione *f.* [*kohm-poh-zee-tsee-oh'-neh*] composition
compostezza [*kohm-pohs-tehts'-tsah*] composure
compositore *m.* [*kohm-poh-zee-toh'-reh*] composer
comprare *v.* [*kohm-prah'-reh*] buy
compratore *m.* [*kohm-prah-toh'-reh*] buyer
comprendere *v.* [*kohm-prehn'-deh-reh*] understand
  Comprende lei? [*kohm-prehn'-deh leh'-ee*] Do you understand?
compromesso [*kohm-proh-mehs'-soh*] compromise
comune *m.* [*koh-moo'-neh*] town
comune [*koh-moo'-neh*] common
comunicare *v.* [*koh-moo-nee-kah'-reh*] communicate
comunicazione *f.* [*koh-moo-nee-kah-tsee-oh'-neh*] communication

piece, pezzo [*pehts'-tsoh*]
pier, molo [*moh'-loh*]
pig, maiale [*mah-ee-ah'-leh*]
pill, pillola [*peel'-loh-lah*]
pillow, cuscino [*koo-shee'-noh*]
pilot *n.*, pilota (m) [*pee-loh'-tah*]
pin *n.*, spilla [*speel'-lah*]
pinch *v.*, pizzicare [*peets-tsee-kah'-reh*]
pipe [smoking], pipa [*pee'-pah*]
pistol, pistola [*pees-toh'-lah*]
pity *n.*, pietà (f, indecl) [*pee-eh-tah'*]
  What a pity! Che peccato! [*keh pehk-kah'-toh*]
place *n.*, luogo [*loo-oh'-goh*]
  in place of, in luogo di [*een loo-oh'-goh dee*]
  take place *v.*, aver luogo [*ah-vehr' loo-oh'-goh*]
place *v.*, collocare [*kohl-loh-kah'-reh*]
plain [simple], semplice [*sehm'-plee-cheh*]
plan *n.*, piano, progetto [*pee-ah'-noh, proh-jeht'-toh*]
plan *v.*, progettare [*proh-jeht-tah'-reh*]
planet, pianeta (m) [*pee-ah-neh'-tah*]
plant *n.*, pianta [*pee-ahn'-tah*]
plant *v.*, piantare [*pee-ahn-tah'-reh*]
plaster *n.*, stucco [*stook'-koh*]
plastic, plastico [*plahs'-tee-koh*]
plate [dish], piatto [*pee-aht'-toh*]
platform, piattaforma [*pee-aht-tah-fohr'-mah*]
play *n.*, dramma (m), gioco [*drahm'-mah, jee-oh'-koh*]
play [a game] *v.*, giocare [*jee-oh-kah'-reh*]
play [an instrument] *v.*, suonare [*soo-oh-nah'-reh*]
playful, scherzoso [*skehr-tsoh'-zoh*]
playground, terreno di gioco [*tehr-reh'-noh dee jee-oh'-koh*]
playmate, compagno di giochi [*kohm-pah'-nyoh dee jee-oh'-kee*]
pleasant, piacevole [*pee-ah-cheh'-voh-leh*]
please *v.*, piacere (irreg) [*pee-ah-cheh'-reh*]
  Please bring me . . . , Per favore, mi porti . . . [*pehr fah-voh'-reh, mee pohr'-tee*]
  Pleased to meet you! Piacere di conoscerla! [*pee-ah-*

cheh'-reh dee koh-noh'-shehr-lah]
Please! Per favore!, Per piacere! [*pehr fah-voh'-reh*, *pehr pee-ah-cheh'-reh*]
Please! [not at all], Prego! [*preh'-goh*]
Please, come in! Prego, entri! [*preh'-goh*, *ehn'-tree*]
pleasure, piacere (m) [*pee-ah-cheh'-reh*]
The pleasure is mine, Il piacere è mio [*eel pee-ah-cheh'-reh eh' mee'-oh*]
With pleasure, Con piacere [*kohn pee-ah-cheh'-reh*]
With much pleasure, Con molto piacere [*kohn mohl'-toh pee-ah-cheh'-reh*]
pleasure trip, viaggio di piacere [*vee-ahj'-jee-oh dee pee-ah-cheh'-reh*]
plenty, in abbondanza [*een ahb-bohn-dahn'-tsah*]
plow *v*., arare [*ah-rah'-reh*]
plug [electric] *n*., presa [*preh'-zah*]
plumber, idraulico [*ee-drah'-oo-lee-koh*]
plural, plurale [*ploo-rah'-leh*]
plus, più [*pee-oo'*]
pneumonia, polmonite (f) [*pohl-moh-nee'-teh*]
pocket, tasca, tasche (pl) [*tahs'-kah*, *tahs'-keh*]
pocketbook, portafoglio [*pohr-tah-foh'-lyoh*]
poem, poema (m) [*poh-eh'-mah*]
poet, poeta (m), poetessa (f) [*poh-eh'-tah*, *poh-eh-tehs'-sah*]
poetry, poesia [*poh-eh-zee'-ah*]
point [abstract] *n*., punto [*poon'-toh*]
point of view, punto di vista [*poon'-toh dee vees'-tah*]
point [of form] *n*., punta [*poon'-tah*]
point *v*., puntare [*poon-tah'-reh*]
point out, far notare [*fahr noh-tah'-reh*]
poison, veleno [*veh-leh'-noh*]
poisonous, velenoso [*veh-leh-noh'-zoh*]
Poland, Polonia [*poh-loh'-nyah*]
pole [stick], palo [*pah'-loh*]
pole [geographical], polo [*poh'-loh*]
police, polizia [*poh-lee-tsee'-ah*]
policeman, poliziotto [*poh-lee-tsee-oht'-toh*]
police station, stazione di polizia [*stah-tsee-oh'-neh dee*

poh-lee-tsee'-ah]
policy [government] *n.*, politica [*poh-lee'-tee-kah*]
policy [insurance] *n.*, polizza [*poh'-leets-tsah*]
Polish, polacco [*poh-lahk'-koh*]
polish *n.*, lucido [*loo'-chee-doh*]
polish *v.*, lucidare [*loo-chee-dah'-reh*]
polite, educato, gentile [*eh-doo-kah'-toh, jehn-tee'-leh*]
political, politico [*poh-lee'-tee-koh*]
politics, politica [*poh-lee'-tee-kah*]
pool [swimming], piscina [*pee-shee'-nah*]
poor *adj.*, povero [*poh'-veh-roh*]
Pope, papa (m) [*pah'-pah*]
popular, popolare [*poh-poh-lah'-reh*]
population, popolazione (f) [*poh-poh-lah-tsee-oh'-neh*]
porch, portico [*pohr'-tee-koh*]
pork, maiale (m) [*mah-ee-ah'-leh*]
port, porto [*pohr'-toh*]
portable, portabile [*pohr-tah'-bee-leh*]
porter [baggage], facchino [*fahk-kee'-noh*]
portrait, ritratto [*ree-traht'-toh*]
Portugal, Portogallo [*pohr-toh-gahl'-loh*]
Portuguese, portoghese [*pohr-toh-geh'-zeh*]
pose *v.*, posare [*poh-zah'-reh*]
position, posizione [*poh-zee-tsee-oh'-neh*]
positive, positivo [*poh-zee-tee'-voh*]
possession, possesso [*pohs-sehs'-soh*]
possible, possibile [*pohs-see'-bee-leh*]
as soon as possible, il più presto possibile [*eel pee-oo' prehs'-toh pohs-see'-bee-leh*]
post, posta [*pohs'-tah*]
postage, affrancatura [*ahf-frahn-kah-too'-rah*]
postage stamp, francobollo [*frahn-koh-bohl'-loh*]
post card, cartolina postale [*kahr-toh-lee'-nah pohs'-tah-leh*]
poster, affisso, manifesto [*ahf-fees'-soh, mah-nee-fehs'-toh*]
post office, ufficio postale [*oof-fee'-chee-oh pohs-tah'-leh*]
post office box, fermo-posta [*fehr-moh-pohs'-tah*]
postpone *v.*, rimandare [*ree-mahn-dah'-reh*]
potato, patata [*pah-tah'-tah*]

pottery, vasellame [*vah-zehl-lah'-meh*]
pound [money], lira sterlina [*lee'-rah stehr-lee'-nah*]
pound [weight], libbra [*leeb'-brah*]
pour *v.*, versare [*vehr-sah'-reh*]
poverty, povertà (f, indecl) [*poh-vehr-tah'*]
powder [cosmetics], cipria, polvere [*chee'-pree-ah, pohl'-veh-reh*]
power, potere (m), forza [*poh-teh'-reh, fohr'-tsah*]
powerful, potente, possente [*poh-tehn'-teh, pohs-sehn'-teh*]
practical, pratico [*prah'-tee-koh*]
practice *v.*, praticare, esercitare [*prah-tee-kah'-reh, eh-zehr-chee-tah'-reh*]
praise *v.*, lodare [*loh-dah'-reh*]
pray *v.*, pregare [*preh-gah'-reh*]
prayer, preghiera [*preh-gee-eh'-rah*]
precaution, precauzione (f) [*preh-kah-oo-tsee-oh'-neh*]
precede *v.*, precedere [*preh-cheh'-deh-reh*]
precious, prezioso [*preh-tsee-oh'-zoh*]
precious stone, pietra preziosa [*pee-eh'-trah preh-tsee-oh'-zah*]
precise, preciso [*preh-chee'-zoh*]
prefer *v.*, preferire [*preh-feh-ree'-reh*]
preference, preferenza [*preh-feh-rehn'-tsah*]
pregnancy, gravidanza [*grah-vee-dahn'-tsah*]
pregnant, incinta [*een-cheen'-tah*]
prejudice, pregiudizio [*preh-jee-oo-dee'-tsee-oh*]
preliminary, preliminare [*preh-lee-mee-nah'-reh*]
preparation, preparazione (f) [*preh-pah-rah-tsee-oh'-neh*]
prepare *v* , preparare [*preh-pah-rah'-reh*]
prescription, ricetta [*ree-cheht'-tah*]
presence, presenza [*preh-zehn'-tsah*]
present [time] *n.*, presente (m) [*preh-zehn'-teh*]
  at present, al momento [*ahl moh-mehn'-toh*]
present [gift] *n.*, regalo [*reh-gah'-loh*]
present *v.*, presentare [*preh-zehn-tah'-reh*]
presentable, presentabile [*preh-zehn-tah'-bee-leh*]
preserve *v.* preservare [*preh-zehr-vah'-reh*]
president, presidente (m) [*preh-zee-dehn'-teh*]

press *v.*, pressare [*prehs-sah'-reh*]
press [clothes] *v.*, stirare [*stee-rah'-reh*]
pressing, urgente [*oor-jehn'-teh*]
pressure, pressione (f) [*prehs-see-oh'-neh*]
prestige, prestigio [*prehs-tee'-jee-oh*]
presume *v.*, presupporre (irreg) [*preh-zoop-pohr'-reh*]
pretend *v.*, pretendere [*preh-tehn'-deh-reh*]
pretentious, pretenzioso [*preh-tehn-tsee-oh'-zoh*]
pretty, graziosa, bella [*grah-tsee-oh'-zah, behl'-lah*]
prevent *v.*, prevenire [*preh-veh-nee'-reh*]
previous, precedente [*preh-cheh-dehn'-teh*]
price *n.*, prezzo [*prehts'-tsoh*]
pride, orgoglio [*ohr-goh'-lyoh*]
priest, prete (m) [*preh'-teh*]
primitive, primitivo [*pree-mee-tee'-voh*]
principal *adj.*, principale [*preen-chee-pah'-leh*]
principles [moral], principi (pl) [*preen-chee'-pee*]
print *v.*, stampare, imprimere [*stahm-pah'-reh, eem-pree'-meh-reh*]
printed matter, stampato [*stahm-pah'-toh*]
printer, tipografo [*tee-poh'-grah-foh*]
prison, prigione (f), carcere (m, f) [*pree-jee-oh'-neh, kahr'-cheh-reh*]
put in prison *v.*, imprigionare [*eem-pree-jee-oh-nah'-reh*]
prisoner, prigioniero [*pree-jee-oh-nee-eh'-roh*]
privacy, intimità (f, indecl) [*een-tee-mee-tah'*]
private, privato [*pree-vah'-toh*]
privilege, privilegio [*pree-vee-leh'-jee-oh*]
prize *n.*, premio [*preh'-mee-oh*]
probable, probabile [*proh-bah'-bee-leh*]
probably, probabilmente [*proh-bah-beel-mehn'-teh*]
problem, problema (m) [*proh-bleh'-mah*]
procedure, procedimento [*proh-cheh-dee-mehn'-toh*]
proceed *v.*, procedere [*proh-cheh'-deh-reh*]
process *n.*, processo [*proh-chehs'-soh*]
produce *v.*, produrre (irreg) [*proh-door'-reh*]
product, prodotto [*proh-doht'-toh*]
production, produzione (f) [*proh-doo-tsee-oh'-neh*]

profession, professione (f) [*proh-fehs-see-oh'-neh*]
professor, professore (m), professoressa (f) [*proh-fehs-soh'-reh, proh-fehs-soh-rehs'-sah*]
profit *n.*, profitto, guadagno [*proh-feet'-toh, goo-ah-dah'-nyoh*]
program *n.*, programma (m) [*proh-grahm'-mah*]
progress *n.*, progresso [*proh-grehs'-soh*]
progressive, progressivo [*proh-grehs-see'-voh*]
prohibit *v.*, proibire [*proh-ee-bee'-reh*]
prohibited, proibito [*proh-ee-bee'-toh*]
project *n.*, progetto [*proh-jeht'-toh*]
project *v.*, progettare [*proh-jeht-tah'-reh*]
prominent, prominente [*proh-mee-nehn'-teh*]
promise *n.*, promessa [*proh-mehs'-sah*]
promise *v.*, promettere [*proh-meht'-teh-reh*]
promotion, promozione (f) [*proh-moh-tsee-oh'-neh*]
prompt, immediato [*eem-meh-dee-ah'-toh*]
pronoun, pronome (m) [*proh-noh'-meh*]
pronounce *v.*, pronunciare [*proh-noon-chee-ah'-reh*]
How do you pronounce . . . ? Come si pronuncia . . . ? [*koh'-meh see proh-noon'-chee-ah*]
pronunciation, pronuncia [*proh-noon'-chee-ah*]
proof, prova [*proh'-vah*]
propaganda, propaganda [*proh-pah-gahn'-dah*]
propeller, elica [*eh'-lee-kah*]
proper, proprio, corretto [*proh'-pree-oh, kohr-reht'-toh*]
property, proprietà (f, indecl) [*proh-pree-eh-tah'*]
prophecy, profezia [*proh-feh-tsee'-ah*]
proportion, proporzione (f) [*proh-pohr-tsee-oh'-neh*]
proposal, proposta [*proh-pohs'-tah*]
propose *v.*, proporre (irreg) [*proh-pohr'-reh*]
proposition, proposizione (f) [*proh-poh-zee-tsee-oh'-neh*]
proprietor, proprietario [*proh-pree-eh-tah'-ree-oh*]
propriety, proprietà (f, indecl) [*proh-pree-eh-tah'*]
prosperity, prosperità (f, indecl) [*prohs-peh-ree-tah'*]
prosperous, prospero [*prohs'-peh-roh*]
protect *v.*, proteggere [*proh-tehj'-jeh-reh*]
protection, protezione (f) [*proh-teh-tsee-oh'-neh*]

protest *n.*, protesta [*proh-tehs'-tah*]
protest *v.*, protestare [*proh-tehs-tah'-reh*]
Protestant, protestante [*proh-tehs-tahn'-teh*]
proud, orgoglioso [*ohr-goh-lyoh'-zoh*]
prove *v.*, provare [*proh-vah'-reh*]
proverb, proverbio [*proh-vehr'-bee-oh*]
provide *v.*, provvedere [*prohv-veh-deh'-reh*]
province, provincia [*proh-veen'-chee-ah*]
provincial, provinciale [*proh-veen-chee-ah'-leh*]
provisions, provviste (pl) [*prohv-vees'-teh*]
psychiatrist, psichiatra (m) [*psee-kee-ah'-trah*]
psychoanalysis, psicoanalisi (f) [*psee-koh-ah-nah'-lee-zee*]
psychological, psicologico [*psee-koh-loh'-jee-koh*]
public *n. &. adj.*, pubblico [*poob'-blee-koh*]
publication, pubblicazione (f) [*poob-blee-kah-tsee-oh'-neh*]
publicity, pubblicità (f, indecl) [*poob-blee-chee-tah'*]
publish *v.*, pubblicare [*poob-blee-kah'-reh*]
pull *v.*, tirare [*tee-rah'-reh*]
  pull out, tirare fuori [*tee-rah'-reh foo-oh'-ree*]
pulse *n.*, polso [*pohl'-soh*]
pump *n.*, pompa [*pohm'-pah*]
punch *n.*, pugno, ponce [*poo'-nyoh, pohn'-cheh*]
punctual, puntuale [*poon-too-ah'-leh*]
punish *v.*, punire [*poo-nee'-reh*]
punishment, punizione (f) [*poo-nee-tsee-oh'-neh*]
pupil, alunno [*ah-loon'-noh*]
puppet, marionetta [*mah-ree-oh-neht'-tah*]
purchase *v.*, acquistare [*ahk-koo-ees-tah'-reh*]
pure, puro [*poo'-roh*]
purple, violetto [*vee-oh-leht'-toh*]
purpose, scopo [*skoh'-poh*]
  on purpose, di proposito [*dee proh-poh'-zee-toh*]
purse, borsa [*bohr'-sah*]
pursue *v.*, perseguire [*pehr-seh-goo-ee'-reh*]
push *v.*, spingere [*speen'-jeh-reh*]
put *v.*, mettere, porre [*meht'-teh-reh, pohr'-reh*]
  put aside, mettere da parte [*meht'-teh-reh dah pahr'-teh*]
  put down, sopprimere [*sohp-pree'-meh-reh*]

put off, rimandare [*ree-mahn-dah'-reh*]
put on [clothes], indossare [*een-dohs-sah'-reh*]
puzzle *n.*, enigma [*eh-neeg'-mah*]

Q

qualification, qualifica [*koo-ah-lee'-fee-kah*]
qualified, qualificato [*koo-ah-lee-fee-kah'-toh*]
qualify *v.*, qualificare [*koo-ah-lee-fee-kah'-reh*]
quality, qualità (f, indecl) [*koo-ah-lee-tah'*]
quantity, quantità (f, indecl) [*koo-ahn-tee-tah'*]
quarrel *n.*, lite (f) [*lee'-teh*]
quarter, quarto, trimestre (m) [*koo-ahr'-toh, tree-mehs'-treh*]
quarter hour, quarto d'ora [*koo-ahr'-toh doh'-rah*]
queen, regina [*reh-jee'-nah*]
queer, strano [*strah'-noh*]
How queer! Che strano! [*keh strah'-noh*]
question *n.*, questione (f), domanda [*koo-ehs-tee-oh'-neh, doh-mahn'-dah*]
questionable, incerto, discutibile [*een-cher'-toh, dees-koo-tee'-bee-leh*]
question mark, punto interrogativo [*poon'-toh een-tehr-roh-gah-tee'-voh*]
quick, svelto, presto, rapido [*zvehl'-toh, prehs'-toh, rah'-pee-doh*]
Quick, quick! Presto, presto! [*prehs'-to, prehs'-toh*]
quickly, rapidamente [*rah-pee-dah-mehn'-teh*]
quiet, tranquillo, quieto [*trahn-koo-eel'-loh, koo-ee-eh'-toh*]
Be quiet! [to many] Zitto!, Silenzio! [*dzeet'-toh, see-lehn'-tsee-oh*; [to one person] Stia calmo! [*stee'-ah kahl'-moh*]
quite, assai, molto [*ahs-sah'-ee, mohl'-toh*]
quite so, precisamente, proprio così [*preh-chee-zah-mehn'-teh, proh'-pree-oh koh-zee'*]

quota, aliquota [*ah-lee'-koo-oh-tah*]
quotation [of words], citazione (f) [*chee-tah-tsee-oh'-neh*]
quotation [of price] quotazione (f) [*koo-oh-tah-tsee-oh'-neh*]
quote *v.*, citare [*chee-tah'-reh*]

R

rabbi, rabbino [*rahb-bee'-noh*]
race [human] *n.*, razza [*rahts'-tsah*]
race [contest] *n.*, corsa, gara [*kohr'-sah, gah'-rah*]
horse race, corsa di cavalli [*kohr'-sah dee kah-vahl'-lee*]
radiator, termosifone (m) [*tehr-moh-see-foh'-neh*]
radical, radicale [*rah-dee-kah'-leh*]
radio, radio (f) [*rah'-dee-oh*]
radio station, stazione radio (f) [*stah-tsee-oh'-neh rah'-dee-oh*]
radish, ravanello [*rah-vah-nehl'-loh*]
rag, straccio [*strach'-chee-oh*]
rage, rabbia, furore (m) [*rahb'-bee-ah, foo-roh'-reh*]
raid *n.*, incursione (f) [*een-koor-see-oh'-neh*]
railroad, railway, ferrovia [*fehr-roh-vee'-ah*]
railroad car, vagone ferroviario (m) [*vah-goh'-neh fehr-roh-vee-ah'-ree-oh*]
railroad crossing, passaggio a livello [*pahs-sahj'-jee-oh ah lee-vehl'-loh*]
railroad station, stazione ferroviaria [*sta-tsee-oh'-neh fehr-roh-vee-ah'-ree-ah*]
rain *n.*, pioggia [*pee-ohj'-jee-ah*]
rain *v.*, piovere [*pee-oh'-veh-reh*]
It's raining, Piove [*pee-oh'-veh*]
rainbow, arcobaleno [*ahr-koh-bah-leh'-noh*]
raincoat, impermeabile (f) [*eem-pehr-meh-ah'-bee-leh*]
rainproof, impermeabile [*eem-pehr-meh-ah'-bee-leh*]
raise [lift] *v.*, sollevare [*sohl-leh-vah'-reh*]
raise [rear] *v.*, allevare [*ahl-leh-vah'-reh*]

random, a casaccio [*ah kah-zahch'-chee-oh*]
range, fila, catena, estensione (f) [*fee'-lah, kah-teh'-nah, ehs-tehn-see-oh'-neh*]
rank *n.*, ordine (m), fila [*ohr'-dee-neh, fee'-lah*]
rape *n.*, violenza carnale [*vee-oh-lehn-tsah kahr-nah'-leh*]
rapid, rapido [*rah'-pee-doh*]
rapidly, rapidamente [*rah-pee-dah-mehn'-teh*]
rare [unusual], raro [*rah'-roh*]
rare [undercooked], poco cotto [*poh'-koh koht'-toh*]
rarely, raramente [*rah-rah-mehn'-teh*]
rash *n.*, eruzione [*eh-roo-tsee-oh'-neh*]
rash *adj.*, precipitoso, temerario [*preh-chee-pee-toh'-zoh, teh-meh-rah'-ree-oh*]
rate [price] *n.*, prezzo, tariffa [*prehts'-tsoh, tah-reef'-fah*]
rather, piuttosto [*pee-oot-tohs'-toh*]
Would you rather . . . , Vorrebbe piuttosto . . . [*vohr-rehb'-beh pee-oot-tohs'-toh*]
rave *v.*, delirare [*deh-lee-rah'-reh*]
raw, grezzo, crudo [*grehdz'-dzoh, kroo'-doh*]
raw material, materiale grezzo [*mah-teh-ree-ah'-leh grehdz'-dzoh*]
ray, raggio [*rahj'-jee-oh*]
razor, rasoio [*rah-zoh'-ee-oh*]
electric razor, rasoio elettrico [*rah-zoh'-ee-oh eh-leht'-tree-koh*]
safety razor, rasoio di sicurezza [*rah-zoh'-ee-oh dee see-koo-rehts'-tsah*]
razor blade, lametta [*lah-meht'-tah*]
reach *v.*, raggiungere [*rahj-jee-oon'-jeh-reh*]
reaction, reazione (f) [*reh-ah-tsee-oh'-neh*]
read *v.*, leggere (irreg) [*lehj'-jeh-reh*]
reading, lettura [*leht-too'-rah*]
ready, pronto [*prohn'-toh*]
ready to wear, già fatto [*jee-ah' faht'-toh*]
real, vero, reale [*veh'-roh, reh-ah'-leh*]
real estate, beni immobili [*beh'-nee eem-moh'-bee-lee*]
realize *v.*, realizzare [*reh-ah-leedz-dzah'-reh*]
really, realmente [*reh-ahl-mehn'-teh*]

rear *v.*, allevare [*ahl-leh-vah'-reh*]
reason *n.*, ragione (f) [*rah-jee-oh'-neh*]
reason *v.*, ragionare [*rah-jee-oh-nah'-reh*]
reasonable, ragionevole [*rah-jee-oh-neh'-voh-leh*]
reassure *v.*, rassicurare [*rahs-see-koo-rah'-reh*]
rebel *n.*, ribelle (m, f) [*ree-behl'-leh*]
rebel *v.*, ribellarsi [*ree-behl-lahr'-see*]
recall *v.*, richiamare (alla memoria) [*ree-kee-ah-mah'-reh (ahl'-lah meh-moh'-ree-ah)*]
receipt, ricevuta [*ree-cheh-voo'-tah*]
receive *v.*, ricevere [*ree-cheh'-veh-reh*]
recent, recente [*reh-chehn'-teh*]
recently, recentemente [*reh-chehn-teh-mehn'-teh*]
reception, accoglienza [*ahk-koh-lyehn'-tsah*]
recession, crisi economica (f) [*kree'-zee eh-koh-noh'-mee-kah*]
recipe, ricetta [*ree-cheht'-tah*]
reciprocate *v.*, contraccambiare [*kohn-trahk-kahm-bee-ah'-reh*]
recite *v.*, recitare [*reh-chee-tah'-reh*]
reckless, imprudente, avventato [*eem-proo-dehn'-teh, ahv-vehn-tah'-toh*]
recline *v.*, reclinare [*reh-klee-nah'-reh*]
recognize *v.*, riconoscere [*ree-koh-noh'-sheh-reh*]
recommend *v.*, raccomandare [*rahk-koh-mahn-dah'-reh*]
recommendation, raccomandazione (f) [*rahk-koh-mahn-dah-tsee-oh'-neh*]
record [for phonograph] *n.*, disco [*dees'-koh*]
record [in sports] *n.*, record (m) [*reh'-kohrd*]
recover [something] *v.*, ritrovare [*ree-troh-vah'-reh*]
recover [from illness] *v.*, ricuperare [*ree-koo-peh-rah'-reh*]
recovery, ricupero [*ree-koo'-peh-roh*]
recreation, ricreazione (f) [*ree-kreh-ah-tsee-oh'-neh*]
red, rosso [*rohs'-soh*]
Red Cross, Croce Rossa [*kroh'-cheh rohs'-sah*]
redeem *v.*, redimere [*reh-dee'-meh-reh*]
red tape, burocrazia [*boo-roh-krah-tsee'-ah*]
reduce *v.*, ridurre (irreg) [*ree-door'-reh*]

reduction, riduzione (f) [*ree-doo-tsee-oh'-neh*]
redundant, superfluo [*soo-pehr'-floo-oh*]
refer *v.*, riferire, indirizzare [*ree-feh-ree'-reh, een-dee-reets-tsah'-reh*]
referee, arbitro [*ahr'-bee-troh*]
reference, riferimento [*ree-feh-ree-mehn'-toh*]
in reference to, in rapporto a [*een rahp-pohr'-toh ah*]
refill *n.*, ricambio [*ree-kahm'-bee-oh*]
refill *v.*, riempire [*ree-ehm-pee'-reh*]
refined, raffinato [*rahf-fee-nah'-toh*]
reflect [light] *v.*, riflettere [*ree-fleht'-teh-reh*]
reflect [think on] *v.*, meditare [*meh-dee-tah'-reh*]
reflection [thought] riflessione (f) [*ree-flehs-see-oh'-neh*]
reflex, riflesso [*ree-flehs'-soh*]
reform *v.*, riformare [*ree-fohr-mah'-reh*]
refrain *v.*, astenersi [*ahs-teh-nehr'-see*]
refresh *v.*, rinfrescare [*reen-frehs-kah'-reh*]
refreshing, rinfrescante [*reen-frehs-kahn'-teh*]
refreshment, rinfresco [*reen-frehs'-koh*]
refrigerator, frigorifero [*free-goh-ree'-feh-roh*]
refuge, rifugio [*ree-foo'-jee-oh*]
refugee, profugo, profughi (pl) [*proh'-foo-goh, proh'-foo-gee*]
refund *n.*, rimborso [*reem-bohr'-soh*]
refusal, rifiuto [*ree-fee-oo'-toh*]
refuse *v.*, rifiutare [*ree-fee-oo-tah'-reh*]
regain *v.*, riacquistare [*ree-ahk-koo-ees-tah'-reh*]
regard *n.*, riguardo [*ree-goo-ahr'-doh*]
with regard to, in riguardo a [*een ree-goo-ahr'-doh ah*]
regardless, incurante, nonostante, a malgrado di [*een-koo-rahn'-teh, nohn-ohs-tahn'-teh, ah mahl-grah'-doh dee*]
regards, complimenti, auguri, saluti [*kohm-plee-mehn'-tee, ah-oo-goo'-ree, sah-loo'-tee*]
kind regards, cordiali saluti, tante belle cose [*kohr-dee-ah'-lee sah-loo'-tee, tahn'-teh behl'-leh koh'-zeh*]
region, regione (f), paese (m) [*reh-jee-oh'-neh, pah-eh-zeh*]
register *n.*, registro [*reh-jees'-troh*]
register *v.*, iscrivere [*ees-kree'-veh-reh*]
registered letter, lettera raccomandata [*leht'-teh-rah rahk-*

koh-mahn-dah'-tah]
regret *n.*, dispiacere [*dees-pee-ah-cheh'-reh*]
regret *v.*, rimpiangere [*reem-pee-ahn'-jeh-reh*]
regular, regolare [*reh-goh-lah'-reh*]
regular gas, ordinario [*ohr-dee-nah'-ree-oh*]
regulate *v.*, regolare [*reh-goh-lah'-reh*]
regulation, regolamento [*reh-goh-lah-mehn'-toh*]
rehearsal, ripetizione, prova [*ree-peh-tee-tsee-oh'-nee, proh'-vah*]
reign *v.*, regnare [*reh-nyah'-reh*]
rejoin *v.*, raggiungere [*rahj-jee-oon'-jeh-reh*]
relate *v.*, raccontare [*rahk-kohn-tah'-reh*]
related, imparentato, connesso [*eem-pah-rehn-tah'-toh, kohn-nehs'-soh*]
be related *v.*, essere imparentato [*ehs'-seh-reh eem-pah-rehn-tah'-toh*]
relationship, parentela, rapporto [*pah-rehn-teh'-lah, rahp-pohr'-toh*]
relative *adj.*, relativo [*reh-lah-tee'-voh*]
relative [family] *n.*, parente (m) [*pah-rehn'-teh*]
relatively, relativamente [*reh-lah-tee-vah-mehn'-teh*]
relax *v.*, rilassare, riposare [*ree-lahs-sah'-reh, ree-poh-zah'-reh*]
relaxation, riposo, distensione (f) [*ree-poh'-zoh, dees-tehn-see-oh'-neh*]
release *v.*, liberare [*lee-beh-rah'-reh*]
relevant, pertinente [*pehr-tee-nehn'-teh*]
reliable, degno di fiducia [*deh'-nyoh dee fee-doo'-chee-ah*]
relief [from discomfort], sollievo [*sohl-lee-eh'-voh*]
relief [aid], soccorso [*sohk-kohr'-soh*]
relieve *v.*, alleviare [*ahl-leh-vee-ah'-reh*]
religion, religione (f) [*reh-lee-jee-oh'-neh*]
religious, religioso [*reh-lee-jee-oh'-zoh*]
reluctant, riluttante [*ree-loot-tahn'-teh*]
rely (on) *v.*, fidarsi di [*fee-dahr'-see dee*]
remain *v.*, rimanere [*ree-mah-neh'-reh*]
remainder, residuo [*reh-zee'-doo-oh*]
remark *n.*, osservazione (f) [*ohs-sehr-vah-tsee-oh'-neh*]

remark *v.*, osservare [*ohs-sehr-vah'-reh*]
remarkable, notevole [*noh-teh'-voh-leh*]
remedy *n.*, rimedio [*ree-meh'-dee-oh*]
remember *v.*, ricordarsi [*ree-kohr-dahr'-see*]
  Do you remember me? Si ricorda di me? [*see ree-kohr'-dah dee meh*]
remind *v.*, ricordare a [*ree-kohr-dah'-reh ah*]
remittance, rimessa [*ree-mehs'-sah*]
remorse, rimorso [*ree-mohr'-soh*]
remote, remoto [*reh-moh'-toh*]
remove *v.*, rimuovere [*ree-moo-oh'-veh-reh*]
renew *v.*, rinnovare [*reen-noh-vah'-reh*]
rent *n.*, affitto [*ahf-feet'-toh*]
  for rent, da affittare [*dah ahf-feet-tah'-reh*]
rent *v.*, affittare [*ahf-feet-tah'-reh*]
repair *n.*, riparazione (f) [*ree-pah-rah-tsee-oh'-neh*]
repair *v.*, riparare [*ree-pah-rah'-reh*]
repay *v.*, rimborsare [*reem-bohr-sah'-reh*]
repeat *v.*, ripetere [*ree-peh'-teh-reh*]
  Please repeat! Per favore ripeta? [*pehr fah-voh'-reh ree-peh'-tah*]
repel *v.*, respingere [*rehs-peen'-jeh-reh*]
replace *v.*, sostituire [*sohs-tee-too-ee'-reh*]
reply *n.*, risposta [*rees-pohs'-tah*]
reply *v.*, rispondere [*rees-pohn'-deh-reh*]
report *n.*, resoconto [*reh-zoh-kohn'-toh*]
report *v.*, riferire, riportare [*ree-feh-ree'-reh, ree-pohr-tah'-reh*]
reporter, cronista (m, f) [*kroh-nees'-tah*]
represent *v.*, rappresentare [*rahp-preh-sehn-tah'-reh*]
representative, rappresentante [*rahp-preh-zehn-tahn-teh*]
reproduction, riproduzione (f) [*ree-proh-doo-tsee-oh'-neh*]
republic, republica [*reh-poob'-lee-kah*]
reputation, reputazione (f) [*reh-poo-tah-tsee-oh'-neh*]
request *n.*, richiesta [*ree-kee-ehs'-tah*]
request *v.*, richiedere [*ree-kee-eh'-deh-reh*]
require *v.*, esigere [*eh-zee'-jeh-reh*]
requirement, requisito [*reh-koo-ee-zee'-toh*]

rescue *n.*, salvamento, soccorso [*sahl-vah-mehn'-toh, sohk-kohr'-soh*]
rescue *v.*, salvare [*sahl-vah'-reh*]
research *n.*, ricerca, ricerche (pl) [*ree-chehr'-kah, ree-chehr'-keh*]
research *v.*, fare ricerche [*fah'-reh ree-chehr'-keh*]
resemblance, rassomiglianza [*rahs-soh-mee-lyahn'-tsah*]
resemble *v.*, rassomigliare [*rahs-soh-mee-lyah'-reh*]
resentment, risentimento [*ree-sehn-tee-mehn'-toh*]
reservation [hotel], prenotazione (f) [*preh-noh-tah-tsee-oh'-neh*]
reserve *v.*, riservare, prenotare [*ree-zehr-vah'-reh, preh-noh-tah'-reh*]
residence, residenza [*reh-zee-dehn'-tsah*]
resident, residente [*reh-zee-dehn'-teh*]
resignation, dimissione (f), rinuncia [*dee-mees-see-oh'-neh, ree-noon'-chee-ah*]
resistance, resistenza [*reh-zees-tehn'-tsah*]
resolution, risoluzione (f) [*ree-zoh-loo-tsee-oh'-neh*]
resolve *v.*, risolvere [*ree-zohl'-veh-reh*]
resort *n.*, stazione climatica [*stah-tsee-oh'-neh klee-mah'-tee-kah*]
resort *v.*, ricorrere a [*ree-kohr'-reh-reh ah*]
respect *n.*, rispetto [*rees-peht'-toh*]
  with respect to, in riguardo a [*een ree-goo-ahr'-doh ah*]
respect *v.*, rispettare [*rees-peht-tah'-reh*]
respectable, rispettabile [*rees-peht-tah'-bee-leh*]
respectful, rispettoso [*rees-peht-toh'-zoh*]
respective, rispettivo [*rees-peht-tee'-voh*]
response, risposta, reazione (f) [*rees-pohs'-tah, reh-ah-tsee-oh'-neh*]
responsibility, responsabilità (f, indecl) [*rehs-pohn-sah-bee-lee-tah'*]
responsible, responsabile [*rehs-pohn-sah'-bee-leh*]
rest *n.*, riposo [*ree-poh'-zoh*]
rest *v.*, riposare [*ree-poh-zah'-reh*]
restaurant, ristorante (m) [*rees-toh-rahn'-teh*]
restless, irrequieto, inquieto [*eer-reh-koo-ee-eh'-toh,*

een-koo-ee-eh'-toh]
restore *v.*, restaurare [*rehs-tah-oo-rah'-reh*]
restrain *v.*, trattenere [*traht-teh-neh'-reh*]
restraint, contegno [*kohn-teh'-nyoh*]
result *n.*, risultato [*ree-zool-tah'-toh*]
resume *v.*, riprendere [*ree-prehn'-deh-reh*]
retail, vendita al minuto [*vehn'-dee-tah ahl mee-noo'-toh*]
retain *v.*, ritenere [*ree-teh-neh'-reh*]
retire *v.*, ritirarsi [*ree-tee-rahr'-see*]
return *n.*, ritorno [*ree-tohr'-noh*]
return *v.*, ritornare [*ree-tohr-nah'-reh*]
When will you return? Quando ritornerà? [*koo-ahn'-doh ree-tohr-neh-rah'*]
reveal *v.*, rivelare [*ree-veh-lah'-reh*]
revenge, vendetta [*vehn-deht'-tah*]
reverence, riverenza [*ree-veh-rehn'-tsah*]
reverse *v.*, rovesciare, invertire [*roh-veh-shee-ah'-reh, een-vehr-tee'-reh*]
review *n.*, rivista [*ree-vees'-tah*]
review *v.*, riesaminare [*ree-eh-zah-mee-nah'-reh*]
revise *v.*, rivedere [*ree-veh-deh'-reh*]
revolution, rivoluzione (f) [*ree-voh-loo-tsee-oh'-neh*]
revolve *v.*, girare [*jee-rah'-reh*]
reward *n.*, ricompensa [*ree-kohm-pehn'-sah*]
reward *v.*, ricompensare [*ree-kohm-pehn-sah'-reh*]
rheumatism, reumatismo [*reh-oo-mah-teez'-moh*]
rhyme, rima [*ree'-mah*]
rhythm *n.*, ritmo [*reet'-moh*]
rib, costola [*kohs'-toh-lah*]
ribbon, nastro [*nahs'-troh*]
rice riso [*ree'-zoh*]
rich, ricco [*reek'-koh*]
rid *v.*, liberare [*lee-beh-rah'-reh*]
get rid of, sbarazzarsi di [*zbah-rahts-tsahr'-see dee*]
ride *n.*, passeggiata [*pahs-sehj-jee-ah'-tah*]
ride [a bicycle] *v.*, andare in bicicletta [*ahn-dah'-reh een bee-chee-kleht'-tah*]
ride [a horse], cavalcare [*kah-vahl-kah'-reh*]

ridicule *n.*, ridicolo [*ree-dee'-koh-loh*]
ridicule *v.*, deridere [*deh-ree'-deh-reh*]
ridiculous, ridicolo [*ree-dee'-koh-loh*]
right [direction] *n.*, destra [*dehs'-trah*]
  on the right, a destra [*ah dehs'-trah*]
right [correct], giusto [*jee-oos'-toh*]
  all right, va bene [*vah beh'-neh*]
  be right *v.*, avere ragione [*ah-veh'-reh rah-jee-oh'-neh*]
  right away, subito [*soo'-bee-toh*]
  right here, proprio qui [*pro'-pree-oh koo-ee'*]
ring [for finger] *r.*, anello [*ah-nehl'-loh*]
ring *v.*, suonare [*soo-oh-nah'-reh*]
  ring up, chiamare al telefono [*kee-ah-mah'-reh ahl teh-leh'-foh-noh*]
ringing *n.*, suonata [*soo-oh-nah'-tah*]
rinse *v.*, risciacquare [*ree-shee-ahk-koo-ah'-reh*]
riot *n.*, tumulto, rivolta [*too-mool'-toh, ree-vohl'-tah*]
riot *v.*, rivoltarsi [*ree-vohl-tahr'-see*]
rip *n.*, strappo [*strahp'-poh*]
rip *v.*, strappare [*strahp-pah'-reh*]
ripe, maturo [*mah-too'-roh*]
rise *v.*, sorgere [*sohr'-jeh-reh*]
rising *n.*, sorgere (m) [*sohr'-jeh-reh*]
risk *n.*, rischio [*rees'-kee-oh*]
ritual *n.*, rituale [*ree-too-ah'-leh*]
rival *adj. & n.*, rivale [*ree-vah'-leh*]
river, fiume (m) [*fee-oo'-meh*]
road, strada, via [*strah'-dah, vee'-ah*]
roadway, autostrada [*ah-oo-toh-strah'-dah*]
roam *v.*, vagare [*vah-gah'-reh*]
roast *n.*, arrosto [*ahr-rohs'-toh*]
roast *v.*, arrostire [*ahr-rohs-tee'-reh*]
roasted, arrostito [*ahr-rohs-tee'-toh*]
rob *v.*, derubare [*deh-roo-bah'-reh*]
robbery, furto [*foor'-toh*]
rock *n.*, roccia, rocca [*rohch'-chee-ah, rohk'-kah*]
rocking chair, sedia a dondolo [*seh'-dee-ah ah dohn'-doh-loh*]
roll *v.*, avvolgere [*ahv-vohl'-jeh-reh*]

Roman, romano [*roh-mah'-noh*]
romance, romanza [*roh-mahn'-tsah*]
Romanesque, romanico [*roh-mah'-nee-koh*]
romantic, romantico [*roh-mahn'-tee-koh*]
Rome, Roma [*roh'-mah*]
roof, tetto [*teht'-toh*]
room [house] *n.*, stanza, camera [*stahn'-tsah, kah'-meh-rah*]
room [space] *n.*, spazio [*spah'-tsee-oh*]
There is no room, Non c'è spazio [*nohn cheh' spah'-tsee-oh*]
root *n.*, radice (f) [*rah-dee'-cheh*]
rope *n.*, corda [*kohr'-dah*]
rose *n.*, rosa [*roh'-sah*]
rotten, marcio [*mahr'-chee-oh*]
rouge, rossetto [*rohs-seht'-toh*]
rough, ruvido, rozzo [*roo'-vee-doh, rohts'-tsoh*]
round *adj.*, rotondo [*roh-tohn'-doh*]
round trip, andata e ritorno [*ahn-dah'-tah eh ree-tohr'-noh*]
route, rotta [*roht'-tah*]
routine, abitudine (f) [*ah-bee-too'-dee-neh*]
row [line] *n.*, fila [*fee'-lah*]
royal, reale [*reh-ah'-leh*]
rub *v.*, fregare, strofinare [*freh-gah'-reh, stroh-fee-nah'-reh*]
rub out *v.*, cancellare [*kahn-chehl-lah'-reh*]
rubber, gomma [*gohm'-mah*]
ruby, rubino [*roo-bee'-noh*]
rude, rude, ruvido [*roo'-deh, roo'-vee-doh*]
rudeness, scortesia [*skohr-teh-zee'-ah*]
rug, tappeto [*tahp-peh'-toh*]
ruin *n.*, rovina [*roh-vee'-nah*]
rule *n.*, regola [*reh'-goh-lah*]
rule *v.*, regolare, governare [*reh-goh-lah'-reh, goh-vehr-nah'-reh*]
ruler [measure], riga [*ree'-gah*]
ruler [governor], governante, sovrano [*goh-vehr-nahn'-teh, soh-vrah'-noh*]
rumor, rumore (m) [*roo-moh'-reh*]
run *v.*, correre [*kohr'-reh-reh*]

run across, incontrare per caso [*een-kohn-trah'-reh pehr kah'-zoh*]
run after, inseguire [*een-seh-goo-ee'-reh*]
run away, scappare [*skahp-pah'-reh*]
run into, scontrarsi [*skohn-trahr'-see*]
run over, investire [*een-vehs-tee'-reh*]
runaway *n., adj.*, fuggitivo [*fooj-jee-tee'-voh*]
running, corsa [*kohr'-sah*]
runway, pista [*pees'-tah*]
rural, rurale [*roo-rah'-leh*]
rush *n.*, afflusso [*ahf-floos'-soh*]
Russia, Russia [*roos'-see-ah*]
Russian, russo [*roos'-soh*]
rust *n.*, ruggine (f) [*rooj'-jee-neh*]
rustic, rustico [*roos'-tee-koh*]
ruthless, spietato [*spee-eh-tah'-toh*]

S

sabotage *n.*, sabotaggio [*sah-boh-tahj'-jee-oh*]
sack, sacco [*sahk'-koh*]
sacred, sacro [*sah'-kroh*]
sacrifice *n.*, sacrificio [*sah-kree-fee'-chee-oh*]
sad, triste [*trees'-teh*]
saddle, sella [*sehl'-lah*]
sadness, tristezza [*trees-tehz'-zah*]
safe *adj.*, salvo [*sahl'-voh*]
safe and sound, sano e salvo [*sah'-noh eh sahl'-voh*]
safe conduct, salva-condotta (m) [*sahl-vah-kohn-doht'-tah*]
safety, sicurezza [*see-koo-rehts'-tsah*]
safety pin, spilla di sicurezza [*speel'-lah dee see-koo-reht'-tsah*]
safety razor, rasoio di sicurezza [*rah-zoh'-ee-oh dee see-koo-rehts'-tsah*]
sail *n.*, vela [*veh'-lah*]
sail *v.*, navigare [*nah-vee-gah'-reh*]

sailboat, barca a vela [*bahr'-kah ah veh'-lah*]
sailor, marinaio [*mah-ree-nah'-ee-oh*]
saint *n. & adj.*, santo [*sahn'-toh*]
sake, scopo, fine (m), amore (m) [*skoh'-poh, fee'-neh, ah-moh'-reh*]
 For heaven's sake! Per l'amor del cielo! [*pehr lah-mohr' dehl chee-eh'-loh*]
 for your sake, per il suo bene [*pehr eel soo'-oh beh'-neh*]
salad, insalata [*een-sah-lah'-tah*]
salary, salario, stipendio [*sah-lah'-ree-oh, stee-pehn'-dee-oh*]
sale, vendita [*vehn'-dee-tah*]
 for sale, in vendita [*een vehn'-dee-tah*]
salesclerk, commesso [*kohm-mehs'-soh*]
salmon, salmone (m) [*sahl-moh'-neh*]
salt, sale (m) [*sah'-leh*]
salty, salato [*sah-lah'-toh*]
same, stesso, medesimo [*stehs'-soh, meh-deh'-zee-moh*]
 all the same, ciononostante [*chee-oh-noh-nohs-tahn'-teh*]
 at the same time, nello stesso tempo [*nehl'-loh stehs'-soh tehm'-poh*]
 It's all the same to me, È lo stesso per me [*eh' loh stehs'-soh pehr meh*]
sample *n.*, campione (m), esempio [*kahm-pee-oh'-neh, eh-zehm'-pee-oh*]
sand, sabbia [*sahb'-bee-ah*]
sandal, sandalo [*sahn'-dah-loh*]
sandwich, panino [*pah-nee'-noh*]
sandy, sabbioso [*sahb-bee-oh'-zoh*]
sane, sano di mente [*sah'-noh dee mehn'-teh*]
sanitary, igienico [*ee-jee-eh'-nee-koh*]
sanitary napkin, pannino igienico [*pah-nee'-noh ee-jee-eh'-nee-koh*]
sapphire, zaffiro [*dzahf'-fee-roh*]
sarcastic, sarcastico [*sahr-kahs'-tee-koh*]
satin, raso [*rah'-soh*]
satire, satira [*sah'-tee-rah*]
satisfaction, soddisfazione (f) [*sohd-dees-fah-tsee-oh'-neh*]
satisfactory, soddisfacente [*sohd-dees-fah-chehn'-teh*]

satisfied, soddisfatto [*sohd-dees-faht'-toh*]
satisfy *v.*, soddisfare [*sohd-dees-fah'-reh*]
Saturday, sabato [*sah'-bah-toh*]
sauce, salsa [*sahl'-sah*]
saucer, piattino [*pee-aht-tee'-noh*]
sausage, salsiccia [*sahl-seech'-chee-ah*]
save [money] *v.*, risparmiare [*rees-pahr-mee-ah'-reh*]
save [life] *v.*, salvare [*sahl-vah'-reh*]
saving, risparmio [*rees-pahr'-mee-oh*]
savings account, libretto di risparmio [*lee-breht'-toh dee rees-pahr'-mee-oh*]
say *v.*, dire (irreg) [*dee'-reh*]
saying, proverbio [*proh-vehr'-bee-oh*]
scale [music, etc.] scala [*skah'-lah*]
scales, bilancia [*bee-lahn'-chee-ah*]
scandal, scandalo [*skahn'-dah-loh*]
scar *n.*, cicatrice (f) [*chee-kah-tree'-cheh*]
scarce, scarso [*skahr'-soh*]
scare *v.*, spaventare [*spah-vehn-tah'-reh*]
scarf, sciarpa [*shee-ahr'-pah*]
scatter *v.*, disperdere [*dees-pehr'-deh-reh*]
scene, scena [*sheh'-nah*]
scenery, scenario [*sheh-nah'-ree-oh*]
scent *n.*, odore (m) [*oh-doh'-reh*]
schedule *n.*, orario [*oh-rah'-ree-oh*]
scheme *n.*, schema (m), disegno [*skeh'-mah, dee-zeh'-nyoh*]
scholar, studioso, erudito [*stoo-dee-oh'-zoh, eh-roo-dee'-toh*]
school, scuola [*skoo-oh'-lah*]
schoolmate, compagno di scuola [*kohm-pah'-nyoh dee skoo-oh'-lah*]
schoolteacher, maestro [*mah-ehs'-troh*]
science, scienza [*shee-ehn'-tsah*]
scientist, scienziato [*shee-ehn-tsee-ah'-toh*]
scissors, forbici [*fohr'-bee-chee*]
scold *v.*, rimproverare [*reem-proh-veh-rah'-reh*]
score *n.*, punteggio [*poon-tehj'-jee-oh*]
score *v.*, segnare [*seh-nyah'-reh*]
scorn *n.*, disprezzo [*dees-prehts'-tsoh*]

scorn *v.*, disprezzare [*dees-prehts-tsah'-reh*]
Scot, Scottish *n. & adj.* scozzese [*skohts-tseh'-zeh*]
Scotland, Scozia [*skoh'-tsee-ah*]
scrape *v.*, raschiare [*rahs-kee-ah'-reh*]
scratch *n.*, graffio [*grahf'-fee-oh*]
scratch *v.*, graffiare [*grahf-fee-ah'-reh*]
scream *n.*, grido [*gree'-doh*]
scream *v.*, gridare [*gree-dah'-reh*]
screen *n.*, schermo [*skehr'-moh*]
screw *n.*, vite (f) [*vee'-teh*]
screwdriver, cacciavite (m) [*kahch-chee-ah-vee'-teh*]
scrub *v.*, strofinare [*stroh-fee-nah'-reh*]
sculpture *n.*, scultura [*skool-too'-rah*]
sea, mare (m) [*mah'-reh*]
seal [animal] *n.*, foca [*foh'-kah*]
seal [stamp] *n.*, sigillo [*see-jeel'-loh*]
seal *v.*, sigillare [*see-jeel-lah'-reh*]
seam *n.*, cucitura [*koo-chee-too'-rah*]
seaport, porto [*pohr'-toh*]
sea shell, conchiglia marina [*kohn-kee'-lyah mah-ree'-nah*]
search *n.*, ricerca [*ree-chehr'-kah*]
search for *v.*, cercare [*chehr-kah'-reh*]
season *n.*, stagione (f) [*stah-jee-oh'-neh*]
season [flavor] *v.*, condire [*kohn-dee'-reh*]
seat *n.*, posto [*pohs'-toh*]
  Have a seat, please! Si sieda, per favore! [*see see-eh'-dah, pehr fah-voh'-reh*]
seated, seduto [*seh-doo'-toh*]
second *adj.*, secondo [*seh-kohn'-doh*]
second [time] *n.*, secondo [*seh-kohn'-doh*]
secondary, secondario [*seh-kohn-dah'-ree-oh*]
secret *n. & adj.*, segreto [*seh-greh'-toh*]
secretary, segretario [*seh-greh-tah'-ree-oh*]
section, sezione (f) [*seh-tsee-oh'-neh*]
secular, laico [*lah'-ee-koh*]
secure *adj.*, sicuro [*see-koo'-roh*]
secure [make sure] *v.*, assicurare [*ahs-see-koo-rah'-reh*]
secure [obtain] *v.*, procurarsi [*proh-koo-rahr'-see*]

security, sicurezza [*see-koo-rehts'-tsah*]
seduce *v.*, sedurre (irreg) [*seh-door'-reh*]
see *v.*, vedere [*veh-deh'-reh*]
Let me see, Mi faccia vedere [*mee fahch'-chee-ah veh-deh'-reh*]
Let's see, vediamo un pò [*veh-dee-ah'-moh oon poh'*]
seed, seme (m) [*seh'-meh*]
seek *v.*, cercare [*chehr-kah'-reh*]
seem *v.*, sembrare [*sehm-brah'-reh*]
How does it seem to you? Come le sembra? [*koh'-meh leh sehm'-brah*]
It seems to me that . . . , Mi sembra che . . . [*mee sehm'-brah keh*]
seize *v.*, afferrare [*ahf-fehr-rah'-reh*]
seldom, raramente [*rah-rah-mehn'-teh*]
select *v.*, scegliere (irreg) [*sheh'-lyeh-reh*]
self, stesso [*stehs'-soh*]
myself, me stesso [*meh stehs'-soh*]
themselves, loro stessi [*loh'-roh stehs'-see*]
self-conscious timido [*tee'-mee-doh*]
selfish, egoista [*eh-goh-ees'-tah*]
sell, vendere [*vehn'-deh-reh*]
senate, senato [*seh-nah'-toh*]
senator, senatore (m) [*seh-nah-toh'-reh*]
send *v.*, mandare [*mahn-dah'-reh*]
send for, mandare a chiamare [*mahn-dah'-reh ah kee-ah-mah'-reh*]
send forth, spedire [*speh-dee'-reh*]
sender, speditore (m) [*speh-dee-toh'-reh*]
senior, più anziano [*pee-oo' ahn-tsee-ah'-noh*]
sense *n.*, senso [*sehn'-soh*]
common sense, buon senso [*boo-ohn' sehn'-soh*]
sensible, sensibile [*sehn-see'-bee-leh*]
sensitive, sensitivo [*sehn-see-tee'-voh*]
sentence [speech] *n.*, frase (f) [*frah'-zeh*]
sentimental, sentimentale [*sehn-tee-mehn-tah'-leh*]
separate *adj.*, separato [*seh-pah-rah'-toh*]
separate *v.*, separare [*seh-pah-rah'-reh*]

separately, separatamente [*seh-pah-rah-tah-mehn'-teh*]
separation, separazione (f) [*seh-pah-rah-tsee-oh'-neh*]
September, settembre (m) [*seht-tehm'-breh*]
serenade *n.*, serenata [*seh-reh-nah'-tah*]
serene, sereno [*seh-reh'-noh*]
series, serie (f, sing & pl) [*seh'-ree-eh*]
serious, serio [*seh'-ree-oh*]
seriously, seriamente [*seh-ree-ah-mehn'-teh*]
sermon, predica [*preh'-dee-kah*]
servant, servitore (m), servitrice (f) [*sehr-vee-toh'-reh, sehr-vee-tree'-cheh*]
serve *v.*, servire [*sehr-vee'-reh*]
service, servizio [*sehr-vee'-tsee-oh*]
at your service, ai suoi ordini [*ah'-ee soo-oh'-ee ohr'-dee-nee*]
session, sessione (f) [*sehs-see-oh'-neh*]
set *n.*, assortimento [*ahs-sohr-tee-mehn'-toh*]
set *v.*, mettere [*meht'-teh-reh*]
set aside, mettere da parte [*meht'-teh-reh dah pahr'-teh*]
set a watch, regolare l'orologio [*reh-goh-lah'-reh loh-roh-loh'-jee-oh*]
set free, mettere in libertà [*meht'-teh-reh een lee-behr-tah'*]
set off, mettere in azione [*meht'-teh-reh een ah-tsee-oh'-neh*]
set up, costruire [*kohs-troo-ee'-reh*]
settle *v.*, regolare [*reh-goh-lah'-reh*]
seven, sette [*seht'-teh*]
seventeen, diciassette [*dee-chee-ah-seht'-teh*]
seventh, settimo [*seht'-tee-moh*]
seventy, settanta [*seht-tahn'-tah*]
sever *v.*, troncare [*trohn-kah'-reh*]
several, parecchi [*pah-rehk'-kee*]
severe, severo [*seh-veh'-roh*]
sew *v.*, cucire [*koo-chee'-reh*]
sewing machine, macchina da cucire [*mahk'-kee-nah dah koo-chee'-reh*]
sex, sesso [*sehs'-soh*]
shade, shadow, ombra [*ohm'-brah*]

shake *v.*, agitare [*ah-jee-tah'-reh*]
shake hands, darsi la mano [*dahr'-see lah mah'-noh*]
shallow, poco profondo [*poh'-koh proh-fohn'-doh*]
shame, vergogna [*vehr-goh'-nyah*]
shameful, vergognoso [*vehr-goh-nyoh'-zoh*]
shampoo *n.*, shampoo [*shahm'-poo*]
shape *n.*, forma [*fohr'-mah*]
shape *v.*, formare [*fohr-mah'-reh*]
share *v.*, spartire, condividere [*spahr-tee'-reh, kohn-dee-vee'-deh-reh*]
sharp, aguzzo, furbo [*ah-goots'-tsoh, foor'-boh*]
shave *n.*, rasatura [*rah-zah-too'-rah*]
shave *v.*, radere, radersi [*rah-deh'-reh, rah-dehr'-see*]
shaving brush, pennello da barba [*pehn-nehl'-loh dah bahr'-bah*]
shaving cream, crema da barba [*kreh'-mah dah bahr'-bah*]
shaving lotion, lozione (f) da barba [*loh-tsee-oh'-neh dah bahr'-bah*]
shawl, scialle (m) [*shee-ahl'-leh*]
she, essa, ella, lei [*ehs'-sah, ehl'-lah, leh'-ee*]
sheep, pecora [*peh'-koh-rah*]
sheet [bedding], lenzuolo, le lenzuola (pl) [*lehn-tsoo-oh'-loh, leh lehn-tsoo-oh'-lah*]
sheet [paper], foglio [*foh'-lyoh*]
shelf, scaffale (m) [*skahf-fah'-leh*]
shell [eggshell], guscio [*goo'-shee-oh*]
shell [seashell], conchiglia [*kohn-kee'-lyah*]
shelter *n.*, rifugio [*ree-foo'-jee-oh*]
shield *v.*, difendere [*dee-fehn'-deh-reh*]
shift *v.*, cambiare [*kahm-bee-ah'-reh*]
shine *v.*, brillare [*breel-lah'-reh*]
shine [shoes] *v.*, lucidare [*loo-chee-dah'-reh*]
ship *n.*, nave (f) [*nah'-veh*]
ship *v.*, imbarcare, spedire [*eem-bahr-kah'-reh, speh-dee'-reh*]
shipment, imbarco, carico [*eem-bahr'-koh, kah'-ree-koh*]
shirt, camicia [*kah-mee'-chee-ah*]
shiver *v.*, tremare [*treh-mah'-reh*]

shock *n.*, urto, scossa [*oor'-toh, skohs'-sah*]
shoe, scarpa [*skahr'-pah*]
shoe laces, lacci di scarpe [*lahch'-chee dee skahr'-peh*]
shoemaker, calzolaio [*kahl-tsoh-lah'-ee-oh*]
shoeshine boy, lustrascarpe (m) [*loos-trah-skahr'-peh*]
shoe store, calzoleria [*kahl-tsoh-leh-ree'-ah*]
shoot [fire] *v.*, sparare [*spah-rah'-reh*]
shop *n.*, negozio, bottega [*neh-goh'-tsee-oh, boht-teh'-gah*]
shop *v.*, fare le compre [*fah'-reh leh kohm'-preh*]
shopping, spesa, compere (f, pl) [*speh'-zah, kohm'-peh-reh*]
shop window, vetrina [*veh-tree'-na*]
shore, riva [*ree'-vah*]
short, corto, basso [*kohr'-toh, bahs'-soh*]
  in a short time, in poco tempo [*een poh'-koh tehm'-poh*]
  in short, in breve [*een breh'-veh*]
shortcut, scorciatoia [*skohr-chee-ah-toh'-ee-ah*]
shorts, calzoncini (m, pl) [*kahl-tsohn-chee'-nee*]
shorten *v.*, abbreviare [*ahb-breh-vee-ah'-reh*]
shortsighted, miope [*mee'-oh-peh*]
should, dovere [*doh-veh'-reh*]
  We should leave, Dovremmo partire [*doh-vrehm'-moh pahr-tee'-reh*]
  You should see it, Lei dovrebbe vederlo [*leh'-ee doh-vrehb'-beh veh-dehr'-loh*]
shoulder, spalla [*spahl'-lah*]
shout *n.*, grido [*gree'-doh*]
shout *v.*, gridare [*gree-dah'-reh*]
show [theater] *n.*, spettacolo [*speht-tah'-koh-loh*]
show [exhibition] *n.*, esposizione (f) [*ehs-poh-zee-tsee-oh'-neh*]
show *v.*, mostrare [*mohs-trah'-reh*]
  Show me! Mi faccia vedere! [*mee fahch'-chee-ah veh-deh'-reh*]
shower [bath], doccia [*dohch'-chee-ah*]
shrewd, astuto, maligno [*ahs-too'-toh, mah-lee'-nyoh*]
shrimp, gamberetto [*gahm-beh-reht'-toh*]
shrine, santuario [*sahn-too-ah'-ree-oh*]
shrink *v.*, contrarsi [*kohn-trahr'-see*]

shut *v.*, chiudere [*kee-oo'-deh-reh*]
Shut up! Silenzio! [*see-lehn'-tsee-oh*]
shy, timido [*tee'-mee-doh*]
Sicilian, siciliano [*see-chee-lee-ah'-noh*]
Sicily, Sicilia [*see-chee'-lee-ah*]
sick, malato [*mah-lah'-toh*]
sickness, malattia [*mah-laht-tee'-ah*]
side, lato, fianco [*lah'-toh*, *fee-ahn'-koh*]
sidewalk, marciapiede (m) [*mahr-chee-ah-pee-eh'-deh*]
sideways, lateralmente [*lah-teh-rahl-mehn'-teh*]
siege, assedio [*ahs-seh'-dee-oh*]
sigh *n.*, sospiro [*sohs-pee'-roh*]
sigh *v.*, sospirare [*sohs-pee-rah'-reh*]
sight, vista, veduta [*vees'-tah*, *veh-doo'-tah*]
sightseeing, giro turistico [*jee'-roh too-rees'-tee-koh*]
sign [mark] *n.*, segno [*seh'-nyoh*]
sign [street] *n.*, cartellone (m) [*kahr-tehl-loh'-neh*]
sign *v.*, firmare [*feer-mah'-reh*]
signal *n.*, segnale (m) [*seh-nyah'-leh*]
signal *v.*, segnalare [*seh-nyah-lah'-reh*]
signature *n.*, firma [*feer'-mah*]
significance, significato [*see-nyee-fee-kah'-toh*]
signpost, palo indicatore [*pah'-loh een-dee-kah-toh'-reh*]
silence *n.*, silenzio [*see-lehn'-tsee-oh*]
silent, silenzioso [*see-lehn-tsee-oh'-zoh*]
silk, seta [*seh'-tah*]
silly, sciocco [*shee-ohk'-koh*]
silver, argento [*ahr-jehn'-toh*]
silverware, argenteria [*ahr-jehn-teh-ree'-ah*]
similar, simile [*see'-mee-leh*]
simple, semplice [*sehm'-plee-cheh*]
simply, semplicemente [*sehm-plee-cheh-mehn'-teh*]
sin *n.*, peccato [*pehk-kah'-toh*]
since *conj.*, poichè [*poh-ee-keh'*]
since *prep.*, da [*dah*]
Since when? Da quando? [*dah koo-ahn'-doh*]
since *adv.*, dopo, di poi [*doh'-poh*, *dee poh'-ee*]

sincere, sincero [*seen-cheh'-roh*]
sincerely, sinceramente [*seen-cheh-rah-mehn'-teh*]
sing *v.*, cantare [*kahn-tah'-reh*]
singer, cantante (m, f) [*kahn-tahn'-teh*]
single [sole], solo, uno [*soh'-loh, oo'-noh*]
not a single one, neanche uno/una [*neh-ahn'-keh oo'-noh/ oo'-nah*]
single [unmarried man], scapolo, celibe (m) [*skah'-poh-loh, cheh'-lee-beh*]
single [unmarried woman], signorina, nubile (f) [*see-nyoh-ree'-nah, noo'-bee-leh*]
sink *v.*, affondare [*ahf-fohn-dah'-reh*]
sir, signore (m) [*see-nyoh'-reh*]
sister, sorella [*soh-rehl'-lah*]
sister [religious], suora [*soo-oh'-rah*]
sister-in-law, cognata [*koh-nyah'-tah*]
sit, sit down *v.*, sedersi [*seh-dehr'-see*]
Sit down, please! Si sieda, per favore! [*see see-eh'-dah, pehr fah-voh'-reh*]
situated, situato [*see-too-ah'-toh*]
situation, situazione (f) [*see-too-ah-tsee-oh'-neh*]
six, sei [*seh'-ee*]
sixteen, sedici [*seh'-dee-chee*]
sixth, sesto [*sehs'-toh*]
sixty, sessanta [*sehs-sahn'-tah*]
size [general], misura [*mee-zoo'-rah*]
size [of clothing], taglia [*tah'-lyah*]
skate *v.*, pattinare [*paht-tee-nah'-reh*]
ice skates, pattini (m, pl) [*paht'-tee-nee*]
skeleton, scheletro [*skeh'-leht-roh*]
sketch *n.*, schizzo [*skeets'-tsoh*]
ski *n.*, sci [*shee*]
ski *v.*, sciare [*shee-ah'-reh*]
skid *n.*, scivolare, slittare [*shee-voh-lah'-reh, zleet-tah'-reh*]
skill, abilità (f, indecl) [*ah-bee-lee-tah'*]
skillful, abile [*ah'-bee-leh*]
skin, pelle (f) [*pehl'-leh*]
skinny, magro [*mah'-groh*]

skirt, sottana, gonna, falda [*soht-tah'-nah, gohn'-nah, fahl'-dah*]
skull, cranio [*krah'-nee-oh*]
sky, cielo [*chee-eh'-loh*]
skyscraper, grattacielo [*graht-tah-chee-eh'-loh*]
slander *v.*, calunniare [*kah-loon-nee-ah'-reh*]
slang, gergo [*jehr'-goh*]
slap *n.*, schiaffo [*skee-ahf'-foh*]
slap *v.*, schiaffeggiare [*skee-ahf-fehj-jee-ah'-reh*]
sleep *n.*, sonno [*sohn'-noh*]
sleep *v.*, dormire [*dohr-mee'-reh*]
  (be) asleep, (essere) addormentato [(*ehs'-seh-reh*) *ahd-dohr-mehn-tah'-toh*]
  be sleepy, avere sonno [*ah-veh'-reh sohn'-noh*]
sleeping car, vagone letto (m) [*vah-goh'-neh leht'-toh*]
sleeve, manica [*mah'-nee-kah*]
slender, snello [*znehl'-loh*]
slice *n.*, fetta [*feht'-tah*]
slide *v.*, slittare [*zleet-tah'-reh*]
slight, tenuo, leggero [*teh'-noo-oh, lehj-jeh'-roh*]
slightly, leggermente [*lehj-jehr-mehn'-teh*]
slip [lingerie] *n.*, sottoveste (f) [*soht-toh-vehs'-teh*]
slippers, pantofole [*pahn-toh'-foh-leh*]
slippery, scivoloso [*shee-voh-loh'-zoh*]
slow, lento, piano [*lehn'-toh, pee-ah'-noh*]
slowly, lentamente [*lehn-tah-mehn'-teh*]
small, piccolo [*peek'-koh-loh*]
smaller, più piccolo [*pee-oo' peek'-koh-loh*]
smart, furbo, intelligente [*foor'-boh, een-tehl-lee-jehn'-teh*]
smash *v.*, fracassare [*frah-kahs-sah'-reh*]
smell *n.*, odore (m) [*oh-doh'-reh*]
smell *v.*, odorare [*oh-doh-rah'-reh*]
smile *n.*, sorriso [*sohr-ree'-zoh*]
smile *v.*, sorridere [*sohr-ree'-deh-reh*]
smoke *n.*, fumo [*foo'-moh*]
smoke *v.*, fumare [*foo-mah'-reh*]
smoking car, scompartimento per fumatori [*skohm-pahr-tee-mehn'-toh pehr foo-mah-toh'-ree*]

smooth, liscio [*lee'-shee-oh*]
smother *v.*, soffocare [*sohf-foh-kah'-reh*]
smuggle *v.*, fare contrabando [*fah'-reh kohn-trah-bahn'-doh*]
snack *n.*, spuntino [*spun-tee'-noh*]
snail, lumaca [*loo-mah'-kah*]
sneeze *n.*, starnuto [*stahr-noo'-toh*]
sneeze *v.*, starnutire [*stahr-noo-tee'-reh*]
snore *v.*, russare [*roos-sah'-reh*]
snow *n.*, neve (f) [*neh'-veh*]
snow *v.*, nevicare [*neh-vee-kah'-reh*]
snowstorm *n.*, bufera di neve [*boo-feh'-rah dee neh'-veh*]
so [thus] *adv.*, così, quindi, perciò [*koh-zee', koo-een'-dee, pehr-chee-oh'*]
  and so forth, e così via [*eh koh-zee' vee'-ah*]
  I don't think so, Credo di no [*kreh'-doh dee noh*]
  I hope so, Lo spero [*loh speh'-roh*]
  I think so, Credo di sì [*kreh'-doh dee see'*]
  Is that so? È vero? [*eh' veh'-roh*]
  just so, proprio così [*proh'-pree-oh koh-zee'*]
  so that, di modo che [*dee moh'-doh keh*]
so [much] *adv.*, tanto [*tahn'-toh*]
  so far, sinora [*seen-oh'-rah*]
  so-so, così, così [*koh-zee', koh-zee'*]
  so much the better, tanto meglio [*tahn'-toh meh'-lyoh*]
soap, sapone (m) [*sah-poh'-neh*]
sober, sobrio [*soh'-bree-oh*]
social, sociale [*soh-chee-ah'-leh*]
socialist, socialista [*soh-chee-ah-lees'-tah*]
society, società (f, indecl) [*soh-chee-eh-tah'*]
sock [apparel], calzino [*kahl-tsee'-noh*]
soda [bicarbonate], soda [*soh'-dah*]
soda water, acqua seltz [*ahk'-koo-ah sehlts*]
soft, morbido, tenero [*mohr'-bee-doh, teh'-neh-roh*]
softness, morbidezza [*mohr-bee-dehts'-tsah*]
soiled, sudicio [*soo-dee'-chee-oh*]
sold, venduto [*vehn-doo'-toh*]
soldier, soldato [*sohl-dah'-toh*]
sole [only] *adj.*, unico [*oo'-nee-koh*]

sole [fish] *n.*, sogliola [*soh-lyee-oh'-lah*]
sole [of shoe] *n.*, suola [*soo-oh'-lah*]
solid, solido [*soh'-lee-doh*]
solitary, solitario [*soh-lee-tah'-ree-oh*]
solution, soluzione (f) [*soh-loo-tsee-oh'-neh*]
solve *v.*, risolvere [*ree-zohl'-veh-reh*]
some [certain], qualche (sing), alcuni (pl) [*koo-ahl'-keh, ahl-koo'-nee*]
some [partitive], del, della, dei [*dehl, dehl'-lah, deh'-ee*]
  some bread, del pane [*dehl pah'-neh*]
  some flowers, dei fiori [*deh'-ee fee-oh'-ree*]
someone, qualcuno [*koo-ahl-koo'-noh*]
something, qualcosa [*koo-ahl-koh'-zah*]
some time, passato, ex [*pahs-sah'-toh, ehks*]
sometimes, qualche volta [*koo-ahl'-keh vohl'-tah*]
somewhat, un poco [*oon poh'-koh*]
somewhere, in qualche luogo [*een koo-ahl'-keh loo-oh'-goh*]
somewhere else, altrove [*ahl-troh'-veh*]
son, figlio [*fee'-lyoh*]
son-in-law, genero [*jeh'-neh-roh*]
song, canzone (f) [*kahn-tsoh'-neh*]
soon, presto [*prehs'-toh*]
  as soon as, non appena [*nohn ahp-peh'-nah*]
  as soon as possible, il più presto possibile [*eel pee-oo' prehs'-toh pohs-see'-bee-leh*]
  How soon? Quando? [*koo-ahn'-doh*]
sooner, più presto [*pee-oo' prehs'-toh*]
sooner or later, presto o tardi [*prehs'-toh oh tahr'-dee*]
sore *adj.*, infiammato [*een-feem-ah-mah'-toh*]
sore *n.*, piaga, ulcera [*pee-ah'-gah, ool'-cheh-rah*]
sore throat, mal di gola [*mahl dee goh'-lah*]
sorrow, dispiacere (m) [*dees-pee-ah-cheh'-reh*]
sorrowful, triste, addolorato [*trees'-teh, ahd-doh-loh-rah'-toh*]
sorry, spiacente [*spee-ah-chehn'-teh*]
  be sorry *v.*, essere spiacente [*ehs'-seh-reh spee-ah-chehn'-teh*]
  I am very sorry, Mi dispiace molto [*mee dees-pee-ah'-cheh mohl'-toh*]

sort *n.*, specie (f) [*speh'-chee-eh*]
soul, anima [*ah'-nee-mah*]
sound [noise] *n.*, suono [*soo-oh'-noh*]
sound *v.*, suonare [*soo-oh-nah'-reh*]
sound proof, antisonoro [*ahn-tee-soh-noh'-roh*]
soup, minestra [*mee-nehs'-trah*]
sour, aspro, acido [*ahs'-proh, ah'-chee-doh*]
south, sud (m) [*sood*]
South America, America del Sud [*ah-meh'-ree-kah dehl sood*]
South American, sudamericano [*sood-ah-meh-ree-kah'-noh*]
southern, meridionale [*meh-ree-dee-oh-nah'-leh*]
souvenir, ricordo [*ree-kohr'-doh*]
sow *v.*, seminare [*seh-mee-nah'-reh*]
space, spazio [*spah'-tsee-oh*]
spacious, spazioso [*spah-tsee-oh'-zoh*]
Spain, Spagna [*spah'-nyah*]
Spaniard, Spanish, spagnolo [*spah-nyoh'-loh*]
spare *adj.*, di ricambio [*dee ree-kahm'-bee-oh*]
spare *v.*, risparmiare [*rees-pahr-mee-ah'-reh*]
spare parts, pezzi di ricambio [*pehts'-tsee dee ree-kahm'-bee-oh*]
spare tire, pneumatico di ricambio [*pneh-oo-mah'-tee-koh dee ree-kahm'-bee-oh*]
sparkling, spumeggiante [*spoo-mehj-jee-ahn'-teh*]
sparkplug, candela d'accensione [*kahn-deh'-lah dahch-chehn-see-oh'-neh*]
speak *v.*, parlare [*pahr-lah'-reh*]
Do you speak English! Parla inglese? [*pahr'-lah een-gleh'-zeh*]
speaker, oratore (m) [*oh-rah-toh'-reh*]
special, speciale [*speh-chee-ah'-leh*]
specialist, specialista [*speh-chee-ah-lees'-tah*]
specially, specialmente [*speh-chee-ahl-mehn'-teh*]
specialty, specialità (f, indecl) [*speh-chee-ah-lee-tah'*]
spectator, spettatore (m), spettatrice (f) [*speht-tah-toh'-reh, speht-tah-tree'-cheh*]
speech, discorso [*dees-kohr'-soh*]

speed, velocità (f, indecl) [*veh-loh-chee-tah'*]
Full speed ahead, A tutta velocità [*ah toot'-tah veh-loh-chee-tah'*]
speed *v.*, accelerare [*ahch-cheh-leh-rah'-reh*]
speed limit, velocità massima [*veh-loh-chee-tah' mahs'-see-mah*]
spell *v.*, scrivere [*skree'-veh-reh*]
How do you spell it? Come si scrive? [*koh'-meh see skree'-veh*]
spelling, ortografia [*ohr-toh-grah-fee'-ah*]
spend [money] *v.*, spendere [*spehn'-deh-reh*]
spend [time] *v.*, passare (il tempo) [*pahs-sah'-reh* (*eel tehm'-poh*)]
spice, spezie (f) [*speh'-tsee-eh*]
spill *v.*, versare [*vehr-sah'-reh*]
spin *v.*, filare [*fee-lah'-reh*]
spinach, spinaci [*spee-nah'-chee*]
spine, spina [*spee'-nah*]
spiral, spirale (f) [*spee-rah'-leh*]
spirit, spirito [*spee'-ree-toh*]
spiritual, spirituale [*spee-ree-too-ah'-leh*]
spit *v.*, sputare [*spoo-tah'-reh*]
spite, dispetto, rancore (m) [*dees-peht'-toh*, *rahn-koh'-reh*]
in spite of, a dispetto di, nonostante [*ah dees-peht'-toh dee*, *noh-nohs-tahn'-teh*]
splendid, splendido [*splehn'-dee-doh*]
split, dividere [*dee-vee'-deh-reh*]
spoil *v.*, guastare [*goo-ahs-tah'-reh*]
spoil [a child] *v.*, viziare [*vee-tsee-ah'-reh*]
sponge, spugna [*spoo'-nyah*]
spontaneous, spontaneo [*spohn-tah'-neh-oh*]
spoon, cucchiaio [*kook-kee-ah'-ee-oh*]
teaspoon, cucchiaino [*kook-kee-ah-ee'-noh*]
sport, sport (m) [*spohrt*]
spot [place] *n.*, posto [*pohs'-toh*]
spot [stain] *n.*, macchia [*mahk'-kee-ah*]
spotless, immacolato [*eem-mah-koh-lah'-toh*]
spouse, sposo, sposa [*spoh'-zoh*, *spoh'-zah*]

sprain *n.*, storta [*stohr'-tah*]
spray *v.*, spruzzare [*sproots-tsah'-reh*]
spread *v.*, spargere [*spahr'-jeh-reh*]
  spread on, spalmare [*spahl-mah'-reh*]
spring [season] *n.*, primavera [*pree-mah-veh'-rah*]
spring [machine] *n.*, molla [*mohl'-lah*]
spring [water] *n.*, fonte (f), sorgente (f) [*fohn'-teh, sohr-jehn'-teh*]
spring up *v.*, scattare [*skaht-tah'-reh*]
spy *n.*, spia [*spee'-ah*]
spy *v.*, spiare [*spee-ah'-reh*]
square *adj.*, quadrato [*koo-ah-drah'-toh*]
square [city] *n.*, piazza [*pee-ahts'-tsah*]
squeeze *v.*, spremere [*spreh'-meh-reh*]
stab *v.*, pugnalare [*poo-nyah-lah'-reh*]
stable *adj.*, stabile [*stah'-bee-leh*]
stadium, stadio [*stah'-dee-oh*]
stage [theater] *n.*, palcoscenico [*pahl-koh-sheh'-nee-koh*]
stain *n.*, macchia [*mahk'-kee-ah*]
stain *v.*, macchiare [*mahk-kee-ah'-reh*]
stairs, staircase, scala [*skah'-lah*]
stamp *n.*, francobollo [*frahn-koh-bohl'-loh*]
stamp *v.*, timbrare [*teem-brah'-reh*]
stand [newspaper], edicola (m) [*eh-dee'-koh-lah*]
stand *v.*, stare in piedi [*stah'-reh een pee-eh'-dee*]
  stand out, eccellere [*ehch-chehl'-leh-reh*]
  stand up, alzarsi in piedi [*ahl-tsahr'-see een pee-eh'-dee*]
standard *n.*, norma, modello [*nohr'-mah, moh-dehl'-loh*]
standing *adj.*, in piedi, fermo [*een pee-eh'-dee, fehr'-moh*]
standing *n.*, posizione (f) [*poh-zee-tsee-oh'-neh*]
standpoint *n.*, punto di vista [*poon'-toh dee vees'-tah*]
star, stella [*stehl'-lah*]
starch, amido [*ah'-mee-doh*]
start *v.*, iniziare [*ee-nee-tsee-ah'-reh*]
starter [auto], messa in moto [*mehs'-sah een moh'-toh*]
starve *v.*, affamare [*ahf-fah-mah'-reh*]
state *n.*, stato [*stah'-toh*]
state *v.*, dichiarare [*dee-kee-ah-rah'-reh*]

statement, dichiarazione (f) [*dee-kee-ah-rah-tsee-oh'-neh*]
stateroom, cabina riservata [*kah-bee'-nah ree-zehr-vah'-tah*]
statesman, statista (m) [*stah-tees'-tah*]
station, stazione (f) [*stah-tsee-oh'-neh*]
railway station, stazione ferroviaria [*stah-tsee-oh'-neh fehr-roh-vee-ah'-ree-ah*]
stationary, fermo [*fehr'-moh*]
stationery, cartoleria [*kahr-toh-leh-ree'-ah*]
statue, statua [*stah'-too-ah*]
stay *v.*, stare (irreg) [*stah'-reh*]
steady, costante [*kohs-tahn'-teh*]
steak, bistecca [*bees-tehk'-kah*]
steal *v.*, rubare [*roo-bah'-reh*]
steam *n.*, vapore (m) [*vah-poh'-reh*]
steamship line, compagnia di navigazione [*kohm-pah-nyee'-ah dee nah-vee-gah-tsee-oh'-neh*]
steel, acciaio [*ahch-chee-ah'-ee-oh*]
steering wheel, volante (m) [*voh-lahn'-teh*]
stenographer, stenografo [*steh-noh'-grah-foh*]
step *n.*, passo [*pahs'-soh*]
sterilized, sterilizzato [*steh-ree-leets-tsah'-toh*]
stern *adj.*, severo [*seh-veh'-roh*]
steward, cameriere di bordo (m) [*kah-meh-ree-eh'-reh dee bohr'-doh*]
stewardess, cameriera di bordo [*kah-meh-ree-eh'-rah dee bohr'-doh*]
sting *n.*, pungiglione (m) [*poon-jee-lyee-oh'-neh*]
sting *v.*, pungere [*poon'-geh-reh*]
stir *v.*, agitare [*ah-jee-tah'-reh*]
stitch *n.*, punto [*poon'-toh*]
stitch *v.*, cucire, suturare [*koo-chee'-reh, soo-too-rah'-reh*]
stock [supply] *n.*, provvista [*prohv-vees'-tah*]
stock [shares] *n.*, azioni (f, pl) [*ah-tsee-oh'-nee*]
stockbroker, agente di cambio [*ah-jehn'-teh dee kahm'-bee-oh*]
stock exchange, borsa valori [*bohr'-sah vah-loh'-ree*]
stockings, calze (per donne) [*kahl'-tseh (pehr dohn'-neh)*]
stolen, rubato [*roo-bah'-toh*]

stomach, stomaco [*stoh'-mah-koh*]
stomachache, mal di stomaco [*mahl dee stoh'-mah-koh*]
stone, pietra [*pee-eh'-trah*]
stop *n.*, fermata [*fehr-mah'-tah*]
stop *v.*, fermare, fermarsi [*fehr-mah'-reh, fehr-mahr'-see*]
  Stop! Alt! [*ahlt*]
  Stop here! Si fermi qui! [*see fehr'-mee koo-ee'*]
  Stop that! La smetta! [*lah zmeht'-tah*]
stop sign, fermata [*fehr-mah'-tah*]
stopwatch, cronometro [*kroh-noh'-meh-troh*]
storage, magazzino [*mah-gahdz-dzee'-noh*]
store *n.*, negozio, deposito [*neh-goh'-tsee-oh, deh-poh'-zee-toh*]
  department store, grande negozio [*grahn'-deh neh-goh'-tsee-oh*]
store *v.*, depositare [*deh-poh-zee-tah'-reh*]
storm *n.*, tempesta [*tehm-pehs'-tah*]
story [tale], storia, racconto [*stoh'-ree-ah, rahk-kohn'-toh*]
story [floor], piano [*pee-ah'-noh*]
stove, stufa [*stoo'-fah*]
straight, diritto, onesto [*dee-reet'-toh, oh-nehs'-toh*]
  straight ahead, diritto avanti [*dee-reet'-toh ah-vahn'-tee*]
strain *n.*, sforzo [*sfohr'-tsoh*]
strange, strano [*strah'-noh*]
stranger, estraneo [*ehs-trah'-neh-oh*]
strap, cinghia [*cheen'-gee-ah*]
straw, paglia [*pah'-lyah*]
strawberry, fragola [*frah'-goh-lah*]
stream, corrente (f) [*kohr-rehn'-teh*]
street, strada [*strah'-dah*]
streetcar, tram [*trahm*]
strength, forza [*fohr'-tsah*]
stress *n.*, tensione (f) [*tehn-see-oh'-neh*]
stretch *v.*, stendere [*stehn'-deh-reh*]
strict, rigido [*ree'-jee-doh*]
strictly, precisamente [*preh-chee-zah-mehn'-teh*]
strike [hit] *v.*, colpire [*kohl-pee'-reh*]
strike [cease working] *v.*, scioperare [*shee-oh-peh-rah'-reh*]

strike [by labor] *n.*, sciopero [*shee-oh'-peh-roh*]
string, corda, laccio [*kohr'-dah, lahch'-chee-oh*]
stripe, striscia [*stree'-shee-ah*]
stroll *v.*, passeggiare [*pahs-sehj-jee-ah'-reh*]
strong, forte [*fohr'-teh*]
structure, struttura [*stroot-too'-rah*]
struggle *n.*, lotta [*loht'-tah*]
struggle *v.*, lottare [*loht-tah'-reh*]
stubborn, ostinato [*ohs-tee-nah'-toh*]
student, studente (m), studentessa (f) [*stoo-dehn'-teh, stoo-dehn-tehs'-sah*]
study *v.*, studiare [*stoo-dee-ah'-reh*]
stumble *v.*, inciampare [*een-chee-ahm-pah'-reh*]
stupid, stupido [*stoo'-pee-doh*]
style, stile (m) [*stee'-leh*]
subject *n.*, soggetto [*sohj-jeht'-toh*]
submit *v.*, sottomettere [*soht-toh-meht'-teh-reh*]
substantial *adj.*, sostanziale [*sohs-tahn-tsee-ah'-leh*]
substitute *v.*, sostituire [*sohs-tee-too-ee'-reh*]
subtraction, sottrazione (f) [*soht-trah-tsee-oh'-neh*]
suburb, sobborgo, periferia [*sohb-bohr'-goh, peh-ree-feh-ree'-ah*]
subway, sotterranea, metropolitana [*soht-tehr-rah'-neh-ah, meh-troh-poh-lee-tah'-nah*]
succeed *v.*, riuscire [*ree-oo-shee'-reh*]
success, successo [*sooch-chehs'-soh*]
successive, successivo [*sooch-chehs-see'-voh*]
such, tale [*tah'-leh*]
  such a good man, un uomo tanto buono [*oon oo-oh'-moh tahn'-toh boo-oh'-noh*]
  Such is life, Cosi è la vita [*koh-zee' eh' lah vee'-tah*]
  There is no such thing, Tale cosa non esiste [*tah'-leh koh'-zah nohn eh-zees-'teh*]
suddenly, improvvisamente, subitamente [*eem-prohv-vee-zah-mehn'-teh, soo-bee-tah-mehn'-teh*]
suffer *v.*, soffrire [*sohf-free'-reh*]
sufficient, sufficiente [*soof-fee-chee-ehn'-teh*]
sugar, zucchero [*dzook'-keh-roh*]

sugar bowl, zuccheriera [*dzook-keh-ree-eh'-rah*]
suggest *v.*, suggerire, proporre (irreg) [*sooj-jeh-ree'-reh, proh-pohr'-reh*]
suggestion, proposta [*proh-pohs'-tah*]
suicide, suicidio [*soo-ee-chee'-dee-oh*]
suit [of clothing] *n.*, abito [*ah'-bee-toh*]
suit [at law] *n.*, petizione (f) [*peh-tee-tsee-oh'-neh*]
suit *v.*, convenire a [*kohn-veh-nee'-reh ah*]
suitable, adatto [*ah-daht'-toh*]
suitcase, valigia [*vah-lee'-jee-ah*]
suitor, corteggiatore (m) [*kohr-tehj-jee-ah-toh'-reh*]
sum *n.*, somma [*sohm'-mah*]
sum up *v.*, sommare [*sohm-mah'-reh*]
summary, sommario [*sohm-mah'-ree-oh*]
summer, estate (f) [*ehs-tah'-teh*]
sun, sole (m) [*soh'-leh*]
sunburn, bruciatura di sole [*broo-chee-ah-too'-rah dee soh'-leh*]
Sunday, domenica [*doh-meh'-nee-kah*]
sunglasses, occhiali da sole (m, pl) [*ohk-kee-ah'-lee dah soh'-leh*]
sunrise, levar del sole (m) [*leh-vahr' dehl soh'-leh*]
sunset, tramonto [*trah-mohn'-toh*]
sunshine, luce del sole (f) [*loo'-cheh dehl soh'-leh*]
suntan, abbronzatura [*ahb-brohn-tsah-too'-rah*]
superficial, superficiale [*soo-pehr-fee-chee-ah'-leh*]
superior, superiore [*soo-peh-ree-oh'-reh*]
superstitious, superstizioso [*soo-pehr-stee'-tsee-oh-zoh*]
supper, cena [*cheh'-nah*]
  have supper *v.*, cenare [*cheh-nah'-reh*]
supply *n.*, provista [*proh-vees'-tah*]
supply *v.*, provvedere [*prohv-veh-deh'-reh*]
support *n.*, appoggio, sostegno [*ahp-pohj'-jee-oh, sohs-teh'-nyoh*]
support *v.*, sostenere [*sohs-teh-neh'-reh*]
suppose *v.*, supporre (irreg) [*soop-pohr'-reh*]
supreme, supremo [*soo-preh'-moh*]
sure, sicuro [*see-koo'-roh*]

Are you sure? È sicuro? [*eh' see-koo'-roh*]
surely, sicuramente [*see-koo-rah-mehn'-teh*]
surface *n.*, superficie (f) [*soo-pehr-fee'-chee-eh*]
surgeon, chirurgo [*kee-roor'-goh*]
surgery, chirurgia [*kee-roor-jee'-ah*]
surprise *n.*, sorpresa [*sohr-preh'-zah*]
surprise *v.*, sorprendere [*sohr-prehn'-deh-reh*]
surrender *v.*, arrendersi [*ahr-rehn'-dehr-see*]
surround *v.*, circondare [*cheer-kohn-dah'-reh*]
surroundings, dintorni [*deen-tohr'-nee*]
survival, sopravvivenza [*soh-prahv-vee-vehn'-tsah*]
survive *v.*, sopravvivere [*soh-prahv-vee'-veh-reh*]
survivor, sopravvivente (m) [*soh-prahv-vee-vehn'-teh*]
suspect *v.*, sospettare [*sohs-peht-tah'-reh*]
suspicious, sospettoso [*sohs-peht-toh'-zoh*]
swallow *v.*, inghiottire [*een-gee-oht-tee'-reh*]
swear *v.*, giurare [*jee-oo-rah'-reh*]
Sweden, Svezia [*zveh'-tsee-ah*]
Swedish, svedese [*zveh-deh'-zeh*]
sweep, *v.*, scopare [*skoh-pah'-reh*]
sweet *adj.*, dolce [*dohl'-cheh*]
sweetheart, innamorato [*een-nah-moh-rah'-toh*]
swell *v.*, gonfiare [*gohn-fee-ah'-reh*]
swim *v.*, nuotare [*noo-oh-tah'-reh*]
swimmer, nuotatore (m) [*noo-oh-tah-toh'-reh*]
swimming pool, piscina [*pee-shee'-nah*]
swimsuit, costume (m) da bagno [*kohs-too'-meh dah bah'-nyoh*]
Swiss, svizzero [*zveets'-tseh-roh*]
switch [electric], interruttore (m) [*een-tehr-root-toh'-reh*]
Switzerland, Svizzera [*zveets'-tseh-rah*]
sympathy, simpatia [*seem-pah-tee'-ah*]
My deepest sympathy, Con sentite condoglianze [*kohn sehn-tee'-teh kohn-doh-lyahn'-tseh*]
symphony, sinfonia [*seen-foh-nee'-ah*]
synthetic, sintetico [*seen-teh'-tee-koh*]
system, sistema (m) [*sees-teh'-mah*]
systematic, sistematico [*sees-teh-mah'-tee-koh*]

T

table, tavola [*tah'-voh-lah*]
set the table *v.*, preparare la tavola [*preh-pah-rah'-reh lah tah'-voh-lah*]
tablecloth, tovaglia [*toh-vah'-lyah*]
tablespoon, cucchiaio [*kook-kee-ah'-ee-oh*]
tack *n.*, bulletta [*boo-leht'-tah*]
tact, tatto [*taht'-toh*]
tactless, indelicato [*een-deh-lee-kah'-toh*]
tail, coda [*koh'-dah*]
tailor, sarto [*sahr'-toh*]
tailor's shop, sartoria [*sahr-toh-ree'-ah*]
take *v.*, prendere [*prehn'-deh-reh*]
take advantage of, approfittare di [*ahp-proh-feet-tah'-reh dee*]
take a walk, fare una passeggiata [*fah'-reh oo'-nah pahs-sehj-jee-ah'-tah*]
take care of, avere cura [*ah-veh'-reh koo'-rah*]
take place, avere luogo [*ah-veh'-reh loo-oh'-goh*]
take the opportunity, cogliere l'opportunità [*koh'-lyeh-reh lohp-pohr-too-nee-tah'*]
take [carry] *v.*, portare [*pohr-tah'-reh*]
tale, racconto [*rahk-kohn'-toh*]
talent, talento [*tah-lehn'-toh*]
talk, *n.*, conversazione (f), parlare (m) [*kohn-vehr-sah-tsee-oh'-neh, pahr-lah'-reh*]
talk *v.*, parlare [*pahr-lah'-reh*]
tall, alto [*ahl'-toh*]
tame *adj.*, mansueto [*mahn-soo-eh'-toh*]
tan, abbronzatura [*ahb-brohn-tsah-too'-rah*]
tape, nastro [*nahs'-troh*]
tapestry, tappezzeria [*tahp-pehts-tseh-ree'-ah*]
tardy, lento [*lehn'-toh*]

tariff, tariffa [*tah-reef'-fah*]
task, compito [*kohm'-pee-toh*]
taste *n.*, sapore (m) [*sah-poh'-reh*]
bad taste, cattivo gusto [*kaht-tee'-voh goos'-toh*]
taste *v.*, assaggiare [*ahs-sahj-jee-ah'-reh*]
tasty, saporito [*sah-poh-ree'-toh*]
tax *n.*, tassa [*tahs'-sah*]
tax *v.*, tassare [*tahs-sah'-reh*]
tax-free, esente da imposte [*eh-zehn'-teh dah eem-pohs'-teh*]
taxi, tassì (m) [*tahs-see'*]
tea, tè (m) [*teh'*]
teach *v.*, insegnare [*een-seh-nyah'-reh*]
teacher, insegnante (m) [*een-seh-nyahn'-teh*]
teacup, tazza di tè [*tahts'-tsah dee teh'*]
team, squadra [*skoo-ah'-drah*]
teapot *n.*, teiera [*teh-ee-eh'-rah*]
tear *v.*, strappare [*strahp-pah'-reh*]
teardrop, lacrima, pianto [*lah'-kree-mah, pee-ahn'-toh*]
teaspoon, cucchiaino da tè [*kook-kee-ah-ee'-noh dah teh'*]
technical, tecnico [*tehk'-nee-koh*]
teeth, denti (m, pl) [*dehn'-tee*]
telegram *n.*, telegramma (m) [*teh-leh-grahm'-mah*]
telephone *n.*, telefono [*teh-leh'-foh-noh*]
telephone *v.*, telefonare [*teh-leh-foh-nah'-reh*]
telephone book, elenco telefonico [*eh-lehn'-koh teh-leh-foh'-nee-koh*]
telephone call, chiamata telefonica, telefonata [*kee-ah-mah'-tah teh-leh-foh'-nee-kah, teh-leh-foh-nah'-tah*]
telephone number, numero di telefono [*nooh'-meh-reh dee teh-leh'-foh-noh*]
telephone operator, telefonista [*teh-leh-foh-nees'-tah*]
telescope, telescopo [*teh-lehs'-koh-poh*]
television, televisione (f) [*teh-leh-vee-zee-oh'-neh*]
television set televisore (m) [*teh-leh-vee-zoh'-reh*]
tell *v.*, dire (irreg) [*dee'-reh*]
Tell me, please, Mi dica, per favore [*mee dee'-kah, pehr fah-voh'-reh*]
Don't tell me, Non mi dica [*nohn mee dee'-kah*]

temperature, temperatura [*tehm-peh-rah-too'-rah*]
temple, tempio [*tehm'-pee-oh*]
temporary, temporaneo [*tehm-poh-rah'-neh-oh*]
temptation tentazione (f) [*tehn-tah-tsee-oh'-neh*]
ten, dieci [*dee-eh'-chee*]
tenant, inquilino [*een-koo-ee-lee'-noh*]
tendency, tendenza [*tehn-dehn'-tsah*]
tender, tenero [*teh'-neh-roh*]
tenth, decimo [*deh'-chee-moh*]
terminal [railroad] *n.*, (stazione) termini [(*stah-tsee-oh'-neh*) *tehr'-mee-nee*]
terms, condizioni (f, pl) [*kohn-dee-tsee-oh'-nee*]
terrible, terribile [*tehr-ree'-bee-leh*]
terrify *v.*, spaventare [*spah-vehn-tah'-reh*]
territory, territorio [*tehr-ree-toh'-ree-oh*]
terror, terrore (m) [*tehr-roh'-reh*]
test *n.*, prova [*proh'-vah*]
test *v.*, esaminare [*eh-zah-mee-nah'-reh*]
testify *v.*, testimoniare [*tehs-tee-moh-nee-ah'-reh*]
text, testo [*tehs'-toh*]
textile, tessile [*tehs'-see-leh*]
than, che, di [*keh*, *dee*]
thank *v.*, ringraziare [*reen-grah-tsee-ah'-reh*]
  Thank you, Grazie [*grah'-tsee-eh*]
  Thanks a lot, Grazie tanto [*grah'-tsee-eh tahn'-toh*]
  Thank you very much, Molte grazie [*mohl'-teh grah'-tsee-eh*]
thankful, grato [*grah'-toh*]
that, *demons. adj. & pron.*, quello, quella, quel [*koo-ehl'-loh*, *koo-ehl'-lah*, *koo-ehl'*]
that, *rel. pron.*, che; il quale, la quale [*keh*; *eel koo-ah'-leh*, *lah koo-ah'-leh*]
that *conj.* che [*keh*]
  that which, quello che [*koo-ehl'-loh keh*]
the, il, lo, l' (m, sing), la, l' (f, sing); i, gli (m, pl), le (f, pl) [*eel*, *loh*, *l*, *la*, *l*, *ee*, *lyee*, *leh*]
theater, teatro [*teh-ah'-troh*]
theft, furto [*foor'-toh*]

their, loro [*loh'-roh*]
theirs, il loro (m, sing), la loro (f, sing); i loro (m, pl), le loro (f, pl) [*eel loh'-roh, lah loh'-roh; ee loh'-roh, leh loh'-roh*]
them, loro (m or f, pl), essi (m, pl), esse (f, pl) [*loh'-roh, ehs'-see, ehs'-seh*]
  to them, a loro [*ah loh'-roh*]
  for them, per loro [*pehr loh'-roh*]
themselves, se stessi (m), se stesse (f), loro stessi (m), loro stesse (f) [*seh stehs'-see, seh stehs'-seh, loh'-roh stehs'-see, loh'-roh stehs'-seh*]
then [at that time], allora [*ahl-loh'-rah*]
then [afterwards], poi [*poh'-ee*]
  now and then, di tanto in tanto [*dee tahn'-toh een tahn'-toh*]
theory, teoria [*teh-oh-ree'-ah*]
there, là, lì [*lah', lee'*]
  there are, ci sono [*chee soh'-noh*]
  there is, c'è [*cheh'*]
therefore, perciò, quindi [*pehr-chee-oh', koo-een'-dee*]
thermometer, termometro [*tehr-moh'-meh-troh*]
these, questi (m, pl), queste (f, pl) [*koo-ehs'-tee, koo-ehs'-teh*]
they, loro (m & f pl), essi (m, pl), esse (f, pl) [*loh'-roh, ehs'-see, ehs'-seh*]
thick, grosso [*grohs'-soh*]
thief, ladro [*lah'-droh*]
thin, sottile [*soht-tee'-leh*]
thing, cosa [*koh'-zah*]
think *v.*, pensare [*pehn-sah'-reh*]
  Don't you think so? Non ci crede? [*nohn chee kreh'-deh*]
  I don't think so, Non ci credo [*nohn chee kreh'-doh*]
third, terzo [*tehr'-tsoh*]
thirst, sete (f) [*seh'-teh*]
thirsty, assetato [*ahs-seh-tah'-toh*]
  be thirsty *v.*, avere sete [*ah-veh'-reh seh'-teh*]
thirteen, tredici [*treh'-dee-chee*]

thirty, trenta [*trehn'-tah*]
this, questo, questa [*koo-ehs'-toh, koo-ehs'-tah*]
What is this? Che cosa è questo [*keh koh'-zah eh' koo-ehs'-toh*]
thoroughly, completamente [*kohm-pleh-tah-mehn'-teh*]
those, quelli (m, pl) quelle (f, pl) [*koo-ehl'-lee, koo-ehl'-leh*]
though, sebbene [*sehb-beh'-neh*]
thought, pensiero [*pehn-see-eh'-roh*]
well-thought, ben pensato [*behn pehn-sah'-toh*]
thoughtful, attento [*aht-tehn'-toh*]
thoughtless, spensierato [*spehn-see-eh-rah'-toh*]
thousand, mille, mila (pl) [*meel'-leh, mee'-lah*]
thread, filo [*fee'-loh*]
threat, minaccia [*mee-nahch'-chee-ah*]
threaten *v.*, minacciare [*mee-nahch-chee-ah'-reh*]
three, tre [*treh*]
thrifty, frugale [*froo-gah'-leh*]
thrilled, emozionato [*eh-moh-tsee-oh-nah'-toh*]
throat, gola [*goh'-lah*]
sore throat, mal (m) di gola [*mahl dee goh'-lah*]
through *prep.*, tramite, attraverso [*trah'-mee-teh, aht-trah-vehr'-soh*]
throughout, durante [*doo-rahn'-teh*]
throw *v.*, gettare [*jeht-tah'-reh*]
throw away, buttar via [*boot-tahr' vee'-ah*]
thunder, tuono [*too-oh'-noh*]
thunderstorm, temporale (m) [*tehm-poh-rah'-leh*]
Thursday, giovedì [*jee-oh-veh-dee'*]
thus, così [*koh-zee'*]
Tiber, Tevere (m) [*teh'-veh-reh*]
ticket, biglietto [*bee-lyeht'-toh*]
round-trip ticket, biglietto di andata e ritorno [*bee-lyeht'-toh dee ahn-dah'-tah eh ree-tohr'-noh*]
ticket office, biglietteria [*bee-lyeht-teh-ree'-ah*]
ticket window, sportello [*spohr-tehl'-loh*]
tie [apparel], cravatta [*krah-vaht'-tah*]
tie *v.*, legare [*leh-gah'-reh*]
tight, stretto [*streht'-toh*]

tighten *v.*, stringere [*streen'-jeh-reh*]
till [until] *prep.*, fino a [*fee'-noh ah*]
till [until] *conj.*, finchè [*feen-keh'*]
time [duration], tempo [*tehm'-poh*]
a long time, molto tempo [*mohl'-toh tehm'-poh*]
at the same time, allo stesso tempo [*ahl'-loh stehs'-soh tehm'-poh*]
At what time? A che ora? [*ah keh oh'-rah*]
How long? Quanto tempo? [*koo-ahn'-toh tehm'-poh*]
How long ago? Quanto tempo fa? [*koo-ahn'-toh tehm'-poh fah*]
for the time being, per il momento [*pehr eel moh-mehn'-toh*]
long ago, molto tempo fa [*mohl'-toh tehm'-poh fah*]
Have a good time! Si diverta! [*see dee-vehr'-tah*]
What time is it? Che ore sono? [*keh oh'-reh soh'-noh*]
time [instance], volta [*vohl'-tah*]
at times, a volte, a ore [*ah vohl'-teh, ah oh'-reh*]
timetable, orario [*oh-rah'-ree-oh*]
timid, timido [*tee'-mee-doh*]
tip [gratuity], mancia [*mahn'-chee-ah*]
tire [of a car], ruota, gomma [*roo-oh'-tah, gohm'-mah*]
flat tire, gomma a terra [*gohm'-mah ah tehr'-rah*]
tired, stanco [*stahn'-koh*]
tiresome, faticoso, noioso [*fah-tee-koh'-zoh, noh-ee-oh'-zoh*]
title, titolo [*tee'-toh-loh*]
to a, per [*ah, pehr*]
to and fro, avanti e dietro [*ah-vahn'-tee eh dee-eh'-troh*]
toast [speech] *n.*, brindisi [*breen'-dee-zee*]
toast [food] *n.*, pane abbrustolito [*pah'-neh ahb-broos-toh-lee'-toh*].
toaster, tostapane (m) [*tohs-tah-pah'-neh*]
tobacco, tabacco [*tah-bahk'-koh*]
today, oggi [*ohj'-jee*]
toe, dito, (le) dita (pl) [*dee'-toh, (leh) dee'-tah*]
together, insieme [*een-see-eh'-meh*]
toilet, toletta [*toh-leht'-tah*]

toilet paper, carta igienica [*kahr'-tah ee-jee-eh'-nee-kah*]
tolerate *v.*, tollerare [*tohl-leh-rah'-reh*]
toll [fee] *n.*, pedaggio, tributo [*peh-dahj'-jee-oh, tree-boo'-toh*]
tomato, pomodoro [*poh-moh-doh'-roh*]
tomato juice, succo di pomodoro [*sook'-koh dee poh-moh-doh'-roh*]
tomb, tomba [*tohm'-bah*]
tomorrow, domani [*doh-mah'-nee*]
  tomorrow morning, domani mattina [*doh-mah'-nee maht-tee'-nah*]
ton, tonnellata [*tohn-neh-lah'-tah*]
tone, tono [*toh'-noh*]
tongue, lingua [*leen'-goo-ah*]
tonight, stasera [*stah-seh'-rah*]
too [also], anche, pure [*ahn'-keh, poo'-reh*]
  too much, too many, troppo, troppi [*trohp'-poh, trohp'-pee*]
tool, strumento [*stroo-mehn'-toh*]
tooth, dente (m) [*dehn'-teh*]
toothache, mal di denti [*mahl dee dehn'-tee*]
toothbrush, spazzolino da denti [*spahts-tsoh-lee'-noh dah dehn'-tee*]
toothpaste, dentifricio [*dehn-tee-free'-chee-oh*]
toothpick, stuzzicadenti [*stoots-tsee-kah-dehn'-tee*]
top [cover] *n.*, coperchio [*koh-pehr'-kee-oh*]
top [high point] *n.*, sommità (f, indecl.) [*sohm-mee-tah'*]
  on top of, in cima a [*een chee'-mah ah*]
topic, soggetto [*sohj-jeht'-toh*]
tornado, burrasca [*boor-rahs'-kah*]
torture *n.*, tortura [*tohr-too'-rah*]
total *n.*, totale [*toh-tah'-leh*]
touch *v.*, toccare [*tohk-kah'-reh*]
touching, commovente [*kohm-moh-vehn'-teh*]
tough, duro [*doo'-roh*]
tour *n.*, giro [*jee'-roh*]
tourist, turista (m, f) [*too-rees'-tah*]
tourist office, agenzia di turismo [*ah-jen-tsee'-ah dee too-*

rees'-moh]
tow *v.*, rimorchiare [*ree-mohr-kee-ah'-reh*]
toward, verso [*vehr'-soh*]
towel [bath], asciugamano [*ah-shee-oo-gah-mah'-noh*]
tower, torre (f) [*tohr'-reh*]
town, città (f, indecl) [*cheet-tah'*]
townhall, palazzo municipale [*pah-lats'-tsoh moo-nee-chee-pah'-leh*]
toy, giocattolo [*jee-oh-kaht'-toh-loh*]
track [train], binario [*bee-nah'-ree-oh*]
track [race], pista [*pees'-tah*]
trade *n.*, commercio [*kohm-mehr'-chee-oh*]
trade [do business] *v.*, negoziare [*neh-goh-tsee-ah'-reh*]
trade [exchange] *v.*, barattare [*bah-raht-tah'-reh*]
trademark, marca di fabbrica [*mahr'-kah dee fahb'-bree-kah*]
tradesman, commerciante (m, f) [*kohm-mehr-chee-ahn'-teh*]
tradition, tradizione (f) [*trah-dee-tsee-oh'-neh*]
traditional, tradizionale [*trah-dee-tsee-oh-nah'-leh*]
traffic, traffico [*trahf'-fee-koh*]
tragedy, tragedia [*trah-jeh'-dee-ah*]
tragic, tragico [*trah'-jee-koh*]
trail *n.*, pista [*pees'-tah*]
train *n.*, treno [*treh'-noh*]
training, addestramento [*ahd-dehs-trah-mehn'-toh*]
trait, caratteristica [*kah-raht-teh-rees'-tee-kah*]
traitor, traditore (m), traditrice (f) [*trah-dee-toh'-reh, trah-dee-three'-cheh*]
tranquil, tranquillo [*trahn-koo-eel'-loh*]
transfer, *n.*, trasferimento [*trahs-feh-ree-mehn'-toh*]
transfer *v.*, trasferire [*trahs-feh-ree'-reh*]
translate *v.*, tradurre (irreg) [*trah-door'-reh*]
translation, traduzione (f) [*trah-doo-tsee-oh'-neh*]
transmission, trasmissione (f) [*trahz-mees-see-oh'-neh*]
transportation, trasporto [*trahs-pohr'-toh*]
trap *n.*, trappola [*trahp'-poh-lah*]
travel *n.*, viaggio [*vee-ahj'-jee-oh*]
travel *v.*, viaggiare [*vee-ahj-jee-ah'-reh*]

travel agency, agenzia di viaggi [*ah-jehn-tsee'-ah dee vee-ahj'-jee*]
traveler, viaggiatore (m), viaggiatrice (f) [*vee-ahj-jee-ah-toh'-reh, vee-ahj-jee-ah-tree'-cheh*]
traveler's check, assegno turistico [*ahs-seh'-nyoh too-rees'-tee-koh*]
tray, vassoio [*vahs-soh'-ee-oh*]
treason, tradimento [*trah-dee-mehn'-toh*]
treasure *n.*, tesoro [*teh-zoh'-roh*]
treasurer, tesoriere (m) [*teh-zoh-ree-eh'-reh*]
treat [deal with] *v.*, trattare [*traht-tah'-reh*]
treatment, trattamento [*trah-tah-mehn'-toh*]
tree, albero [*ahl'-beh-roh*]
tremendous, tremendo [*treh-mehn'-doh*]
trespass *v.*, trasgredire [*trahz-greh-dee'-reh*]
trial [test], prova [*proh'-vah*]
trial [at law], processo [*proh-chehs'-soh*]
tribute, tributo, omaggio [*tree-boo'-toh, oh-mahj'-jee-oh*]
trick *n.*, trucco [*trook'-koh*]
trim *v.*, guarnire [*goo-ahr-nee'-reh*]
trip *n.*, viaggio, gita [*vee-ahj'-jee-oh, jee'-tah*]
trip [stumble] *v.*, inciampare [*een-chee-ahm-pah'-reh*]
triple, triplice [*tree'-plee-cheh*]
triumphant, trionfante [*tree-ohn-fahn'-teh*]
trivial, triviale [*tree-vee-ah'-leh*]
tropical, tropicale [*troh-pee-kah'-leh*]
trouble *n.*, disturbo [*dees-toor'-boh*]
trouble *v.*, disturbare [*dees-toor-bah'-reh*]
  Don't trouble yourself, Non si disturbi [*nohn see dees-toor'-bee*]
trousers, pantaloni lunghi (m, pl) [*pahn-tah-loh'-nee loon'-gee*]
truck, camion (m) [*kah-mee-ohn'*]
true, vero [*veh'-roh*]
  It is true, È vero [*eh' veh'-roh*]
  It isn't true, Non è vero [*nohn eh' veh'-roh*]
trunk [container], baule (m) [*bah-oo'-leh*]
trust *n.*, fiducia, credito [*fee-doo'-chee-ah, kreh'-dee-toh*]

trust *v.*, fidarsi [*fee-dahr'-see*]
truth, verità (f, indecl) [*veh-ree-tah'*]
try *v.*, tentare, provare [*tehn-tah'-reh, proh-vah'-reh*]
try on, provare [*proh-vah'-reh*]
tube, tubo [*too'-boh*]
Tuesday, martedì [*mahr-teh-dee'*]
tugboat, rimorchiatore (m) [*ree-mohr-kee-ah-toh'-reh*]
tune [melody] *n.*, aria [*ah'-ree-ah*]
tunnel, galleria sotterranea [*gahl-leh-ree'-ah soht-tehr-rah'-neh-ah*]
Turkey, Turchia [*toor-kee'-ah*]
Turkish, turco [*toor'-koh*]
turmoil, confusione (f) [*kohn-foo-zee-oh'-neh*]
Turin, Torino [*toh-ree'-noh*]
turn [order] *n.*, turno, giro [*toor'-noh, jee'-roh*]
turn [curve] *n.*, svolta, curva [*zvohl'-tah, koor'-vah*]
turn *v.*, girare [*jee-rah'-reh*]
turn around, rivoltarsi [*ree-vohl-tahr'-see*]
turn off, spegnere [*speh'-nyeh-reh*]
turn on, accendere [*ahch-chehn'-deh-reh*]
twelfth, dodicesimo [*doh-dee-cheh'-zee-moh*]
twelve, dodici [*doh'-dee-chee*]
twenty, venti [*vehn'-tee*]
twice, due volte [*doo'-eh vohl'-teh*]
twilight, crepuscolo [*kreh-poos'-koh-loh*]
twin, gemello [*jeh-mehl'-loh*]
twist *v.*, torcere [*tohr'-cheh-reh*]
two, due [*doo'-eh*]
type *n.*, tipo [*tee'-poh*]
type(write) *v.*, scrivere a macchina [*skree'-veh-reh ah mahk'-kee-nah*]
typewriter, macchina da scrivere [*mahk'-kee-nah dah skree'-veh-reh*]
typical, tipico [*tee'-pee-koh*]
typist, dattilografo [*daht-tee-loh'-grah-foh*]
tyrant, tiranno [*tee-rahn'-noh*]

U

ugly, brutto [*broot'-toh*]
ultimate, ultimo, finale [*ool'-tee-moh, fee-nah'-leh*]
umbrella, ombrello [*ohm-brehl'-loh*]
unable, incapace [*een-kah-pah'-cheh*]
be unable to . . . , non potere . . . [*nohn poh-teh'-reh*]
I am unable to come, Non posso venire [*nohn pohs'-soh veh-nee'-reh*]
unanimous, unanime [*oo-nah'-nee-meh*]
unbearable, insopportabile [*een-sohp-pohr-tah'-bee-leh*]
uncertain, incerto [*een-chehr'-toh*]
uncle, zio, zii (pl) [*dzee'-oh, dzee'-ee*]
uncomfortable scomodo [*skoh'-moh-doh*]
unconscious, inconsapevole [*een-kohn-sah-peh'-voh-leh*]
uncover *v.*, scoprire [*skoh-pree'-reh*]
undecided, indeciso [*een-deh-chee'-zoh*]
under, underneath, sotto [*soht'-toh*]
underground, sottosuolo [*soht-toh-soo-oh'-loh*]
understand *v.*, comprendere, capire [*kohm-prehn'-deh-reh, kah-pee'-reh*]
Do you understand? Comprende lei? [*kohm-prehn'-deh leh'-ee*]
It is understood, È inteso [*eh' een-teh'-zoh*]
understanding *n.*, intesa [*een-teh'-zah*]
undertake *v.*, intraprendere [*een-trah-prehn'-deh-reh*]
undertaking, impresa [*eem-preh'-zah*]
underwear, biancheria personale [*bee-ahn-keh-ree'-ah pehr-soh-nah'-leh*]
undress *v.*, svestire [*zvehs-tee'-reh*]
undress oneself, svestirsi, spogliarsi [*zvehs-teer'-see, spoh-lyahr'-see*]
uneasy, inquieto [*een-koo-ee-eh'-toh*]
unemployed, disoccupato [*deez-ohk-koo-pah'-toh*]

unequal, disuguale [*deez-oo-goo-ah'-leh*]
unexpected, inatteso [*een-aht-teh'-zoh*]
unfair, ingiusto [*een-jee-oos'-toh*]
unfaithful, infedele [*een-feh-deh'-leh*]
unfavorable, sfavorevole [*sfah-voh-reh'-voh-leh*]
unforeseen, imprevisto [*eem-preh-vees'-toh*]
unforgettable, indimenticabile [*een-dee-mehn-tee-kah'-bee-leh*]
unforgiving, implacabile [*eem-plah-kah'-bee-leh*]
unforgivable, imperdonabile [*eem-pehr-doh-nah'-bee-leh*]
unfortunate, disgraziato [*deez-grah-tsee-ah'-toh*]
unfortunately, disgraziatamente [*deez-grah-tsee-ah-tah-mehn'-teh*]
ungrateful, ingrato [*een-grah'-toh*]
unhappy, infelice [*een-feh-lee'-cheh*]
unharmed, illeso [*eel-leh'-zoh*]
unhealthy, malsano [*mahl-sah'-noh*]
uniform, uniforme [*oo-nee-fohr'-meh*]
unimportant, insignificante [*een-see-nyee-fee-kahn'-teh*]
uninteresting, non interessante [*nohn een-teh-rehs-sahn'-teh*]
union [labor union], sindicato [*seen-dee-kah'-toh*]
unit, **unity**, unità (f, indecl) [*oo-nee-tah'*]
unite *v.*, unire [*oo-nee'-reh*]
united, unito [*oo-nee'-toh*]
United States, gli Stati Uniti [*lyee stah'-tee oo-nee'-tee*]
universal, universale [*oo-nee-vehr-sah'-leh*]
universe, universo [*oo-nee-vehr'-soh*]
university, università (f, indecl) [*oo-nee-vehr-see-tah'*]
unjust, ingiusto [*een-jee-oos'-toh*]
unkind, scortese [*skohr-teh'-zeh*]
unknown, sconosciuto [*skoh-noh-shee-oo'-toh*]
unlawful, illegale [*eel-leh-gah'-leh*]
unless, a meno che, eccetto [*ah meh'-noh keh, ehch-cheht'-toh*]
unlike, dissimile, a differenza di [*dees-see'-mee-leh, ah deef-feh-rehn'-tsah dee*]
unlikely, improbabile [*eem-proh-bah'-bee-leh*]
unload *v.*, scaricare [*skah-ree-kah'-reh*]

unlock *v.*, aprire [*ah-pree'-reh*]
unlucky, sfortunato [*sfohr-too-nah'-toh*]
unoccupied, disoccupato [*deez-ohk-koo-pah'-toh*]
unorganized, disorganizzato [*deez-ohr-gah-needz-dzah'-toh*]
unpack *v.*, disfare [*dees-fah'-reh*]
unpleasant, sgradevole [*zgrah-deh'-voh-leh*]
unprepared, impreparato [*eem-preh-pah-rah'-toh*]
unselfish, disinteressato [*deez-een-teh-rehs-sah'-toh*]
until, finchè [*feen-keh'*]
untrue, falso, non vero, inesatto [*fahl'-soh, nohn veh'-roh, een-eh-zaht'-toh*]
unusual, insolito [*een-soh'-lee-toh*]
unwelcome, sgradito [*zgrah-dee'-toh*]
unwilling, maldisposto [*mahl-dees-pohs'-toh*]
unyielding, inflessibile [*een-flehs-see'-bee-leh*]
up, sopra, su [*soh'-prah, soo*]
get up *v.*, alzarsi [*ahl-tsahr'-see*]
go up *v.*, salire [*sah-lee'-reh*]
up and down, su e giù [*soo eh jee-oo'*]
up to now, fino ad ora [*fee'-noh ahd oh'-rah*]
upbringing, educazione (f) [*eh-doo-kah-tsee-oh'-neh*]
uphill, ripido [*ree'-pee-doh*]
uphold *v.*, sostenere [*sohs-teh-neh'-reh*]
upon, su, sopra [*soo, soh'-prah*]
upper, superiore [*soo-peh-ree-oh'-reh*]
upper floor, piano di sopra [*pee-ah'-noh dee soh'-prah*]
uproar, tumulto [*too-mool'-toh*]
ups and downs (of life), gli alti e bassi (della vita) [*lyee ahl'-tee eh bahs'-see (deh'-lah vee-tah)*]
upset *adj.*, preoccupato [*preh-ohk-koo-pah'-toh*]
upside down, sotto sopra, capovolto [*soht-toh-soh'-prah, kah-poh-vohl'-toh*]
upstairs, al piano superiore [*ahl pee-ah'-noh soo-peh-ree-oh'-reh*]
up-to-date, aggiornato [*ahj-jee-ohr-nah'-toh*]
urban, urbano [*oor-bah'-noh*]
urgent, urgente [*oor-jehn'-teh*]
us, noi, ci [*noh'-ee, chee*]

to us, a noi [*ah noh'-ee*]
They call us, Ci chiamano [*chee kee-ah'-mah-noh*]
use *n.*, uso [*oo'-zoh*]
use *v.*, usare [*oo-zah'-reh*]
What is this used for! A che cosa serve questo? [*ah keh koh'-zah sehr'-veh koo-ehs'-toh*]
be used to *v.*, essere abituato [*ehs'-seh-reh ah-bee-too-ah'-toh*]
used, usato [*oo-zah'-to*]
useful, utile [*oo'-tee-leh*]
useless, inutile [*een-oo'-tee-leh*]
usher, usciere (m) [*oo-shee-eh'-reh*]
usual, abituale [*ah-bee-too-ah'-leh*]
usually, di solito, abitualmente [*dee soh'-lee-toh, ah-bee-too-ahl-mehn'-teh*]
utmost, massimo [*mahs'-see-moh*]

V

vacancy, disponibilità (f, indecl), posto vacante [*dees-poh-nee-bee-lee-tah', pohs'-toh vah-kahn'-teh*]
no vacancy, nessuna camera libera [*nehs-soo'-nah kah'-meh-rah lee'-beh-rah*]
vacant, vacante [*vah-kahn'-teh*]
vacation, vacanza [*vah-kahn'-tsah*]
vaccination, vaccinazione (f) [*vahch-chee-nah-tsee-oh'-neh*]
vacuum cleaner, aspirapolvere (m) [*ahs-pee-rah-pohl'-veh-reh*]
vague, vago [*vah'-goh*]
vain, vano, vanitoso [*vah'-noh, vah-nee-toh'-zoh*]
in vain, invano [*een-vah'-noh*]
valid, valido [*vah'-lee-doh*]
valley, valle (f) [*vahl'-leh*]
valuable, prezioso [*preh-tsee-oh'-zoh*]
value *n.*, valore (m) [*vah-loh'-reh*]

value *v.*, stimare, apprezzare [*stee-mah'-reh, ahp-prehts-tsah'-reh*]
vanish *v.*, svanire, sparire [*zvah-nee'-reh, spah-ree'-reh*]
vanity, vanità (f, indecl) [*van-nee-tah'*]
variety, varietà (f, indecl) [*vah-ree-eh-tah'*]
various, vari, diversi [*vah'-ree, dee-vehr'-see*]
vast, vasto [*vahs'-toh*]
Vatican, Vaticano [*vah-tee-kah'-noh*]
vault, volta [*vohl'-tah*]
veal, carne (f) di vitello [*kahr'-neh dee vee-tehl'-loh*]
vegetables, legumi [*leh-goo'-mee*]
vehicle, veicolo [*veh-ee'-koh-loh*]
veil *n.*, velo [*veh'-loh*]
vein, vena [*veh'-nah*]
velvet, velluto [*vehl-loo'-toh*]
Venice, Venezia [*veh-neh'-tsee-ah*]
verb, verbo [*vehr'-boh*]
verdict, verdetto, sentenza [*vehr-deht'-toh, sehn-tehn'-tsah*]
verge *n.*, bordo, orlo [*bohr'-doh, ohr'-loh*]
verify *v.*, verificare [*veh-ree-fee-kah'-reh*]
versatile, versatile [*vehr-sah'-tee-leh*]
verse, verso [*vehr'-soh*]
version, versione (f) [*vehr-see-oh'-neh*]
vertical, verticale [*vehr-tee-kah'-leh*]
very, molto, troppo [*mohl'-toh, trohp'-poh*]
  very bad, malissimo [*mah-lees'-see-moh*]
  very much, moltissimo [*mohl-tees'-see-moh*]
  very well, benissimo [*beh-nees'-see-moh*]
veteran, veterano [*veh-teh-rah'-noh*]
veterinary, veterinario [*veh-teh-ree-nah'-ree-oh*]
vibrate *v.*, vibrare [*vee-brah'-reh*]
vice, vizio [*vee'-tsee-oh*]
vicinity, vicinanza [*vee-chee-nahn'-tsah*]
vicious, vizioso, corrotto [*vee-tsee-oh'-zoh, kohr-roht'-toh*]
victim, vittima [*veet'-tee-mah*]
victory, vittoria [*veet-toh'-ree-ah*]
view *n.*, vista, veduta [*vees'-tah, vee-doo'-tah*]
viewpoint, punto di vista [*poon'-toh dee vees'-tah*]

vigorous, vigoroso [*vee-goh-roh'-zoh*]
villa, villa [*veel'-lah*]
village, villaggio [*veel-lahj'-jee-oh*]
villain, furfante (m) [*foor-fahn'-teh*]
vine, vigna [*vee'-nyah*]
vinegar, aceto [*ah-cheh'-toh*]
violate *v.*, violare [*vee-oh-lah'-reh*]
violence, violenza [*vee-oh-lehn'-tsah*]
violin, violino [*vee-oh-lee'-noh*]
virgin, vergine [*vehr'-jee-neh*]
virtue, virtù (f, indecl) [*veer-too'*]
visa, visto [*vees'-toh*]
visible, visibile [*vee-zee'-bee-leh*]
vision, visione (f) [*vee-zee-oh'-neh*]
visit *n.*, visita [*vee'-zee-tah*]
  pay a visit to *v.*, fare una visita [*fah'-reh oo'-nah vee'-zee-tah*]
visit *v.*, visitare [*vee-zee-tah'-reh*]
visiting-card, biglietto da visita [*bee-lyeht'-toh dah vee'-zee-tah*]
visitor, visitatore (m), visitatrice (f) [*vee-zee-tah-toh'-reh, vee-zee-tah-tree'-cheh*]
vocabulary, vocabolario [*voh-kah-boh-lah'-ree-oh*]
vocal, vocale [*voh-kah'-leh*]
vocation, vocazione (f) [*voh-kah-tsee-oh'-neh*]
vocational, professionale [*proh-fehs-see-oh-nah'-leh*]
voice *n.*, voce (f) [*voh'-cheh*]
volcano, vulcano [*vool-kah'-noh*]
volume, volume (m) [*voh-loo'-meh*]
vomit *v.*, vomitare [*voh-mee-tah'-reh*]
vote *n.*, voto [*voh'-toh*]
vote *v.*, votare [*voh-tah'-reh*]
voucher, garante (m) [*gah-rahn'-teh*]
vow *n.*, voto (sacro) [*voh'-toh (sah'-kroh)*]
vowel, vocale (f) [*voh-kah'-leh*]
voyage *n.*, viaggio (per mare) [*vee-ahj'-jee-oh (pehr mah'-reh)*]
vulgar, volgare [*vohl-gah'-reh*]
vulnerable, vulnerabile [*vool-neh-rah'-bee-leh*]

W

wages, salario (m, sing) [*sah-lah'-ree-oh*]
wagon, vagone (m) [*vah-goh'-neh*]
waist, vita [*vee-tah*]
wait *v.*, aspettare [*ahs-peht-tah'-reh*]
  Wait a moment! Aspetti un momento! [*ahs-peht'-tee oon moh-mehn'-toh*]
  Wait for me, Mi aspetti [*mee ahs-peht'-tee*]
waiter, cameriere (m) [*kah-meh-ree-eh'-reh*]
waiting room, sala d'aspetto [*sah'-lah dahs-peht'-toh*]
waitress, cameriera [*kah-meh-ree-eh'-rah*]
wake up *v.*, svegliare [*zveh-lyah'-reh*]
wake up [oneself], svegliarsi [*zveh-lyahr'-see*]
walk *n.*, passeggiata [*pahs-sehj-jee-ah'-tah*]
  take a walk *v.*, fare una passeggiata [*fah'-reh oo'-nah pahs-sehj-jee-ah'-tah*]
walk *v.*, camminare [*kahm-mee-nah'-reh*]
  walk in, entrare [*ehn-trah'-reh*]
  walk out, uscire [*oo-shee'-reh*]
wall, muro, parete (f) [*moo'-roh, pah-reh'-teh*]
wallet, portafoglio [*pohr-tah-foh'-lyoh*]
wander, *v.* vagare [*vah-gah'-reh*]
want *v.*, volere (irreg) [*voh-leh'-reh*]
war, guerra [*goo-ehr'-rah*]
wardrobe, armadio [*ahr-mah'-dee-oh*]
warehouse, magazzino [*mah-gahdz-dzee'-noh*]
warm *adj.*, caldo [*kahl'-doh*]
warm *v.*, riscaldare [*rees-kahl-dah'-reh*]
warmth, calore (m) [*kah-loh'-reh*]
warn *v.*, avvertire [*ahv-vehr-tee'-reh*]
warning, avvertimento [*ahv-vehr-tee-mehn'-toh*]
warrant *n.*, mandato, autorizzazione (f) [*mahn-dah'-toh, ah-oo-toh-reedz-dzah-tsee-oh'-neh*]

was, ero, era [*eh'-roh, eh'-rah*]
  There was . . . , C'era . . . [*cheh'-rah*]
wash *v.*, lavare [*lah-vah'-reh*]
  wash [oneself], lavarsi [*lah-vahr'-see*]
washbasin, lavabó [*lah-vah-boh'*]
waste *v.*, sciupare, sprecare [*shee-oo-pah'-reh, spreh-kah'-reh*]
wastebasket, cestino [*chehs-tee'-noh*]
watch *n.*, orologio [*oh-roh-loh'-jee-oh*]
  wind a watch *v.*, caricare l'orologio [*kah-ree-kah'-reh loh-roh-loh'-jee-oh*]
  wristwatch, orologio da polso [*oh-roh-loh'-jee-oh dah pohl'-soh*]
watch *v.*, sorvegliare, osservare [*sohr-veh-lyah'-reh, ohs-sehr-vah'-reh*]
  Watch out! Attento! [*aht-tehn'-toh*]
watchmaker, orologiaio [*oh-roh-loh-jee-ah'-ee-oh*]
watchman, guardiano [*goo-ahr-dee-ah'-noh*]
water, acqua [*ahk'-koo-ah*]
  fresh water, acqua fresca [*ahk'-koo-ah frehs'-kah*]
  mineral water, acqua minerale [*ahk'-koo-ah mee-neh-rah'-leh*]
  running water, acqua corrente [*ahk'-koo-ah kohr-rehn'-teh*]
water bottle, borraccia [*bohr-rahch'-chee-ah*]
water closet, latrina [*lah-tree'-nah*]
watercolors, acquarello [*ahk-koo-ah-rehl'-loh*]
waterfall, cascata [*kahs-kah'-tah*]
watermelon, cocomero [*koh-koh'-meh-roh*]
wave *n.*, onda, ondata, cenno [*ohn'-dah, ohn-dah'-tah, chehn'-noh*]
  short wave, onde corte (f, pl) [*ohn'-deh kohr'-teh*]
wave *v.*, ondeggiare, ondulare [*ohn-dehj-jee-ah'-reh, ohn-doo-lah'-reh*]
  wave [one's hand], fare cenno [*fah'-reh chehn'-noh*]
wax *n.*, cera [*cheh'-rah*]
way [route] *n.*, via [*vee'-ah*]
  Is this the right way? È questa la via giusta? [*eh' koo-*

ehs'-tah lah vee'-ah jee-oos'-tah]
way [manner] *n.*, modo, maniera [*moh'-doh, mah-nee-eh'-rah*]
by the way, a proposito [*ah proh-poh'-zee-toh*]
in no way, in nessun modo [*een nehs-soon' moh'-doh*]
in this way, in questa maniera [*een koo-ehs'-tah mah-nee-eh'-rah*]
we, noi [*noh'-ee*]
weak, debole [*deh'-boh-leh*]
weakness, debolezza [*deh-boh-lehts'-tsah*]
wealth, ricchezza [*reek-kehts'-tsah*]
wealthy, ricco [*reek'-koh*]
weapon, arma [*ahr'-mah*]
wear [clothes] *v.*, indossare [*een-dohs-sah'-reh*]
wear [glasses] *v.*, portare [*pohr-tah'-reh*]
wear out, consumare [*kohn-soo-mah'-reh*]
weary, stanco [*stahn'-koh*]
weather *n.*, tempo [*tehm'-poh*]
How is the weather? Come è il tempo? [*koh'-meh eh' eel tehm'-poh*]
wedding, nozze (f, pl) [*nohts'-tseh*]
wedding cake, torta nuziale [*tohr'-tah noo-tsee-ah'-leh*]
wedding ring, fede (f) [*feh'-deh*]
Wednesday, mercoledì [*mehr-koh-leh-dee'*]
weed *n.*, erbaccia [*ehr-bahch'-chee-ah*]
week, settimana [*seht-tee-mah'-nah*]
last week, la settimana scorsa [*lah seht-tee-mah'-nah skohr'-sah*]
next week, la settimana prossima [*lah seht-tee-mah'-nah prohs'-see-mah*]
weekend, fine-settimana [*fee-neh-seht-tee-mah'-nah*]
weekly, settimanale [*seht-tee-mah-nah'-leh*]
weep *v.*, piangere [*pee-ahn'-jeh-reh*]
weigh *v.*, pesare [*peh-zah'-reh*]
weight, peso [*peh'-zoh*]
welcome *n.*, benvenuto [*behn-veh-noo'-toh*]
You're welcome! Prego! [*preh'-goh*]
welcome *v.*, dare il benvenuto, accogliere [*dah'-reh eel behn-veh-noo'-toh, ahk-koh'-lyeh-reh*]
welfare, benessere (m) [*behn-ehs'-seh-reh*]

well *n.*, pozzo [*pohts'-tsoh*]
well *adv. & adj.*, bene [*beh'-neh*]
be well *v.*, stare bene [*stah'-reh beh'-neh*]
Well! Bene! [*beh'-neh*]
well-bred, educato [*eh-doo-kah'-toh*]
well-known, molto conosciuto [*mohl'-toh koh-noh-shee-oo'-toh*]
well-off, benestante [*beh-neh-stahn'-teh*]
were, eravamo, eravate, erano (1st, 2nd & 3rd person pl) [*eh-rah-vah'-moh, eh-rah-vah'-teh, eh'-rah-noh*]
There were . . . C'erano . . . [*cheh'-rah-noh*]
west, ovest (m), occidente (m) [*oh'-vehst, ohch-chee-dehn'-teh*]
western *adj.*, occidentale [*ohch-chee-dehn-tah'-leh*]
wet *adj.*, bagnato [*bah-nyah'-toh*]
get wet *v.*, bagnarsi [*bah-nyahr'-see*]
what, che, che cosa, quale [*keh, keh koh'-zah, koo-ah'-leh*]
What a pity! Che peccato! [*keh pehk-kah'-toh*]
What else? Che altro? [*keh ahl'-troh*]
What for? Perchè? [*pehr-keh'*]
What is the matter? Che succede? [*keh sooch-cheh'-deh*]
whatever, qualunque [*koo-ah-loon'-koo-eh*]
whatever you wish, quello che desidera [*koo-ehl'-loh keh deh-zee'-deh-rah*]
wheel, ruota [*roo-oh'-tah*]
steering wheel, volante (m) [*voh-lahn'-teh*]
when, quando [*koo-ahn'-doh*]
since when, da quando [*dah koo-ahn'-doh*]
When will you (he, she) return? Quando ritornerà? [*koo-ahn'-doh ree-tohr-neh-rah'*]
whenever, ogni volta che [*oh'-nyee vohl'-tah keh*]
where, dove [*doh'-veh*]
Where is it (he, she)? Dov'è? [*doh-veh'*]
Wherever, dovunque [*doh-voon'-koo-eh*]
whether, se [*seh*]
Whether he comes or not . . . Se viene oppure non viene . . [*seh vee-eh'-neh ohp-poo'-reh nohn vee-eh'-neh*]
which [of several] *adj. & pron.*, quale [*koo-ah'-leh*]
which *rel. pron.*, chi [*kee*]
while *cons.*, mentre [*mehn'-treh*]

While I was eating, Mentre mangiavo [*mehn'-treh mahn-jee-ah'-voh*]
a while ago, poco tempo fa [*poh'-koh tehm'-poh fah*]
whisper *n.*, mormorio [*mohr-moh-ree'-oh*]
whisper *v.*, sussurrare [*soos-soor-rah'-reh*]
whistle *n.*, fischio [*fees'-kee-oh*]
whistle *v.*, fischiare [*fees-kee-ah'-reh*]
white, bianco [*bee-ahn'-koh*]
who, che [*keh*]
who? chi? [*kee*]
whoever, chiunque [*kee-oon'-koo-eh*]
whole *n. & adj.*, tutto, intero [*toot'-toh, een-teh'-roh*]
wholehearted, cordiale, sincero, leale [*kohr-dee-ah'-leh, seen-cheh'-roh, leh-ah'-leh*]
wholesale, vendita all'ingrosso [*vehn'-dee-tah ahl-leen-grohs'-soh*]
whom, chi, che, cui [*kee, keh, koo'-ee*]
whom? chi?, che? [*kee, keh*]
whose, di chi? di cui? [*dee kee, dee koo'-ee*]
why, perchè [*pehr-keh'*]
why not? perchè no? [*pehr-keh' noh*]
wicked, malvagio [*mahl-vah'-jee-oh*]
wide, largo, ampio [*lahr'-goh, ahm'-pee-oh*]
wide-awake, tutto sveglio [*toot'-toh sveh'-lyoh*]
wide-open, spalancato [*spah-lahn-kah'-toh*]
widespread, diffuso [*deef-foo'-zoh*]
widow, vedova [*veh'-doh-vah*]
widower, vedovo [*veh'-doh-voh*]
width, larghezza [*lahr-gehts'-tsah*]
wife, moglie (f) [*moh'-lyeh*]
wig, parrucca [*pahr-rook'-kah*]
wild, selvaggio [*sehl-vahj'-jee-oh*]
will *n.*, volontà (f, indecl), desiderio [*voh-lohn-tah', deh-zee-deh'-ree-oh*]
will *v.*, volere (irreg), desiderare [*voh-leh'-reh, deh-zee-deh-rah'-reh*]
I will go, (io) andrò [(*ee'-oh*) *ahn-droh'*]
Will you have a cigarette? Desidera una sigaretta? [*deh-zee'-deh-rah oo'-nah see-gah-reht'-tah*]
willing, disposto [*dees-pohs'-toh*]

I am willing to . . . Sono disposto a . . . [*soh'-noh dees-pohs'-toh ah*]
willingly, volentieri [*voh-lehn-tee-eh'-ree*]
willpower, forza di volontà [*fohr'-tsah dee voh-lohn-tah'*]
win *v.*, vincere [*veen'-cheh-reh*]
wind *n.*, vento [*vehn'-toh*]
windmill, mulino a vento [*moo-lee'-noh ah vehn'-toh*]
window [car, train], finestrino [*fee-nehs-tree'-noh*]
window [house], finestra [*fee-nehs'-trah*]
windowpane, vetro della finestra [*veh'-troh dehl'-lah fee-nehs'-trah*]
windshield, parabrezza [*pah-rah-brehts'-tsah*]
wine, vino [*vee'-noh*]
red wine, vino rosso [*vee'-noh rohs'-soh*]
white wine, vino bianco [*vee'-noh bee-ahn'-koh*]
wing, ala, le ali (pl), [*ah'-lah, leh ah'-lee*]
winner, vincitore (m), vincitrice (f) [*veen-chee-toh'-reh, veen-chee-tree'-cheh*]
winter, inverno [*een-vehr'-noh*]
wipe *v.*, asciugare, pulire [*ah-shee-oo-gah'-reh, poo-lee'-reh*]
wipe off, cancellare [*kahn-chehl-lah'-reh*]
wire [filament] *n.*, filo [*fee'-loh*]
wire [telegraph] *v.*, telegrafare [*teh-leh-grah-fah'-reh*]
wireless, radio (f), senza filo [*rah'-dee-oh, sehn'-tsah fee'-loh*]
wisdom, saggezza, prudenza [*sahj-jehts'-tsah, proo-dehn'-tsah*]
wise, saggio [*sahj'-jee-oh*]
wish *n.*, desiderio [*deh-zee-deh'-ree-oh*]
wish *v.*, desiderare [*deh-zee-deh-rah'-reh*]
What do you wish? Cosa desidera? [*koh'-zah deh-zee'-deh-rah*]
wit, ingegno, spirito [*een-jeh'-nyoh, spee'-ree-toh*]
with, con [*kohn*]
withdraw *v.*, ritirare [*ree-tee-rah'-reh*]
withhold *v.*, trattenere (irreg) [*traht-teh-neh'-reh*]
within, dentro, fra [*dehn'-troh, frah*]
without, senza [*sehn'-tsah*]
withstand *v.*, resistere [*reh-zees'-teh-reh*]
witness *n.*, testimone (m, f) [*tehs-tee-moh'-neh*]
witness *v.*, testimoniare [*tehs-tee-moh-nee-ah'-reh*]

witty, intelligente [*een-tehl-lee-jehn'-teh*]
woman, donna [*dohn'-nah*]
wonder *v.*, meravigliarsi [*meh-rah-vee-lyahr'-see*]
wonderful, meraviglioso [*meh-rah-vee-lyoh'-zoh*]
wood, legno [*leh'-nyoh*]
wooden, di legno [*dee leh'-nyoh*]
woods, bosco [*bohs'-koh*]
wool, lana [*lah'-nah*]
word, parola [*pah-roh'-lah*]
work *n.*, lavoro [*lah-voh'-roh*]
  work of art, opera d'arte [*oh'-peh-rah dahr'-teh*]
work *v.*, lavorare [*lah-voh-rah'-reh*]
  Where do you work? Dove lavora? [*doh'-veh lah-voh'-rah*]
workday, giorno feriale [*jee-ohr'-noh feh-ree-ah'-leh*]
worker, lavoratore (m), lavoratrice (f) [*lah-voh-rah-toh'-reh, lah-voh-rah-tree'-cheh*]
working, lavoro, lavorando [*lah-voh'-roh, lah-voh-rahn'-doh*]
  This isn't working, Questo non funziona [*koo-ehs'-toh nohn foon-tsee-oh'-nah*]
workshop, officina, corso di specializzazione [*ohf-fee-chee'-nah, kohr'-soh dee speh-chee-ah-leedz-dzah-tsee-oh'-neh*]
world, mondo [*mohn'-doh*]
worldwide, diffuso [*deef-foo'-zoh*]
world war, guerra mondiale [*goo-ehr'-rah mohn-dee-ah'-leh*]
worn-out [objects], consumato [*kohn-soo-mah'-toh*]
worn-out [persons], esausto [*eh-zah'-oos-toh*]
worried, preoccupato [*preh-ohk-koo-pah'-toh*]
worry *n.*, preoccupazione (f) [*preh-ohk-koo-pah-tsee-oh'-neh*]
worry *v.*, preoccuparsi [*preh-ohk-koo-pahr'-see*]
  Don't worry! Non si preoccupi! [*nohn see preh-ohk'-koo-pee*]
worse, peggio, peggiore [*pehj'-jee-oh, pehj-jee-oh'-reh*]
  worse than, peggiore di [*pehj-jee-oh'-reh dee*]
worship *n.*, adorazione (f) [*ah-doh-rah-tsee-oh'-neh*]
worship *v.*, adorare [*ah-doh-rah'-reh*]
worst *adj.*, il peggiore, la peggiore [*eel pehj-jee-oh'-reh, lah pehj-jee-oh'-reh*]
  the worst of all, il peggiore di tutti [*eel pehj-jee-oh'-reh dee toot'-tee*]

worth, valore (m) [*vah-loh'-reh*]
be worth *v.*, valere [*vah-leh'-reh*]
How much is this worth? Quanto vale questo? [*koo-ahn'-toh vah'-leh koo-ehs'-toh*]
worthwhile, (che) ne vale la pena [(*keh*) *neh vah'-leh lah peh'-nah*]
It is not worthwhile, Non ne vale la pena [*nohn neh vah'-leh lah peh'-nah*]
wounded, ferito [*feh-ree'-toh*]
wrinkle *n.*, ruga [*roo'-gah*]
wrist, polso [*pohl'-soh*]
wristwatch, orologio da polso [*oh-roh-loh'-jee-oh dah pohl'-soh*]
write *v.*, scrivere [*skree'-veh-reh*]
writer, scrittore (m), scrittrice (f) [*skreet-toh'-reh, skreet-tree'-cheh*]
writing, scrittura, scritto [*skreet-too'-rah, skreet'-toh*]
writing paper, carta da scrivere [*kahr'-tah dah skree'-veh-reh*]
written, scritto [*skreet'-toh*]
wrong *adj.*, sbagliato [*zbah-lyah'-toh*]
be wrong *v.*, avere torto [*ah-veh'-reh tohr'-toh*]

X, Y, Z

x-ray, raggi x (pl) [*rahj'-jee ehks*]

yacht, panfilo [*pahn-fee'-loh*]
yard [courtyard], cortile (m) [*kohr-tee'-leh*]
yard [measure], iarda [*ee-ahr'-dah*]
yawn *v.*, sbadigliare [*zbah-dee-lyah'-reh*]
year, anno [*ahn'-noh*]
last year, l'anno scorso [*lahn'-noh skohr'-soh*]
next year, l'anno prossimo [*lahn'-noh prohs'-see-moh*]
yearly, annualmente [*ahn-noo-ahl-mehn'-teh*]
yell *v.*, gridare [*gree-dah'-reh*]
yes, sì [*see'*]

Yes indeed! Per davvero! [*pehr dahv-veh'-roh*]
yesterday, ieri [*ee-eh'-ree*]
the day before yesterday, l'altro ieri [*lahl'-troh ee-eh'-ree*]
yesterday evening, ieri sera [*ee-eh'-ree seh'-rah*]
yet *conj.*, tuttavia [*toot-tah-vee'-ah*]
not yet, non ancora [*nohn ahn-koh'-rah*]
yield *v.*, produrre (irreg), cedere [*proh-door'-reh, cheh'-deh-reh*]
you [polite form], lei (3rd pers. sing); loro (3rd pers. pl) [*leh'-ee, loh'-roh*]
you [informal address], tu (2nd person sing); voi (2nd person pl) [*too, voh'-ee*]
young, giovane [*jee-oh'-vah-neh*]
(the) young man, il giovane [*eel jee-oh'-vah-neh*]
(the) young woman, la giovane [*lah jee-oh'-vah-neh*]
your [formal & polite form], suo, sua (m & f sing); suoi, sue (m & f pl) [*soo'-oh, soo'-ah, soo-oh'-ee, soo'-eh*]
your [plural; polite form], il loro, la loro (m & f sing); i loro, le loro (m & f pl) [*eel loh'-roh, lah loh'-roh, ee loh'-roh, leh loh'-roh*]
your [informal form], tuo, tua (m & f sing); tuoi, tue (m & f pl) [*too'-oh, too'-ah, too-oh'-ee, too'-eh*]
your [plural; familiar], vostro, vostra (m & f sing); vostri, vostre (m & f pl) [*vohs'-troh, vohs'-trah, vohs'-tree, vohs'-treh*]
yourself, tu stesso (sing, informal form); lei stesso (sing, polite form) [*too stehs'-soh, leh'-ee stehs'-soh*]
yourselves, voi stessi (pl, informal form); loro stessi (pl, polite form) [*voh'-ee stehs'-see, loh'-roh stehs'-see*]
youth, gioventù (f, indecl) [*jee-oh-vehn-too'*]
youthful, giovanile [*jee-oh-vah-nee'-leh*]

zeal, zelo [*dzeh'-loh*]
zero, zero [*dzeh'-roh*]
zipper, chiusura lampo [*kee-oo-zoo'-rah lahm'-poh*]
zone, zona [*dzoh'-nah*]
zoo, giardino zoologico [*jee-ahr-dee'-noh dzoh-oh-loh'-jee-koh*]

Italian/English

A

a [*ah*] at, to, in
abbaiare *v.* [*ahb-bah-ee-ah'-reh*] bark
abbacchio [*ahb-bahk'-kee-oh*] lamb [food]
abbandonare *v.* [*ahb-bahn-doh-nah'-reh*] abandon
abbasso [*ahb-bahs'-soh*] below
abbastanza [*ahb-bahs-tahn'-tsah*] enough
  più che abbastanza [*pee-oo' keh ahb-bahs-tahn'-tsah*] more than enough
abbigliamento [*ahb-bee-lyah-mehn'-toh*] attire
abbonamento [*ahb-boh-nah-mehn'-toh*] subscription
abbondante [*ahb-bohn-dahn'-teh*] abundant
abbondanza [*ahb-bohn-dahn'-tsah*] abundance
  in abbondanza [*een ahb-bohn-dahn'-tsah*] plenty
abbottonare *v.* [*ahb-boht-toh-nah'-reh*] button
abbracciare *v.* [*ahb-brahch-chee-ah'-reh*] hug
abbraccio [*ahb-brach'-chee-oh*] hug
abbreviare *v.* [*ahb-breh-vee-ah'-reh*] shorten
abbronzato [*ahb-brohn-tsah'-toh*] sunburned
abbronzatura [*ahb-brohn-tsah-too'-rah*] tan
abbrustolire *v.* [*ahb-broos-toh-lee'-reh*] toast
abile [*ah'-bee-leh*] skillful, able
abilità *f. indecl.* [*ah-bee-lee-tah'*] ability
abitante [*ah-bee-tahn'-teh*] inhabitant
abitare *v.* [*ah-bee-tah'-reh*] live, inhabit
abitazione *f.* [*ah-bee-tah-tsee-oh'-neh*] home, residence
abito [*ah'-bee-toh*] suit, dress
  abito da sera [*ah'-bee-toh dah seh'-rah*] evening dress
abituale [*ah-bee-too-ah'-leh*] usual, customary
abitualmente [*ah-bee-too-ahl-mehn'-teh*] usually
abituato [*ah-bee-too-ah'-toh*] accustomed
abituarsi *v.* [*ah-bee-too-ahr'-see*] get accustomed
  essere abituato [*ehs'-seh-reh ah-bee-too-ah'-toh*] be accustomed
abitudine [*ah-bee-too'-dee-neh*] habit, costume, routine

abolire *v.* [*ah-boh-lee'-reh*] abolish
aborto [*ah-bohr'-toh*] abortion
abusare *v.* [*ah-boo-zah'-reh*] abuse
abuso [*ah-boo'-zoh*] abuse
accademia [*ahk-kah-deh'-mee-ah*] academy
accadere *v.* [*ahk-kah-deh'-reh*] happen, occur
accanto [*ahk-kahn'-toh*] near, beside
accendere *v. irreg.* [*ahch-chehn'-deh-reh*] light, turn on [light]
accendi-sigaro [*ahch-chehn-dee-see'-gah-roh*] (cigarette) lighter
accenno [*ahch-chen'-noh*] hint
accento [*ahch-chehn'-toh*] accent
accessibile [*ahch-chehs-see'-bee-leh*] accessible
accesso [*ahch-chehs'-soh*] access
accettare *v.* [*ahch-cheht-tah'-reh*] accept
accettazione *f.* [*ahch-cheht-tah-tsee-oh'-neh*] acceptance
acciaio [*ahch-chee-ah'-ee-oh*] steel
accidentale [*ahch-chee-dehn-tah'-leh*] accidental
acciuga [*ahch-chee-oo'-gah*] anchovy
acclamazione *f.* [*ahk-klah-mah-tsee-oh'-neh*] cheer
accludere *v. irreg.* [*ahk-kloo'-deh-reh*] inclose
accoglienza [*ahk-koh-lyehn'-tsah*] reception
accogliere *v. irreg.* [*ahk-koh'-lyeh-reh*] receive, welcome
accomodamento [*ahk-koh-moh-dah-mehn'-toh*] accommodation
accomodare *v.* [*ahk-koh-moh-dah'-reh*] accommodate
accomodarsi *v.* [*ahk-koh-moh-dahr'-see*] make oneself comfortable
Si accomodi! [*see ahk-koh'-moh-dee*] Sit down! Make yourself at home!
accompagnare *v.* [*ahk-kohm-pah-nyah'-reh*] accompany
acconsentire *v.* [*ahk-kohn-sehn-tee'-reh*] consent
accoppiare *v.*, [*ahk-kohp-pee-ah'-reh*] match
accordare *v.* [*ahk-kohr-dah'-reh*] grant, tune
accordo [*ahk-kohr'-doh*] agreement
essere *v.* **d'accordo** [*ehs'-seh-reh dahk-kohr'-doh*] agree
non essere *v.* **d'accordo** [*nohn ehs'-seh-reh dahk-kohr'-doh*] disagree
accorgersi *v.* [*ahk-kohr'-jehr-see*] notice, perceive

accuratezza [*ahk-koo-rah-tehts'-tsah*] accuracy
accurato [*ahk-koo-rah'-toh*] elaborate
accusa [*ahk-koo'-zah*] accusation
accusare *v.* [*ahk-koo-zah'-reh*] accuse
accusato [*ahk-koo-zah'-toh*] accused
accusatore *m.* [*ahk-koo-zah-toh'-reh*] accuser
aceto [*ah-cheh'-toh*] vinegar
acido [*ah'-chee-doh*] sour, acid
acqua [*ahk'-koo-ah*] water
  acqua corrente [*ahk'-koo-ah kohr-rehn'-teh*] running water
  acqua fresca [*ahk'-koo-ah frehs'-kah*] fresh water
  acqua minerale [*ahk'-koo-ah mee-neh-rah'-leh*] mineral water
  acqua ossigenata [*ahk'-koo-ah ohs-see-jeh-nah'-tah*] peroxide
  acqua seltz [*ahk'-koo-ah sehlts*] soda water
acquarello [*ahk-koo-ah-rehl'-loh*] water colors
acquistare *v.* [*ahk-koo-ees-tah'-reh*] purchase, acquire
acquisto [*ahk-koo-ees'-toh*] acquisition, purchase
adattamento [*ah-daht-tah-mehn'-toh*] adjustment
adattare *v.* [*ah-daht-tah'-reh*] adapt, fit
adatto [*ah-daht'-toh*] suitable
addebitare *v.* [*ahd-deh-bee-tah'-reh*] charge [a customer]
addestramento [*ahd-dehs-trah-mehn'-toh*] training
addestrare *v.* [*ahd-dehs-trah'-reh*] train
addizionare *v.* [*ahd-dee-tsee-oh-nah'-reh*] add up
addizione *f.* [*ahd-dee-tsee-oh'-neh*] addition
addormentarsi *v.* [*ahd-dohr-mehn-tahr'-see*] fall asleep
addormentato [*ahd-dohr-mehn-tah'-toh*] asleep
adeguato [*ah-deh-goo-ah'-toh*] adequate
adesso [*ah-dehs'-soh*] now
adorabile [*ah-doh-rah'-bee-leh*] adorable
adorare *v.* [*ah-doh-rah'-reh*] worship, adore
adorazione *f.* [*ah-doh-rah-tsee-oh'-neh*] worship
adornare *v.* [*ah-dohr-nah'-reh*] adorn
adottare *v.* [*ah-doht-tah'-reh*] adopt
adozione *f.* [*ah-doh-tsee-oh'-neh*] adoption
adulare *v.* [*ah-doo-lah'-reh*] flatter
adulatore *m.*, **adulatrice** *f.* [*ah-doo-lah-toh'-reh, ah-doo-lah-tree'-cheh*] flatterer

adulazione [*ah-doo-lah-tsee-oh'-neh*] flattery
adulto [*ah-dool'-toh*] adult
aereo, aeroplano [*ah-eh'-reh-oh, ah-eh-roh-plah'-noh*] airplane
aeroporto [*ah-eh-roh-pohr'-toh*] airport
affamare *v.* [*ahf-fah-mah'-reh*] starve
affamato [*ahf-fah-mah'-toh*] hungry
affare *m.* [*ahf-fah'-reh*] business, affair
  uomo d'affari [*oo-oh'-moh dahf-fah'-ree*] businessman
affascinante [*ahf-fah-shee-nahn'-teh*] charming
affascinare *v.* [*ahf-fah-shee-nah'-reh*] fascinate, charm
affatto [*ahf-faht'-toh*] at all
  niente affatto [*nee-ehn'-teh ahf-faht'-toh*] not at all
affermare *v.* [*ahf-fehr-mah'-reh*] affirm
affermativo [*ahf-fehr-mah-tee'-voh*] affirmative
afferrare *v.* [*ahf-fehr-rah'-reh*] grasp, apprehend
affetto [*ahf-feht'-toh*] affection
affettuosamente [*ahf-feht-too-oh-zah-mehn'-teh*] affectionately
affettuoso [*ahf-feht-too-oh'-zoh*] affectionate
affezione *f.* [*ahf-feh-tsee-oh'-neh*] affection
affinchè [*ahf-feen-keh'*] in order that
affittare *v.* [*ahf-feet-tah'-reh*] let, rent, lease
  contratto d'affitto [*kohn-traht'-toh dahf-feet'-toh*] lease
  da affittare [*dah ahf-feet-tah'-reh*] for rent
  stanza d'affittare [*stahn'-tsah dahf-feet-tah'-reh*] room to let
affitto [*ahf-feet'-toh*] rent
affliggere *v. irreg.* [*ahf-fleej'-jeh-reh*] afflict, grieve
afflusso [*ahf-floos'-soh*] rush
affollato [*ahf-fohl-lah'-toh*] crowded
affondare *v.* [*ahf-fohn-dah'-reh*] sink
affrancatura [*ahf-frahn-kah-too'-rah*] postage
Africa [*ah'-free-kah*] Africa
africano [*ah-free-kah'-noh*] African
affrontare *v.* [*ahf-frohn-tah'-reh*] face
agente *m.* [*ah-jehn'-teh*] agent
  agente di cambio [*ah-jehn'-teh dee kahm'-bee-oh*] stockbroker, money changer
  agente investigativo [*ah-jehn'-teh een-vehs-tee-gah-tee'-voh*] detective

agenzia [*ah-jehn-tsee'-ah*] agency
agenzia di collocamento [*ah-jehn-tsee'-ah dee kohl-loh-kah-mehn'-toh*] employment agency
agenzia di viaggi [*ah-jehn-tsee'-ah dee vee-ahj'-jee*] travel agency
aggettivo [*ahj-jeht-tee'-voh*] adjective
aggiornato [*ahj-jee-ohr-nah'-toh*] up-to-date
aggiungere *v.* [*ahj-jee-oon'-jeh-reh*] add
aggiustare *v.* [*ahj-jee-oos-tah'-reh*] adjust
aggressione *f.* [*ahg-grehs-see-oh'-neh*] aggression
aggressivo [*ahg-grehs-see'-voh*] aggressive
agiato [*ah-jee-ah'-toh*] well-off
agile [*ah'-jee-leh*] agile, nimble
agio [*ah'-jee-oh*] leisure
agire *v.* [*ah-jee'-reh*] act
agitare *v.* [*ah-jee-tah'-reh*] agitate, shake
agitarsi *v.* [*ah-jee-tahr'-see*] get excited
Non si agiti! [*nohn see ah'-jee-tee*] Don't get excited!
agitato [*ah-jee-tah'-toh*] agitated, excited
agli: a gli *m. pl.* [*ah'-lyee*] to the, at the
aglio [*ah'-lyoh*] garlic
agnello [*ah-nyehl'-loh*] lamb [animal]
ago [*ah'-goh*] needle
agonia [*ah-goh-nee'-ah*] agony
agosto [*ah-gohs'-toh*] August
agricoltura [*ah-gree-kohl-too'-rah*] agriculture
ai *m. pl.* [*ah'-ee*] to the, at the
aiutare *v.* [*ah-ee-oo-tah'-reh*] aid, help
aiuto [*ah-ee-oo'-toh*] help, assistance
Aiuto! [*ah-ee-oo'-toh*] Help!
al: a il [*ahl*] to the, at the
ala, le ali *pl.* [*ah'-lah, leh ah'-lee*] wing
alba [*ahl'-bah*] dawn
albanese [*ahl-bah-neh'-zeh*] Albanian
Albania [*ahl-bah-nee'-ah*] Albania
albergo [*ahl-behr'-goh*] hotel
all'albergo [*ahl-lahl-behr'-goh*] at the hotel
albero [*ahl'-beh-roh*] tree
alcool [*ahl'-koh-ohl*] alcohol
alcuni *pl.* [*ahl-koo'-nee*] some

alcuni uomini [*ahl-koo'-nee oo-oh'-mee-nee*] some men
alcune volte [*ahl-koo'-neh vohl'-teh*] sometimes
alcuno [*ahl-koo'-noh*] any, anyone
alfabeto [*ahl-fah-beh'-toh*] alphabet
alimentare *v.* [*ah-lee-mehn-tah'-reh*] feed, nourish
aliquota [*ah-lee'-koo-oh-tah*] quota
alito [*ah'-lee-toh*] breath
alla: a la [*ahl*] to the, at the
alla, all' [*ahl-lah, ahl*] in the manner of
all'americana [*ahl-lah-meh-ree-kah'-nah*] in the American way
allarmare *v.* [*ahl-lahr-mah'-reh*] alarm
allarmarsi *v.* [*ahl-lahr-mahr'-see*] get alarmed
allarme *m.* [*ahl-lahr'-meh*] alarm
alle: a le *f. pl.* [*ahl'-leh*] to the, at the
alleanza [*ahl-leh-ahn'-tsah*] alliance
alleato [*ahl-leh-ah'-toh*] allied
allegria [*ahl-leh-gree'-ah*] joy
allegro [*ahl-leh'-groh*] cheerful, gay, merry
allergico [*ahl-lehr'-jee-koh*] allergic
allevare *v.* [*ahl-leh-vah'-reh*] rear
alleviare *v.* [*ahl-leh-vee-ah'-reh*] relieve
allievo [*ahl-lee-eh'-voh*] pupil
alloggiare *v.* [*ahl-lohj-jee-ah'-reh*] lodge
alloggio [*ahl-lohj'-jee-oh*] lodging
allontanarsi *v.* [*ahl-lohn-tah-nahr'-see*] go away
allora [*ahl-loh'-rah*] then
fin da allora [*feen dah ahl-loh'-rah*] since then
da allora in poi [*dah ahl-loh'-rah een poh'-ee*] from that time
alludere *v.* [*ahl-loo'-deh-reh*] hint
allusione *f.* [*ahl-loo-zee-oh'-neh*] allusion, hint
Alpi *f. pl.* [*ahl'-pee*] Alps
alquanto [*ahl-koo-ahn'-toh*] somewhat, rather
Alt! [*ahlt*] Stop!
altare *m.* [*ahl-tah'-reh*] altar
altezza [*ahl-tehts'-tsah*] height
altitudine *f.* [*ahl-tee-too'-dee-neh*] altitude
alto [*ahl'-toh*] high, tall
ad alta voce [*ahd ahl'-tah voh'-cheh*] aloud

più alto [*pee-oo' ahl'-toh*] higher, taller
altoparlante [*ahl-toh-pahr-lahn'-teh*] loudspeaker
altretanto [*ahl-treh-tahn'-toh*] likewise
altrimenti [*ahl-tree-mehn'-tee*] otherwise
altro [*ahl'-troh*] other, else
in un altro posto [*een oon ahl'-troh pohs'-toh*] somewhere else
l'un l'altro [*loon lahl'-troh*] each other
nessun altro [*nehs-soon' ahl'-troh*] nobody else
Nient' altro? [*nee-ehnt-ahl'-troh*] Nothing else?
Qualche altra cosa? [*koo-ahl'-keh ahl'-trah koh'-zah*] Anything else?
qualcun altro [*koo-ahl-koon' ahl'-troh*] somebody else
un altro [*oon ahl'-troh*] another
un' altra persona [*oon ahl'-trah pehr-soh'-nah*] someone else
altrove [*ahl-troh'-veh*] somewhere else
alunno [*ah-loon'-noh*] pupil
alveare *m.* [*ahl-veh-ah'-reh*] beehive
alzare *v.* [*ahl-tsah'-reh*] raise, lift up
alzarsi *v.* [*ahl-tsahr'-see*] get up
Mi sono alzato alle sei [*mi soh'-noh ahl-tsa'-toh ahl'-leh seh'-ee*] I got up at six
amante *m., f.* [*ah-mahn'-teh*] lover
amante *adj.* [*ah-mahn'-teh*] fond
amare *v.* [*ah-mah'-reh*] love, like, please
Ti amo! [*tee ah'-moh*] I love you!
non amare [*nohn ah-mah'-reh*] dislike
amaro [*ah-mah'-roh*] bitter
ambasciata [*ahm-bah-shee-ah'-tah*] embassy
ambasciatore *m.*, **ambasciatrice** *f.* [*ahm-bah-shee-ah-toh'-reh, ahm-bah-shee-ah-tree'-cheh*] ambassador
ambedue [*ahm-beh-doo'-eh*] both
ambiente *m.* [*ahm-bee-ehn'-teh*] environment
ambiguità *f. indecl.* [*ahm-bee-goo-ee-tah'*] ambiguity
ambizione *f.* [*ahm-bee-tsee-oh'-neh*] ambition
ambizioso [*ahm-bee-tsee-oh'-zoh*] ambitious
ambulanza [*ahm-boo-lahn'-tsa*] ambulance
America [*ah-meh'-ree-kah*] America
America del Nord [*ah-meh'-ree-kah dehl nohrd*] North

America

America del Sud [*ah-meh'-ree-kah dehl sood*] South America

americano [*ah-meh-ree-kah'-noh*] American
amichevole [*ah-mee-keh'-voh-leh*] friendly
amico [*ah-mee'-koh*] friend
amicizia [*ah-mee-chee'-tsee-ah*] friendship
amido [*ah'-mee-doh*] starch
ammalarsi *v.* [*ahm-mah-lahr'-see*] fall ill
ammalato [*ahm-mah-lah'-toh*] ill
ammazzare *v.* [*ahm-mahts-tsah'-reh*] kill
ammettere *v.* [*ahm-meht'-teh-reh*] admit
ammesso che [*ahm-mehs'-soh keh*] granted that
amministrare *v.* [*ahm-mee-nees-trah'-reh*] manage, administer
amministrazione *f.* [*ahm-mee-nees-trah-tsee-oh'-neh*] administration
ammirabile [*ahm-mee-rah'-bee-leh*] admirable
ammiraglio [*ahm-mee-rah'-lyoh*] admiral
ammirare *v.* [*ahm-mee-rah'-reh*] admire
ammiratore *m.* [*ahm-mee-rah-toh'-reh*] admirer, fan
ammirazione *f.* [*ahm-mee-rah-tsee-oh'-neh*] admiration
ammissione *f.* [*ahm-mees-see-oh'-neh*] admission, fee
ammobiliare *v.* [*ahm-moh-bee-lee-ah'-reh*] furnish [a house]
ammoniaca [*ahm-moh-nee'-ah-kah*] ammonia
ammonire *v.* [*ahm-moh-nee'-reh*] admonish
ammontare *v.* [*ahm-mohn-tah'-reh*] amount
amnistia [*ahm-nees-tee'-ah*] amnesty
amore *m.* [*ah-moh'-reh*] love, affection
amor proprio [*ah-mohr' proh'-pree-oh*] self-respect
amoreggiare *v.* [*ah-moh-rehj-jee-ah'-reh*] flirt
ampio [*ahm'-pee-oh*] ample
analfabeta [*ah-nahl-fah-beh'-tah*] illiterate
analisi *f. indecl.* [*ah-nah'-lee-zee*] analysis
analisi di sangue [*ah-nah'-lee-zee dee sahn'-goo-eh*] blood test
analizzare *v.* [*ah-nah-leedz-dzah'-reh*] analyze
ananasso [*ah-nah-nahs'-soh*] pineapple
anarchia [*ah-nahr-kee'-ah*] anarchy
anche [*ahn'-keh*] and, also, even
anche allora [*ahn'-keh ahl-loh'-rah*] even then

anche lui [*ahn'-keh loo'-ee*] also him, even him
anche se [*ahn'-keh seh*] even if
ancora [*ahn'-koh-rah*] anchor
ancora [*ahn-koh'-rah*] still, again
ancora una volta [*ahn-koh'-rah oo'-nah vohl'-tah*] once more
non ancora [*nohn ahn-koh'-rah*] not yet
andare *v. irreg.* [*ahn-dah'-reh*] go
andare a piedi [*ahn-dah'-reh ah pee-eh'-dee*] walk
andare in automobile [*ahn-dah'-reh een ah-oo-toh-moh'-bee-leh*] drive
andare via [*ahn-dah'-reh vee'-ah*] go away
Vada via! [*vah'-dah vee'-ah*] Go away!
anello [*ah-nehl'-loh*] ring [jewelry]
angelo [*ahn'-jeh-loh*] angel
angolo [*ahn'-goh-loh*] angle, corner
anguria [*ahn-goo'-ree-ah*] watermelon
anima [*ah'-nee-mah*] soul
animale *m.* [*ah-nee-mah'-leh*] animal
animare *v.* [*ah-nee-mah'-reh*] animate
anitra [*ah'-nee-trah*] duck
annegarsi *v.* [*ahn-neh-gahr'-see*] drown
anniversario [*ahn-nee-vehr-sah'-ree-oh*] anniversary
anno [*ahn'-noh*] year
Buon anno! [*boo-ohn' ahn'-noh*] Happy New Year!
il primo dell'anno [*eel pree'-moh dehl-lahn'-noh*] New Year's day
l'anno scorso [*lahn'-noh skohr'-soh*] last year
l'anno prossimo [*lahn'-noh prohs'-see-moh*] next year
Quanti anni ha? [*koo-ahn'-tee ahn'-nee ah*] How old are you?
annoiare *v.* [*ahn-noh-ee-ah'-reh*] bore, annoy, bother
annoiarsi [*ahn-noh-ee-ahr'-see*] become bored
annoiato [*ahn-noh-ee-ah'-toh*] bored, disturbed
annotare *v.* [*ahn-noh-tah'-reh*] note, take down
annuale [*ahn-noo-ah'-leh*] annual
annualmente [*ahn-noo-ahl-mehn'-teh*] yearly
annullamento [*ahn-nool-lah-mehn'-toh*] annulment
annunciare *v.* [*ahn-noon-chee-ah'-reh*] announce
annunciatore *m.*, **annunciatrice** *f.* [*ahn-noon-chee-ah-toh'-reh,*

ahn-noon-chee-ah-tree'-cheh] announcer
annuncio [*ahn-noon'-chee-oh*] announcement
anonimo [*ah-noh'-nee-moh*] anonymous
ansioso [*ahn-see-oh'-zoh*] anxious
antenato [*ahn-teh-nah'-toh*] ancestor
antichità *f. indecl.* [*ahn-tee-kee-tah'*] antiquity, antique
anticipare *v.* [*ahn-tee-chee-pah'-reh*] anticipate
in anticipo, anticipato [*een ahn-tee'-chee-poh, ahn-tee-chee-pah'-toh*] in advance
antico [*ahn-tee'-koh*] ancient
antipatia [*ahn-tee-pah-tee'-ah*] dislike
antipasto [*ahn-tee-pahs'-toh*] appetizer
antipatico [*ahn-tee-pah'-tee-koh*] unpleasant person
anzi [*ahn'-tsee*] on the contrary
anziano [*ahn-tsee-ah'-noh*] senior, elderly
più anziano [*pee-oo' ahn-tsee-ah'-noh*] senior
anzichè [*ahn-tsee-keh'*] instead
anzitutto *adv.* [*ahn-tsee-toot'-toh*] first of all
apatia [*ah-pah-tee'-ah*] apathy
ape *f.* [*ah'-peh*] bee
aperitivo [*ah-peh-ree-tee'-voh*] appetizer [liquor]
aperto [*ah-pehr'-toh*] open
all'aperto [*ahl-lah-pehr'-toh*] outdoors
apertura [*ah-pehr-too'-rah*] opening
apostolo [*ah-pohs'-toh-loh*] apostle
apparato, apparecchio [*ahp-pah-rah'-toh, ahp-pah-rehk'-kee-oh*] apparatus
apparente [*ahp-pah-rehn'-teh*] apparent
apparire *v.* [*ahp-pah-ree'-reh*] appear
apparizione *f.* [*ahp-pah-ree-tsee-oh'-neh*] appearance
appartamento [*ahp-pahr-tah-mehn'-toh*] apartment
appartenere *v. irreg.* [*ahp-pahr-teh-neh'-reh*] belong
Mi appartiene [*mee ahp-pahr-tee-eh'-neh*] It belongs to me
appassionato [*ahp-pahs-see-oh-nah'-toh*] passionate, fond
appello [*ahp-pehl'-loh*] appeal
fare *v.* **appello** [*fah'-reh ahp-pehl'-loh*] appeal
appena [*ahp-peh'-nah*] as soon as, barely
Sono appena arrivato [*soh'-noh ahp-peh'-nah ahr-ree-vah'-toh*] I just arrived
appendere *v. irreg.* [*ahp-pehn'-deh-reh*] hang [an object]

appendicite *f.* [*ahp-pehn-dee-chee'-teh*] appendicitis
Appennini *m. pl.* [*ahp-peh-nee'-nee*] Appennines
appetito [*ahp-peh-tee'-toh*] appetite
appetitoso [*ahp-peh-tee-toh'-zoh*] appetizing
applaudire *v.* [*ahp-plah-oo-dee'-reh*] applaud
applauso [*ahp-plah'-oo-zoh*] applause
applicare *v.* [*ahp-plee-kah'-reh*] apply
appoggiare [*ahp-pohj-jee-ah'-reh*] lean, support
appoggio [*ahp-pohj'-jee-oh*] support
apposta [*ahp-pohs'-tah*] on purpose
apprendere *v. irreg.* [*ahp-prehn'-deh-reh*] learn
apprendista [*ahp-prehn-dees'-tah*] apprentice
apprezzare *v.* [*ahp-preh-tsah'-reh*] appreciate, value
approdo [*ahp-proh'-doh*] landing [of ship]
approfittare di *v.* [*ahp-proh-feet-tah'-reh dee*] take advantage of
appropriato [*ahp-proh-pree-ah'-toh*] appropriate
approssimativamente [*ahp-prohs-see-mah-tee-vah-mehn'-teh*] approximately
approvare *v.* [*ahp-proh-vah'-reh*] approve
approvazione *f.* [*ahp-proh-vah-tsee-oh'-neh*] approval
appuntamento [*ahp-poon-tah-mehn'-toh*] appointment, date
appuntare *v.* [*ahp-poon-tah'-reh*] pin
appunto [*ahp-poon'-toh*] note, remark
aprile *m.* [*ah-pree'-leh*] April
aprire *v. irreg.* [*ah-pree'-reh*] open, unlock
apriscatola [*ah-pree-skah'-toh-lah*] can opener
aquila [*ah'-koo-ee-lah*] eagle
Arabia [*ah-rah'-bee-ah*] Arabia
arabo [*ah'-rah-boh*] Arab, Arabic
aragosta [*ah-rah-gohs'-tah*] lobster
arancia [*ah-ràhn'-chee-ah*] orange
  succo d'arancia [*sook'-koh dah-rahn'-chee-ah*] orange juice
aranciata [*ah-rahn-chee-ah'-tah*] orangeade
arare *v.* [*ah-rah'-reh*] plow
arbitrario [*ahr-bee-trah'-ree-oh*] arbitrary
arbitro [*ahr'-bee-troh*] referee
architetto [*ahr-kee-teht'-toh*] architect
architettura [*ahr-kee-teht-too'-rah*] architecture
archivio [*ahr-kee'-vee-oh*] archives, file

arcipelago [*ahr-chee-peh'-lah-goh*] archipelago
arcivescovo [*ahr-chee-vehs'-koh-voh*] archbishop
arco [*ahr'-koh*] arch, arc, bow
arcobaleno [*ahr-koh-bah-leh'-noh*] rainbow
ardere *v. irreg.* [*ahr'-deh-reh*] burn
area [*ah'-reh-ah*] area, ground
Argentina [*ahr-jehn-tee'-nah*] Argentina
argentino [*ahr-jehn-tee'-noh*] Argentine
argento [*ahr-jehn'-toh*] silver
argine *m.* [*ahr'-jee-neh*] embankment, limit
argomento [*ahr-goh-mehn'-toh*] subject, matter
aria [*ah'-ree-ah*] air, tune
  aria condizionata [*ah'-ree-ah kohn-dee-tsee-oh-nah'-tah*] air conditioning
  darsi *v.* **delle arie** [*dahr'-see dehl'-leh ah'-ree-eh*] show off
  mal d'aria [*mahl dah'-ree-ah*] airsickness
arido [*ah'-ree-doh*] arid
aristocratico [*ah-rees-toh-krah'-tee-koh*] aristocratic
aristocrazia [*ah-rees-toh-krah-tsee'-ah*] aristocracy
aritmetica [*ah-reet-meh'-tee-kah*] arithmetic
arma, le armi *pl.* [*ahr'-mah, leh ahr'-mee*] weapon, arms
armadio [*ahr-mah'-dee-oh*] wardrobe, closet
armata [*ahr-mah'-tah*] army
armato [*ahr-mah'-toh*] armed
armonia [*ahr-moh-nee'-ah*] harmony
aroma [*ah-roh'-mah*] flavor
arrabbiarsi *v.* [*ahr-rahb-bee-ahr'-see*] get angry
arrabbiato [*ahr-rahb-bee-ah'-toh*] angry
arrendersi *v.* [*ahr-rehn'-dehr-see*] surrender
arrestare *v.* [*ahr-rehs-tah'-reh*] arrest
arresto [*ahr-rehs'-toh*] arrest
arretrato [*ahr-reh-trah'-toh*] backward
arricchire *v.* [*ahr-reek-kee'-reh*] enrich
arrivare *v.* [*ahr-ree-vah'-reh*] arrive
  Arrivederci! [*ahr-ree-veh-dehr'-chee*] Goodbye! [familiar form]
  Arrivederla! [*ahr-ree-veh-dehr'-lah*] Goodbye! [polite form]
arrivo [*ahr-ree'-voh*] arrival
arroganza [*ahr-roh-gahn'-tsah*] arrogance

arrossire *v.* [*ahr-rohs-see'-reh*] blush
arrostire *v.* [*ahr-rohs-tee'-reh*] roast, broil
arrostito [*ahr-rohs-tee'-toh*] roasted, broiled
arrosto [*ahr-rohs'-toh*] roast
arrugginito [*ahr-rooj-jee-nee'-toh*] rusted
arruolare *v.* [*ahr-roo-oh-lah'-reh*] enroll
arte *f.* [*ahr'-teh*] art
  le belle arti [*leh behl'-leh ahr'-tee*] the fine arts
arteria [*ahr-teh'-ree-ah*] artery
articolo [*ahr-tee'-koh-loh*] item [of things], article
artificiale [*ahr-tee-fee-chee-ah'-leh*] artificial
artificialmente [*ahr-tee-fee-chee-ahl-mehn'-teh*] artificially
artigiano [*ahr-tee-jee-ah'-noh*] craftsman
artista *m.*, *f.* [*ahr-tees'-tah*] artist
artistico [*ahr-tees'-tee-koh*] artistic
arto [*ahr'-toh*] limb
ascensore *m.* [*ah-shehn-soh'-reh*] elevator
ascesso [*ah-shehs'-soh*] abscess
asciugamano [*ah-shee-oo-gah-mah'-noh*] towel
asciugare *v.* [*ah-shee-oo-gah'-reh*] dry
asciutto [*ah-shee-oot'-toh*] dry
ascoltare *v.* [*ahs-kohl-tah'-reh*] listen
Asia [*ah'-zee-ah*] Asia
asiatico [*ah-zee-ah'-tee-koh*] Asiatic
asilo [*ah-zee'-loh*] asylum
asino [*ah'-zee-noh*] donkey
asparagi *m. pl.* [*ahs-pah'-rah-jee*] asparagus
aspettare *v.* [*ahs-peht-tah'-reh*] expect, wait
  Aspetti un momento [*ahs-peht'-tee oon moh-mehn'-toh*] Wait a moment
  Mi aspetti [*mee ahs-peht'-tee*] Wait for me
aspetto [*ahs-peht'-toh*] aspect, looks
  bell'aspetto [*behl-lahs-peht'-toh*] good looks
aspirapolvere *m.* [*ahs-pee-rah-pohl'-veh-reh*] vacuum cleaner
aspirare *v.* [*ahs-pee-rah'-reh*] aspire
aspirazione *f.* [*ahs-pee-rah-tsee-oh'-neh*] aspiration
aspirina [*ahs-pee-ree'-nah*] aspirin
aspro [*ahs'-proh*] harsh
assaggiare *v.* [*ahs-sahj-jee-ah'-reh*] taste
assai [*ahs-sah'-ee*] quite, very much

assalire *v.* [*ahs-sah-lee'-reh*] assault
assalto [*ahs-sahl'-toh*] assault
assassinare *v.* [*ahs-sahs-see-nah'-reh*] murder
assassinio [*ahs-sahs-see'-nee-oh*] murder
assassino [*ahs-sahs-see'-noh*] murderer
assedio [*ahs-seh'-dee-oh*] siege
assegnare *v.* [*ahs-seh-nyah'-reh*] assign
assegno [*ahs-seh'-nyoh*] check [bank]
  assegno fisso [*ahs-seh'-nyoh fees'-soh*] allowance
  assegno turistico [*ahs-seh'-nyoh too-rees'-tee-koh*] traveler's check
assemblea [*ahs-sehm-bleh'-ah*] assembly
assente [*ahs-sehn'-teh*] absent
assenza [*ahs-sehn'-tsah*] absence
assetato [*ahs-seh-tah'-toh*] thirsty
assicurare *v.* [*ahs-see-koo-rah'-reh*] assure, insure, secure
assicurazione *f.* [*ahs-see-koo-rah-tsee-oh'-neh*] assurance, insurance
assistente [*ahs-sees-tehn'-teh*] assistant
assistere *v.* [*ahs-sees'-teh-reh*] assist
  assistere a [*ahs-sees'-teh-reh ah*] attend to
asso [*ahs'-soh*] ace, champion
associare *v.* [*ahs-soh-chee-ah'-reh*] associate
associazione *f.* [*ahs-soh-chee-ah-tsee-oh'-neh*] association
assolutamente [*ahs-soh-loo-tah-mehn'-teh*] absolutely
assoluto [*ahs-soh-loo'-toh*] absolute
assolvere *v.* [*ahs-sohl'-veh-reh*] acquit
assorbente [*ahs-sohr-behn'-teh*] absorbent
assorbire *v.* [*ahs-sohr-bee'-reh*] absorb
assortimento [*ahs-sohr-tee-mehn'-toh*] assortment, set
assumere *v.* [*ahs-soo'-meh-reh*] assume, appoint
assunzione [*ahs-soon-tsee-oh'-neh*] assumption
assurdo [*ahs-soor'-doh*] absurd
asta [*ahs'-tah*] auction; lance, pole
astratto [*ahs-traht'-toh*] abstract
astrazione *f.* [*ahs-trah-tsee-oh'-neh*] abstraction
astronomia [*ahs-troh-noh-mee'-ah*] astronomy
astuto [*ahs-too'-toh*] cunning
Atlantico [*aht-lahn'-tee-koh*] Atlantic
atletica [*aht-leh'-tee-kah*] athletics

atmosfera [*aht-mohs-feh'-rah*] atmosphere
atomico [*ah-toh'-mee-koh*] atomic
atroce [*ah-troh'-cheh*] terrible, outrageous
attaccapanni *m. pl.* [*aht-tahk-kah-pahn'-nee*] hanger [clothes]
attaccare *v.* [*aht-tahk-kah'-reh*] attack, attach
attacco [*aht-tahk'-koh*] attack
atteggiamento [*aht-tehj-jee-ah-mehn'-toh*] attitude
attendere *v.* [*aht-tehn'-deh-reh*] attend, await
attentamente [*aht-tehn-tah-mehn'-teh*] carefully
attento [*aht-tehn'-toh*] attentive, careful
  Attento! [*aht-tehn'-toh*] Watch out!
attenzione *f.* [*aht-tehn-tsee-oh'-neh*] attention
  Attenzione! [*aht-tehn-tsee-oh'-neh*] Caution!
  fare *v.* **attenzione** [*fah'-reh aht-tehn-tsee-oh'-neh*] beware
  Faccia attenzione! [*fahch'-chee-ah aht-tehn-tsee-oh'-neh*] Be careful!
atterraggio [*aht-tehr-rahj'-jee-oh*] landing [of airplane]
atterrare *v.* [*aht-tehr-rah'-reh*] land [an airplane]
attesa [*aht-teh'-zah*] wait, waiting
attiguo [*aht-tee'-goo-oh*] adjoining
attimo [*aht'-tee-moh*] instant, moment
attività *f. indecl.* [*aht-tee-vee-tah'*] activity
attivo [*aht-tee'-voh*] active
atto [*aht'-toh*] act, action; document
  atto di nascita [*aht'-toh dee nah'-shee-tah*] birth certificate
attore *m.*, **attrice** *f.* [*aht-toh'-reh*, *aht-tree'-cheh*] actor, actress
attraente [*aht-trah-ehn'-teh*] attractive
attrarre *v. irreg.* [*aht-trahr'-reh*] attract
attraversare *v.* [*aht-trah-vehr-sah'-reh*] cross
attraverso [*aht-trah-vehr'-soh*] across, through
attuale [*aht-too-ah'-leh*] actual
attualmente [*aht-too-ahl-mehn'-teh*] actually
augurare *v.* [*ah-oo-goo-rah'-reh*] wish
Auguri! [*ah-oo-goo'-ree*] Best wishes!
aula [*ah'-oo-lah*] classroom, hall
aumentare *v.* [*ah-oo-mehn-tah'-reh*] increase
aumento [*ah-oo-mehn'-toh*] increase
aurora [*ah-oo-roh'-rah*] dawn
Australia [*ah-oos-trah'-lee-ah*] Australia
australiano [*ah-oos-trah-lee-ah'-noh*] Australian

Austria [*ah'-oos-tree-ah*] Austria
austriaco [*ah-oos-tree'-ah-koh*] Austrian
autentico [*ah-oo-tehn'-tee-koh*] authentic
autista *m.* [*ah-oo-tees'-tah*] driver
autobus *m.* [*ah-oo'-toh-boos*] bus
automatico [*ah-oo-toh-mah'-tee-koh*] automatic
automobile *f.* [*ah-oo-toh-moh'-bee-leh*] automobile, car
autonomia [*ah-oo-toh-noh-mee'-ah*] autonomy
autore *m.*, **autrice** *f.* [*ah-oo-toh'-reh, ah-oo-tree'-cheh*] author
autorimessa [*ah-oo-toh-ree-mehs'-sah*] garage
autorità *f. indecl.* [*ah-oo-toh-ree-tah'*] authority
autorizzare *v.* [*ah-oo-toh-reedz-dzah'-reh*] authorize
autostop [*ah'-oo-toh-stohp*] hitchhiking
autostrada [*ah-oo-toh-strah'-dah*] roadway, highway
autunno [*ah-oo-toon'-noh*] autumn
avanti [*ah-vahn'-tee*] ahead, before
  Avanti! [*ah-vahn'-tee*] Come in!
  da ora in avanti [*dah oh'-rah een ah-vahn'-tee*] from this time on
  Vada avanti! [*vah'-dah ah-vahn'-tee*] Go ahead [in front]!
  avanti e dietro [*ah-vahn'-tee eh dee-eh'-troh*] to and fro
avanzamento [*ah-vahn-tsah-mehn'-toh*] advancement
avanzare *v.* [*ah-vahn-tsah'-reh*] advance
avarizia [*ah-vah-ree'-tsee-ah*] greediness
avaro [*ah-vah'-roh*] miser, stingy
avere *v. irreg.* [*ah-veh'-reh*] have
  Che cosa ha? [*keh koh'-zah ah*] What's up?
avido [*ah'-vee-doh*] eager, greedy
avorio [*ah-voh'-ree-oh*] ivory
avvenimento [*ahv-veh-nee-mehn'-toh*] event, occurrence
avvenire *v.* [*ahv-veh-nee'-reh*] happen
avvenire *m.* [*ahv-veh-nee'-reh*] future
  in avvenire [*een ahv-veh-nee'-reh*] in the future
avventura [*ahv-vehn-too'-rah*] adventure
avventuriero [*ahv-vehn-too-ree-eh'-roh*] adventurer
avverbio [*ahv-vehr'-bee-oh*] adverb
avversario [*ahv-vehr-sah'-ree-oh*] adversary
avvertimento [*ahv-vehr-tee-mehn'-toh*] warning
avvertire *v.* [*ahv-vehr-tee'-reh*] warn

avvicinare *v.* [*ahv-vee-chee-nah'-reh*] approach
avvisare *v.* [*ahv-vee-zah'-reh*] inform
avviso [*ahv-vee'-zoh*] notice
  a mio avviso [*ah mee'-oh ahv-vee'-zoh*] in my opinion
  avviso pubblicitario [*ahv-vee'-zoh poo-blee-chee-tah'-ree-oh*] poster, advertisement
avvocato [*ahv-voh-kah'-toh*] lawyer, attorney
avvolgere *v.* [*ahv-vohl'-jeh-reh*] wrap up, roll
azienda [*ah-dzee-ehn'-dah*] business, firm
azione *f.* [*ah-tsee-oh'-neh*] action, deed
azioni *f. pl.* [*ah-tsee-oh'-nee*] stocks, shares
azzardo [*ahdz-dzahr'-doh*] hazard
  gioco d'azzardo [*jee-oh'-koh dahdz-dzahr'-doh*] gambling
azzurro [*ahdz-dzoor'-roh*] azure, light blue

B

baciare *v.* [*bah-chee-ah'-reh*] kiss
bacio [*bah'-chee-oh*] kiss
badare a *v.* [*bah-dah'-reh ah*] mind
baffi *m. pl.* [*bahf'-fee*] moustache
bagaglio [*bah-gah'-lyoh*] luggage
  ufficio-bagagli [*oof-fee'-chee-oh bah-gah'-lyee*] luggage counter
bagnarsi *v.* [*bah-nyahr'-see*] get wet, bathe
bagnato [*bah-nyah'-toh*] wet
bagnino [*bah-nyee'-noh*] lifeguard
bagno [*bah'-nyoh*] bath
  costume *m.* **da bagno** [*kohs-too'-meh dah bah'-nyoh*] bathing suit
  fare *v.* **il bagno** [*fah'-reh eel bah'-nyoh*] take a bath
  stanza da bagno [*stahn'-tsah dah bah'-nyoh*] bathroom
  vasca da bagno [*vahs'-kah da bah'-nyoh*] bathtub
baia [*bah'-ee-ah*] bay
balcone [*bahl-koh'-neh*] balcony
balena [*bah-leh'-nah*] whale
balia [*bah'-lee-ah*] nurse [for babies]

ballare *v.* [*bahl-lah'-reh*] dance
ballerino [*bahl-leh-ree'-noh*] dancer
balletto [*bahl-leht'-toh*] ballet
ballo [*bahl'-loh*] dance
bambinaia [*bahm-bee-nah'-ee-ah*] nursemaid
bambino [*bahm-bee'-noh*] child
bambola [*bahm'-boh-lah*] doll
banana [*bah-nah'-nah*] banana
banca [*bahn'-kah*] bank
banchetto [*bahn-keht'-toh*] banquet
banchiere *m.* [*bahn-kee-eh'-reh*] banker
banchina [*bahn-kee'-nah*] quay, dock
banco [*bahn'-koh*] bench
banconota [*bahn-koh-noh'-tah*] bank note
banda [*bahn'-dah*] band, gang
bandiera [*bahn-dee-eh'-rah*] flag
bandito [*bahn-dee'-toh*] bandit
barba [*bahr'-bah*] beard
  crema da barba [*kreh'-mah dah bahr'-bah*] shaving cream
  farsi *v.* **la barba** [*fahr'-see lah bahr'-bah*] shave
  pennello da barba [*pehn-nehl'-loh dah bahr'-bah*] shaving brush
barbiere *m.* [*bahr-bee-eh'-reh*] barber
barca [*bahr'-kah*] boat
  barca da pesca [*bahr'-kah dah pehs'-kah*] fishing boat
  barca a vela [*bahr'-kah ah veh'-lah*] sailboat
barco [*bahr'-koh*] rowboat
barile *m.* [*bah-ree'-leh*] barrel
barone *m.*, **baronessa** [*bah-roh'-neh, bah-roh-nehs'-sah*] baron, baroness
barzelletta [*bahr-dzehl-leht'-tah*] joke
base *f.* [*bah'-zeh*] base
basico [*bah'-zee-koh*] basic
bassifondi *m. pl.* [*bahs-see-fohn'-dee*] gutter
basso [*bahs'-soh*] low, short
  in basso [*een bahs'-soh*] down
bastare *v.* [*bahs-tah'-reh*] suffice
  Basta! [*bahs'-tah*] That's enough!
bastone [*bahs-toh'-neh*] cane, stick
battaglia [*baht-tah'-lyah*] battle

battello [*baht-tehl'-loh*] boat, skiff
  battello a vapore [*baht-tehl'-loh ah vah-poh'-reh*] steamboat
battere *v.* [*baht'-teh-reh*] beat, hit; vanquish, overcome
batteria [*baht-teh-ree'-ah*] battery
battesimo [*baht-teh'-zee-moh*] baptism
  nome *m.* **di battesimo** [*noh'-meh dee baht-teh'-zee-moh*] Christian name
battezzare *v.* [*baht-tehdz-dzah'-reh*] baptize
battito [*baht'-tee-toh*] beat, pulse
battuta [*baht-too'-tah*] beating, beat
battuto [*baht-too'-toh*] beaten
baule *m.* [*bah-oo'-leh*] trunk
becco [*behk'-koh*] beak
belga [*behl'-gah*] Belgian
Belgio [*behl'-jee-oh*] Belgium
bellezza [*behl-lehts'-tsah*] beauty
bello [*behl'-loh*] good looking, beautiful
belva [*behl'-vah*] wild beast
benchè [*behn-keh'*] although
benda [*behn'-dah*] band, bandage
bene [*beh'-neh*] well, good
  Bene! [*beh'-neh*] Fine!
  abbastanza bene [*ahb-bahs-tahn'-tsah beh'-neh*] fairly well
  stare *v.* **bene** [*stah'-reh beh'-neh*] be well
  Va bene! [*vah beh'-neh*] All right!
benedire *v.* [*beh-neh-dee'-reh*] bless
benedizione *f.* [*beh-neh-dee-tsee-oh'-neh*] blessing
beneficenza [*beh-neh-fee-chehn'-tsah*] charity
beneficio [*beh-neh-fee'-chee-oh*] advantage, benefit
benessere *m.* [*behn-ehs'-seh-reh*] welfare, comfort
benestante [*beh-neh-stahn'-teh*] well-off
beni *m. pl.* [*beh'-nee*] property
  beni immobili [*beh'-nee eem-moh'-bee-lee*] real estate
benissimo [*beh-nees'-see-moh*] very well
benvenuto [*behn-veh-noo'-toh*] welcome
  dare *v.* **il benvenuto** [*dah'-reh eel behn-veh-noo'-toh*] welcome
benzina [*behn-dzee'-nah*] gasoline
  pompa di benzina [*pohm'-pah dee behn-dzee'-nah*] gasoline station

bere *v. irreg.* [*beh'-reh*] drink
berretto [*behr-reht'-toh*] cap
bersaglio [*behr-sah'-lyoh*] target
bestemmiare *v.* [*behs-tehm-mee-ah'-reh*] swear
bestia [*behs'-tee-ah*] beast
bestiame *m.* [*behs-tee-ah'-meh*] cattle
bevanda [*beh-vahn'-dah*] drink
biancheria [*bee-ahn-keh-ree'-ah*] linen
bianco [*bee-ahn'-koh*] white
  in bianco [*een bee-ahn'-koh*] blank
Bibbia [*beeb'-bee-ah*] Bible
biberon *m.* [*bee-beh-rohn'*] baby bottle
bibita [*bee'-bee-tah*] drink
biblioteca [*bee-blee-oh-teh'-kah*] library
bicchiere *m.* [*beek-kee-eh'-reh*] glass [for drinking]
bicicletta [*bee-chee-kleht'-tah*] bicycle
  andare *v.* **in bicicletta** [*ahn-dah'-reh een bee-chee-kleht'-tah*] ride a bicycle
biglietteria [*bee-lyeht-teh-ree'-ah*] ticket office
biglietto [*bee-lyeht'-toh*] ticket
  biglietto da visita [*bee-lyeht'-toh dah vee'-zee-tah*] calling card
  bigietto di andata e ritorno [*bee-lyeht'-toh dee ahn-dah'-tah eh ree-tohr'-noh*] round trip ticket
bilancia [*bee-lahn'-chee-ah*] balance
bilancio [*bee-lahn'-chee-oh*] budget
bimbo [*beem'-boh*] baby
binario [*bee-nah'-ree-oh*] track [for a train]
biondo [*bee-ohn'-doh*] blond
birra [*beer'-rah*] beer, ale
biscotto [*bees-koht'-toh*] biscuit
bisogno [*bee-zoh'-nyoh*] need
  aver *v.* **bisogno** [*ah-vehr' bee-zoh'-nyoh*] need
bistecca [*bees-tehk'-kah*] steak
blu [*bloo*] blue
blusa [*bloo'-zah*] blouse
bocca [*bohk'-kah*] mouth
  In bocca al lupo! [*een bohk'-kah ahl loo'-poh*] Good luck!
boccone *m.* [*bohk-koh'-neh*] mouthful
bolla [*bohl'-lah*] blister

bollettino [*bohl-leht-tee'-noh*] bulletin
bollire *v.* [*bohl-lee'-reh*] boil
bollo [*bohl'-loh*] stamp, seal
bomba [*bohm'-bah*] bomb
bontà *f. indecl.* [*bohn-tah'*] goodness
bordo [*bohr'-doh*] edge, limit
  a bordo [*ah bohr'-doh*] aboard
borghese [*bohr-geh'-zeh*] civilian
borghesia [*bohr-geh-zee'-ah*] bourgeoisie
borsa [*bohr'-sah*] purse, bag
  borsa di studio [*bohr'-sah dee stoo'-dee-oh*] scholarship
  borsa valori [*bohr'-sah vah-loh'-ree*] stock exchange
borsaiuolo [*bohr-sah-ee-oh'-loh*] pickpocket
bosco [*bohs'-koh*] woods
bottiglia [*boht-tee'-lyah*] bottle
bottino [*boht-tee'-noh*] booty
bottone *m.* [*boht-toh'-neh*] button
braccialetto [*brahch-chee-ah-leht'-toh*] bracelet
braccio, le braccia *pl.* [*brahch'-chee-oh, leh brahch'-chee-ah*] arm [of body]
branda [*brahn'-dah*] cot
Brasile *m.* [*brah-zee'-leh*] Brazil
brasiliano [*brah-zee-lee-ah'-noh*] Brazilian
bravo [*brah'-voh*] nice, good-natured
  Bravo! [*brah'-voh*] Magnificent!
breve [*breh'-veh*] brief
  in breve [*een breh'-veh*] in short
  tra breve [*trah breh'-veh*] in a short time
brevetto [*breh-veht'-toh*] patent
brezza [*brehts'-tsah*] breeze
briciola [*bree'-chee-oh-lah*] crumb
brigante [*bree-gahn'-teh*] brigand
brillante [*breel-lahn'-teh*] bright, brilliant
brillare *v.* [*breel-lah'-reh*] shine [sun]
brina [*bree'-nah*] frost
brindare *v.* [*breen-dah'-reh*] toast [to one's health]
brindisi *m.* [*breen'-dee-zee*] toast [to one's health]
brio [*bree'-oh*] humor, fine spirits
brivido [*bree'-vee-doh*] shiver
brocca [*brohk'-kah*] jug

brodo di carne [*broh'-doh dee kahr'-neh*] broth
brontolio [*brohn-toh-lee'-oh*] grumble
bronzo [*brohn'-tsoh*] bronze
bruciare *v.* [*broo-chee-ah'-reh*] burn
bruciatura [*broo-chee-ah-too'-rah*] burn
  bruciatura di sole [*broo-chee-ah-too'-rah dee soh'-leh*] sunburn
brunetta [*broo-neht'-tah*] brunette
bruno [*broo'-noh*] brunette, dark
brutale [*broo-tah'-leh*] brutal
brutto [*broot'-toh*] ugly
buca (delle lettere) [*boo'-kah* (*dehl'-leh leht'-teh-reh*)] (letter) box
bucare *v.* [*boo-kah'-reh*] pierce
bucato [*boo-kah'-reh*] washing [of linen]
buccia [*booch'-chee-ah*] peel, skin
buco [*boo'-koh*] hole
bue *m.* **buoi** *pl.* [*boo'-eh*, *boo-oh'-ee*] ox
  carne *f.* **di bue** [*kahr'-neh dee boo'-eh*] beef
bufera (di neve) [*boo-feh'-rah* (*dee neh'-veh*)] (snow)storm
buffo [*boof'-foh*] funny
bugia [*boo-jee'-ah*] lie
bugiardo [*boo-jee-ahr'-doh*] liar
buio [*boo'-ee-oh*] dark [not clear]
  al buio [*ahl boo'-ee-oh*] in the dark
bulbo [*bool'-boh*] eyeball
Bulgaria [*bool-gah-ree'-ah*] Bulgaria
bulgaro [*bool'-gah-roh*] Bulgarian
buongustaio [*boo-ohn-goos-tah'-ee-oh*] connoisseur [of food, drink]
buono [*boo-oh'-noh*] good, nice
  buona fortuna [*boo-oh'-na fohr-too'-nah*] good luck
  buon giorno [*boo-ohn' jee-ohr'-noh*] good day, good morning
  buona notte [*boo-oh'-nah noht'-teh*] good night
  buon pomeriggio [*boo-ohn' poh-meh-reej'-jee-oh*] good afternoon
  buona sera [*boo-oh'-nah seh'-rah*] good evening
buontempone *m.* [*boo-ohn-tehm-poh'-neh*] jolly fellow
burla [*boor'-lah*] jest, trick

burocrazia [*boo-roh-krah-tsee'-ah*] red tape
burrasca [*boor-rahs'-kah*] tornado
burro [*boor'-roh*] butter
bussare *v.* [*boos-sah'-reh*] knock
bussata [*boos-sah'-tah*] knock
bussola [*boos'-soh-lah*] compass
busta [*boos'-tah*] envelope
busto [*boos'-toh*] bust, corset
buttare *v.* [*boot-tah'-reh*] throw
  buttar via [*boot-tahr' vee'-ah*] throw away

C

cabina [*kah-bee'-nah*] cabin, booth
  cabina telefonica [*kah-bee'-nah teh-leh-foh'-nee-kah*] telephone booth
cablogramma *m.* [*kah-bloh-grahm'-mah*] cable
cacao [*kah-kah'-oh*] cocoa
caccia [*kahch'-chee-ah*] hunting
cacciare *v.* [*kahch-chee-ah'-reh*] chase, hunt
cacciatore *m.* [*kahch-chee-ah-toh'-reh*] hunter
cacciavite *m.* [*kahch-chee-ah-vee'-teh*] screwdriver
cadavere [*kah-dah'-veh-reh*] corpse
cadere *v. irreg.* [*kah-deh'-reh*] fall
  lasciar cadere [*lah-shee-ahr' kah-deh'-reh*] drop
caduta [*kah-doo'-tah*] fall, collapse
caduto [*kah-doo'-toh*] fallen
caffè *m.* [*kahf-feh'*] cafè, coffeehouse, coffee
calcagno [*kahl-kah'-nyoh*] heel [of foot]
calcio [*kahl'-chee-oh*] football
calcolare *v.* [*kahl-koh-lah'-reh*] calculate
calcolo [*kahl'-koh-loh*] calculation
caldo *n.* [*kahl'-doh*] heat
caldo *adj.* [*kahl'-doh*] warm, hot
  Fa caldo [*fah kahl'-doh*] It is hot [weather]
  avere *v.* **caldo** [*ah-veh'-reh kahl'-doh*] be warm [for persons]

calendario [*kah-lehn-dah'-ree-oh*] calendar
calma [*kahl'-mah*] calmness
Con calma! [*kohn kahl'-mah*] Take it easy!
calmante *m. & adj.* [*kahl-mahn'-teh*] sedative
calmare *v.* [*kahl-mah'-reh*] calm
calmo [*kahl'-moh*] calm, quiet
Stia calmo! [*stee'-ah kahl'-moh*] Be quiet! [to one person]
calore *m.* [*kah-loh'-reh*] heat, warmth
calorifero [*kah-loh-ree'-feh-roh*] heater
calunnia [*kah-loon'-nee-ah*] slander
calunniare *v.* [*kah-loon-nee-ah'-reh*] slander
calvo [*kahl'-voh*] bald
calza [*kahl'-tsah*] stocking
calzino [*kahl-tsee'-noh*] sock
calzolaio [*kahl-tsoh-lah'-ee-oh*] shoemaker
calzoleria [*kahl-tsoh-leh-ree'-ah*] shoe store
calzoni [*kahl-tsoh'-nee*] pants
cambiale *f.* [*kahm-bee-ah'-leh*] draft [commercial]
cambiamento [*kahm-bee-ah-mehn'-toh*] change
cambiare *v.* [*kahm-bee-ah'-reh*] change, shift
cambiare idea [*kahm-bee-ah'-reh ee-deh'-ah*] change one's mind
cambio [*kahm'-bee-oh*] change, exchange
corso del cambio [*kohr'-soh dehl kahm'-bee-oh*] rate of exchange
in cambio di [*een kahm'-bee-oh dee*] in exchange for
camera [*kah'-meh-rah*] room
camera da affittare [*kah'-meh-rah dah ahf-fee-tah'-reh*] furnished room
camera da letto [*kah'-meh-rah dah leht'-toh*] bedroom
camera d'albergo [*kah'-meh-rah dahl-behr'-goh*] hotel room
cameriera, cameriere *m.* [*kah-meh-ree-eh'-rah, kah-meh-ree-eh'-reh*] maid, waitress, waiter
cameriera d'albergo [*kah-meh-ree-eh'-rah dahl-behr'-goh*] chambermaid
cameriera di bordo [*kah-meh-ree-eh'-rah dee bohr'-doh*] stewardess
cameriere di bordo [*kah-meh-ree-eh'-reh dee bohr'-doh*] steward

camicia [*kah-mee'-chee-ah*] shirt
camino [*kah-mee'-noh*] chimney
camion *m.* [*kah-mee-ohn'*] truck
camminare *v.* [*kahm-mee-nah'-reh*] walk
cammino [*kahm-mee'-noh*] way, road, walk
campagna [*kahm-pah'-nyah*] countryside
campana, campanello [*kahm-pah'-nah, kahm-pah-nehl'-loh*] bell
campeggio [*kahm-pehj'-jee-oh*] camping
campione *m.*, **campionessa** [*kahm-pee-oh'-neh, kahm-pee-oh-nehs'-sah*] sample, champion
campo [*kahm'-poh*] camp, field
Canada *m.* [*kah'-nah-dah*] Canada
canadese [*kah-nah-deh'-zeh*] Canadian
canale *m.* [*kah-nah'-leh*] canal, channel
canarino [*kah-nah-ree'-noh*] canary
cancellare *v.* [*kahn-chehl-lah'-reh*] erase, cancel
cancello [*kahn-chehl'-loh*] gate
cancro [*kahn'-kroh*] cancer
candela [*kahn-deh'-lah*] candle
  candela d'accensione [*kahn-deh'-lah dahch-chehn-see-oh'-neh*] spark plug
candelabro [*kahn-deh-lah'-broh*] candlestick
candidato [*kahn-dee-dah'-toh*] candidate
cane *m.* [*kah'-neh*] dog
cannocchiali [*kahn-nohk-kee-ah'-lee*] field glasses
cannone *m.* [*kahn-noh'-neh*] gun, cannon
canottaggio [*kah-noht-tahj'-jee-oh*] boating
cantante *m., f.* [*kahn-tahn'-teh*] singer
cantare *v.* [*kahn-tah'-reh*] sing
cantina [*kahn-tee'-nah*] cellar
canzone *f.* [*kahn-tsoh'-neh*] song
capace [*kah-pah'-cheh*] able, capable
capacità *f. indecl.* [*kah-pah-chee-tah'*] capacity
capella [*kah-pehl'-lah*] chapel
capello, capelli [*kah-pehl'-loh, kah-pehl'-lee*] hair
  taglio di capelli [*tah'-lyoh dee kah-pehl'-lee*] haircut
capezzolo [*kah-pehts'-tsoh-loh*] nipple
capire *v.* [*kah-pee'-reh*] understand
  Capite? [*kah-pee'-teh*] Do you understand?

Non capisco [*nohn kah-pees'-koh*] I don't understand
capire male [*kah-pee'-reh mah'-leh*] be mistaken, misunderstand
capitale *m.* [*kah-pee-tah'-leh*] capital [money]
capitale *f.* [*kah-pee-tah'-leh*] capital [city]
capitano [*kah-pee-tah'-noh*] captain
capitolo [*kah-pee'-toh-loh*] chapter
capo [*kah'-poh*] head, chief, leader
da capo [*dah kah'-poh*] again
capodanno [*kah-poh-dahn'-noh*] New Year's Day
Buon capodanno [*boo-ohn' kah-poh-dahn'-noh*] Happy New Year
capolavoro [*kah-poh-lah-voh'-roh*] masterpiece
capolinea [*kah-poh-lee'-neh-ah*] terminal [bus, train]
capovolgere *v.* [*kah-poh-vohl'-jeh-reh*] overturn
capovolto [*kah-poh-vohl'-toh*] upside down
cappello [*kahp-pehl'-loh*] hat
cappotto [*kahp-poht'-toh*] overcoat
cappuccino [*kahp-pooch-chee'-noh*] capuchin [friar]
capriccio [*kah-preech'-chee-oh*] caprice, fancy
caramella [*kah-rah-mehl'-lah*] candy
caramente [*kah-rah-mehn'-teh*] dearly
carattere *m.* [*kah-raht'-teh-reh*] character
caratteristica [*kah-raht-teh-rees'-tee-kah*] trait
caratteristico [*kah-raht-teh-rees'-tee-koh*] characteristic
carbone *m.* [*kahr-boh'-neh*] charcoal
carburante *m.* [*kahr-boo-rahn'-teh*] gas, fuel
carcere *m.* [*kahr'-cheh-reh*] jail
cardinale *m.* [*kahr-dee-nah'-leh*] cardinal
carezza [*kah-rehts'-tsah*] caress
carezzare *v.* [*kah-rets-tsah'-reh*] caress
carica [*kah'-ree-kah*] charge, office
caricare *v.* [*kah-ree-kah'-reh*] load, wind [a watch]
caricatura [*kah-ree-kah-too'-rah*] cartoon
carico [*kah'-ree-koh*] load, burden, freight
carino [*kah-ree'-noh*] nice, dear, pretty
carità *f. indef.* [*kah-ree-tah'*] charity
Per carità! [*pehr kah-ree-tah'*] For pity's sake!
carnagione *f.* [*kahr-nah-jee-oh'-neh*] complexion
carne *f.* [*kahr'-neh*] meat, flesh

carnevale *m.* [*kahr-neh-vah'-leh*] carnival
caro [*kah'-roh*] dear, darling, expensive
carota [*kah-roh'-tah*] carrot
carpentiere *m.* [*kahr-pehn-tee-eh'-reh*] carpenter
carriera [*kahr-ree-eh'-rah*] career
carro [*kahr'-roh*] truck, cart
carrozza [*kahr-rohts'-tsah*] carriage
carta [*kahr'-tah*] paper
  carta carbone [*kahr'-tah kahr-boh'-neh*] carbon paper
  carta geografica [*kahr'-tah jeh-oh-grah'-fee-kah*] map
  carta igienica [*kahr'-tah ee-jee-eh'-nee-kah*] toilet paper
  carte da giuoco [*kahr'-teh dah jee-oh'-koh*] playing cards
  mazzo di carte [*mahts'-tsoh dee kahr'-teh*] pack of cards
  carta da scrivere [*kahr'-tah dah skree'-veh-reh*] writing paper
  carta velina [*kahr'-tah veh-lee'-nah*] tissue paper
cartellone *m.* [*kahr-tehl-loh'-neh*] sign [street]
cartoleria [*kahr-toh-leh-ree'-ah*] stationery
cartolina [*kahr-toh-lee'-nah*] card
  cartolina di natale [*kahr-toh-lee'-nah dee nah-tah'-leh*] Christmas card
  cartolina postale [*kahr-toh-lee'-nah pohs-tah'-leh*] postcard
  cartolina vaglia [*kahr-toh-lee'-nah vah'-lyah*] money order
cartone *m.* [*kahr-toh'-neh*] cardboard
casa [*kah'-zah*] home, house
  casa di campagna [*kah'-zah dee kahm-pah'-nyah*] cottage
cascata [*kahs-kah'-tah*] waterfall
casella postale [*kah-zehl'-lah pohs-tah'-leh*] post-office box
caso [*kah'-zoh*] case, chance
  in tal caso [*een tahl kah'-zoh*] in that case
  nel caso che [*nehl kah'-zoh keh*] in the event of
  per caso [*pehr kah'-zoh*] by chance
  per puro caso [*pehr poo'-roh kah'-zoh*] by mere chance
cassa [*kahs'-sah*] case
cassetto [*kahs-seht'-toh*] drawer
cassettone *m.* [*kahs-seht-toh'-neh*] chest of drawers
cassiere *m.* [*kahs-see-eh'-reh*] cashier
castagna [*kahs-tah'-nyah*] chestnut
castello [*kahs-tehl'-loh*] castle
casualmente [*kah-zoo-ahl-mehn'-teh*] casually

catalogo [*kah-tah'-loh-goh*] catalog
categoria [*kah-teh-goh-ree'-ah*] category
catena [*kah-teh'-nah*] chain
cattedrale [*kaht-teh-drah'-leh*] cathedral
cattiveria [*kaht-tee-veh'-ree-ah*] mischief
cattivo [*kaht-tee'-voh*] bad, evil
  più cattivo, il più cattivo [*pee-oo' kaht-tee'-voh, eel pee-oo' kaht-tee'-voh*] worse, worst
cattolico [*kaht-toh'-lee-koh*] catholic
causa [*kah'-oo-zah*] cause
  a causa di . . . [*ah kah'-oo-zah dee*] due to . . .
causare *v.* [*kah-oo-zah'-reh*] cause
cavalcare *v.* [*kah-vahl-kah'-reh*] ride a horse
cavaliere *m.* [*kah-vah-lee-eh'-reh*] knight
cavalleria [*kah-vahl-leh-ree'-ah*] cavalry
cavallo [*kah-vahl'-loh*] horse
  andare *v.* **a cavallo** [*ahn-dah'-reh ah kah-vahl'-loh*] go horseback riding
cavatappi *m. sing.* [*kah-vah-tahp'-pee*] corkscrew
caverna [*kah-vehr'-nah*] cave
caviglia [*kah-vee'-lyah*] ankle
cavità *f. indecl.* [*kah-vee-tah'*] cavity
cavo [*kah'-voh*] cable
cavolfiore *m.* [*kah-vohl-fee-oh'-reh*] cauliflower
cavolo [*kah'-voh-loh*] cabbage
c'e, ci sono [*cheh, chee soh'-noh*] there is, there are
Cecoslovacchia [*cheh-kohs-loh-vahk'-kee-ah*] Czechoslovakia
cecoslovacco [*cheh-koh-sloh-vahk'-koh*] Czechoslovak
cedere *v.* [*cheh'-deh-reh*] give up
celebrare *v.* [*cheh-leh-brah'-reh*] celebrate
celebrità *f. indecl.* [*cheh-leh-bree-tah'*] celebrity
celibe [*cheh'-lee-beh*] single, bachelor
cella [*chehl'-lah*] cell
cementare *v.* [*cheh-mehn-tah'-reh*] cement
cemento [*cheh-mehn'-toh*] cement
cena [*cheh'-nah*] dinner, supper
cenare *v.* [*cheh-nah'-reh*] have supper, dinner
cenere *f.* [*cheh'-neh-reh*] ash
cenno [*chehn'-noh*] sign, wave, nod
  fare *v.* **cenno** [*fah'-reh chehn'-noh*] wave [one's hand]

censura [*chehn-soo'-rah*] censorship
centesimo [*chehn-teh'-zee-moh*] cent
centimetro [*chehn-tee'-meh-troh*] centimeter
cento [*chehn'-toh*] hundred, one hundred
  due cento [*doo'-eh chehn'-toh*] two hundred
centrale [*chehn-trah'-leh*] central
centro [*chehn'-troh*] center
cera [*cheh'-rah*] wax
cercare *v.* [*chehr-kah'-reh*] search for, seek
cerchio [*chehr'-kee-oh*] circle, ring, hoop
cereale *m.* [*cheh-reh-ah'-leh*] cereal
cerimonia [*cheh-ree-moh'-nee-ah*] ceremony
cerino [*cheh-ree'-noh*] match [made of wax]
certamente [*chehr-tah-mehn'-teh*] certainly
certificare *v.* [*chehr-tee-fee-kah'-reh*] certify
certificato [*chehr-tee-fee-kah'-toh*] certificate
  certificato medico [*chehr-tee-fee-kah'-toh meh'-dee-koh*] health certificate
certo [*chehr'-toh*] certain
  fino ad un certo punto [*fee'-noh ahd oon chehr'-toh poon'-toh*] to a certain extent
cervello [*chehr-vehl'-loh*] brain
cespuglio [*chehs-poo'-lyoh*] bush
cessare *v.* [*chehs-sah'-reh*] cease
cestino [*chehs-tee'-noh*] wastebasket
cesto [*chehs'-toh*] basket
cetriolo [*cheh-tree-oh'-loh*] cucumber
che *pron.* [*keh*] what, who, whom, which
  Che altro? [*keh ahl'-troh*] What else?
  Che peccato! [*keh pehk-kah'-toh*] What a pity!
  Che succede? [*keh sooch-cheh'-deh*] What is the matter?
che *conj.* [*keh*] than, that
chi [*kee*] who, the one who, which, whom
  Chi parla? [*kee pahr'-lah*] Who is talking?
  Di chi è questo? [*dee kee eh' koo-ehs'-toh*] Whose is this?
chiacchierare *v.* [*chee-ahk-kee-eh-rah'-reh*] chat
chiamare *v.* [*kee-ah-mah'-reh*] call
  Ci chiamano [*chee kee-ah'-mah-noh*] They call us
chiamarsi *v.* [*kee-ah-mahr'-see*] be called, be named
  Come si chiama? [*koh'-meh see kee-ah'-mah*] What is your

name?
chiamata [*kee-ah-mah'-tah*] call
chiamata telefonica [*kee-ah-mah'-tah teh-leh-foh'-nee-kah*] telephone call
chiaramente [*kee-ah-rah-mehn'-teh*] clearly
chiarire *v.* [*kee-ah-ree'-reh*] make clear
chiaro [*kee-ah'-roh*] clear
chiave *f.*, [*kee-ah'-veh*] key
chiedere *v.* [*kee-eh'-deh-reh*] ask [for something]
chiedere il permesso [*kee-eh'-deh-reh eel pehr-mehs'-soh*] ask permission to
chiedere scusa [*kee-eh'-deh-reh skoo'-zah*] beg pardon
chiesa [*kee-eh'-zah*] church
chilo [*kee'-loh*] kilogram
chilometro [*kee-loh'-meh-troh*] kilometer [0.621 mile]
chimico [*kee'-mee-koh*] chemical
chinino [*kee-nee'-noh*] quinine
chiodo [*kee-oh'-doh*] nail [carpentry]
chirurgia [*kee-roor-jee'-ah*] surgery
chirurgo [*kee-roor'-goh*] surgeon
chitarra [*kee-tahr'-rah*] guitar
chiudere *v.* [*kee-oo'-deh-reh*] shut, close
chiudere a chiave [*kee-oo'-deh-reh ah kee-ah'-veh*] lock up
chiunque [*kee-oon'-koo-eh*] whoever, anybody
chiuso [*kee-oo'-zoh*] shut, closed
chiusura [*kee-oo-zoo'-rah*] closing
chiusura lampo [*kee-oo-zoo'-rah lahm'-poh*] zipper
ci [*chee*] here, there, of it, to it
ci sono [*chee soh'-noh*] there are
ci [*chee*] us, to us, ourselves
Ciao! [*chee-ah'-oh*] So long!
ciascuno [*chee-ahs-koo'-noh*] each one, everyone
cibo [*chee'-boh*] food
cicatrice *f.* [*chee-kah-tree'-cheh*] scar
cieco [*chee-eh'-koh*] blind
cielo [*chee-eh'-loh*] sky, heaven
cifra [*chee'-frah*] figure, amount
ciglia *f. pl.* [*chee'-lyah*] eyelashes
Cile [*chee'-leh*] Chile
cileno [*chee-leh'-noh*] Chilean

comunista *m., f.* [*koh-moo-nees'-tah*] communist
comunità *f. indecl.* [*koh-moo-nee-tah'*] community
comunque [*koh-moon'-koo-eh*] however
con [*kohn*] with, by, to
concedere *v.* [*kohn-cheh'-deh-reh*] grant, concede
concentrare *v.* [*kohn-chehn-trah'-reh*] concentrate
concepire *v.* [*kohn-cheh-pee'-reh*] conceive
concerto [*kohn-chehr'-toh*] concert
concetto [*kohn-cheht'-toh*] concept
conchiglia [*kohn-kee'-lyah*] shell [sea]
conciliazione *f.* [*koh-chee-lee-ah-tsee-oh'-neh*] conciliation
conciso [*kohn-chee'-zoh*] concise
concludere *v.* [*kohn-kloo'-deh-reh*] conclude
conclusione *f.* [*kohn-kloo-zee-oh'-neh*] conclusion
concorrenza [*kohn-kohr-rehn'-tsah*] competition
concorso [*kohn-kohr'-soh*] contest
condanna [*kohn-dahn'-nah*] condemnation
condannare *v.* [*kohn-dahn-nah'-reh*] condemn
condannato [*kohn-dah-nah'-toh*] convict(ed)
condensare *v.* [*kohn-dehn-sah'-reh*] condense
condizione *f.* [*kohn-dee-tsee-oh'-neh*] condition
condizioni *pl.* [*kohn-dee-tsee-oh'-nee*] terms
condotta [*kohn-doht'-tah*] conduct, behavior
condurre *v.* [*kohn-door'-reh*] conduct, lead
conduttore *m.* [*kohn-doot-toh'-reh*] conductor [of train]
conferenza [*kohn-feh-rehn'-tsah*] conference
  tenere *v.* **una conferenza** [*teh-neh'-reh oo'-nah kohn-feh-rehn'-tsah*] lecture
confermare *v.* [*kohn-fehr-mah'-reh*] confirm
conferire *v.* [*kohn-feh-ree'-reh*] confer
confessare *v.* [*kohn-fehs-sah'-reh*] confess
confessione *f.* [*kohn-fehs-see-oh'-neh*] confession
confidenziale [*kohn-fee-dehn-tsee-ah'-leh*] confidential
confine [*kohn-fee'-neh*] border
conflitto [*kohn-fleet'-toh*] conflict
confondere *v.* [*kohn-fohn'-deh-reh*] confuse
confortare *v.* [*kohn-fohr-tah'-reh*] comfort
conforto [*kohn-fohr'-toh*] comfort
confusione *f.* [*kohn-foo-zee-oh'-neh*] confusion
confuso [*kohn-foo'-zoh*] confused

congelare *v.* [*kohn-jeh-lah'-reh*] freeze
congratularsi *v.* [*kohn-grah-too-lahr'-see*] congratulate
  Congratulazioni! [*kohn-grah-too-lah-tsee-oh'-nee*] Congratulations!
congresso [*kohn-grehs'-soh*] congress
coniglio [*koh-nee'-lyoh*] rabbit
connessione *f.* [*kohn-nehs-see-oh'-neh*] connection
conoscente [*koh-noh-shehn'-teh*] acquaintance
conoscenza [*koh-noh-shehn'-tsah*] knowledge, acquaintance
conoscere *v.* [*koh-noh'-sheh-reh*] know [somebody or something]
conosciuto [*koh-noh-shee-oo'-toh*] well-known
conquistare *v.* [*kohn-koo-ees-tah'-reh*] conquer
consacrare *v.* [*kohn-sah-krah'-reh*] dedicate
consapevole [*kohn-sah-peh'-voh-leh*] self-conscious
conscio [*kohn'-shee-oh*] conscious
consecutivo [*kohn-seh-koo-tee'-voh*] consecutive
consegnare *v.* [*kohn-seh-nyah'-reh*] deliver
conseguenza [*kohn-seh-goo-ehn'-tsah*] consequence
  di consequenza [*dee kohn-seh-goo-ehn'-tsah*] accordingly
consenso [*kohn-sehn'-soh*] consent
conservare *v.* [*kohn-sehr-vah'-reh*] preserve
conservativo [*kohn-sehr-vah-tee'-voh*] conservative
considerabile [*koh-see-deh-rah'-bee-leh*] considerable
considerare *v.* [*kohn-see-deh-rah'-reh*] consider
considerazione *f.* [*kohn-see-deh-rah-tsee-oh'-neh*] consideration
consigliare *v.* [*kohn-see-lyah'-reh*] advise
consiglio [*kohn-see'-lyoh*] advice, counsel
consistere *v.* [*kohn-sees'-teh-reh*] consist
consolare *v.* [*kohn-soh-lah'-reh*] comfort
consolato [*kohn-soh-lah'-toh*] consulate
console *m.* [*kohn'-soh-leh*] consul
consultare *v.* [*kohn-sool-tah'-reh*] consult
consumare *v.* [*kohn-soo-mah'-reh*] consume
consumato [*kohn-soo-mah'-toh*] worn out
consumatore *m.* [*kohn-soo-mah-toh'-reh*] consumer
contabile *m.* [*kohn-tah'-bee-leh*] bookkeeper
contadino [*kohn-tah-dee'-noh*] farmer, peasant
contagioso [*kohn-tah-jee-oh'-zoh*] contagious

contare *v.* [*kohn-tah'-reh*] count
contare su [*kohn-tah'-reh soo*] count on
denaro contante [*deh-nah'-roh kohn-tahn'-teh*] cash
pagare *v.* **in contanti** [*pah-gah'-reh een kohn-tahn'-tee*] pay cash
contatore *m.* [*kohn-tah-toh'-reh*] meter
conte *m.*, **contessa** *f.* [*kohn'-teh, kohn-tehs'-sah*] count, countess
contegno [*kohn-teh'-nyoh*] restraint
contemporaneo [*kohn-tehm-poh-rah'-neh-oh*] contemporary
contenere *v.* [*kohn-teh-neh'-reh*] contain
contento [*kohn-tehn'-toh*] glad, content
contenuto [*kohn-teh-noo'-toh*] contents
contiguo [*kon-tee'-goo-oh*] adjacent
continente *m.* [*kohn-tee-nehn'-teh*] continent
continuare *v.* [*kohn-tee-noo-ah'-reh*] continue
continuazione *f.* [*kohn-tee-noo-ah-tsee-oh'-neh*] continuation
conto [*kohn'-toh*] check, bill, account
conto corrente [*kohn'-toh kohr-rehn'-teh*] checking account
conto in banca [*kohn'-toh een bahn'-kah*] bank account
pagare *v.* **il conto** [*pah-gah'-reh eel kohn'-toh*] pay the bill
regolare *v.* **un conto** [*reh-goh-lah'-reh oon kohn'-toh*] settle an account
rendere *v.* **conto di** [*rehn'-deh-reh kohn'-toh dee*] account for
contrabbandiere *m.* [*kohn-trahb-bahn-dee-eh'-reh*] smuggler
contraccambiare *v.* [*kohn-trahk-kahm-bee-ah'-reh*] reciprocate
contradizione *f.* [*kohn-trah-dee-tsee-oh'-neh*] contradiction
contrariamente [*kohn-trah-ree-ah-mehn'-teh*] on the contrary
contrario [*kohn-trah'-ree-oh*] contrary
al contrario [*ahl kohn-trah'-ree-oh*] on the contrary
contrasto [*kohn-trahs'-toh*] contrast
contratto [*kohn-traht'-toh*] contract
contravvenzione [*kohn-trah-vehn-tsee-oh'-neh*] fine, violation
contribuire *v.* [*kohn-tree-boo-ee'-reh*] contribute
contribuzione *f.* [*kohn-tree-boo-tsee-oh'-neh*] contribution
contro [*kohn'-troh*] against
controllare *v.* [*kohn-trohl-lah'-reh*] control, check
controllo [*kohn-trohl'-loh*] control

controversia [*kohn-troh-vehr'-see-ah*] controversy
contusione *f.* [*kohn-too-zee-oh'-neh*] bruise
conveniente [*kohn-veh-nee-ehn'-teh*] convenient
convento [*kohn-vehn'-toh*] convent
conversazione *f.* [*kohn-vehr-sah-tsee-oh'-neh*] conversation, talk
convertire *v.* [*kohn-vehr-tee'-reh*] convert
convertito [*kohn-vehr-tee'-toh*] convert
convincere *v.* [*kohn-veen'-cheh-reh*] convince
convinto [*kohn-veen'-toh*] convinced
convitto [*kohn-veet'-toh*] boarding school
convocare *v.* [*kohn-voh-kah'-reh*] summon
cooperazione [*koh-oh-peh-rah-tsee-oh'-neh*] cooperation
coperchio [*koh-pehr'-kee-oh*] lid, cover
coperta [*koh-pehr'-tah*] blanket
coperto [*koh-pehr'-toh*] covered
copertura [*koh-pehr-too'-rah*] cover
copia [*koh'-pee-ah*] copy
copiare *v.* [*koh-pee-ah'-reh*] copy
coppia [*kohp'-pee-ah*] couple
coprire *v. irreg.* [*koh-pree'-reh*] cover
coraggio [*koh-rahj'-jee-oh*] courage
  Che coraggio! [*keh koh-rahj'-jee-oh*] What a nerve!
coraggioso [*koh-rahj-jee-oh'-zoh*] courageous
corallo [*koh-rahl'-loh*] coral
corda [*kohr'-dah*] rope
cordiale [*kohr-dee-ah'-leh*] cordial
coricarsi *v.* [*koh-ree-kahr'-see*] lie down, go to bed
cornice *f.* [*kohr-nee'-cheh*] frame
corno, le corna *pl.* [*kohr'-noh, leh kohr'-nah*] horn [of animal]
coro [*koh'-roh*] chorus
corona [*koh-roh'-nah*] crown
corpo [*kohr'-poh*] body
corporazione *f.* [*kohr-poh-rah-tsee-oh'-neh*] corporation
correggere *v. irreg.* [*kohr-rehj'-jeh-reh*] correct
corrente *f.* [*kohr-rehn'-teh*] current, stream
  al corrente [*ahl koh-rehn'-teh*] well informed
  corrente d'aria [*kohr-rehn'-teh dah'-ree-ah*] draft (of air)
  moneta corrente [*moh-neh'-tah kohr-rehn'-teh*] currency
correre *v. irreg.* [*kohr'-reh-reh*] run

correttezza [*kohr-reht-tehts'-tsah*] decency
corretto [*kohr-reht'-toh*] correct
correzione *f.* [*kohr-reh-tsee-oh'-neh*] correction
corridoio [*kohr-ree-doh'-ee-oh*] corridor
corrispondenza [*kohr-rees-pohn-dehn'-tsah*] correspondence
corrompere *v.* [*kohr-rohm'-peh-reh*] corrupt, bribe
corrotto [*kohr-roht'-toh*] corrupt
corruzione *f.* [*kohr-roo-tsee-oh'-neh*] corruption
corsa [*kohr'-sah*] run, race, trip
  corsa di cavalli [*kohr'-sah dee kah-vahl'-lee*] horse race
corso [*kohr'-soh*] course
corte *f.* [*kohr'-teh*] court
corteggiare *v.* [*kohr-tehj-jee-ah'-reh*] court
corteggiatore *m., f.* [*kohr-tehj-jee-ah-toh'-reh*] suitor
cortese [*kohr-teh'-zeh*] courteous
cortesia [*kohr-teh-zee'-ah*] politeness, kindness
cortile *m.* [*kohr-tee'-leh*] courtyard
corto [*kohr'-toh*] short, brief
cosa [*koh'-zah*] thing, what
  che, che cosa [*keh, keh koh'-zah*] what
  Che cosa c'e? [*keh koh'-zah cheh'*] What's the matter?
  Cosa desidera? [*koh'-zah deh-zee'-deh-rah*] What do you wish?
  Che cosa vi prende? [*keh koh'-zah vee prehn'-deh*] What is the matter with you?
  Che cosa significa? [*keh koh'-zah see-nyee'-fee-kah*] What does it mean?
  Cos' ha? [*kohz-ah'*] What is the matter with him (her, you)?
  Cos'è? [*kohz-eh'*] What is it?
coscienza [*koh-shee-ehn'-tsah*] conscience
coscienzioso [*kohn-shee-ehn-tsee-oh'-zoh*] conscientious
così [*koh-zee'*] so, thus, like this
  così così [*koh-zee' koh-zee'*] so so
  e così via [*eh koh-zee' vee'-ah*] and so forth
cosmetici [*kohz-meh'-tee-chee*] cosmetics
costa [*kohs'-tah*] coast
costare *v.* [*kohs-tah'-reh*] cost
  Quanto costa questo? [*koo-ahn'-toh kohs'-tah koo-ehs'-toh*] How much does this cost?
costante [*kohs-tahn'-teh*] constant

costituire *v.* [*kohs-tee-too-ee'-reh*] constitute
costituzione *f.* [*kohs-tee-too-tsee-oh'-neh*] constitution
costo [*kohs'-toh*] cost
costo della vita [*kohs'-toh dehl'-lah vee'-tah*] cost of living
costola [*kohs'-toh-lah*] rib
costoletta d'agnello [*kohs-toh-leht'-tah dah-nyehl'-loh*] lamb chop
costoletta di maiale [*kohs-toh-leht'-tah dee mah-ee-ah'-leh*] pork chop
costoso [*kohs-toh'-zoh*] expensive
costringere *v.* [*kohs-treen'-jeh-reh*] compel
costrizione *f.* [*kohs-tree-tsee-oh'-neh*] compulsion
costruire *v.* [*kohs-troo-ee'-reh*] build, construct
costruzione *f.* [*kohs-troo-tsee-oh'-neh*] building, construction
costume *m.* [*kohs-too'-meh*] custom
costume da bagno *m.* [*kohs-too'-meh dah bah'-nyoh*] bathing suit
cotoletta [*koh-toh-leht'-tah*] cutlet
cotone *m.* [*koh-toh'-neh*] cotton
cotto [*koht'-toh*] done, cooked
ben cotto [*behn koht'-toh*] well-done [cooking]
poco cotto [*poh'-koh koht'-toh*] rare [cooking]
cranio [*krah'-nee-oh*] skull
cravatta [*krah-vaht'-tah*] necktie
creare *v.* [*kreh-ah'-reh*] create
creatura [*kreh-ah-too'-rah*] creature
creazione *f.* [*kreh-ah-tsee-oh'-neh*] creation
credente [*kreh-dehn'-teh*] believer
credere *v.* [*kreh'-deh-reh*] believe
credito [*kreh'-dee-toh*] credit
creditore *m.* [*kreh-dee-toh'-reh*] creditor
crema [*kreh'-mah*] cream
crepuscolo [*kreh-poos'-koh-loh*] twilight
crescere *v. irreg.* [*kreh'-sheh-reh*] grow [up, bigger, taller), increase
criminale [*kree-mee-nah'-leh*] criminal
crimine *m.* [*kree'-mee-neh*] crime
crisi *f.* [*kree'-zee*] crisis
crisi economica *f.* [*kree'-zee eh-koh-noh'-mee-kah*] recession

cristallo [*krees-tahl'-loh*] crystal
cristianesimo [*krees-tee-ah-neh'-zee-moh*] Christianity
cristiano [*krees-tee-ah'-noh*] Christian
Cristo [*krees'-toh*] Christ
criterio [*kree-teh'-ree-oh*] criterion
criticare *v.* [*kree-tee-kah'-reh*] criticize
critico [*kree'-tee-koh*] critical
croce *f.* [*kroh'-cheh*] cross
  Croce Rossa [*kroh'-cheh rohs'-sah*] Red Cross
crociera [*kroh-chee-eh'-rah*] cruise
crollo [*krohl'-loh*] collapse
cronista *m.* [*kroh-nees'-tah*] reporter
cronometro [*kroh-noh'-meh-troh*] stopwatch
crudele [*kroo-deh'-leh*] cruel
crudeltà *f. indecl.* [*kroo-dehl-tah'*] cruelty
crudo [*kroo'-doh*] raw, crude
cubo [*koo'-boh*] cube
cucchiaio [*kook-kee-ah'-ee-oh*] spoon, spoonful
cucchiaino [*kook-kee-ah-ee'-noh*] teaspoon
cucina [*koo-chee'-nah*] kitchen
cucinare *v.* [*koo-chee-nah'-reh*] cook
cucire *v.* [*koo-chee'-reh*] sew, seam
cucitura [*koo-chee-too'-rah*] seam
cugino *m.*, **cugina** *f.* [*koo-jee'-noh*, *koo-jee'-nah*] cousin
cui [*koo'-ee*] whom, whose, which
culla [*kool'-lah*] cradle
cultura [*kool-too'-rah*] culture
cuocere *v. irreg.* [*koo-oh'-cheh-reh*] bake, cook
cuoco [*koo-oh'-koh*] cook
cuoio [*koo-oh'-ee-oh*] leather
cuore *m.* [*koo-oh'-reh*] heart
cupola [*koo'-poh-lah*] dome
cura [*koo'-rah*] care, cure
  avere *v.* **cura** [*ah-veh'-reh koo'-rah*] take care of
curare *v.* [*koo-rah'-reh*] cure, care
curiosità *f. indecl.* [*koo-ree-oh-zee-tah'*] curiosity
curioso [*koo-ree-oh'-zoh*] curious
curva [*koor'-vah*] curve
cuscino [*koo-shee'-noh*] pillow
custodia [*koos-toh'-dee-ah*] custody

D

da [*dah*] from, by, since, to, for
  da ora in poi [*dah oh'-rah een poh'-ee*] from now on
  Da dove viene? [*dah doh'-veh vee-eh'-neh*] Where do you come from?
  da lontano [*dah lohn-tah'-noh*] from far
dabbene [*dahb-beh'-neh*] good, honest, well educated
dadi [*dah'-dee*] dice
dal, dalla, dallo, dall' [*dahl*, *dahl'-lah*, *dahl'-loh*, *dahl*] from the
damigella d'onore [*dah-mee-jehl'-lah doh-noh'-reh*] bridesmaid
danese [*dah-neh'-zeh*] Danish
danneggiare *v.* [*dahn-nehj-jee-ah'-reh*] damage
danno [*dahn'-noh*] damage
dannoso [*dahn-noh'-zoh*] harmful
danza [*dahn'-tsah*] dance
dappertutto [*dahp-pehr-toot'-toh*] everywhere
dare *v. irreg.* [*dah'-reh*] give
  Me lo da [*meh loh dah*] He, she gives it to me
  Mi dia . . . [*mee dee'-ah*] Give me . . .
  Ci dia . . . [*chee dee'-ah*] Give us . . .
  Dia loro . . . [*dee'-ah loh'-roh*] Give them . . .
  Gli dia . . . , Le dia . . . [*lyee dee'-ah*, *leh dee'-ah*] Give him . . . , Give her . . .
data [*dah'-tah*] date [day of month]
dato [*dah'-toh*] given
dattilografo [*daht-tee-loh'-grah-foh*] typist
davanti [*dah-vahn'-tee*] before, in front of
  davanti all'albergo [*dah-vahn'-tee ahl-lahl-behr'-goh*] in front of the hotel
Davvero [*dahv-veh'-roh*] Yes, indeed
dazio [*dah'-tsee-oh*] duty [customs]
debito [*deh'-bee-toh*] debt
debole [*deh'-boh-leh*] weak
debolezza [*deh-boh-lehts'-tsah*] weakness

decadenza [*deh-kah-dehn'-tsah*] decay, decline
decadere *v.* [*deh-kah-deh'-reh*] decay, decline
decennio [*deh-chehn'-nee-oh*] decade
decente [*deh-chehn'-teh*] decent
decidere *v. irreg.* [*deh-chee'-deh-reh*] decide
decimo [*deh'-chee-moh*] tenth
decisione *f.* [*deh-chee-zee-oh'-neh*] decision
declarazione *f.* [*deh-klah-rah-tsee-oh'-neh*] declaration
declinare *v.* [*deh-klee-nah'-reh*] decline
decollare *v.* [*deh-kohl-lah'-reh*] take off [plane]
decorare *v.* [*deh-koh-rah'-reh*] decorate
decorazione *f.* [*deh-koh-rah-tsee-oh'-neh*] decoration
decreto [*deh-kreh'-toh*] decree
dedicare *v.* [*deh-dee-kah'-reh*] dedicate
deficiente [*deh-fee-chee-ehn'-teh*] deficient
definire *v.* [*deh-fee-nee'-reh*] define
definitivamente [*deh-fee-nee-tee-vah-mehn'-teh*] definitely
definito [*deh-fee-nee'-toh*] definite
definizione *f.* [*deh-fee-nee-tsee-oh'-neh*] definition
defunto [*deh-foon'-toh*] deceased
degno [*deh'-nyoh*] worthy
deliberare *v.* [*deh-lee-beh-rah'-reh*] deliberate
delicato [*deh-lee-kah'-toh*] delicate
delinquente [*deh-leen-koo-ehn'-teh*] delinquent
delitto [*deh-leet'-toh*] crime
delizioso [*deh-lee-tsee-oh'-zoh*] delicious
deludere *v.* [*deh-loo'-deh-reh*] disappoint
deluso [*deh-loo'-zoh*] disappointed
democratico [*deh-moh-krah'-tee-koh*] democratic, democrat
democrazia [*deh-moh-krah-tsee'-ah*] democracy
demolire *v.*, [*deh-moh-lee'-reh*] take down, demolish
demoralizzante [*deh-moh-rah-leedz-dzahn'-teh*] discouraging
demoralizzato [*deh-moh-rah-leedz-dzah'-toh*] discouraged
denaro [*deh-nah'-roh*] money
densità *f. indecl.* [*dehn-see-tah'*] density
denso [*dehn'-soh*] dense, thick
dente *m.* [*dehn'-teh*] tooth
  mal *m.* **di denti** [*mahl dee dehn'-tee*] toothache
dentifricio [*dehn-tee-free'-chee-oh*] toothpaste

dentista *m.* [*dehn-tees'-tah*] dentist
dentro [*dehn'-troh*] inside, within
depositare *v.* [*deh-poh-zee-tah'-reh*] deposit
deposito [*deh-poh'-zee-toh*] deposit, stock
depresso [*deh-prehs'-soh*] depressed
deputato [*deh-poo-tah'-toh*] deputy
derubare *v.* [*deh-roo-bah'-reh*] rob
descrivere *v.* [*dehs-kree'-veh-reh*] describe
descrizione *f.* [*dehs-kree-tsee-oh'-neh*] description
deserto [*deh-zehr'-toh*] desert
desiderabile [*deh-zee-deh-rah'-bee-leh*] desirable
desiderare *v.*, [*deh-zee-deh-rah'-reh*] desire
desiderio [*deh-zee-deh'-ree-oh*] wish, desire
destinatario [*dehs-tee-nah-tah'-ree-oh*] addressee
destinazione *f.* [*dehs-tee-nah-tsee-oh'-neh*] destination
destino [*dehs-tee'-noh*] destiny, fate
destra [*dehs'-trah*] right [direction]
determinare *v.* [*deh-tehr-mee-nah'-reh*] determine
dettaglio [*deht-tah'-lyoh*] detail
dettare *v.* [*deht-tah'-reh*] dictate
dettato [*deht-tah'-toh*] dictation
deviazione *f.* [*deh-vee-ah-tsee-oh'-neh*] detour
devoto [*deh-voh'-toh*] devoted
devozione *f.* [*deh-voh-tsee-oh'-neh*] devotion
di *prep.* [*dee*] of
  di cotone [*dee koh-toh'-neh*] made of cotton
  di lana [*dee lah'-nah*] woolen
  di legno [*dee leh'-nyoh*] wooden
  la sorella di Maria [*lah soh-rehl'-lah dee mah-ree'-ah*] Mary's sister
  di quando in quando [*dee koo-ahn'-doh een koo-ahn'-doh*] now and then
diagnosi *f.* [*dee-ahg-noh'-zee*] diagnosis
diagramma *m.* [*dee-ah-grahm'-mah*] diagram
dialetto [*dee-ah-leht'-toh*] dialect
dialogo [*dee-ah'-loh-goh*] dialogue
diamante *m.* [*dee-ah-mahn'-teh*] diamond
diametro [*dee-ah'-meh-troh*] diameter
diario [*dee-ah'-ree-oh*] diary
diavolo [*dee-ah'-voh-loh*] devil

dicembre *m.* [*dee-chehm'-breh*] December
dichiarare *v.* [*dee-kee-ah-rah'-reh*] declare, state
dichiarazione *f.* [*dee-kee-ah-rah-tsee-oh'-neh*] statement
dichiarazione di dogana [*dee-kee-ah-rah-tsee-oh'-neh dee doh-gah'-nah*] customs declaration
dicianove [*dee-chee-ah-noh'-veh*] nineteen
diciassette [*dee-chee-ah-seht'-teh*] seventeen
diciotto [*dee-chee-oht'-toh*] eighteen
dieci [*dee-eh'-chee*] ten
dieta [*dee-eh'-tah*] diet
dietro [*dee-eh'-troh*] behind
difendere *v. irreg.* [*dee-fehn'-deh-reh*] defend
difesa [*dee-feh'-zah*] defense
difetto [*dee-feht'-toh*] defect
difettoso [*dee-feht-toh'-zoh*] defective
differente [*deef-feh-rehn'-teh*] different
differenza [*deef-feh-rehn'-tsah*] difference
a differenza di [*ah deef-feh-rehn'-tsah dee*] unlike
difficile [*deef-fee'-chee-leh*] difficult
difficoltà *f. indecl.* [*deef-fee-kohl-tah'*] difficulty
diffidare *v.* [*deef-fee-dah'-reh*] distrust
diffuso [*deef-foo'-zoh*] widespread
diga [*dee'-gah*] dam
digerire *v.* [*dee-jeh-ree'-reh*] digest
digestione *f.* [*dee-jehs-tee-oh'-neh*] digestion
dignità *f. indecl.* [*dee-nyee-tah'*] dignity
digiunare *v.* [*dee-jee-oo-nah'-reh*] fast
digiuno [*dee-jee-oo'-noh*] fast
dilettare *v.* [*dee-leht-tah'-reh*] delight
diletto [*dee-leht'-toh*] delight
dimagrire *v.* [*dee-mah-gree'-reh*] grow thin, reduce
dimensione *f.* [*dee-mehn-see-oh'-neh*] dimension
dimenticare *v.* [*dee-mehn-tee-kah'-reh*] forget
dimenticato [*dee-mehn-tee-kah'-toh*] forgotten
dimettersi *v.* [*dee-meht'-tehr-see*] resign
diminuire *v.* [*dee-mee-noo-ee'-reh*] diminish
dimissione [*dee-mees-see-oh'-neh*] resignation
dimostrare *v.* [*dee-mohs-trah'-reh*] demonstrate
dimostrazione *f.* [*dee-mohs-trah-tsee-oh'-neh*] demonstration

dinamite *f.* [*dee-nah-mee'-teh*] dynamite
dintorni [*deen-tohr'-nee*] surroundings
Dio [*dee'-oh*] God
dipartimento [*dee-pahr-tee-mehn'-toh*] department
dipendente [*dee-pehn-dehn'-teh*] dependent
dipendere da *v.* [*dee-pehn'-deh-reh dah*] depend on
  dipende [*dee-pehn'-deh*] that depends
dipingere *v. irreg.* [*dee-peen'-jeh-reh*] paint
diploma *m.* [*dee-ploh'-mah*] diploma
diplomatico [*dee-ploh-mah'-tee-koh*] diplomat, diplomatic
diplomato [*dee-ploh-mah'-toh*] graduate
diplomazia [*dee-ploh-mah-tsee'-ah*] diplomacy
dire *v. irreg.* [*dee'-reh*] tell, say
  Mi dica, per favore [*mee dee'-kah, pehr fah-voh'-reh*] Tell me, please
  Non mi dica [*nohn mee dee'-kah*] Don't tell me
direttamente [*dee-reht-tah-mehn'-teh*] directly
direttissimo [*dee-reht-tees'-see-moh*] express (train)
diretto [*dee-reht'-toh*] direct
direttore *m.*, **direttrice** *f.* [*dee-reht-toh'-reh, dee-reht-tree'-cheh*] director
direzione *f.* [*dee-reh-tsee-oh'-neh*] direction
dirigere *v. irreg.* [*dee-ree'-jeh-reh*] direct
diritto [*dee-reet'-toh*] right, law
diritto *adj.* [*dee-reet'-toh*] straight, right
  andare *v.* **diritto** [*ahn-dah'-reh dee-reet'-toh*] go straight on
disaccordo [*deez-ahk-kohr'-doh*] disagreement
disagio [*dee-zah'-jee-oh*] discomfort
disapprovare *v.* [*deez-ahp-proh-vah'-reh*] disapprove
disastro [*dee-zahs'-troh*] disaster
discendere *v.* [*dee-shehn'-deh-reh*] descend, come down
disciplina [*dee-shee-plee'-nah*] discipline
disco [*dees'-koh*] record [phono]
discorso [*dees-kohr'-soh*] speech
discussione *f.* [*dees-koos-see-oh'-neh*] discussion
discutere *v. irreg.* [*dees-koo'-teh-reh*] discuss
discutibile [*dees-koo-tee'-bee-leh*] questionable
disegnare *v.* [*dee-zeh-nyah'-reh*] draw [a picture], outline
disegno [*dee-zeh'-nyoh*] design
disertare *v.* [*dee-zehr-tah'-reh*] desert

disfare *v.* [*dees-fah'-reh*] unpack, undo
disgrazia [*deez-grah'-tsee-ah*] disgrace, bad luck
disgraziatamente [*deez-grah-tsee-ah-tah-mehn'-teh*] unfortunately
disgraziato [*deez-grah-tsee-ah'-toh*] unfortunate
disgustato [*deez-goos-tah'-toh*] disgusted
disinteressato [*deez-een-teh-rehs-sah'-toh*] unselfish
disobbedire *v.* [*deez-ohb-beh-dee'-reh*] disobey
disoccupato [*deez-ohk-koo-pah'-toh*] unemployed
disonesto [*deez-oh-nehs'-toh*] dishonest
disonorare *v.* [*deez-oh-noh-rah'-reh*] disgrace
disonore *m.* [*deez-oh-noh'-reh*] disgrace
disordine *m.* [*deez-ohr'-dee-neh*] disorder
disorganizzato [*deez-ohr-gah-needz-dzah'-toh*] unorganized
dispari [*dees'-pah-ree*] odd [number]
disperare *v.* [*dees-peh-rah'-reh*] despair
disperato [*dees-peh-rah'-toh*] desperate
disperazione *f.* [*dees-peh-rah-tsee-oh'-neh*] despair
dispetto [*dees-peht'-toh*] spite, vexation
dispiacere *m.* [*dees-pee-ah-cheh'-reh*] sorrow, regret
dispiacersi *v.* [*dees-pee-ah-chehr'-see*] be sorry
Le dispiace se mi siedo qui? [*leh dees-pee-ah'-cheh seh mee see-eh'-doh koo-ee'*] Do you mind if I sit here?
Mi dispiace molto [*mee dees-pee-ah'-cheh mohl'-toh*] I am very sorry
disponibile [*dees-poh-nee'-bee-leh*] available
disporre *v. irreg.* [*dees-pohr'-reh*] dispose
disposizione *f.* [*dees-poh-zee-tsee-oh'-neh*] disposition, arrangement
disposto [*dees-pohs'-toh*] willing
Sono disposto a . . . [*soh'-noh dees-pohs'-toh ah*] I am willing to . . .
disprezzare *v.* [*dees-prehts-tsah'-reh*] despise, scorn
disprezzo [*dees-prehts'-tsoh*] contempt, scorn
disputa, [*dees'-poo-tah*] dispute
disputare *v.* [*dees-poo-tah'-reh*] argue
dissenteria [*dees-sehn-teh-ree'-ah*] dysentery
dissimile [*dees-see'-mee-leh*] unlike
dissolvere *v.* [*dees-sohl'-veh-reh*] dissolve
distante [*dees-tahn'-teh*] distant

distanza [*dees-tahn'-tsah*] distance
distensione *f.* [*dees-tehn-see-oh'-neh*] relaxation
distinguere *v.* [*dees-teen'-goo-eh-reh*] distinguish
distintivo [*dees-teen-tee'-voh*] badge, distinctive
distinto [*dees-teen'-toh*] distinct, distinguished
distratto [*dees-traht'-toh*] absent-minded
distrazione *f.* [*dees-trah-tsee-oh'-neh*] distraction
distretto [*dees-treht'-toh*] district
distribuire *v.* [*dees-tree-boo-ee'-reh*] distribute
distribuzione *f.* [*dees-tree-boo-tsee-oh'-neh*] distribution
distruggere *v.* [*dees-trooj'-jeh-reh*] destroy
distruzione *f.* [*dees-troo-tsee-oh'-neh*] destruction
disturbare *v.* [*dees-toor-bah'-reh*] disturb, annoy
  Non si disturbi [*nohn see dees-toor'-bee*] Don't trouble yourself
disturbato [*dees-toor-bah'-toh*] annoyed, disturbed
disturbo [*dees-toor'-boh*] trouble, disturbance
disubbidire *v.* [*deez-oo-bee-dee'-reh*] disobey
disuguale [*deez-oo-goo-ah'-leh*] unequal
dito, le dita *pl.* [*dee'-toh, leh dee'-tah*] finger, toe
ditta [*deet'-tah*] firm, company
diurno [*dee-oor'-noh*] daily
divano [*dee-vah'-noh*] couch, sofa
diventare, divenire *v. irreg.* [*dee-vehn-tah'-reh, dee-veh-nee'-reh*] become, get, grow
diversi [*dee-vehr'-see*] various
divertente [*dee-vehr-tehn'-teh*] entertaining, amusing
divertimento [*dee-vehr-tee-mehn'-toh*] amusement, fun
  Buon divertimento! [*boo-ohn' dee-vehr-tee-mehn'-toh*] Have a good time!
divertire *v.* [*dee-vehr-tee'-reh*] amuse
divertirsi *v.* [*dee-vehr-teer'-see*] amuse oneself
  Si diverta! [*see dee-vehr'-tah*] Enjoy yourself!
dividere *v. irreg.* [*dee-vee'-deh-reh*] split, divide
divino [*dee-vee'-noh*] divine
divisione *f.* [*dee-vee-zee-oh'-neh*] division
diviso [*dee-vee'-zoh*] divided
divorziare *v.* [*dee-vohr-tsee-ah'-reh*] divorce
divorziato [*dee-vohr-tsee-ah'-toh*] divorced
divorzio [*dee-vohr'-tsee-oh*] divorce

dizionario [*dee-tsee-oh-nah'-ree-oh*] dictionary
doccia [*dohch'-chee-ah*] shower
documento [*doh-koo-mehn'-toh*] document
dodicesimo [*doh-dee-cheh'-zee-moh*] twelfth
dodici [*doh'-dee-chee*] twelve
dogana [*doh-gah'-nah*] customs
  agente *m.* **di dogana** [*ah-jehn'-teh dee doh-gah'-nah*] customs officer
  dazio di dogana [*dah'-tsee-oh dee doh-gah'-nah*] customs duty
dolce [*dohl'-cheh*] sweet, cake, dessert
dolore *m.* [*doh-loh'-reh*] ache, pain, grief
doloroso [*doh-loh-roh'-zoh*] painful
dollaro [*dohl'-lah-roh*] dollar
domanda [*doh-mahn'-dah*] question, demand
domandare *v.* [*doh-mahn-dah'-reh*] ask
domandarsi *v.* [*doh-mahn-dahr'-see*] ask [oneself]
domani [*doh-mah'-nee*] tomorrow
  domani mattina [*doh-mah'-nee maht-tee'-nah*] tomorrow morning
  dopodomani [*doh-poh-doh-mah'-nee*] day after tomorrow
domenica [*doh-meh'-nee-kah*] Sunday
domestico [*doh-mehs'-tee-koh*] valet, domestic
domicilio [*doh-mee-chee'-lee-oh*] residence
dominare *v.* [*doh-mee-nah'-reh*] dominate
donare *v.* [*doh-nah'-reh*] donate
donna [*dohn'-nah*] woman, lady
dopo [*doh'-poh*] after, later
doppio [*dohp'-pee-oh*] double
dormire *v.* [*dohr-mee'-reh*] sleep
dormitorio [*dohr-mee-toh'-ree-oh*] dormitory
dose *f.* [*doh'-zeh*] dose
dotato [*doh-tah'-toh*] gifted
dote *f.* [*doh'-teh*] dowry, quality
dottore *m.*, **dottoressa** *f.* [*doht-toh'-reh, doht-toh-rehs'-sah*] doctor, physician
dove [*doh'-veh*] where
  Dov'è? [*doh-veh'*] Where is it (he, she)?
dovere *m.* [*doh-veh'-reh*] duty
dovere *v. irreg., aux.* [*doh-veh'-reh*] have to, ought to, must

Devo andare a casa [*deh'-voh ahn-dah'-reh ah kah'-zah*] I must go home
Dovrei andare [*doh-vreh'-ee ahn-dah'-reh*] I ought to go
Lei dovrebbe riposare [*leh'-ee doh-vrehb'-beh ree-poh-zah'-reh*] You ought to rest
dovunque [*doh-voon'-koo-eh*] anywhere, wherever
dovuto [*doh-voo'-toh*] due
dozzina [*dohdz-dzee'-nah*] dozen
dramma *m.* [*drahm'-mah*] drama, play
drammatico [*drahm-mah'-tee-koh*] dramatic
droga [*droh'-gah*] drug
drogheria [*droh-geh-ree'-ah*] grocery
dubbio [*doob'-bee-oh*] doubt
senza dubbio [*sehn'-tsah doob'-bee-oh*] without a doubt
dubbioso [*doob-bee-oh'-zoh*] doubtful
dubitare *v.* [*doo-bee-tah'-reh*] doubt
duca *m.*, **duchessa** [*doo'-kah, doo-kehs'-sah*] duke, duchess
duce *m.* [*doo'-cheh*] leader
due [*doo'-eh*] two
le due e mezzo [*leh doo'-eh eh mehdz'-dzoh*] half past two
due volte [*doo'-eh vohl'-teh*] twice
duello [*doo-ehl'-loh*] duel
dunque [*doon'-koo-eh*] then
duomo [*doo-oh'-moh*] cathedral
durante [*doo-rahn'-teh*] during
durare *v.* [*doo-rah'-reh*] last
durata [*doo-rah'-tah*] duration
durevole [*doo-reh'-voh-leh*] durable
duro [*doo'-roh*] hard, tough

E

e, ed [*eh, ehd*] and
è [*eh'*] is
ebbene [*ehb-beh'-neh*] well!, well then
ebreo [*eh-breh'-oh*] Jew, Jewish
eccedere *v.* [*ehch-cheh'-deh-reh*] exceed

eccellente [*ehch-chehl-lehn'-teh*] excellent
eccentrico [*ehch-chehn'-tree-koh*] eccentric
eccessivo [*ehch-chehs-see'-voh*] excessive
eccesso [*ehch-chehs'-soh*] excess
eccetera [*ehch-cheht'-teh-rah*] et cetera
eccetto [*ehch-cheht'-toh*] except
eccezionale [*ehch-cheh-tsee-oh-nah'-leh*] exceptional
eccezione *f.* [*ehch-cheh-tsee-oh'-neh*] exception
eccitato [*ehch-chee-tah'-toh*] excited
ecco [*ehk'-koh*] here is, there is
  Ecco fatto! [*ehk'-koh faht'-toh*] It is done, Here it is!
  Eccoci! [*ehk'-koh-chee*] Here we are!
  Eccomi! [*ehk'-koh-mee*] Here I am!
  Eccola! [*ehk'-koh-lah*] There she (it) is!
  Eccolo! [*ehk'-koh-loh*] There he (it) is!
eco [*eh'-koh*] echo
economico [*eh-koh-noh'-mee-koh*] economical
edicola [*eh-dee'-koh-lah*] newsstand
edifico [*eh-dee-fee'-chee-oh*] building
edizione *f.* [*eh-dee-tsee-oh'-neh*] edition
educato [*eh-doo-kah'-toh*] polite, well mannered
educazione *f.* [*eh-doo-kah-tsee-oh'-neh*] upbringing
effetti personali [*ehf-feht'-tee pehr-soh-nah'-lee*] belongings
effettivo [*ehf-feht-tee'-voh*] effective
effetto [*ehf-feht'-toh*] effect
efficace [*ehf-fee-kah'-cheh*] effective
efficiente [*ehf-fee-chee-ehn'-teh*] efficient
Egitto [*eh-jeet'-toh*] Egypt
egiziano [*eh-jee-tsee-ah'-noh*] Egyptian
egli [*eh'-lyee*] he
egoista [*eh-goh-ees'-tah*] selfish
egregio [*eh-greh'-jee-oh*] distinguished
  Egregio Signore: [*eh-greh'-jee-oh see-nyoh'-reh*] Dear Sir:
eguaglianza [*eh-goo-ah-lyahn'-tsah*] equality
eguale [*eh-goo-ah'-leh*] same, equal
elastico [*eh-lahs'-tee-koh*] elastic
elaborare *v.* [*eh-lah-boh-rah'-reh*] elaborate
elefante *m.* [*eh-leh-fahn'-teh*] elephant
elegante [*eh-leh-gahn'-teh*] elegant
eleganza [*eh-leh-gahn'-tsah*] elegance

eleggere *v.* [*eh-lehj'-jeh-reh*] elect
elementare [*eh-leh-mehn-tah'-reh*] elementary
elemento [*eh-leh-mehn'-toh*] element
elenco [*eh-lehn'-koh*] list
  elenco telefonico [*eh-lehn'-koh teh-leh-foh'-nee-koh*] telephone directory
elettricità *f. indecl.* [*eh-leht-tree-chee-tah'*] electricity
elettrico [*eh-leht'-tree-koh*] electric
elevato [*eh-leh-vah'-toh*] elevated, high
elezione *f.* [*eh-leh-tsee-oh'-neh*] election
elica [*eh'-lee-kah*] propeller
eliminare *v.* [*eh-lee-mee-nah'-reh*] eliminate
ella [*ehl'-lah*] she
embargo [*ehm-bahr'-koh*] embargo
emergenza [*eh-mehr-jehn'-tsah*] emergency
  in caso di emergenza [*een kah'-zoh dee eh-mehr-jehn'-tsah*] in case of emergency
emigrante *m.* [*eh-mee-grahn'-teh*] emigrant
emigrazione *f.* [*eh-mee-grah-tsee-oh'-neh*] emigration
emotivo [*eh-moh-tee'-voh*] emotional
emozionato [*eh-moh-tsee-oh-nah'-toh*] thrilled
emozione *f.* [*eh-moh-tsee-oh'-neh*] emotion
energia [*eh-nehr-jee'-ah*] energy
energico [*eh-nehr'-jee-koh*] energetic
enigma [*eh-neeg'-mah*] puzzle
enorme [*eh-nohr'-meh*] huge
ente *m.*[*ehn'-teh*] institution, corporation
entrare *v.* [*ehn-trah'-reh*] enter
  No entri [*noh ehn'-tree*] Do not enter
entrata [*ehn-trah'-tah*] entrance
entro [*ehn'-troh*] in, within
entusiasmo [*ehn-too-zee-ahz'-moh*] enthusiasm
episodio [*eh-pee-soh'-dee-oh*] episode
epoca [*eh'-poh-kah*] epoch
eppure [*ehp-poo'-reh*] even so, yet, and still
equilibrare *v.* [*eh-koo-ee-lee-brah'-reh*] balance
equilibrio [*eh-koo-ee-lee'-bree-oh*] balance
equipaggiamento [*eh-koo-ee-pahj-jee-ah-mehn'-toh*] equipment
equipaggio [*eh-koo-ee-pahj'-jee-oh*] crew
equivalente [*eh-koo-ee-vah-lehn'-teh*] equivalent

equivoco [*eh-koo-ee'-voh-koh*] misunderstanding
equo [*eh'-koo-oh*] just, fair
era [*eh'-rah*] age, era
erba [*ehr'-bah*] grass
erede [*eh-reh'-deh*] heir, heiress
eredità *f. indecl.* [*eh-reh-dee-tah'*] inheritance
ereditare *v.* [*eh-reh-dee-tah'-reh*] inherit
eroe *m.* [*eh-roh'-eh*] hero
eroico [*eh-roh'-ee-koh*] heroic
errore *m.* [*ehr-roh'-reh*] error, mistake
  errore di stampa [*ehr-roh'-reh dee stahm'-pah*] misprint
esagerare *v.* [*eh-zah-jeh-rah'-reh*] exaggerate
esagerazione *f.* [*eh-zah-jeh-rah-tsee-oh'-neh*] exaggeration
esame *m.* [*eh-zah'-meh*] examination
esaminare *v.* [*eh-zah-mee-nah'-reh*] examine
esattamente [*eh-zaht-tah-mehn'-teh*] exactly
esatto [*eh-zaht'-toh*] accurate, exact
esaurito [*eh-zah-oo-ree'-toh*] exhausted
  tutto esaurito [*toot'-toh eh-zah-oo-ree'-toh*] sold out
escludere *v.* [*ehs-kloo'-deh-reh*] exclude
esclusivo [*ehs-kloo-zee'-voh*] exclusive
escursione *f.* [*ehs-koor-see-oh'-neh*] excursion
esempio [*eh-zehm'-pee-oh*] example
  per esempio [*pehr eh-zehm'-pee-oh*] for example
esente [*eh-zehn'-teh*] exempt, free
esercitare *v.* [*eh-zehr-chee-tah'-reh*] exercise, practice
esercito [*eh-zehr'-chee-toh*] army
esercizio [*eh-zehr-chee'-tsee-oh*] exercise
esibire *v.* [*eh-zee-bee'-reh*] exhibit
esibizione *f.* [*eh-zee-bee-tsee-oh'-neh*] exhibition
esigenza [*eh-zee-jehn'-tsah*] requirement
esigere *v.* [*eh-zee'-jeh-reh*] require
esilio [*eh-zee'-lee-oh*] exile
esistente [*eh-zees-tehn'-teh*] existent, living
esistenza [*eh-zees-tehn'-tsah*] existence
esistere *v.* [*eh-zees'-teh-reh*] exist
esitare *v.* [*eh-zee-tah'-reh*] hesitate
esperienza [*ehs-peh-ree-ehn'-tsah*] experience
esperimento [*ehs-peh-ree-mehn'-toh*] experiment
esperto [*ehs-pehr'-toh*] expert

esplodere *v.* [*ehs-ploh'-deh-reh*] burst
esplorare *v.* [*ehs-ploh-rah'-reh*] explore
esplosione *f.* [*ehs-ploh-zee-oh'-neh*] explosion
esporre *v. irreg.* [*ehs-pohr'-reh*] display
esportare *v.* [*ehs-pohr-tah'-reh*] export
esportazione *f.* [*ehs-pohr-tah-tsee-oh'-neh*] export
esposizione *f.* [*ehs-poh-zee-tsee-oh'-neh*] show, exhibition
espressione *f.* [*ehs-prehs-see-oh'-neh*] expression
espresso [*ehs-prehs'-soh*] express
esprimere *v. irreg.* [*ehs-pree'-meh-reh*] express
essa [*ehs'-sah*] she, it
esse *f.* [*ehs'-seh*] they
essenza [*ehs-sehn'-tsah*] essence
essenziale [*ehs-sehn-tsee-ah'-leh*] essential
essere *v. irreg.* [*ehs'-seh-reh*] be
essere umano [*ehs'-seh-reh oo-mah'-noh*] human being
essi *m.* [*ehs'-see*] they
esso [*ehs'-soh*] he, it
est *m.* [*ehst*] East
estate *f.* [*ehs-tah'-teh*] summer
estendere *v.* [*ehs-tehn'-deh-reh*] extend
estensione *f.* [*ehs-tehn-see-oh'-neh*] extent, extension
esteriore [*ehs-teh-ree-oh'-reh*] exterior
esterno [*ehs-tehr'-noh*] external
estero [*ehs'-teh-roh*] foreign
  all'estero [*ahl-lehs'-teh-roh*] abroad
estinguere *v.* [*ehs-teen'-goo-eh-reh*] extinguish
estivo *adj.* [*ehs-tee'-voh*] summer, summery
estraneo [*ehs-trah'-neh-oh*] stranger
estrarre *v. irreg.* [*ehs-trahr'-reh*] extract
estremamente [*ehs-treh-mah-mehn'-teh*] extremely
estremo [*ehs-treh'-moh*] extreme
età *f. indecl.* [*eh-tah'*] age
eterno [*eh-tehr'-noh*] eternal
etichetta [*eh-tee-keht'-tah*] label
Europa [*eh-oo-roh'-pah*] Europe
Europeo [*eh-oo-roh-peh'-oh*] European
evacuare *v.* [*eh-vah-koo-ah'-reh*] evacuate
evento [*eh-vehn'-toh*] event
eventualmente [*eh-vehn-too-ahl-mehn'-teh*] eventually

evidente [*eh-vee-dehn'-teh*] evident
evidentemente [*eh-vee-dehn-teh-mehn'-teh*] evidently
evidenza [*eh-vee-dehn'-tsah*] evidence
evitare *v.* [*eh-vee-tah'-reh*] avoid
evo [*eh'-voh*] age, era
  medio evo [*meh'-dee-oh eh'-voh*] middle ages

F

fa [*fah*] he (she, it) makes, does
  Cosa fa? [*koh'-zah fah*] What are you doing?
  Fa caldo [*fah kahl'-doh*] It is warm
  Fa freddo [*fah frehd'-doh*] It is cold
  Non fa niente [*nohn fah nee-ehn'-teh*] It doesn't matter
fa [*fah*] ago
  due settimane fa [*doo'-eh seht-tee-mah'-ne fah*] two weeks ago
  molto tempo fa [*mohl'-toh tehm'-poh fah*] long ago
fabbrica [*fahb'-bree-kah*] factory
fabbricante [*fahb-bree-kahn'-teh*] manufacturer
fabbricare *v.* [*fahb-bree-kah'-reh*] manufacture
faccenda [*fahch-chehn'-dah*] business, matter
facchino [*fahk-kee'-noh*] porter
faccia [*fahch'-chee-ah*] face
facile [*fah'-chee-leh*] easy
facilità *f. indecl.* [*fah-chee-lee-tah'*] ease, facility
facilmente [*fah-cheel-mehn'-teh*] easily
facoltà *f. indecl.* [*fah-kohl-tah'*] faculty
faggioli *m. pl.* [*fahj-jee-oh'-lee*] beans
fagotto [*fah-goht'-toh*] bundle
fallimento [*fahl-lee-mehn'-toh*] failure
fallire *v.* [*fahl-lee'-reh*] fail
falsità *f. indecl.* [*fahl-see-tah'*] falsehood
falso [*fahl'-soh*] false
fama [*fah'-mah*] fame
fame *f.* [*fah'-meh*] hunger
  avere *v.* **fame** [*ah-veh'-reh fah'-meh*] be hungry

famiglia [*fah-mee'-lyah*] family
familiare [*fah-mee-lee-ah'-reh*] familiar
famoso [*fah-moh'-zoh*] famous
fanciullezza [*fahn-chee-oo-lehts'-tsah*] childhood
fanciullo, fanciulla [*fahn-chee-ool'-loh, fahn-chee-ool'-lah*] young boy, young girl
fango [*fahn'-goh*] mud
fantasia [*fahn-tah-zee'-ah*] fantasy, fancy
fantasma [*fahn-tahz'-mah*] ghost
fantastico [*fahn-tahs'-tee-koh*] fantastic
fare *v. irreg.* [*fah'-reh*] make, do
Faccia attenzione! [*fahch'-chee-ah aht-tehn-tsee-oh'-neh*] Pay attention!, Look out!
Faccia presto! [*fahch'-chee-ah prehs'-toh*] Hurry up!
farfalla [*fahr-fahl'-lah*] butterfly
farina [*fah-ree'-nah*] flour
farmacia [*fahr-mah-chee'-ah*] pharmacy
faro [*fah'-roh*] lighthouse
fascino [*fah'-shee-noh*] charm
fase *f.* [*fah'-zeh*] phase
fastidio [*fahs-tee'-dee-oh*] annoyance
fatale [*fah-tah'-leh*] fatal
fatica [*fah-tee'-kah*] fatigue
faticoso [*fah-tee-koh'-zoh*] tiresome
fatto [*faht'-toh*] fact, deed, made, done
fatto a mano [*faht'-toh ah mah'-noh*] handmade
fattoria [*faht-toh-ree'-ah*] farm
fattura [*faht-too'-rah*] invoice
favore *m.* [*fah-voh'-reh*] favor
per favore [*pehr fah-voh'-reh*] please
favorire *v.* [*fah-voh-ree'-reh*] favor, please
Favorisca! [*fah-voh-rees'-kah*] Please!
favorito [*fah-voh-ree'-toh*] favorite
fazzoletto [*fahts-tsoh-leht'-toh*] handkerchief
febbraio [*fehb-brah'-ee-oh*] February
febbre *f.* [*fehb'-breh*] fever
febbrile [*fehb-bree'-leh*] feverish
fede *f.* [*feh'-deh*] faith, wedding ring
fedele [*feh-deh'-leh*] faithful
federale [*feh-deh-rah'-leh*] federal

fegato [*feh'-gah-toh*] liver
felice [*feh-lee'-cheh*] happy
felicità *f. indecl.* [*feh-lee-chee-tah'*] happiness
felicitazioni [*feh-lee-chee-tah-tsee-oh'-nee*] congratulations
femmina [*fehm'-mee-nah*] female
femminile [*fehm-mee-nee'-leh*] feminine
ferire *v.* [*feh-ree'-reh*] wound, injure
ferita [*feh-ree'-tah*] wound, injury
ferito [*feh-ree'-toh*] wounded
fermare *v.* [*fehr-mah'-reh*] stop
fermarsi *v.* [*fehr-mahr'-see*] stop [oneself]
  Si fermi qui! [*see fehr'-mee koo-ee'*] Stop here!
fermata [*fehr-mah'-tah*] stop
fermo [*fehr'-meh*] firm, closed
feroce [*feh-roh'-cheh*] ferocious, fierce
ferro [*fehr'-roh*] iron [metal]
  ferro da stiro [*fehr'-roh dah stee'-roh*] flat iron
ferrovia [*fehr-roh-vee'-ah*] railroad, railway
festa [*fehs'-tah*] feast, party
festival *m.* [*fehs'-tee-vahl*] festival
fetta [*feht'-tah*] slice
fettuccine *f. pl.* [*feht-tooch-chee'-neh*] fettucine
fiamma [*fee-ahm'-mah*] flame
fiammifero [*fee-ahm-mee'-feh-roh*] (safety) match
fianco [*fee-ahn'-koh*] side, hip
fiaschetta [*fees-ahs-keht'-tah*] flask
fiato [*fee-ah'-toh*] breath, breathing
fico [*fee'-koh*] fig
fidanzamento [*fee-dahn-tsah-mehn'-toh*] engagement
fidanzato [*fee-dahn-tsah'-toh*] fiancé
fidarsi *v.* [*fee-dahr'-see*] rely, trust
fiducia [*fee-doo'-chee-ah*] trust
  degno di fiducia [*deh'-nyoh dee fee-doo'-chee-ah*] reliable
fiducioso [*fee-doo-chee-oh'-zoh*] confident
fiero [*fee-eh'-roh*] proud
figlia [*fee'-lyah*] daughter
figliastra [*fee-lyahs'-trah*] stepdaughter
figliastro [*fee-lyahs'-troh*] stepson
figli [*fee'-lyee*] children
figlio [*fee'-lyoh*] son

figura [*fee-goo'-rah*] figure
figurarsi *v.* [*fee-goo-rahr'-see*] imagine
Si figuri!, Figurati! [*see fee-goo'-ree, fee-goo'-rah-tee*] Just imagine!
fila [*fee'-lah*] file, line, row
filo [*fee'-loh*] wire [metal], thread
filobus [*fee'-loh-boos*] trolley bus
filosofia [*fee-loh-zoh-fee'-ah*] philosophy
filosofo [*fee-loh'-zoh-foh*] philosopher
filtro [*feel'-troh*] filter
finale [*fee-nah'-leh*] final
finalmente [*fee-nahl-mehn'-teh*] finally
finanziario [*fee-nahn-tsee-ah'-ree-oh*] financial
finchè [*feen-keh'*] until, till
fine *adj.*, [*fee'-neh*] fine, thin, subtle
fine *m.* [*fee'-neh*] purpose, sake, aim
fine *f.* [*fee'-neh*] end, ending
alla fine [*ahl'-lah fee'-neh*] at last
finestra [*fee-nehs'-trah*] window [of house]
finestrino [*fee-nehs-tree'-noh*] window [of car or train]
fingere *v. irreg.* [*feen'-jeh-reh*] pretend
finire *v.* [*fee-nee'-reh*] end, finish
finito [*fee-nee'-toh*] finished
fino a [*fee'-noh ah*] until, up to
finora [*fee-noh'-rah*] as yet
fintanto che [*feen-tahn'-toh keh*] as long as
fioraio [*fee-oh-rah'-ee-oh*] flower shop
fiore *m.* [*fee-oh'-reh*] flower
dei fiori [*deh'-ee fee-oh'-ree*] some flowers
Firenze [*fee-rehn'-tseh*] Florence
fiorire *v.* [*fee-oh-ree'-reh*] blossom
fioritura [*fee-oh-ree-too'-rah*] blossom
firma [*feer'-mah*] signature
firmare *v.* [*feer-mah'-reh*] sign
fischiare *v.* [*fees-kee-ah'-reh*] whistle
fischio [*fees'-kee-oh*] whistle
fisica [*fee'-zee-kah*] physics
fisico [*fee'-zee-koh*] physical
fissare *v.* [*fees-sah'-reh*] fix, set, fasten
fiume *m.* [*fee-oo'-meh*] river

fisso [*fees'-soh*] fixed, regular
prezzo fisso [*prehts'-tsoh fees'-soh*] fixed price
flanella [*flah-nehl'-lah*] flannel
flauto [*flah'-oo-toh*] flute
flessibile [*flehs-see'-bee-leh*] flexible
flotta [*floht'-tah*] fleet
fluente [*floo-ehn'-teh*] fluent
fluentemente [*floo-ehn-teh-mehn'-teh*] fluently
fluido [*floo'-ee-doh*] fluid
focolare *m.* [*foh-koh-lah'-reh*] fireplace
fodera [*foh'-deh-rah*] lining
foglia [*foh'-lyah*] leaf
foglio [*foh'-lyoh*] sheet [paper]
folla [*fohl'-lah*] crowd
fondamentale [*fohn-dah-mehn-tah'-leh*] fundamental
fondare *v.* [*fohn-dah'-reh*] found, establish
fondazione *f.* [*fohn-dah-tsee-oh'-neh*] foundation
fondi [*fohn'-dee*] funds
fondo [*fohn'-doh*] bottom
fonografo [*foh-noh'-grah-foh*] phonograph
fontana [*fohn-tah'-nah*] fountain
fonte *f.* [*fohn'-teh*] spring [of water]
forbici [*fohr'-bee-chee*] scissors
forchetta [*fohr-keht'-tah*] fork
foresta [*foh-rehs'-tah*] forest
forare *v.* [*foh-rah'-reh*] bore [a hole]
forma [*fohr'-mah*] form, shape
formaggio [*fohr-mahj'-jee-oh*] cheese
formale [*fohr-mah'-leh*] formal
formalità *f. indecl.* [*fohr-mah-lee-tah'*] formality
formare *v.* [*fohr-mah'-reh*] form, shape
formica [*fohr'-mee-kah*] ant
formidabile [*fohr-mee-dah'-bee-leh*] formidable
formula [*fohr'-moo-lah*] formula
fornire *v.* [*fohr-nee'-reh*] furnish
forno [*fohr'-noh*] oven
foro [*foh'-roh*] forum
forse [*fohr'-seh*] maybe
forte [*fohr'-teh*] strong
fortezza [*fohr-tehts'-tsah*] fortress

fortuna [*fohr-too'-nah*] fortune, luck
  Buona fortuna! [*boo-oh'-nah fohr-too'-nah*] Good luck!
  per fortuna [*pehr fohr-too'-nah*] luckily
fortunatamente [*fohr-too-nah-tah-mehn'-teh*] fortunately
fortunato [*fohr-too-nah'-toh*] fortunate, lucky
forza [*fohr'-tsah*] strength, force, power
forzare *v.* [*fohr-tsah'-reh*] force
fossa [*fohs'-sah*] ditch, pit
fotografare *v.* [*foh-toh-grah-fah'-reh*] photograph
fotografia [*foh-toh-grah-fee'-ah*] photograph, picture
fotografo [*foh-toh'-grah-foh*] photographer
fra [*frah*] between, among
  fra poco [*frah poh'-koh*] in a short while
  fra noi [*frah noh'-ee*] between us
fracassare *v.* [*frah-kahs-sah'-reh*] smash
fragile [*frah'-jee-leh*] fragile, frail
fragola [*frah'-goh-lah*] strawberry
fragranza [*frah-grahn'-tsah*] fragrance
francese [*frahn-cheh'-zeh*] French, Frenchman
Francia [*frahn'-chee-ah*] France
Franco [*frahn'-koh*] frank
francobollo [*frahn-koh-bohl'-loh*] stamp
frase [*frah'-zeh*] sentence, phrase
fratello [*frah-tehl'-loh*] brother
frattanto [*fraht-tahn'-toh*] meanwhile
freccia [*frehch'-chee-ah*] arrow
freddo [*frehd'-doh*] cold
  avere *v.* **freddo** [*ah-veh'-reh frehd'-doh*] be cold
  prendere *v.* **freddo** [*prehn'-deh-reh frehd'-doh*] catch cold
fremere *v.* [*freh'-meh-reh*] shudder
frenare *v.* [*freh-nah'-reh*] brake
frenetico [*freh-neh'-tee-koh*] frantic
freno [*freh'-noh*] brake
frequente [*freh-koo-ehn'-teh*] frequent
frequentemente [*freh-koo-ehn-teh-mehn'-teh*] frequently
fresco [*frehs'-koh*] cool, fresh
fretta [*freht'-tah*] haste, hurry
  avere *v.* **fretta** [*ah-veh'-reh freht'-tah*] be in a hurry
friggere *v.* [*freej'-jeh-reh*] fry
frigorifero [*free-goh-ree'-feh-roh*] refrigerator

frittata [*freet-tah'-tah*] omelet
frittella [*free-tehl'-lah*] pancake
fritto [*freet'-toh*] fried
fronte *m.* [*frohn'-teh*] front
fronte *f.* [*frohn'-teh*] forehead
frode *f.* [*froh'-deh*] fraud
frugale [*froo-gah'-leh*] thrifty
frusta [*froos'-tah*] whip
frutta [*froot'-tah*] fruit
fruttivendolo [*froot-tee-vehn'-doh-loh*] fruit store
fucile *m.* [*foo-chee'-leh*] gun, rifle
fuga [*foo'-gah*] escape, flight
fuggire *v.* [*fooj-jee'-reh*] flee
fuggitivo [*fooj-jee-tee'-voh*] runaway
fulmine *f.* [*fool'-mee-neh*] lightning
fumare *v.* [*foo-mah'-reh*] smoke
fumo [*foo'-moh*] smoke
fune *f.* [*foo'-neh*] rope
fungo [*foon'-goh*] mushroom
funerale *m.* [*foo-neh-rah'-leh*] funeral
funzione *f.* [*foon-tsee-oh'-neh*] function
fuoco [*foo-oh'-koh*] fire
fuori [*foo-oh'-ree*] out, outside
furbo [*foor'-boh*] smart, crafty
furfante [*foor-fahn'-teh*] villain
furioso [*foo-ree-oh'-zoh*] furious
furore *m.* [*foo-roh'-reh*] rage, fury
furia [*foo'-ree-ah*] fury, anger
furto [*foor'-toh*] theft
futuro [*foo-too'-roh*] future

G

gabbia [*gahb'-bee-ah*] cage
gabinetto [*kah-bee-neht'-toh*] cabinet
galleggiare *v.* [*gahl-lehj-jee-ah'-reh*] float
galleria [*gahl-leh-ree'-ah*] gallery

galleria sotterranea [*gahl-leh-ree'-ah soht-tehr-rah'-neh-ah*] tunnel
gallina [*gahl-lee'-nah*] hen
gallo [*gahl'-loh*] rooster
gallone *m.* [*gahl-loh'-neh*] gallon
gamba [*gahm'-bah*] leg
gambero [*gahm'-beh-roh*] shrimp
gancio [*gahn'-chee-oh*] hook
gara [*gah'-rah*] race, competition
garante *m.* [*gah-rahn'-teh*] voucher
garantire *v.* [*gah-rahn-tee'-reh*] guarantee
garanzia [*gah-rahn-tsee'-ah*] guarantee
gattino [*gaht-tee'-noh*] kitten
gatto [*gaht'-toh*] cat
gelatina [*jeh-lah-tee'-nah*] jelly
gelato [*jeh-lah'-toh*] ice cream
gelato [*jeh-lah'-toh*] frozen
gelo [*jeh'-loh*] frost
geloso [*jeh-loh'-zoh*] jealous
gemello [*jeh-mehl'-loh*] twin
gemito [*jeh'-mee-toh*] groan
gemma [*jehm'-mah*] gem
generale [*jeh-neh-rah'-leh*] general
in generale [*een jeh-neh-rah'-leh*] in general
generalmente [*jeh-neh-rahl-mehn'-teh*] generally
generatore *m.* [*jeh-neh-rah-toh'-reh*] generator
generazione *f.* [*jeh-neh-rah-tsee-oh'-neh*] generation
genere *m.* [*jeh'-neh-reh*] kind, gender, sort
genero [*jeh'-neh-roh*] son-in-law
generoso [*jeh-neh-roh'-zoh*] generous
gengiva [*jehn-jee'-vah*] gum [anat.]
genio [*jeh'-nee-oh*] genius
genitori [*jeh-nee-toh'-ree*] parents
gennaio [*jehn-nah'-ee-oh*] January
Genova [*jeh'-noh-vah*] Genoa
gente *f.* [*jehn'-teh*] people
gentile [*jehn-tee'-leh*] kind, gentle, polite
gentilezza [*jehn-tee-lehts'-tsah*] kindness
genuino [*jeh-noo-ee'-noh*] genuine
geografia [*jeh-oh-grah-fee'-ah*] geography

geometria [*jeh-oh-meh-tree'-ah*] geometry
gergo [*jehr'-goh*] slang
Germania [*jehr-mah'-nee-ah*] Germany
germe *m.* [*jehr'-meh*] germ
gettare *v.* [*jeht-tah'-reh*] throw
ghiaccio [*gee-ahch'-chee-oh*] ice
già [*jee-ah'*] already
giacca, giacche *pl.* [*jee-ahk'-kah, jee-ahk'-keh*] jacket
giallo [*jee-ahl'-loh*] yellow
Giappone *m.* [*jee-ahp-poh'-neh*] Japan
giapponese [*jee-ahp-poh-neh'-zeh*] Japanese
giardiniere *m.* [*jee-ahr-dee-nee-eh'-reh*] gardener
giardino [*jee-ahr-dee'-noh*] garden
  giardino d'infanzia [*jee-ahr-dee'-noh deen-fahn'-tsee-ah*] kindergarten
  giardino zoologico [*jee-ahr-dee'-noh dzoh-oh-loh'-jee-koh*] zoo
ginocchio [*jee-nohk'-kee-oh*] knee
giocare *v.* [*jee-oh-kah'-reh*] play [a game]
  giocare d'azzardo [*jee-oh-kah'-reh dahdz-dzahr'-doh*] gamble
giocattolo [*jee-oh-kaht'-toh-loh*] toy
gioco [*jee-oh'-koh*] game, play
  gioco del calcio [*jee-oh'-koh dehl kahl'-chee-oh*] football
gioia [*jee-oh'-ee-ah*] joy
gioielliere *m.* [*jee-oh-ee-ehl-lee-eh'-reh*] jeweller
gioielleria [*jee-oh-ee-ehl-leh-ree'-ah*] jeweller's shop
gioiello [*jee-oh-ee-ehl'-loh*] jewel
gioioso [*jee-oh-ee-oh'-zoh*] joyful
giornale *m.* [*jee-ohr-nah'-leh*] newspaper
giornalismo [*jee-ohr-nah-leez'-moh*] journalism
giornalista *m.* [*jee-ohr-nah-lees'-tah*] journalist
giornalmente [*jee-ohr-nahl-mehn'-teh*] daily
giornata [*jee-ohr-nah'-tah*] daylong
giorno [*jee-ohr'-noh*] day
  buon giorno [*boo-ohn' jee-ohr'-noh*] good morning
  giorno feriale [*jee-ohr'-noh feh-ree-ah'-leh*] workday
  ogni giorno [*oh'-nyee jee-ohr'-noh*] every day
  tutto il giorno [*toot'-toh eel jee-ohr'-noh*] all day
giovane [*jee-oh'-vah-neh*] young

(il) giovane [*(eel) jee-oh'-vah-neh*] (the) young man
(la) giovane [*(lah) jee-oh'-vah-neh*] (the) young woman
più giovane [*pee-oo' jee-oh'-vah-neh*] junior
giovanile [*jee-oh-vah-nee'-leh*] youthful
giovanotto [*jee-oh-vah-noht'-toh*] young man
giovedì *m. indecl.* [*jee-oh-veh-dee'*] Thursday
gioventù *f. indecl.* [*jee-oh-vehn-too'*] youth
gioviale [*jee-oh-vee-ah'-leh*] jovial
girare *v.* [*jee-rah'-reh*] turn; tour; endorse [a check]
giro [*jee'-roh*] tour, turn
gita [*jee'-tah*] short trip, picnic
giù [*jee-oo'*] down, below
giubilante [*jee-oo-bee-lahn'-teh*] jubilant
giubileo [*jee-oo-bee-leh'-oh*] jubilee
giudeo [*jee-oo-deh'-oh*] Jewish
giudicare *v.* [*jee-oo-dee-kah'-reh*] judge
giudice [*jee-oo'-dee-cheh*] judge
giudizio [*jee-oo-dee'-tsee-oh*] judgment
giugno [*jee-oo'-nyoh*] June
giungere *v.* [*jee-oon'-jeh-reh*] arrive, reach
giuramento [*jee-oo-rah-mehn'-toh*] oath
giurare *v.* [*jee-oo-rah'-reh*] swear
giuria [*jee-oo-ree'-ah*] jury
giurisdizione *f.* [*jee-oo-reez-dee-tsee-oh'-neh*] jurisdiction
giustamente [*jee-oos-tah-mehn'-teh*] justly
giustezza [*jee-oos-tehts'-tsah*] fairness
giustizia [*jee-oos-tee'-tsee-ah*] justice
giusto [*jee-oos'-toh*] just, fair
Sono giusto arrivato [*soh'-noh jee-oos'-toh ahr-ree-vah'-toh*] I just arrived
glandola [*glahn'-doh-lah*] gland
gli *art., m. pl.* [*lyee*] the
gli: a lui *obj. pron., m. sing.* [*lyee, ah loo'-ee*] to him
globo [*gloh'-boh*] globe
gloria [*gloh'-ree-ah*] glory
goccia [*gohch'-chee-ah*] drop
godere *v.* [*goh-deh'-reh*] enjoy
godere la vita [*goh-deh'-reh lah vee'-tah*] enjoy life
gola [*goh'-lah*] throat
mal *m.* **di gola** [*mahl dee goh'-lah*] sore throat

gomito [*goh'-mee-toh*] elbow
gomma [*gohm'-mah*] tire [of car]
gomma [*gohm'-mah*] rubber
gomma da cancellare [*gohm'-mah dah kahn-chehl-lah'-reh*] eraser
gonfiare *v.* [*gohn-fee-ah'-reh*] swell
governante *f.* **di casa** [*goh-vehr-nahn'-teh dee kah'-zah*] housekeeper
governare *v.* [*goh-vehr-nah'-reh*] govern
governatore *m.* [*goh-vehr-nah-toh'-reh*] governor
governo [*goh-vehr'-noh*] government
gradito [*grah-dee'-toh*] appreciated
grado [*grah'-doh*] grade, degree
gradualmente [*grah-doo-ahl-mehn'-teh*] gradually
graffio [*grahf'-fee-oh*] scratch
grammatica [*grahm-mah'-tee-kah*] grammar
Gran Bretagna [*grahn breh-tah'-nyah*] Great Britain
granchio [*grahn'-kee-oo*] crab
grande [*grahn'-deh*] big, great
più grande, il (la) più grande [*pee-oo' grahn'-deh, eel (lah) pee-oo' grahn'-deh*] bigger, (the) biggest
grandissimo [*grahn-dees'-see-moh*] very big
grandezza [*grahn-dehts'-tsah*] greatness
grandine *f.* [*grahn'-dee-neh*] hail
grano [*grah'-noh*] wheat, grain
grappa [*grahp'-pah*] brandy
grasso *n. & adj.* [*grahs'-soh*] fat, grease
gratitudine *f.* [*grah-tee-too'-dee-neh*] gratitude
grato [*grah'-toh*] thankful
grattacielo [*graht-tah-chee-eh'-loh*] skyscraper
gratuito [*grah-too-ee'-toh*] free, granted
grave *adj.* [*grah'-veh*] grave
gravidanza [*grah-vee-dahn'-tsah*] pregnancy
gravità *f. indecl.* [*grah-vee-tah'*] gravity
grazia [*grah'-tsee-ah*] grace
Grazie [*grah'-tsee-eh*] Thank you
Grazie tanto [*grah'-tsee-eh tahn'-toh*] Thanks a lot
grazioso [*grah-tsee-oh'-zoh*] lovely
Grecia [*greh'-chee-ah*] Greece
greco [*greh'-koh*] Greek

grembiule *m.* [*grehm-bee-oo'-leh*] apron
grezzo [*grehdz'-dzoh*] raw
materiale grezzo [*mah-teh-ree-ah'-leh grehdz'-dzoh*] raw material
gridare *v.* [*gree-dah'-reh*] yell
grido [*gree'-doh*] shout
grigio [*gree'-jee-oh*] grey
grosso [*grohs'-soh*] big, bulky
gruppo [*groop'-poh*] group
guadagnare *v.* [*goo-ah-dah-nyah'-reh*] earn, gain
guadagno [*goo-ah-dah'-nyoh*] gain
Guai! [*goo-ah'-ee*] Beware!, Woe!
guancia [*goo-ahn'-chee-ah*] cheek
guanto [*goo-ahn'-toh*] glove
guardare *v.* [*goo-ahr-dah'-reh*] watch, look
Guardi! [*goo-ahr'-dee*] Look!
guardarobiere *m.* [*goo-ahr-dah-roh-bee-eh'-reh*] dresser
guardia [*goo-ahr'-dee-ah*] guard
guardiano [*goo-ahr-dee-ah'-noh*] guardian
guarire *v.* [*goo-ah-ree'-reh*] heal, get well
guastare *v.* [*goo-ahs-tah'-reh*] spoil
guerra [*goo-ehr'-rah*] war
guerra mondiale [*goo-ehr'-rah mohn-dee-ah'-leh*] world war
guida [*goo-ee'-dah*] guide
guidare *v.* [*goo-ee-dah'-reh*] drive, lead
guscio [*goo-'shee-oh*] nutshell
gusto [*goos'-toh*] taste
gustoso [*goos-toh'-zoh*] tasty, agreeable

H

ha [*ah*] he (she, it) has, (you) have
hai [*ah'-ee*] you have
hanno [*ahn'-noh*] they have
ho [*oh*] I have

I

i *m. pl.* [*ee*] the
iarda [*ee-ahr'-dah*] yard
Iddio [*ee-dee'-oh*] God
idea [*ee-deh'-ah*] idea
ideale [*ee-deh-ah'-leh*] ideal
identico [*ee-dehn'-tee-koh*] identical
identificare *v.* [*ee-dehn-tee-fee-kah'-reh*] identify
identità *f. indecl.* [*ee-dehn-tee-tah'*] identity
  carta d'identità [*kahr'-tah dee-dehn-tee-tah'*] identification card
idiota [*ee-dee-oh'-tah*] idiot
idolo [*ee'-doh-loh*] idol
ieri [*ee-eh'-ree*] yesterday
  l'altro ieri [*lahl'-troh ee-eh'-ree*] the day before yesterday
  ieri sera [*ee-eh'-ree seh'-rah*] yesterday evening
igienico [*ee-jee-eh'-nee-koh*] sanitary
ignorante [*ee-nyoh-rahn'-teh*] ignorant
ignoto [*ee-nyoh'-toh*] unknown
il, lo, l' *m. sing.* [*eel, loh, l*] the
illecito [*eel-leh'-chee-toh*] illicit
illegale [*eel-leh-gah'-leh*] unlawful, illegal
illegibile [*eel-leh-jee'-bee-leh*] illegible
illeso [*eel-leh'-zoh*] unharmed
illogico [*eel-loh'-jee-koh*] irrational
illusione *f.* [*eel-loo-zee-oh'-neh*] illusion
illustrazione *f.* [*eel-loos-trah-tsee-oh'-neh*] illustration
illustre [*eel-loos'-treh*] distinguished
imballaggio [*eem-bahl-lahj'-jee-oh*] packing
imbarazzare *v.* [*eem-bah-rahts-tsah'-reh*] embarrass
imbarazzato [*eem-bah-rahts-tsah'-toh*] embarrassed
imbarcare *v.* [*eem-bahr-kah'-reh*] ship
imbarcarsi *v.* [*eem-bahr-kahr'-see*] embark
imbarco [*eem-bahr'-koh*] shipment
imbroglione *m.* [*eem-broh-lyoh'-neh*] crook

imbucare *v.* [*em-boo-kah'-reh*] mail
imitare *v.* [*ee-mee-tah'-reh*] imitate
imitazione *f.* [*ee-mee-tah-tsee-oh'-neh*] imitation
immacolato [*eem-mah-koh-lah'-toh*] spotless
immaginare *v.* [*eem-mah-jee-nah'-reh*] imagine
immaginazione *f.* [*eem-mah-jee-nah-tsee-oh'-neh*] imagination
immagine *f.* [*eem-mah'-jee-neh*] image
immateriale [*eem-mah-teh-ree-ah'-leh*] immaterial
immaturo [*eem-mah-too'-roh*] immature
immediatamente [*eem-meh-dee-ah-tah-mehn'-teh*] immediately
immediato [*eem-meh-dee-ah'-toh*] immediate
immenso [*eem-mehn'-soh*] immense
immigrazione *f.* [*eem-mee-grah-tsee-oh'-neh*] immigration
imminente [*eem-mee-nehn'-teh*] impending, imminent
immondizia [*eem-mohn-dee'-tsee-ah*] garbage
immorale [*eem-moh-rah'-leh*] immoral
immunità *f. indecl.* [*eem-moo-nee-tah'*] immunity
impaccare *v.* [*eem-pahk-kah'-reh*] pack
imparare *v.* [*eem-pah-rah'-reh*] learn
imparentato [*eem-pah-rehn-tah'-toh*] related
imparziale [*eem-pahr-tsee-ah'-leh*] impartial
impaurito [*eem-pah-oo-ree'-toh*] afraid
impaziente [*eem-pah-tsee-ehn'-teh*] impatient
impedire [*eem-peh-dee'-reh*] prevent
impegnarsi *v.*, [*eem-peh-nyahr'-see*] engage [oneself]
impegno [*eem-peh'-nyoh*] engagement
imperdonabile [*eem-pehr-doh-nah'-bee-leh*] unforgivable
imperfetto [*eem-pehr-feht'-toh*] imperfect
imperialismo [*eem-pehr-ee-ah-leez'-moh*] imperialism
impermeabile [*eem-pehr-meh-ah'-bee-leh*] waterproof
impero [*eem-peh'-roh*] empire
impiegare *v.* [*eem-pee-eh-gah'-reh*] employ
impiegato [*eem-pee-eh-gah'-toh*] employee, clerk
impiego [*eem-pee-eh'-goh*] job, employment, use
imporre *v.* [*eem-pohr'-reh*] impose
importante [*eem-pohr-tahn'-teh*] important
  Che importa? [*keh eem-pohr'-tah*] What difference does it make?
  Non importa [*nohn eem-pohr'-tah*] It doesn't matter
importanza [*eem-pohr-tahn'-tsah*] importance

importare *v.* [*eem-pohr-tah'-reh*] import
importato [*eem-pohr-tah'-toh*] imported
impossibile [*eem-pohs-see'-bee-leh*] impossible
impreparato [*eem-preh-pah-rah'-toh*] unprepared
impresa [*eem-preh'-zah*] enterprise
impressione *f.* [*eem-prehs-see-oh'-neh*] impression
impressionante [*eem-prehs-see-oh-nahn'-teh*] impressive
imprevisto [*eem-preh-vees'-toh*] unforseen
imprigionare *v.* [*eem-pree-jee-oh-nah'-reh*] imprison
imprimere *v.* [*eem-pree'-meh-reh*] print
improbabile [*eem-proh-bah'-bee-leh*] unlikely
improvvisamente [*eem-prohv-vee-zah-mehn'-teh*] suddenly
improvviso [*eem-prohv-vee'-zoh*] sudden
impronta [*eem-prohn'-tah*] print, mark, footprint
  impronta digitale [*eem-prohn'-tah dee-jee-tah'-leh*] fingerprint
imprudente [*eem-proo-dehn'-teh*] careless
in [*een*] in, into, at
inatteso [*ee-naht-teh'-zoh*] unexpected
incapace [*een-kah-pah'-cheh*] unable
incapacità *f. indecl.* [*een-kah-pah-chee-tah'*] inability
incarico [*een-kah'-ree-koh*] appointment, task
incassare *v.* [*een-kahs-sah'-reh*] cash
incerto [*een-chehr'-toh*] uncertain
inchiesta [*een-kee-ehs'-tah*] inquiry
inchinarsi *v.* [*een-kee-nahr'-see*] bow
inchino [*een-kee'-noh*] bow, curtsey
inchiodare *v.* [*een-kee-oh-dah'-reh*] nail
inchiostro [*een-kee-ohs'-troh*] ink
inciampare *v.* [*een-chee-ahm-pah'-reh*] trip, stumble
incidentalmente [*een-chee-dehn-tahl-mehn'-teh*] incidentally
incidente *m.* [*een-chee-dehn'-teh*] accident, incident
incinta [*een-cheen'-tah*] pregnant
inclinazione *f.* [*een-klee-nah-tsee-oh'-neh*] inclination
includere *v.* [*een-kloo'-deh-reh*] include
incluso [*een-kloo'-zoh*] included
incombustibile [*een-kohm-boos-tee'-bee-leh*] fireproof
incomparabile [*een-kohm-pah-rah'-bee-leh*] incomparable
incompleto [*een-kohm-pleh'-toh*] incomplete
inconsapevole [*een-kohn-sah-peh'-voh-leh*] unconscious,

unaware
incontestabile [*een-kohn-tehs-tah'-bee-leh*] unquestionable
incontrare *v.* [*een-kohn-trah'-reh*] encounter
incontrare per caso [*een-kohn-trah'-reh pehr kah'-zoh*] run across
L'incontro ogni domenica [*leen-kohn'-troh oh'-nyee doh-meh'-nee-kah*] I meet him every Sunday
incontro [*een-kohn'-troh*] match [sport], meeting
incoraggiamento [*een-koh-rahj-jee-ah-mehn'-toh*] encouragement
incoraggiare *v.* [*een-koh-rahj-jee-ah'-reh*] encourage
incredibile [*een-kreh-dee'-bee-leh*] incredible
incrocio [*een-kroh'-chee-oh*] intersection
incubo [*een'-koo-boh*] nightmare
incursione *f.* [*een-koor-see-oh'-neh*] raid
indecente [*een-deh-chehn'-teh*] indecent
indeciso [*een-deh-chee'-zoh*] undecided
indefinito [*een-deh-fee-nee'-toh*] indefinite
indelicato [*een-deh-lee-kah'-toh*] tactless
India [*een'-dee-ah*] India
indiano [*een-dee-ah'-noh*] Indian
indicare *v.* [*een-dee-kah'-reh*] indicate
indicatore *m.* [*een-dee-kah-toh'-reh*] gauge
indice *m.* [*een'-dee-cheh*] index
indietro [*een-dee-eh'-troh*] back, backwards
indifferente [*een-deef-feh-rehn'-teh*] indifferent
indigestione *f.* [*een-dee-jehs-tee-oh'-neh*] indigestion
indignato [*een-dee-nyah'-toh*] indignant
indimenticabile [*een-dee-mehn-tee-kah'-bee-leh*] unforgettable
indipendente [*een-dee-pehn-dehn'-teh*] independent
indipendenza [*een-dee-pehn-dehn'-tsah*] independence
indiretto [*een-dee-reht'-toh*] indirect
indirizzare (una lettera) *v.* [*een-dee-reets-tsah'-reh* (*oo'-nah leht'-teh-rah*)] address (a letter)
indirizzo [*een-dee-reets'-tsoh*] address, direction
indiscreto [*een-dees-kreh'-toh*] indiscreet
individuale [*een-dee-vee-doo-ah'-leh*] individual
indossare *v.* [*een-dohs-sah'-reh*] wear [clothes]
indovinare *v.* [*een-doh-vee-nah'-reh*] guess
indubbiamente [*een-doob-bee-ah-mehn'-teh*] doubtlessly

indumento [*een-doo-mehn'-toh*] garment
industria [*een-doos'-tree-ah*] industry
industriale [*een-doos-tree-ah'-leh*] industrial
inesatto [*een-ehz-aht'-toh*] inaccurate
inefficiente [*een-ehf-fee-chee-ehn'-teh*] inefficient
inesprimibile [*een-ehs-pree-mee'-bee-leh*] unspeakable
inestimabile [*een-ehs-tee-mah'-bee-leh*] invaluable
inetto [*een-eht'-toh*] unfit
infatti [*een-faht'-tee*] in fact
infedele [*een-feh-deh'-leh*] unfaithful
infelice [*een-feh-lee'-cheh*] unhappy
inferiore [*een-feh-ree-oh'-reh*] inferior
infermiera [*een-fehr-mee-eh'-rah*] nurse [medical]
inferno [*een-fehr'-noh*] hell
infezione *f.* [*een-feh-tsee-oh'-neh*] infection
infine [*een-fee'-neh*] after all, at last
infinito [*een-fee-nee'-toh*] infinite, infinitive
inflessibile [*een-flehs-see'-bee-leh*] unyielding
influenza [*een-floo-ehn'-tsah*] influence
influenzare *v.* [*een-floo-ehn-tsah'-reh*] influence
informare *v.* [*een-fohr-mah'-reh*] inform, acquaint
informarsi *v.* [*een-fohr-mahr'-see*] inquire
informazione *f.* [*een-fohr-mah-tsee-oh'-neh*] information
infrequente [*een-freh-koo-ehn'-teh*] infrequent
ingannare *v.* [*een-gahn-nah'-reh*] deceive
inganno [*een-gahn'-noh*] deceit
ingegnere *m.* [*een-jeh-nyeh'-reh*] engineer
ingegno [*een-jeh'-nyoh*] wit
ingenuo [*een-jeh'-noo-oh*] naive
Inghilterra [*een-geel-tehr'-rah*] England
inghiottire *v.* [*een-gee-oht-tee'-reh*] swallow
inginocchiarsi *v.* [*een-jee-nohk-kee-ahr'-see*] kneel
ingiusto [*een-jee-oos'-toh*] unjust
ingiustizia [*een-jee-oos-tee'-tsee-ah*] injustice
inglese [*een-gleh'-zeh*] British, English
ingranaggio [*een-grah-nahj'-jee-oh*] gear [of a car]
ingrato [*een-grah'-toh*] ungrateful
ingresso [*een-grehs'-soh*] entrance
  Vietato l'ingresso [*vee-eh-tah'-toh leen-grehs'-soh*]
    No admittance

iniezione *f.* [*ee-nee-eh-tsee-oh'-neh*] injection
inimmaginabile [*een-eem-mah-jee-nah'-bee-leh*] unimagined
iniziale *f.* [*ee-nee-tsee-ah'-leh*] initial
iniziare *v.* [*ee-nee-tsee-ah'-reh*] start
inizio [*ee-nee'-tsee-oh*] beginning
innamorarsi *v.* [*een-nah-moh-rahr'-see*] fall in love
innanzi [*een-nahn'-tsee*] before
innocente [*een-noh-chehn'-teh*] innocent
inoltre [*ee-nohl'-treh*] furthermore, besides
inondazione *f.* [*ee-nohn-dah-tsee-oh'-neh*] flood
inquieto [*een-koo-ee-eh'-toh*] uneasy
inquilino [*een-koo-ee-lee'-noh*] tenant
insalata [*een-sah-lah'-tah*] salad
insegnamento [*een-seh-nyah-mehn'-toh*] teaching
insegnante *m.* [*een-seh-nyahn'-teh*] teacher
insegnare *v.* [*een-seh-nyah'-reh*] teach
inseguire *v.* [*een-seh-goo-ee'-reh*] run after
insetto [*een-seht'-toh*] insect
insieme [*een-see-eh'-meh*] together
  nell' insieme [*nehl-een-see-eh'-meh*] altogether
insignificante [*een-see-nyee-fee-kahn'-teh*] unimportant
insistere *v.* [*een-sees'-teh-reh*] insist
insolito [*een-soh'-lee-toh*] unusual
insomma [*een-sohm'-mah*] in conclusion, after all
insopportabile [*een-sohp-pohr-tah'-bee-leh*] unbearable
installare *v.* [*een-stahl-lah'-reh*] install
insufficiente [*een-soo-fee-chee-ehn'-teh*] insufficient
insultare *v.* [*een-sool-tah'-reh*] insult
insulto [*een-sool'-toh*] insult
intanto [*een-tahn'-toh*] meanwhile
inttato [*een-taht'-toh*] intact
integrale [*een-teh-grah'-leh*] unabridged
intellettuale [*een-tehl-leht-too-ah'-leh*] intellectual
intelligente [*een-tehl-lee-jehn'-teh*] intelligent
intendere *v.* [*een-tehn'-deh-reh*] intend, mean
intenso [*een-tehn'-soh*] intense
intenzione *f.* [*een-tehn-tsee-oh'-neh*] intention
internazionale [*een-tehr-nah-tsee-oh-nah'-leh*] international
interno [*een-tehr'-noh*] internal
  all'interno [*ahl-leen-tehr'-noh*] inside

interamente [*een-teh-rah-mehn'-teh*] entirely
interdire *v.* [*een-tehr-dee'-reh*] ban
interessante [*een-teh-rehs-sahn'-teh*] interesting
non interessante [*nohn een-teh-rehs-sahn'-teh*] uninteresting
interessarsi *v.* [*een-teh-rehs-sahr'-see*] care for
interessato in [*een-teh-rehs-sah'-toh een*] interested in
interesse *m.* [*een-teh-rehs'-seh*] interest
interferire *v.* [*een-tehr-feh-ree'-reh*] interfere
interiore [*een-teh-ree-oh'-reh*] interior
intero [*een-teh'-roh*] entire
interprete *m.* [*een-tehr'-preh-teh*] interpreter
interrompere *v.* [*een-tehr-rohm'-peh-reh*] discontinue
interruttore *m.* [*een-tehr-root-toh'-reh*] switch [electric]
intervallo [*een-tehr-vahl'-loh*] intermission
intervista [*een-tehr-vees'-tah*] interview
intervistare *v.* [*een-tehr-vees-tah'-reh*] interview
intesa [*een-teh'-zah*] understanding
E inteso [*eh' een-teh'-zoh*] It is understood
intestini *m. pl.* [*een-tehs-tee'-nee*] bowels
intimità *f. indecl.* [*een-tee-mee-tah'*] privacy
intimo [*een'-tee-moh*] intimate
intorno [*een-tohr'-noh*] around
intraprendere *v.* [*een-trah-prehn'-deh-reh*] undertake
intrattenere *v.* [*een-traht-teh-neh'-reh*] entertain
intrudere *v.* [*een-troo'-deh-reh*] intrude
intuito [*een-too'-ee-toh*] intuition
inumano [*een-oo-mah'-noh*] inhuman
inutile [*ee-noo'-tee-leh*] useless
invalido [*een-vah'-lee-doh*] invalid
invano [*een-vah'-noh*] in vain
invasione *f.* [*een-vah-zee-oh'-neh*] invasion
invecchiare *v.* [*een-vehk-kee-ah'-reh*] age
invece (di) [*een-veh'-cheh* (*dee*)] instead (of)
inventore *m.* [*een-vehn-toh'-reh*] inventor
invenzione *f.* [*een-vehn-tsee-oh'-neh*] invention
inverno [*een-vehr'-noh*] winter
investigare *v.* [*een-vehs-tee-gah'-reh*] investigate
investire *v.* [*een-vehs-tee'-reh*] invest, run over
invidia [*een-vee'-dee-ah*] envy
invidiare *v.* [*een-vee-dee-ah'-reh*] envy

invisibile [*een-vee-zee'-bee-leh*] invisible
invitare *v.* [*een-vee-tah'-reh*] invite
invito [*een-vee'-toh*] invitation
invocare *v.* [*een-voh-kah'-reh*] plead
involontario [*een-voh-lohn-tah'-ree-oh*] involuntary
io [*ee'-oh*] I
iodio [*ee-oh'-dee-oh*] iodine
ipnotizzare *v.* [*eep-noh-teedz-dzah'-reh*] hypnotize
ipocrisia [*ee-poh-kree-zee'-ah*] hypocrisy
ipoteca [*ee-poh'-teh-kah*] mortgage
ira [*ee'-rah*] anger
Irlanda [*eer-lahn'-dah*] Ireland
irlandese [*eer-lahn-deh'-zeh*] Irish
ironico [*ee-roh'-nee-koh*] ironic
irregolare [*eer-reh-goh-lah'-reh*] irregular
irrequieto [*eer-reh-koo-ee-eh'-toh*] restless
irresistibile [*eer-reh-zees-tee'-bee-leh*] irresistible
irrigazione *f.* [*eer-ree-gah-tsee-oh'-neh*] irrigation
irritare *v.* [*eer-ree-tah'-reh*] irritate
irritazione *f.* [*eer-ree-tah-tsee-oh'-neh*] irritation
isola [*ee'-zoh-lah*] island
ispettore *m.* [*ees-peht-toh'-reh*] inspector
ispezionare *v.* [*ees-peh-tsee-oh-nah'-reh*] inspect
ispezione *f.* [*ees-peh-tsee-oh'-neh*] inspection
ispirazione *f.* [*ees-pee-rah-tsee-oh'-neh*] inspiration
isterico [*ees-teh'-ree-koh*] hysterical
istanza [*ees-tahn'-tsah*] instance
istinto [*ees-teen'-toh*] instinct
istituzione *f.* [*ees-tee-too-tsee-oh'-neh*] institution
istruire *v.* [*ees-troo-ee'-reh*] instruct, teach
istruito [*ees-troo-ee'-toh*] learned
istruttore *m.* [*ees-troot-toh'-reh*] instructor
istruzione *f.* [*ees-troo-tsee-oh'-neh*] instruction, education
Italia [*ee-tah'-lee-ah*] Italy
italiano [*ee-tah-lee-ah'-noh*] Italian
itinerario [*ee-tee-neh-rah'-ree-oh*] itinerary
Iugoslavia [*ee-oo-gohs-lah'-vee-ah*] Yugoslavia
iugoslavo [*ee-oo-gohs-lah'-voh*] Yugoslav
ivi [*ee'-vee*] there

L

la *art., f. sing.* [*lah*] the
la *obj. pron. f. sing.* [*lah*] her, it, you [polite form]
là, lì [*lah', lee'*] there
  al di là [*ahl dee lah'*] beyond
labbro, le labbra *pl.* [*lahb'-broh, leh lahb'-brah*] lip
laboratorio [*lah-boh-rah-toh'-ree-oh*] laboratory
laccio [*lahch'-chee-oh*] string, shoe lace
lacrima [*lah'-kree-mah*] teardrop
ladro [*lah'-droh*] thief
laggiù [*lahj-jee-oo'*] down there
lagnarsi *v.* [*lah-nyahr'-see*] complain
lago, laghi *pl.* [*lah'-goh, lah'-gee*] lake
laico [*lah'-ee-koh*] secular
lama [*lah'-mah*] blade
lamentare *v.* [*lah-mehn-tah'-reh*] lament, regret
lamentarsi *v.* [*lah-mehn-tahr'-see*] complain, moan
lametta [*lah-meht'-tah*] razor blade
lampada [*lahm'-pah-dah*] lamp
lampadina [*lahm-pah-dee'-nah*] light bulb
lampo [*lahm'-poh*] lightning, flash
lana [*lah'-nah*] wool
lanciare *v.* [*lahn-chee-ah'-reh*] throw, fling
lanterna [*lahn-tehr'-nah*] lantern
lapide *m.* [*lah'-pee-deh*] tombstone
lapis [*lah'-pees*] pencil
lardo [*lahr'-doh*] lard, bacon
larghezza [*lahr-gehts'-tsah*] width
largo [*lahr'-goh*] wide, large
lasagne *f. pl.* [*lah-zah'-nyeh*] lasagna
lasciare *v.* [*lah-shee-ah'-reh*] leave, let
  lasciar stare [*lah-shee-ahr' stah'-reh*] let alone
lassù [*lahs-soo'*] up there
lateralmente [*lah-teh-rahl-mehn'-teh*] sideways
latino [*lah-tee'-noh*] Latin

lato [*lah'-toh*] side
latrina [*lah-tree'-nah*] water closet
latte *m.* [*laht'-teh*] milk
latteria [*laht-teh-ree'-ah*] dairy
laurea [*lah'-oo-reh-ah*] degree
laurearsi *v.* [*lah-oo-reh-ahr'-see*] graduate
laureato [*lah-oo-reh-ah'-toh*] graduate
lavabo [*lah-vah-boh'*] washbasin
lavandaia [*lah-vahn-dah'-ee-ah*] laundress
lavanderia [*lah-vahn-deh-ree'-ah*] laundry
lavare *v.* [*lah-vah'-reh*] wash
  lavarsi [*lah-vahr'-see*] wash [oneself]
lavorare *v.* [*lah-voh-rah'-reh*] work
lavoratore *m.*, **lavoratrice** *f.* [*lah-voh-rah-toh'-reh, lah-voh-rah-tree'-cheh*] worker
lavoro [*lah-voh'-roh*] work, working
  datore *m.* **di lavoro** [*dah-toh'-reh dee lah-voh'-roh*] employer
le *art., f. pl.* [*leh*] the
le *pron., f. pl.* [*leh*] to you, you, her, to her, them
leale [*leh-ah'-leh*] loyal
lega [*leh'-gah*] league
legale [*leh-gah'-leh*] legal
legame *m.*, [*leh-gah'-meh*] bond
legare *v.* [*leh-gah'-reh*] bind, tie
legge *f.* [*lehj'-jeh*] law
leggere *v. irreg.* [*lehj'-jeh-reh*] read
leggermente [*lehj-jehr-mehn'-teh*] slightly
leggero [*lehj-jeh'-roh*] light [not heavy]
leggibile [*lehj-jee'-bee-leh*] legible
legione *f.* [*leh-jee-oh'-neh*] legion
legittimo [*leh-jeet'-tee-moh*] lawful
legno [*leh'-nyoh*] wood
legumi [*leh-goo'-mee*] vegetables
lei *3d pers. sing., f.* [*leh'-ee*] she, her, you [polite form]
  lei scrive [*leh'-ee skree'-veh*] she/you write(s)
  a lei [*ah leh'-ee*] to her, to you
lentamente [*lehn-tah-mehn'-teh*] slowly
lente *m. sing.* [*lehn'-teh*] lens
lento [*lehn'-toh*] slow
lenzuolo, le lenzuola *pl.* [*lehn-tsoo-oh'-loh, leh lehn-tsoo-*

oh'-lah] bedsheet

lettera [*leht'-teh-rah*] letter

cassetta da lettere [*kahs-seht'-tah dah leht'-teh-reh*] letter box

lettera di presentazione [*leht'-teh-rah dee preh-zehn-tah-tsee-oh'-neh*] letter of introduction

lettera raccomandata [*leht'-teh-rah rahk-koh-mahn-dah'-tah*] registered letter

letteralmente [*leht-teh-rahl-mehn'-teh*] literally

letteratura [*leht-teh-rah-too'-rah*] literature

letto [*leht'-toh*] bed

lettura [*leht-too'-rah*] reading

leva [*leh'-vah*] draft [military], lever

levante *m.* [*leh-vahn'-teh*] Near East

lezione *f.* [*leh-tsee-oh'-neh*] lesson

li *pron., m. pl.* [*lee*] them

lí [*lee'*] there

lì per lì [*lee' pehr lee'*] at first

libbra [*leeb'-brah*] pound [weight]

liberale [*lee-beh-rah'-leh*] liberal

liberare *v.* [*lee-beh-rah'-reh*] free

libero [*lee'-beh-roh*] free

libertà *f. indecl.* [*lee-behr-tah'*] freedom

libreria [*lee-breh-ree'-ah*] bookstore

libro [*lee'-broh*] book

licenza [*lee-chehn'-tsah*] permit

licenziare *v.* [*lee-chehn-tsee-ah'-reh*] dismiss

lido [*lee'-doh*] seashore

lieto [*lee-eh'-toh*] glad, happy

Molto lieto di conoscerla! [*mohl'-toh lee-eh'-toh dee koh-noh'-shehr-lah*] Very happy to meet you!

lima [*lee'-mah*] file [tool]

limitare *v.* [*lee-mee-tah'-reh*] limit

limite [*lee'-mee-teh*] boundary

limonata [*lee-moh-nah'-tah*] lemonade

limone *m.* [*lee-moh'-neh*] lemon

linea [*lee'-neh-ah*] line

linea aerea [*lee'-neh-ah ah-eh'-reh-ah*] airline

lineamenti *m. pl.* [*lee-neh-ah-mehn'-tee*] features

lingua [*leen'-goo-ah*] tongue, language

liquido [*lee'-koo-ee-doh*] liquid
liquore *m.* [*lee-koo-oh'-reh*] liquor
lira sterlina [*lee'-rah stehr-lee'-nah*] pound [money]
liscio [*lee'-shee-oh*] smooth
lista [*lees'-tah*] list, menu
  lista delle vivande [*lees'-tah dehl'-leh vee-vahn'-deh*] bill of fare
lite *f.* [*lee'-teh*] quarrel
litorale [*lee-toh-rah'-leh*] waterfront
litro [*lee'-troh*] liter [approx. 1 quart]
livello [*lee-vehl'-loh*] level
  passaggio a livello [*pahs-sahj'-jee-oh ah lee-vehl'-loh*] railroad crossing
lo *art., m. sing.* [*loh*] the
lo *pron., m. sing.* [*loh*] him, it
locale [*loh-kah'-leh*] local
località *f. indecl.* [*loh-kah-lee-tah'*] location
locomotiva [*loh-koh-moh-tee'-vah*] locomotive
locanda [*loh-kahn'-dah*] inn
lodare *v.* [*loh-dah'-reh*] praise
logico [*loh'-jee-koh*] logical
lontano [*lohn-tah'-noh*] far
  Quanto lontano? [*koo-ahn'-toh lohn-tah'-noh*] How far?
  molto lontano [*mohl'-toh lohn-tah'-noh*] far away
loro *subj. pron., m. & f. pl.* [*loh'-roh*] they, you [polite form]
loro *m., f. pl.*, **essi** *m. pl.*, **esse** *f. pl.* [*loh'-roh, ehs'-see, ehs'-seh*] them
  il loro *m. sing.*, **la loro** *f. sing.*, **i loro** *m. pl.*, **le loro** *f. pl.* [*eel loh'-roh, lah loh'-roh, ee loh'-roh, leh loh'-roh*] theirs, yours [polite form]
  a loro [*ah loh'-roh*] to them, to you
  per loro [*pehr loh'-roh*] for them, for you
lotta [*loht'-tah*] struggle
  lotta libera [*loht'-tah lee'-beh-rah*] wrestling
lottare *v.* [*loht-tah'-reh*] fight
lotto [*loht'-toh*] lot [real estate]
lozione *f.* [*loh-tsee-oh'-neh*] lotion
  lozione da barba [*loh-tsee-oh'-neh dah bahr'-bah*] shaving lotion
lubrificare *v.* [*loo-bree-fee-kah'-reh*] lubricate

luce *f.* [*loo'-cheh*] light
  accendere *v.* **la luce** [*ahch-chehn'-deh-reh lah loo'-cheh*] turn on the light
  spegnere *v.* **la luce** [*speh'-nyeh-reh lah loo'-cheh*] turn out the light
lucidare *v.* [*loo-chee-dah'-reh*] polish
lucido [*loo'-chee-doh*] polish
luglio [*loo'-lyoh*] July
lui [*loo'-ee*] he, him
luna [*loo'-nah*] moon
  chiaro di luna [*kee-ah'-roh dee loo'-nah*] moonlight
  luna di miele [*loo'-nah dee mee-eh'-leh*] honeymoon
lunedì [*loo-neh-dee'*] Monday
lunghezza [*loon-gehts'-tsah*] length
lungo [*loon'-goh*] long
  più a lungo [*pee-oo' ah loon'-goh*] longer [time]
  più lungo [*pee-oo' loon'-goh*] longer [measure]
luogo [*loo-oh'-goh*] place
  aver *v.* **luogo** [*ah-vehr' loo-oh'-goh*] take place, happen
  in luogo di [*een loo-oh'-goh dee*] in place of
lupo [*loo'-poh*] wolf
lusingare *v.* [*loo-zeen-gah'-reh*] flatter
lusso [*loos'-soh*] luxury
lussuoso [*loos-soo-oh'-zoh*] luxurious
lustrascarpe *m.* [*loos-trah-skahr'-peh*] shoeshine boy
lutto [*loot'-toh*] mourning

M

ma [*mah*] but, however, yet
macchia [*mahk'-kee-ah*] spot, stain
macchina [*mahk'-kee-nah*] car, machine, engine
  macchina da scrivere [*mahk'-kee-nah dah skree'-veh-reh*] typewriter
  macchina da cucire [*mahk'-kee-nah dah koo-chee'-reh*] sewing machine
  macchina fotografica [*mahk'-kee-nah foh-toh-grah'-fee-kah*]

camera
macchinario [*mahk-kee-nah'-ree-oh*] machinery
macellaio [*mah-chehl-lah'-ee-oh*] butcher
macelleria [*mah-chehl-leh-ree'-ah*] butcher shop
macinare *v.* [*mah-chee-nah'-reh*] grind
madre *f.* [*mah'-dreh*] mother
madrigna [*mah-dree'-nyah*] stepmother
madrina [*mah-dree'-nah*] godmother
maestà *f. indecl.* [*mah-ehs-tah'*] majesty
maestro *m.*, **maestra** *f.* [*mah-ehs'-troh, mah-ehs'-trah*] schoolteacher
magazzino [*mah-gahdz-dzee'-noh*] warehouse, storage
maggio [*mahj'-jee-oh*] May
maggiore [*mahj-jee-oh'-reh*] bigger, greater, elder
la maggior parte [*lah mahj'-jee-ohr pahr'-teh*] most, the majority
maggioranza [*mahj-jee-oh-rahn'-tsah*] majority
maggiorenne [*mahj-jee-oh-rehn'-neh*] of age
magico [*mah'-jee-koh*] magic
magnifico [*mah-nyee'-fee-koh*] magnificent
magro [*mah'-groh*] skinny, thin
mai [*mah'-ee*] never, ever
maiale *m.* [*mah-ee-ah'-leh*] pork
malato [*mah-lah'-toh*] sick, ill
malattia [*mah-laht-tee'-ah*] sickness, disease
malattia del cuore [*mah-laht-tee'-ah del koo-oh'-reh*] heart disease
maldisposto [*mahl-dees-pohs'-toh*] unwilling
male *m.* [*mah'-leh*] evil, ill
male *adj. & adv.* [*mah'-leh*] bad, badly
far male *v.* [*fahr mah'-leh*] ache
fare male a [*fah'-reh mah'-le ah*] hurt [somebody]
mal di denti [*mahl dee dehn'-tee*] toothache
mal di stomaco [*mahl dee stoh'-mah-koh*] stomachache
mal di testa [*mahl dee tehs'-tah*] headache
maledire *v.* [*mah-leh-dee'-reh*] curse
maledizione *f.* [*mah-leh-dee-tsee-oh'-neh*] curse
malgrado [*mahl-grah'-doh*] regardless, despite
maligno [*mah-lee'-nyoh*] evil, bad
malinteso [*mahl-een-teh'-zoh*] misunderstanding

malissimo [*mah-lees'-see-moh*] very bad
malsano [*mahl-sah'-noh*] unhealthy
malvagio [*mahl-vah'-jee-oh*] wicked
mancanza [*mahn-kahn'-tsah*] lack
  sentire *v.* **la mancanza** [*sehn-tee'-reh lah mahn-kahn'-tsah*] miss [someone]
  Sento molto la sua mancanza [*sehn'-toh mohl'-toh lah soo'-ah mahn-kahn'-tsah*] I miss you very much
mancare *v.* [*mahn-kah'-reh*] be lacking
mancia [*mahn'-chee-ah*] tip, gratuity
mandare *v.* [*mahn-dah'-reh*] send
  mandare a chiamare [*mahn-dah'-reh ah kee-ah-mah'-reh*] send for
mandato [*mahn-dah'-toh*] warrant
maneggiare *v.* [*mah-nehj-jee-ah'-reh*] handle
mangiare *v.* [*mahn-jee-ah'-reh*] eat
mania [*mah-nee'-ah*] fad
manica [*mah'-nee-kah*] sleeve
manicure *f.* [*mah-nee-koo'-reh*] manicure
maniera [*mah-nee-eh'-rah*] manner, way
manifesto [*mah-nee-fehs'-toh*] poster, bill
maniglia [*mah-nee'-lyah*] handle
mano, le mani *pl.* [*mah'-noh, leh mah'-nee*] hand
  darsi *v.* **la mano** [*dahr'-see lah mah'-noh*] shake hands
manoscritto [*mah-nohs-kreet'-toh*] manuscript
mansueto [*mahn-soo-eh'-toh*] tame
mantenere *v. irreg.* [*mahn-teh-neh'-reh*] maintain, keep, support
manuale [*mah-noo-ah'-leh*] manual
manzo [*mahn'-tsoh*] beef
marca [*mahr'-kah*] brand
  marca di fabbrica [*mahr'-kah dee fahb'-bree-kah*] trademark
marchese *m.*, **marchesa** *f.* [*mahr-keh'-zeh, mahr-keh'-zah*] marquis, marchioness
marcia [*mahr'-chee-ah*] march
marciapiede *m.* [*mahr-chee-ah-pee-eh'-deh*] sidewalk
marcio [*mahr'-chee-oh*] rotten
mare *m.* [*mah'-reh*] sea
marea [*mah-reh'-ah*] tide

margherita [*mahr-geh-ree'-tah*] daisy
marina [*mah-ree'-nah*] navy
marinaio [*mah-ree-nah'-ee-oh*] sailor
marionetta [*mah-ree-oh-neht'-tah*] puppet
marito [*mah-ree'-toh*] husband
marmellata [*mahr-mehl-lah'-tah*] jam
marmo [*mahr'-moh*] marble
marrone [*mahr-roh'-neh*] brown
martedì [*mahr-teh-dee'*] Tuesday
martello [*mahr-tehl'-loh*] hammer
marzo [*mahr'-tsoh*] March
mascella [*mah-shehl'-lah*] jaw
maschera [*mahs'-keh-rah*] mask
maschio [*mahs'-kee-oh*] male
massa [*mahs'-sah*] mass [quantity]
massaggio [*mahs-sahj'-jee-oh*] massage
massaia [*mahs-sah'-ee-ah*] housewife
massimo [*mahs'-see-moh*] greatest
masticare *v.* [*mahs-tee-kah'-reh*] chew
matematica [*mah-teh-mah'-tee-kah*] mathematics
materasso [*mah-teh-rahs'-soh*] mattress
materia [*mah-teh'-ree-ah*] matter
materiale *m.* [*mah-teh-ree-ah'-leh*] material
maternità *f. indecl.* [*mah-tehr-nee-tah'*] motherhood
materno [*mah-tehr'-noh*] maternal
matita [*mah-tee'-tah*] pencil
mattina [*maht-tee'-nah*] morning
mattone *m.* [*maht-toh'-neh*] brick
matrimonio [*mah-tree-moh'-nee-oh*] marriage
matto [*maht'-toh*] crazy
maturità *f. indecl.* [*mah-too-ree-tah'*] maturity
maturo [*mah-too'-roh*] mature, ripe
me [*meh*] me
meccanico [*mehk-kah'-nee-koh*] mechanic, mechanical
meccanismo [*mehk-kah-neez'-moh*] device
medaglia [*meh-dah'-lyah*] medal
medesimo [*meh-deh'-zee-moh*] same
media [*meh'-dee-ah*] average
medicina [*meh-dee-chee'-nah*] medicine
medico *adj.* [*meh'-dee-koh*] medical

medico *n.* [*meh'-dee-koh*] physician
professione medica [*proh-fehs-see-oh'-neh meh'-dee-kah*] medical profession
medio [*meh'-dee-oh*] medium
mediterraneo [*meh-dee-tehr-rah'-neh-oh*] Mediterranean
meglio [*meh'-lyoh*] better, best
meglio così [*meh'-lyoh koh-zee'*] better like that
tanto meglio [*tahn'-toh meh'-lyoh*] so much the better
mela [*meh'-lah*] apple
torta di mele [*tohr'-tah dee meh'-leh*] apple pie
melodia [*meh-loh-dee'-ah*] melody
melone *m.* [*meh-loh'-neh*] melon
membro [*mehm'-broh*] member
memoria [*meh-moh'-ree-ah*] memory
a memoria [*ah meh-moh'-ree-ah*] by heart
mendicante *m.* [*mehn-dee-kahn'-teh*] beggar
meno [*meh'-noh*] less, minus
a meno che [*ah meh'-noh keh*] unless
al meno [*ahl meh'-noh*] at least
di meno [*dee meh'-noh*] fewer
il meno possibile [*eel meh'-noh pohs-see'-bee-leh*] the least possible
mensile [*mehn-see'-leh*] monthly
mentale [*mehn-tah'-leh*] mental
mente *f.* [*mehn'-teh*] mind
mentire *v.* [*mehn-tee'-reh*] lie, tell a lie
mento [*mehn'-toh*] chin
mentre *conj.* [*mehn'-treh*] while, as
Mentre mangiavo [*mehn'-treh mahn-jee-ah'-voh*] While I was eating
menzionare *v.* [*mehn-tsee-oh-nah'-reh*] mention
meraviglia [*meh-rah-vee'-lyah*] amazement, wonder
Che meraviglia! [*keh meh-rah-vee'-lyah*] How wonderful!
meravigliare *v.* [*meh-rah-vee-lyah'-reh*] amaze, astonish
meravigliarsi *v.* [*meh-rah-vee-lyahr'-see*] wonder
meraviglioso [*meh-rah-vee-lyoh'-zoh*] wonderful
mercante *m.* [*mehr-kahn'-teh*] merchant
mercato [*mehr-kah'-toh*] market
a buon mercato [*ah boo-ohn' mehr-kah'-toh*] cheap
merce *f.* [*mehr'-cheh*] merchandise, goods

mercoledì [*mehr-koh-leh-dee'*] Wednesday
meridionale [*meh-ree-dyoh-nah'-leh*] southern
meritare *v.* [*meh-ree-tah'-reh*] deserve, merit
merito [*meh'-ree-toh*] merit
meschino [*mehs-kee'-noh*] mean, wretched
mescolare *v.* [*mehs-koh-lah'-reh*] mix
mescuglio [*mehs-koo'-lyoh*] mixture
mese *m.* [*meh'-zeh*] month
messa [*mehs'-sah*] mass [eccl.]
messaggero [*mehs-sahj-jeh'-roh*] messenger
messaggio [*mehs-sahj'-jee-oh*] message
messicano [*mehs-see-kah'-noh*] Mexican
Messico [*mehs'-see-koh*] Mexico
meta [*meh'-tah*] goal
metà *f. indecl.* [*meh-tah'*] half
  a metà strada [*ah meh-tah' strah'-dah*] halfway
  la metà [*lah meh-tah'*] one half
metallo [*meh-tahl'-loh*] metal
metodo [*meh'-toh-doh*] method
metro [*meh'-troh*] meter
  sistema *m.* **metrico** [*sees-teh'-mah meh'-tree-koh*] metric system
mettere *v. irreg.* [*meht'-teh-reh*] set, put, lay
  mettere da parte [*meht'-teh-reh dah pahr'-teh*] set aside
  mettere in azione [*meht'-teh-reh een ah-tsee-oh'-neh*] set off
mezzo [*mehdz'-dzoh*] half, middle
  mezz'ora [*mehdz-dzoh'-rah*] half an hour
  in mezzo a [*een mehdz'-dzoh ah*] among, between
mezzogiorno [*mehdz-dzoh-jee-ohr'-noh*] noon
mezzanotte *f.* [*mehdz-dzah-noht'-teh*] midnight
mi [*mee*] me, to me
  Mi dia [*mee dee'-ah*] Give me
  Mi dica [*mee dee'-kah*] Tell me
  Mi scusi [*mee skoo'-zee*] Excuse me
miele *m.* [*mee-eh'-leh*] honey [food]
mietere *v.* [*mee-eh'-teh-reh*] harvest
miglio, miglia *pl.* [*mee'-lyoh, mee'-lyah*] mile
miglioramento [*mee-lyoh-rah-mehn'-toh*] improvement
migliorare *v.* [*mee-lyoh-rah'-reh*] improve
migliore *adj.*, [*mee-lyoh'-reh*] better

il (la) migliore [*eel (lah) mee-lyoh'-reh*] (the) best
Milano [*mee-lah'-noh*] Milan
milionario [*mee-lee-oh-nah'-ree-oh*] millionaire
milione *m.* [*mee-lee-oh'-neh*] million
un milione, due milioni [*oon mee-lee-oh'-neh, doo'-eh mee-lee-oh-nee*] one million, two millions
militare [*mee-lee-tah'-reh*] military
mille, mila *pl.* [*meel'-leh, mee'-lah*] thousand, one thousand
due mila [*doo'-eh mee'-lah*] two thousand
minaccia [*mee-nahch'-chee-ah*] threat
minacciare *v.* [*mee-nahch-chee-ah'-reh*] threaten
minatore *m.* [*mee-nah-toh'-reh*] miner
minerale *m.* [*mee-neh-rah'-leh*] mineral
minestra [*mee-nehs'-trah*] soup
miniera [*mee-nee-eh'-rah*] mine
minimo [*mee'-nee-moh*] least, minimum
ministero [*mee-nees-teh'-roh*] ministry, office
ministero degli affari esteri [*mee-nees-teh'-roh deh'-lyee ahf-fah'-ree ehs'-teh-ree*] foreign office
ministro [*mee-nees'-troh*] minister
minoranza [*mee-noh-rahn'-tsah*] minority
minore [*mee-noh'-reh*] minor [of age]
minorenne [*mee-noh-rehn'-neh*] underage, minor
minuto *m. & adj.* [*mee-noo'-toh*] minute
Aspetti un minuto! [*ahs-peht'-tee oon mee-noo'-toh*] Wait a minute!
mio *m.*, **mia** *f.*; **miei, mie** *pl.* [*mee'-oh, mee'-ah, mee-eh'-ee, mee'-eh*] my, mine
miope [*mee'-oh-peh*] shortsighted
miracolo [*mee-rah'-koh-loh*] miracle
mirare *v.* [*mee-rah'-reh*] aim
miscela [*mee-sheh'-lah*] blend
miserabile [*mee-zeh-rah'-bee-leh*] miserable
miseria [*mee-zeh'-ree-ah*] misery
misericordia [*mez-zeh-ree-kohr'-dee-ah*] mercy
misero [*mee'-zeh-roh*] woeful, wretched
missionario [*mees-see-oh-nah'-ree-oh*] missionary
missione *f.* [*mees-see-oh'-neh*] mission
misterioso [*mees-teh-ree-oh'-zoh*] mysterious
mistero [*mees-teh'-roh*] mystery

mistico [*mees'-tee-koh*] mystic
misura [*mee-zoo'-rah*] measure, size
misurare *v.* [*mee-zoo-rah'-reh*] measure
mite [*mee'-teh*] mild
mittente *m.* [*mee-tehn'-teh*] sender
mito [*mee'-toh*] myth
mobili *pl. m.* [*moh'-bee-lee*] furniture
moda [*moh'-dah*] fashion
  di moda [*dee moh'-dah*] fashionable
modello [*moh-dehl'-loh*] model, pattern
moderno [*moh-dehr'-noh*] modern
modestia [*moh-dehs'-tee-ah*] modesty
modesto [*moh-dehs'-toh*] modest
modificare *v.* [*moh-dee-fee-kah'-reh*] modify, alter
modo [*moh'-doh*] way, manner
  ad ogni modo [*ahd oh'-nyee moh'-doh*] in any case
  di modo che [*dee moh'-doh keh*] so that
  in nessun modo [*een nehs-soon' moh'-doh*] in no way
moglie [*moh'-lyeh*] wife
molo [*moh'-loh*] dock, pier, wharf
molti [*mohl'-tee*] many
moltissimo [*mohl-tees'-see-moh*] very much, a great many
molto [*mohl'-toh*] much, a lot, very
  Molto male! [*mohl'-toh mah'-leh*] Too bad!
  molto tempo [*mohl'-toh tehm'-poh*] a long time
  molto tempo fa [*mohl'-toh tehm'-poh fah*] long ago
momento [*moh-mehn'-toh*] moment
  al momento [*ahl moh-mehn'-toh*] at present
monaca [*moh'-nah-kah*] nun
monarchia [*moh-nahr-kee'-ah*] monarchy
monastero [*moh-nahs-teh'-roh*] monastery
mondo [*mohn'-doh*] world
moneta [*moh-neh'-tah*] coin, currency
monotono [*moh-noh'-toh-noh*] monotonous
montagna [*mohn-tah'-nyah*] mountain
  catena di montagne [*kah-teh'-nah dee mohn-tah'-nyeh*] mountain range
montare *v.* [*mohn-tah'-reh*] mount, set up
monte *m.* [*mohn'-teh*] mountain
monumento [*moh-noo-mehn'-toh*] monument

morale [*moh-rah'-leh*] moral, morale
moralità *f. indecl.* [*moh-rah-lee-tah'*] morality
morbido [*mohr'-bee-doh*] soft
morbillo [*mohr-beel'-loh*] measles
mordere *v. irreg.* [*mohr'-deh-reh*] bite
morire *v. irreg.* [*moh-ree'-reh*] die
mormorio [*mohr-moh-ree'-oh*] whisper, murmur
morso [*mohr'-soh*] bite, bitten
mortale [*mohr-tah'-leh*] deadly
morte *f.* [*mohr'-teh*] death
morto [*mohr'-toh*] dead
mosca [*mohs'-kah*] fly
mostarda [*mohs-tahr'-dah*] mustard
mostra [*mohs'-trah*] exhibition
mostrare *v.* [*mohs-trah'-reh*] show
mostruoso [*mohs-troo-oh'-zoh*] monstrous
motivo [*moh-tee'-voh*] motive
motocicletta [*moh-toh-chee-kleht'-tah*] motorcycle
motore *m.* [*moh-toh'-reh*] motor, engine
movimento [*moh-vee-mehn'-toh*] motion
mucchio [*mook'-kee-oh*] pile
mulino a vento [*moo-lee'-noh ah vehn'-toh*] windmill
multa [*mool'-tah*] fine, penalty
municipio [*moo-nee-chee'-pee-oh*] city hall
munizione *f.* [*moo-nee-tsee-oh'-neh*] ammunition
muovere *v. irreg.* [*moo-oh'-veh-reh*] move
muro [*moo'-roh*] wall
muscolo [*moos'-koh-loh*] muscle
museo [*moo-zeh'-oh*] museum
musica [*moo'-zee-kah*] music
musicale [*moo-zee-kah'-leh*] musical
musicista *m., f.* [*moo-zee-chees'-tah*] musician
muto [*moo'-toh*] dumb, mute

N

Napoli [*nah'-poh-lee*] Naples
narcotico [*nahr-koh'-tee-koh*] drug

narrativa [*nahr-rah-tee'-vah*] fiction
narrare *v.* [*nahr-rah'-reh*] narrate
nascere *v. irreg.* [*nah'-sheh-reh*] be born
Dove è nato? [*doh'-veh eh' nah'-toh*] Where were you born?
nascita [*nah'-shee-tah*] birth
nascondere *v. irreg.* [*nahs-kohn'-deh-reh*] hide
naso [*nah'-zoh*] nose
nastro [*nahs'-troh*] ribbon, tape
Natale *m.* [*nah-tah'-leh*] Christmas
Buon Natale! [*boo-ohn' nah-tah'-leh*] Merry Christmas!
nativo [*nah-tee'-voh*] native
nato [*nah'-toh*] born
Dove è nato Lei? [*doh'-veh eh nah'-toh leh'-ee*] Where were you born?
natura [*nah-too'-rah*] nature
naturale [*nah-too-rah'-leh*] natural
naturalmente [*nah-too-rahl-mehn'-teh*] naturally
navale [*nah-vah'-leh*] naval
nave *f.* [*nah'-veh*] ship
nave da carico [*nah'-veh dah kah'-ree-koh*] cargo ship
nave da guerra [*nah'-veh dah goo-ehr'-rah*] warship
nave traghetto [*nah'-veh trah-geht'-toh*] ferryboat
navigare *v.* [*nah-vee-gah'-reh*] sail
nazionale [*nah-tsee-oh-nah'-leh*] national
nazionalità *f. indecl.* [*nah-tsee-oh-nah-lee-tah'*] nationality
nazione *m.* [*nah-tsee-oh'-neh*] nation, country
nè, neppure [*neh, nehp-poo'-reh*] nor
nè . . . nè [*neh' . . . neh'*] neither . . . nor
nè l'uno nè l'altro [*neh loo'-noh neh lahl'-troh*] neither
ne [*neh*] from there, from it
ne vengono [*neh vehn'-goh-noh*] they come (from there)
ne [*neh*] of (about, from) him (her, it, you, them); some, any
Di Pietro, ne abbiamo parlato [*dee pee-eh'-troh neh ahb-bee-ah'-moh pahr-lah'-toh*] Of Peter [of him] we spoke
neanche [*neh-ahn'-keh*] neither, not even
nebbia [*nehb'-bee-ah*] fog
nebbioso [*nehb-bee-oh'-zoh*] foggy
necessario [*neh-chehs-sah'-ree-oh*] necessary

necessità *f. indecl.* [*neh-chehs-see-tah'*] need, necessity
negare *v.* [*neh-gah'-reh*] deny
negativo [*neh-gah-tee'-voh*] negative
negligenza [*neh-glee-jehn'-tsah*] neglect
negli: in gli *m. pl.* [*neh'-lyee*] in the
negoziante *m.* [*neh-goh-tsee-ahn'-teh*] dealer
negoziare *v.* [*neh-goh-tsee-ah'-reh*] trade
negozio [*neh-goh'-tsee-oh*] store, shop
negro [*neh'-groh*] Negro
nemico [*neh-mee'-koh*] enemy
nemmeno [*nehm-meh'-noh*] not even
neppure [*nehp-poo'-reh*] not even
nero [*neh'-roh*] black
nervi [*nehr'-vee*] nerves
nervoso [*nehr-voh'-zoh*] nervous
nessuno [*nehs-soo'-noh*] nobody, none
  Non c'è nessuno [*nohn cheh' nehs-soo'-noh*] There is none
  per nessun motivo [*pehr nehs-soon' moh-tee'-voh*] by no means
netto *adj.*, [*neht'-toh*] net
neutrale [*neh-oo-trah'-leh*] neutral
neve *f.* [*neh'-veh*] snow
nevicare *v.* [*neh-vee-kah'-reh*] snow
nido [*nee'-doh*] nest
niente [*nee-ehn'-teh*] nothing
  niente affatto [*nee-ehn'-teh ahf-faht'-toh*] not in the least
  Non fa niente! [*nohn fah nee-ehn'-teh*] Never mind!
nipote *m.* [*nee-poh'-teh*] nephew
nipote *f.* [*nee-poh'-teh*] niece
nipotino *m.*, **nipotina** *f.* [*nee-poh-tee'-noh, nee-poh-tee'-nah*] grandchild
no [*noh*] no
nobile [*noh'-bee-leh*] noble
nocivo [*noh-chee'-voh*] harmful
nodo [*noh'-doh*] knot
noi [*noh'-ee*] we, us
  a noi [*ah noh'-ee*] to us
noia [*noh'-ee-ah*] boredom
noioso [*noh-ee-oh'-zoh*] boring
noleggiare *v.* [*noh-lehj-jee-ah'-reh*] charter

nome *m.* [*noh'-meh*] name, noun

Quale è il suo nome? [*koo-ah'-leh eh' eel soo'-oh noh'-meh*] What is your name?

Mi chiamo . . . [*mee kee-ah'-moh*] My name is . . .

primo nome [*pree'-moh noh'-meh*] first name

nomignolo [*noh-mee'-nyoh-loh*] nickname

nominare *v.* [*noh-mee-nah'-reh*] name, elect

non [*nohn*] not

Non . . . [*nohn*] Don't . . .

No, non ci vado [*noh, nohn chee vah'-doh*] No, I don't go

Non è buono [*nohn eh' boo-oh'-noh*] It is no good

non più [*nohn pee-oo'*] no longer, no more

non una volta [*nohn oo'-nah vohl'-tah*] not once

nondimeno [*nohn-dee-meh'-noh*] nevertheless

nonna [*nohn'-nah*] grandmother

nonno [*nohn'-noh*] grandfather

nono [*noh'-noh*] ninth

nonostante [*noh-nohs-tahn'-teh*] in spite of

ciò nonostante [*chee-oh' noh-nohs-tahn'-teh*] even so

nord *m.* [*nohrd*] north

nord-est [*nohrd-ehst'*] northeast

nord-ovest [*nohrd-oh'-vehst*] northwest

normale [*nohr-mah'-leh*] normal

norvegese [*nohr-veh-jeh'-zeh*] Norwegian

Norvegia [*nohr-veh'-jee-ah*] Norway

nostalgico [*nohs-tahl'-jee-koh*] homesick

nostro *m.*, **nostra** *f.* [*nohs'-troh, nohs'-trah*] our

il nostro, la nostra [*eel nohs'-troh, lah nohs'-trah*] ours

nostri *m. pl.*, **nostre** *f. pl.* [*nohs'-tree, nohs'-treh*] our

i nostri, le nostre [*ee nohs'-tree, leh nohs'-treh*] ours

nota [*noh'-tah*] note

notare *v.* [*noh-tah'-reh*] notice

far notare *v.* [*fahr noh-tah'-reh*] point out

notevole [*noh-teh'-voh-leh*] remarkable

notifica [*noh-tee'-fee-kah*] notice

notificare *v.* [*noh-tee-fee-kah'-reh*] notify

notizia [*noh-tee'-tsee-ah*] news

notte *f.* [*noht'-teh*] night

Buona notte! [*boo-oh'-nah noht'-teh*] Good night!

la notte scorsa [*lah noht'-teh skohr'-sah*] last night

locale notturno [*loh-kah'-leh noht-toor'-noh*] nightclub
novanta [*noh-vahn'-tah*] ninety
nove [*noh'-veh*] nine
novecento [*noh-veh-chehn'-toh*] nine hundred
novembre *m.* [*noh-vehm'-breh*] November
novità *f. indecl.* [*noh-vee-tah'*] novelty, news
Che novità? [*keh noh-vee-tah'*] What's new?
nozione *f.* [*noh-tsee-oh'-neh*] notion
nozze *f. pl.* [*nohts'-tseh*] wedding
nubile [*noo'-bee-leh*] single, unmarried woman
nudo [*noo'-doh*] naked
nulla [*nool'-lah*] nothing
Non c'è nulla [*nohn cheh' nool'-lah*] There is nothing
Non serve a nulla [*nohn sehr'-veh ah nool'-lah*] It's good for nothing
nulla di particolare [*nool'-lah dee pahr-tee-koh-lah'-reh*] nothing special
nullaosta [*nool-lah-ohs'-tah*] official permission
numero [*noo'-meh-roh*] number
numeroso [*noo-meh-roh'-zoh*] numerous
numberare *v.* [*noo-meh-rah'-reh*] number
nuocere *v.* [*noo-oh'-cheh-reh*] harm
nuora [*noo-oh'-rah*] daughter-in-law
nuotare *v.* [*nooh-oh-tah'-reh*] swim
nuotatore *m.* [*noo-oh-tah-toh'-reh*] swimmer
nuovo [*noo-oh'-voh*] new
di nuovo [*dee noo-oh'-voh*] again
niente di nuovo [*nee-ehn'-teh dee noo-oh'-voh*] nothing new
nutrimento [*noo-tree-mehn'-toh*] nourishment
nutrire *v.* [*noo-tree'-reh*] feed
nuvola [*noo'-voh-lah*] cloud
nuvoloso [*noo-voh-loh'-zoh*] cloudy
nylon *m.* [*nah'-ee-lohn*] nylon

O

o, od [*oh, ohd*] or, either
obbedire *v.* [*ohb-beh-dee'-reh*] obey

obbligare *v.* [*ohb-blee-gah'-reh*] oblige
obbligato [*ohb-blee-gah'-toh*] obliged
  molto obbligato [*mohl'-toh ohb-blee-gah'-toh*] much obliged
obbligo [*ohb'-blee-goh*] obligation
obiezione *f.* [*oh-bee-eh-tsee-oh'-neh*] objection
occasione *f.* [*ohk-kah-zee-oh'-neh*] occasion
occhiali *m. pl.* [*ohk-kee-ah'-lee*] eyeglasses
occhiata [*ohk-kee-ah'-tah*] glance
  dare *v.* **un'occhiata** [*dah'-reh oon ohk-kee-ah'-tah*] glance
occhio, occhi *pl.* [*ohk'-kee-oh, ohk'-kee*] eye
occorrere *v. irreg.* [*ohk-kohr'-reh-reh*] occur, need
occidentale [*ohch-chee-dehn-tah'-leh*] western
occidente [*ohch-chee-dehn'-teh*] west
occupare *v.* [*ohk-koo-pah'-reh*] occupy
occupato [*ohk-koo-pah'-toh*] busy, engaged, occupied
occupazione *f.* [*ohk-koo-pah-tsee-oh'-neh*] occupation
oceano [*oh-cheh'-ah-noh*] ocean
oculista *m.* [*oh-koo-lees'-tah*] eye doctor
odiare *v.* [*oh-dee-ah'-reh*] hate
odio [*oh'-dee-oh*] hate
odorare *v.* [*oh-doh-rah'-reh*] smell
odore *m.* [*oh-doh'-reh*] smell, odor
offendere *v. irreg.* [*ohf-fehn'-deh-reh*] offend
offendersi *v.* [*ohf-fehn'-dehr-see*] feel offended
offensivo [*ohf-fehn-see'-voh*] offensive
offerta [*ohf-fehr'-tah*] offer
offesa [*ohf-feh'-zah*] offence
officina [*ohf-fee-chee'-nah*] workshop
offrire *v. irreg.* [*ohf-free'-reh*] offer
oggetto [*ohj-jeht'-toh*] object
oggi [*ohj'-jee*] today
oggigiorno [*ohj-jee-jee-ohr'-noh*] nowadays
ogni [*oh'-nyee*] every, each, any
  ogni altro giorno [*oh'-nyee ahl'-troh jee-ohr'-noh*] every other day
  ogni cosa [*oh'-nyee koh'-zah*] everything
  ogni giorno [*oh'-nyee jee-ohr'-noh*] every day
  ogni volta [*oh'-nyee vohl'-tah*] every time
ognuno [*oh-nyoo'-noh*] everybody

Olanda [*oh-lahn'-dah*] Holland
olandese [*oh-lahn-deh'-zeh*] Dutch
olio [*oh'-lee-oh*] oil
  olio di oliva [*oh'-lee-oh dee oh-lee'-vah*] olive oil
oliva [*oh-lee'-vah*] olive
oltremare [*ohl-treh-mah'-reh*] overseas
ombra [*ohm'-brah*] shade, shadow
ombrello [*ohm-brehl'-loh*] umbrella
omettere *v.* [*oh-meht'-teh-reh*] omit
omissione *f.* [*oh-mees-see-oh'-neh*] omission
onda, ondata [*ohn'-dah, ohn-dah'-tah*] wave
ondeggiare *v.* [*ohn-dehj-jee-ah'-reh*] wave
onesto [*oh-nehs'-toh*] honest
onorare *v.* [*oh-noh-rah'-reh*] honor
onorario [*oh-noh-rah'-ree-oh*] fee
onore *m.* [*oh-noh'-reh*] honor
opera [*oh'-peh-rah*] opera, work
  mano d'opera [*mah'-noh doh'-peh-rah*] labor
  opera d'arte [*oh'-peh-rah dahr'-teh*] work of art
operaio [*oh-peh-rah'-ee-oh*] laborer
operare *v.* [*oh-peh-rah'-reh*] operate [surgery]
operazione *f.* [*oh-peh-rah-tsee-oh'-neh*] operation
opinione *f.* [*oh-pee-nee-oh'-neh*] opinion
opporre *v. irreg.* [*ohp-pohr'-reh*] oppose
opportunità *f. indecl.* [*ohp-pohr-too-nee-tah'*] opportunity
opposto [*ohp-pohs'-toh*] opposite
oppure [*ohp-poo'-reh*] or (else)
ora [*oh'-rah*] hour, now, time
  or sono [*ohr soh'-noh*] ago
  Che ore sono? [*keh oh'-reh soh'-noh*] What time is it?
orale [*oh-rah'-leh*] oral
orario [*oh-rah'-ree-oh*] schedule
oratore *m.* [*oh-rah-toh'-reh*] speaker
orchestra [*ohr'-kehs-trah*] orchestra
ordinare *v.* [*ohr-dee-nah'-reh*] order, arrange, command
ordinariamente [*ohr-dee-nah-ree-ah-mehn'-teh*] ordinarily
ordinario [*ohr-dee-nah'-ree-oh*] ordinary
ordinato [*ohr-dee-nah'-toh*] orderly
ordine *m.* [*ohr'-dee-neh*] order
  ai suoi ordini [*ah'-ee soo-oh'-ee ohr'-dee-nee*] at your

service
orecchino [*oh-rehk-kee'-noh*] earring
orecchio, le orecchie *pl.* [*oh-rehk'-kee-oh, leh oh-rehk'-kee-eh*] ear
organico [*ohr-gah'-nee-koh*] organic
organizzare *v.* [*ohr-gah-needz-dzah'-reh*] organize
organizzazione *f.* [*ohr-gah-needz-dzah-tsee-oh'-neh*] organization
organo [*ohr'-gah-noh*] organ
orgoglio [*ohr-goh'-lyoh*] pride
orgoglioso [*ohr-goh-lyoh'-zoh*] proud
orfano [*ohr'-fah-noh*] orphan
orientale [*oh-ree-ehn-tah'-leh*] eastern
Oriente *m.* [*oh-ree-ehn'-teh*] Far East
Medio Oriente [*meh'-dee-oh oh-ree-ehn'-teh*] Middle East
originale [*oh-ree-jee-nah'-leh*] original
originalmente [*oh-ree-jee-nahl-mehn'-teh*] originally
orizzonte *m.* [*oh-reedz-dzohn'-teh*] horizon
orlo [*ohr'-loh*] edge
ormai [*ohr-mah'-ee*] by now, already
ornamento [*ohr-nah-mehn'-toh*] ornament
oro [*oh'-roh*] gold
d'oro [*doh'-roh*] golden
orologiaio [*oh-roh-loh-jee-ah'-ee-oh*] watchmaker
orologio [*oh-roh-loh'-jee-oh*] watch, clock
orologio da polso [*oh-roh-loh'-jee-oh dah pohl'-soh*] wristwatch
orribile [*ohr-ree'-bee-leh*] horrible
orso [*ohr'-soh*] bear
ortografia [*ohr-toh-grah-fee'-ah*] spelling
osare *v.* [*oh-zah'-reh*] dare
osceno [*oh-sheh'-noh*] obscene
oscurità *f. indecl.* [*ohs-koo-ree-tah'*] darkness
oscuro [*ohs-koo'-roh*] obscure, dim
ospedale *m.* [*ohs-peh-dah'-leh*] hospital
ospitalità *f. indecl.* [*ohs-pee-tah-lee-tah'*] hospitality
ospite *m.* [*ohs'-pee-teh*] host, guest
osservare *v.* [*ohs-sehr-vah'-reh*] observe
osservatore *m.*, **osservatrice** *f.* [*ohs-sehr-vah-toh'-reh, ohs-sehr-vah-tree'-cheh*] observer

osservazione *f.* [*ohs-sehr-vah-tsee-oh'-neh*] observation
ossigeno [*ohs-see'-jeh-noh*] oxygen
osso, le ossa *pl.* [*ohs'-soh, leh ohs'-sah*] bone
ostacolo [*ohs-tah'-koh-loh*] obstacle
oste [*ohs'-teh*] innkeeper
ostile [*ohs-tee'-leh*] hostile
ostinato [*ohs-tee-nah'-toh*] stubborn
ostrica [*ohs'-tree-kah*] oyster
ottanta [*oht-tahn'-tah*] eighty
ottavo [*oht-tah'-voh*] eighth
ottenere *v. irreg.* [*oht-teh-neh'-reh*] obtain, get
ottimista *m., f.* [*oht-tee-mees'-tah*] optimistic, optimist
ottimo [*oht'-tee-moh*] excellent
otto [*oht'-toh*] eight
ottobre *m.* [*oht-toh'-breh*] October
ottocento [*oht-toh-chehn'-toh*] eight hundred
ottone *m.* [*oht-toh'-neh*] brass
ovale [*oh-vah'-leh*] oval
ovest *m.* [*oh'-vehst*] west
ovunque [*oh-voon'-koo-eh*] everywhere
ovvio [*ohv'-vee-oh*] obvious
ozioso [*oh-tsee-oh'-zoh*] lazy

P

pacchetto [*pahk-keht'-toh*] package
  pacchetto di sigarette [*pahk-keht'-toh dee see-gah-reht'teh*] pack of cigarettes
pacco [*pahk'-koh*] pack, package, parcel
pace *f.* [*pah'-cheh*] peace
pacifico [*pah-chee'-fee-koh*] peaceful, easy-going
padella [*pah-dehl'-lah*] frying pan
padre *m.* [*pah'-dreh*] father
padrigno [*pah-dree'-nyoh*] stepfather
padrino [*pah-dree'-noh*] godfather
padrona *f.* [*pah-droh'-nah*] boss, owner [female]
  padrona di casa [*pah-droh'-nah dee kah'-zah*] landlady

padrone *m.* [*pah-droh'-neh*] boss, owner, master
  padrone di casa [*pah-droh'-neh dee kah'-zah*] landlord
paesaggio [*pah-eh-zahj'-jee-oh*] landscape
paese *m.* [*pah-eh'-zeh*] country
paga [*pah'-gah*] pay
pagamento [*pah-gah-mehn'-toh*] payment, pay
  tratta di pagamento [*traht'-tah dee pah-gah-mehn'-toh*] draft [bank]
pagare *v.* [*pah-gah'-reh*] pay
  pagare in contanti [*pah-gah'-reh een kohn-tahn'-tee*] pay cash
  pagare mensilmente [*pah-gah'-reh mehn-seel-mehn'-teh*] pay by instalments
  pagare una multa [*pah-gah'-reh oo'-nah mool'-tah*] pay a fine
pagina [*pah'-jee-nah*] page
paglia [*pah'-lyah*] straw
paio, paia *pl.* [*pah'-ee-oh, pah'-ee-ah*] pair
palazzo [*pah-lahts'-tsoh*] palace, mansion
palcoscenico [*pahl-koh-sheh'-nee-koh*] stage [theater]
palestra [*pah-lehs'-trah*] gymnasium [sports]
palla [*pahl'-lah*] ball [for playing]
pallido [*pahl'-lee-doh*] pale
pallone *m.* [*pahl-loh'-neh*] balloon
palma [*pahl'-mah*] palm
palo [*pah'-loh*] pole, post
palpebra [*pahl'-peh-brah*] eyelid
pane *m.* [*pah'-neh*] bread
  del pane [*dehl pah'-neh*] some bread
pane abbrustolito [*pah'-neh ahb-broos-toh-lee'-toh*] toast
panetteria [*pah-neht-teh-ree'-ah*] bakery
panfilo [*pahn-fee'-loh*] yacht
panico [*pah'-nee-koh*] panic
panino [*pah-nee'-noh*] sandwich, bun
panna [*pahn'-nah*] cream
  panna montata [*pahn'-nah mohn-tah'-tah*] whipped cream
panno [*pahn'-noh*] cloth
pantaloni lunghi *m. pl.* [*pahn-tah-loh'-nee loon'-gee*] trousers
pantofole *f. pl.* [*pahn-toh'-foh-leh*] slippers

papa *m.* [*pah'-pah*] pope
papà [*pah-pah'*] dad, daddy
parabrezza [*pah-rah-brehts'-tsah*] windshield
paracadute *m.* [*pah-rah-kah-doo'-teh*] parachute
paradiso [*pah-rah-dee'-zoh*] paradise
paragonare *v.* [*pah-rah-goh-nah'-reh*] compare
paragone *m.* [*pah-rah-goh'-neh*] comparison
paragrafo [*pah-rah'-grah-foh*] paragraph
paralizzare *v.* [*pah-rah-leedz-dzah'-reh*] paralyze
parallelo [*pah-rahl-leh'-loh*] parallel
parata [*pah-rah'-tah*] parade
parcheggiare *v.* [*pahr-kehj-jee-ah'-reh*] park
parcheggio [*pahr-kehj'-jee-oh*] parking
parco [*pahr'-koh*] park
parecchi [*pah-rehk'-kee*] several
parente *m.* [*pah-rehn'-teh*] relative
parere *v. irreg.* [*pah-reh'-reh*] seem
  Che le pare? [*keh leh pah'-reh*] How does it seem to you?
  Mi pare che . . . [*mee pah'-reh keh*] It seems to me that . . .
parete *f.* [*pah-reh'-teh*] wall
pari [*pah'-ree*] even, equal, same
  numero pari [*noo'-meh-roh pah'-ree*] even number
parlare *v.* [*pahr-lah'-reh*] speak, talk
  Parla italiano? [*pahr'-lah ee-tah-lee-ah'-noh*] Do you speak Italian?
parlamento [*pahr-lah-mehn'-toh*] parliament
parola [*pah-roh'-lah*] word
  parola d'ordine [*pah-roh'-lah dohr'-dee-neh*] watchword
parrocchia [*pahr-rohk'-kee-ah*] parish
parrucca [*pahr-rook'-kah*] wig
parrucchiere *m.* [*pahr-rook-kee-eh'-reh*] hairdresser
parte *f.* [*pahr'-teh*] part, share
  a parte [*ah pahr'-teh*] beside
  da parte [*dah pahr'-teh*] aside
  d'altra parte [*dahl'-trah pahr'-teh*] on the other hand
  da parte mia [*dah pahr'-teh mee'-ah*] on my part
  in parte [*een pahr'-teh*] partly
partecipare *v.* [*pahr-teh-chee-pah'-reh*] participate
partenza [*pahr-tehn'-tsah*] departure

particolare [*pahr-tee-koh-lah'-reh*] particular
particolarmente [*pahr-tee-koh-lahr-mehn'-teh*] particularly
partire *v.* [*pahr-tee'-reh*] leave, depart
partita [*pahr-tee'-tah*] game, shipment [commerce]
partito [*pahr-tee'-toh*] party [political]
parto [*pahr'-toh*] childbirth, delivery
partorire *v.* [*pahr-toh-ree'-reh*] give birth
patria [*pah'-tree-ah*] native land
parzialmente [*pahr-tsee-ahl-mehn'-teh*] partially
Pasqua [*pahs'-koo-ah*] Easter
passaggio [*pahs-sahj'-jee-oh*] passage
  passaggio a livello [*pahs-sahj'-jee-oh ah lee-vehl'-loh*] railroad crossing
passante *m.* [*pahs-sahn'-teh*] passerby
passaporto [*pahs-sah-pohr'-toh*] passport
passare *v.* [*pahs-sah'-reh*] pass, come by
  passare il tempo [*pahs-sah'-reh eel tehm'-poh*] spend time
passato [*pahs-sah'-toh*] past
  la settimana passata [*lah seht-tee-mah'-nah pahs-sah'-tah*] last week
passeggero [*pahs-sehj-jeh'-roh*] passenger
  treno passeggeri [*treh'-noh pahs-sehj-jeh'-ree*] passenger train
passeggiare *v.* [*pahs-sehj-jee-ah'-reh*] stroll
passeggiata [*pahs-sehj-jee-ah'-tah*] ride, walk
  fare *v.* **una passeggiata** [*fah'-reh oo'-nah pahs-sehj-jee-ah'-tah*] take a walk
passione *f.* [*pahs-see-oh'-neh*] passion
passivo [*pahs-see'-voh*] passive
passo [*pahs'-soh*] pace, step, pass [mountain]
pasta [*pahs'-tah*] paste, pastry
pasticceria [*pahs-teech-cheh-ree'-ah*] pastry shop
pasto [*pahs'-toh*] meal
patata [*pah-tah'-tah*] potato
patente *f.* [*pah-tehn'-teh*] license
patetico [*pah-teh'-tee-koh*] pathetic
patria [*pah'-tree-ah*] fatherland, country
patriotico [*pah-tree-oh'-tee-koh*] patriotic
pattinare *v.* [*paht-tee-nah'-reh*] skate
pattini *m. pl.* [*paht'-tee-nee*] skates

paura [*pah-oo'-rah*] fear
  avere *v.* **paura** [*ah-veh'-reh pah-oo'-rah*] be afraid
pausa [*pah'-oo-zah*] pause
pavimento [*pah-vee-mehn'-toh*] floor, pavement
paziente *n. & adj.* [*pah-tsee-ehn'-teh*] patient
pazienza [*pah-tsee-ehn'-tsah*] patience
pazzo [*pahts'-tsoh*] crazy, mad
peccato [*pehk-kah'-toh*] sin
  Che peccato! [*keh pehk-kah'-toh*] That's too bad!, What a pity!
pecora [*peh'-koh-rah*] sheep
pedaggio [*peh-dahj'-jee-oh*] toll
pedale *m.* [*peh-dah'-leh*] pedal
pedata [*peh-dah'-tah*] kick
pedestre *adj.* [*peh-dehs'-treh*] pedestrian
peggio [*pehj'-jee-oh*] worse
peggiore [*pehj-jee-oh'-reh*] worse
  il, la peggiore [*eel, lah pehj-jee-oh'-reh*] (the) worst
  peggiore di [*pehj-jee-oh'-reh dee*] worse than
pelare *v.* [*peh-lah'-reh*] peel, skin
pelle *f.* [*pehl'-leh*] skin
pellicia [*pehl-lee'-chee-ah*] fur
pellicola [*pehl-lee'-koh-lah*] film
pelo [*peh'-loh*] hair, fur
peloso [*peh-loh'-zoh*] hairy
pena [*peh'-nah*] pain
  a mala pena [*ah mah'-lah peh'-nah*] hardly
  Non vale la pena [*nohn vah'-leh lah peh'-nah*] It isn't worthwhile
penalità *f. indecl.* [*peh-nah-lee-tah'*] penalty
pendente [*pehn-dehn'-teh*] leaning
penisola [*peh-nee'-zoh-lah*] peninsula
penna [*pehn'-nah*] pen
pennello [*pehn-nehl'-loh*] paintbrush
pensare *v.* [*pehn-sah'-reh*] think
pensato [*pehn-sah'-toh*] thought
  ben pensato [*behn pehn-sah'-toh*] well-thought
pensiero [*pehn-see-eh'-roh*] thought, thinking
pensione *f.* [*pehn-see-oh'-neh*] boardinghouse, pension
pentola [*pehn'-toh-lah*] pot

pentolino [*pehn-toh-lee'-noh*] kettle
pepe *m.* [*peh'-peh*] pepper
per [*pehr*] for
  per esempio [*pehr eh-zehm'-pee-oh*] for example
  Per favore! [*pehr fah-voh'-reh*] Please!
  per me, per lei [*pehr meh, pehr leh'-ee*] for me, for you
pera [*peh'-rah*] pear
percento [*pehr-chehn'-toh*] percent
percentuale *m.* [*pehr-chehn-too-ah'-leh*] percentage
percepire *v.* [*pehr-cheh-pee'-reh*] perceive
perchè [*pehr-keh'*] why, because
  Perchè? [*pehr-keh'*] What for?, Why?
  Perchè no? [*pehr-keh' noh*] Why not?
  Perchè non voglio [*pehr-keh' nohn voh'-lyoh*] Because I don't want to
perciò [*pehr-chee-oh'*] therefore
perdere *v. irreg.* [*pehr'-deh-reh*] lose
  perdere (l'autobus, ecc.) [*pehr'-deh-reh*] miss (the bus, etc.)
  Ho perduto l'autobus [*oh pehr-doo'-toh lah'-oo-toh-boos*] I missed the bus
perdita [*pehr'-dee-tah*] loss, leakage
perdonare *v.* [*pehr-doh-nah'-reh*] pardon, forgive
perdonato [*pehr-doh-nah'-toh*] forgiven
perdono [*pehr-doh'-noh*] pardon
perduto [*pehr-doo'-toh*] lost
perfetto [*pehr-feht'-toh*] perfect
perfezione *f.* [*pehr-feh-tsee-oh'-neh*] perfection
pericolo [*peh-ree'-koh-loh*] danger
pericoloso [*peh-ree-koh-loh'-zoh*] dangerous, unsafe
periferia [*peh-ree-feh-ree'-ah*] suburb
periodico [*peh-ree-oh'-dee-koh*] periodical
periodo [*peh-ree'-oh-doh*] period
perla [*pehr'-lah*] pearl
permaloso [*pehr-mah-loh'-zoh*] touchy
permanente [*pehr-mah-nehn'-teh*] permanent
  ondulazione permanente [*ohn-doo-lah-tsee-oh'-neh pehr-mah-nehn'-teh*] permanent wave
permesso [*pehr-mehs'-soh*] permission, permit
permettere *v.* [*pehr-meht'-teh-reh*] permit, allow
  Mi permetta di . . . [*mee pehr-meht'-tah dee*] Allow me

to . . .

però [*peh-roh'*] but

persecuzione *f.* [*pehr-seh-koo-tsee-oh'-neh*] persecution

perseguire *v.* [*pehr-seh-goo-ee'-reh*] pursue

persiana di finestra [*pehr-see-ah'-nah dee fee-nehs'-trah*] shutter

persiano [*pehr-see-ah'-noh*] Persian

persistere *v.* [*pehr-sees'-teh-reh*] persist

persona [*pehr-soh'-nah*] person

personale [*pehr-soh-nah'-leh*] personal

personale *m.* [*pehr-soh-nah'-leh*] personnel

personalità *f. indecl.* [*pehr-soh-nah-lee-tah'*] personality

personalmente [*pehr-soh-nahl-mehn'-teh*] personally

persuadere *v. irreg.* [*pehr-soo-ah-deh'-reh*] persuade

persuasivo [*pehr-soo-ah-zee'-voh*] persuasive

pertinente [*pehr-tee-nehn'-teh*] relevant

pesante [*peh-zahn'-teh*] heavy

pesare *v.* [*peh-zah'-reh*] weigh

pesca [*pehs'-kah*] peach

pesca [*pehs'-kah*] fishing

pescare *v.* [*pehs-kah'-reh*] fish

pescatore *m.* [*pehs-kah-toh'-reh*] fisherman

pesce *m.* [*peh'-sheh*] fish

peso [*peh'-zoh*] weight

pessimista [*pehs-see-mees'-tah*] pessimist, pessimistic

peste *f.* [*pehs'-teh*] pest

petizione *f.* [*peh-tee-tsee-oh'-neh*] petition

petrolio [*peh-troh'-lee-oh*] oil [fuel]

pettegolo [*peht-teh'-goh-loh*] gossip

pettinare *v.* [*peht-tee-nah'-reh*] comb

  pettinarsi [*peht-tee-nahr'-see*] comb [oneself]

  Mi pettino i capelli [*mee peht'-tee-noh ee kah-pehl'-lee*] I comb my hair

pettine *m.* [*peht'-tee-neh*] comb

petto [*peht'-toh*] bosom, breast

pezzetto [*pehts-tseht'-toh*] bit, little bit

pezzo [*pehts'-tsoh*] piece, part [of a machine]

  pezzi di ricambio [*pehts'-tsee dee ree-kahm'-bee-oh*] spare parts

  pezzo grosso [*pehts'-tsoh grohs'-soh*] big shot

piacere *v. irreg.* [*pee-ah-cheh'-reh*] like, please, be pleasing
piacere *m.* [*pee-ah-cheh'-reh*] pleasure, favor
con piacere [*kohn pee-ah-cheh'-reh*] with pleasure
con molto piacere [*kohn mohl'-toh pee-ah-cheh'-reh*] with much pleasure
Il piacere è mio [*eel pee-ah-cheh'-reh eh' mee'-oh*] The pleasure is mine
Le fa piacere? [*leh fah pee-ah-cheh'-reh*] Does it please you?
Le piacerebbe . . . ? [*leh pee-ah-cheh-rehb'-beh*] Would you like . . . ?
Mi piace moltissimo [*mee pee-ah'-cheh mohl-tees'-see-moh*] I like it very much
Non mi piace [*nohn mee pee-ah'-cheh*] I don't like it
Per piacere! [*pehr pee-ah-cheh'-reh*] Please!
Piacere di conoscerla! [*pee-ah-cheh'-reh dee koh-noh'-shehr-lah*] Pleased to meet you!
vaggio di piacere [*vee-ahj'-jee-oh dee pee-ah-cheh'-reh*] pleasure trip
piacevole [*pee-ah-cheh'-voh-leh*] pleasant, likeable
piaga [*pee-ah'-gah*] sore, wound
pianeta *m.* [*pee-ah-neh'-tah*] planet
piangere *v. irreg.* [*pee-ahn'-jeh-reh*] cry, weep
pianista *m., f.* [*pee-ah-nees'-tah*] pianist
piano *adj.* [*pee-ah'-noh*] level, plane
piano *adv.* [*pee-ah'-noh*] slowly, softly
piano (di casa) [*pee-ah'-noh* (*dee kah'-zah*)] floor, plan
al piano superiore [*ahl pee-ah'-noh soo-peh-ree-oh'-reh*] upstairs
pianoforte *m.* [*pee-ah-noh-fohr'-teh*] piano
pianta [*pee-ahn'-tah*] plant
pianterreno [*pee-ahn-tehr-reh'-noh*] ground floor
piattaforma [*pee-aht-tah-fohr'-mah*] platform
piattino [*pee-aht-tee'-noh*] saucer
piatto [*pee-aht'-toh*] plate, dish
piatto [*pee-aht'-toh*] plain, flat
piazza [*pee-ahts'-tsah*] square [of a city]
piccione *m.* [*peech-chee-oh'-neh*] pigeon
piccolo [*peek'-koh-loh*] small, little
più piccolo [*pee-oo' peek'-koh-loh*] smaller

piede *m.* [*pee-eh'-deh*] foot
a piedi [*ah pee-eh'-dee*] on foot
piegare *v.* [*pee-eh-gah'-reh*] bend, fold
pieno [*pee-eh'-noh*] full
pietà *f. indecl.* [*pee-eh-tah'*] mercy, pity
pietra [*pee-eh'-trah*] stone
pigiama *m.* [*pee-jee-ah'-mah*] pajamas
pigione *f.* [*pee-jee-oh'-neh*] rent
pigro [*pee'-groh*] lazy
pillola [*peel'-loh-lah*] pill
pilota *m.* [*pee-loh'-tah*] pilot
pinta [*peen'-tah*] pint
pio [*pee'-oh*] pious
pioggia [*pee-ohj'-jee-ah*] rain
piombo [*pee-ohm'-boh*] lead [metal]
piovere *v.* [*pee-oh'-veh-reh*] rain
Piove [*pee-oh'-veh*] It is raining
pipa [*pee'-pah*] pipe [smoking]
piroscafo [*pee-rohs'-kah-foh*] steamship
piscina [*pee-shee'-nah*] swimming pool
pista [*pees'-tah*] track, runway
pistola [*pees-toh'-lah*] pistol
pittore *m.*, **pittrice** *f.* [*peet-toh'-reh*, *peet-tree'-cheh*] painter
pittura [*peet-too'-rah*] painting
più [*pee-oo'*] more, most, plus
il più [*eel pee-oo'*] the most
mai più [*mah'-ee pee-oo'*] nevermore
non più [*nohn pee-oo'*] no more
più o meno [*pee-oo' oh meh'-noh*] more or less
tanto più [*tahn'-toh pee-oo'*] all the more
piuma [*pee-oo'-mah*] feather
piuttosto [*pee-oot-tohs'-toh*] rather
Vorrebbe piuttosto . . . ? [*vohr-rehb'-beh pee-oot-tohs'-toh*] Would you rather . . . ?
Io preferisco piuttosto . . . [*ee'-oh preh-feh-rees'-koh pee-oo-tohs'-toh*] I rather prefer . . .
pizzicare *v.* [*peets-tsee-kah'-reh*] pinch
pizzicotto [*peets-tsee-koht'-toh*] pinching
plastico [*plahs'-tee-koh*] plastic
pleurite *f.* [*pleh-oo-ree'-teh*] pleurisy

plurale [*ploo-rah'-leh*] plural
pneumatico (di ricambio) [*pneh-oo-mah'-tee-koh* (*dee ree-kahm'-bee-oh*)] (spare) tire
pochi *m.*, **poche** *f.* [*poh'-kee*, *poh'-keh*] few
pochissimo [*poh-kees'-see-moh*] very little
poco [*poh'-koh*] little
dopo poco [*doh'-poh poh'-koh*] shortly afterwards
in poco tempo [*een poh'-koh tehm'-poh*] in a short time
poco a poco [*poh'-koh ah poh'-koh*] little by little
un poco [*oon poh'-koh*] somewhat
poema *m.* [*poh-eh'-mah*] poem
poesia [*poh-eh-zee'-ah*] poetry
poeta *m.*, **poetessa** *f.* [*poh-eh'-tah*, *poh-eh-tehs'-sah*] poet
poi [*poh'-ee*] then, afterwards
poichè *conj.* [*poh-ee-keh'*] since
polacco [*poh-lahk'-koh*] Polish
polare [*poh-lah'-reh*] polar
politica [*poh-lee'-tee-kah*] politics, policy
politico [*poh-lee'-tee-koh*] political
polizia [*poh-lee-tsee'-ah*] police
poliziotto [*poh-lee-tsee-oht'-toh*] policeman
polizza di assicurazione [*poh-leets'-tsah dee ahs-see-koo-rah-tsee-oh'-neh*] insurance policy
pollice *m.* [*pohl'-lee-cheh*] thumb, inch
pollo [*pohl'-loh*] chicken
polmone *m.* [*pohl-moh'-neh*] lung
polmonite *f.* [*pohl-moh-nee'-teh*] pneumonia
polo [*poh'-loh*] pole [geog.]
Polonia [*poh-loh'-nee-ah*] Poland
polpetta [*pohl-peht'-tah*] meatball
polso [*pohl'-soh*] pulse, wrist
poltrona [*pohl-troh'-nah*] armchair
polvere *f.* [*pohl'-veh-reh*] dust
polveroso [*pohl-veh-roh'-zoh*] dusty
pomeriggio [*poh-meh-reej'-jee-oh*] afternoon
pomodoro [*poh-moh-doh'-roh*] tomato
sugo di pomodoro [*soo'-goh dee poh-moh-doh'-roh*] tomato juice
pompa [*pohm'-pah*] pump
pompare *v.* [*pohm-pah'-reh*] pump

pompelmo [*pohm-pehl'-moh*] grapefruit
pompiere *m.* [*pohm-pee-eh'-reh*] fireman
ponte *m.* [*pohn'-teh*] bridge, deck [of ship]
popolare [*poh-poh-lah'-reh*] popular
popolarità *f. indecl.* [*poh-poh-lah-ree-tah'*] popularity
popolazione *f.* [*poh-poh-lah-tsee-oh'-neh*] population
popolo [*poh'-poh-loh*] people
porcellana [*pohr-chehl-lah'-nah*] porcelain, china
porco [*pohr'-koh*] pig
porpora [*pohr'-poh-rah*] purple
porre *v. irreg.* [*pohr'-reh*] put, place
porta [*pohr'-tah*] door, gate
  Apra la porta [*ah'-prah lah pohr'-tah*] Open the door
  Chiuda la porta! [*kee-oo'-dah lah pohr'-tah*] Close the door!
portabile [*pohr-tah'-bee-leh*] portable
portacenere *m.* [*pohr-tah-cheh'-neh-reh*] ashtray
portafoglio [*pohr-tah-foh'-lyoh*] wallet
portare *v.* [*pohr-tah'-reh*] carry, bring, wear
  Per favore, mi porti . . . [*pehr fah-voh'-reh, mee pohr'-tee*] Please bring me . . .
  Portamelo [*pohr'-tah-meh-loh*] Bring it to me
portata [*pohr-tah'-tah*] reach
portico [*pohr'-tee-koh*] porch
portiere *m.* [*pohr-tee-eh'-reh*] janitor, doorman
porto [*pohr'-toh*] seaport, harbor
Portogallo [*pohr-toh-gahl'-loh*] Portugal
portoghese [*pohr-toh-geh'-zeh*] Portuguese
porzione *f.* [*pohr-tsee-oh'-neh*] portion, part
posa [*poh'-zah*] pose
posare *v.* [*poh-zah'-reh*] pose
positivo [*poh-zee-tee'-voh*] positive
posizione [*poh-zee-tsee-oh'-neh*] position
possedere *v. irreg.* [*pohs-seh-deh'-reh*] own, possess
possesso [*pohs-sehs'-soh*] possession
possible [*pohs-see'-bee-leh*] possible
possibilità *f. indecl.* [*pohs-see-bee-lee-tah'*] possibility
possibilmente [*pohs-see-beel-mehn'-teh*] possibly
posta [*pohs'-tah*] mail, post
  fermo-posta [*fehr-moh-pohs'-tah*] post-office box,

general delivery
postino [*pohs-tee'-noh*] mailman
posto [*pohs'-toh*] place, spot, seat
in nessun posto [*een nehs-soon' pohs'-toh*] nowhere
potente [*poh-tehn'-teh*] powerful
potere *m.* [*poh-teh'-reh*] power [authority]
potere *v. irreg., aux.* [*poh-teh'-reh*] be able, can, may
Può essere [*poo-oh' ehs'-seh-reh*] It may be
Può darsi che . . . [*poo-oh' dahr'-see keh*] It may be that . . .
Può venire Lei? [*poo-oh' veh-nee'-reh leh'-ee*] Can you come?
Sì io posso [*see', ee'-oh pohs'-soh*] Yes, I can
Posso entrare? [*pohs'-soh ehn-trah'-reh*] May I come in?
potere (fare qualcosa) *v.* [*poh-teh'-reh* (*fah'-reh koo-ahl-koh'-zah*)] afford to
Non posso pagare [*nohn pohs'-soh pah-gah'-reh*] I can't afford to pay
Non posso bere [*nohn pohs'-soh beh'-reh*] I can't afford to drink
Io potrei andare domani [*ee'-oh poh-treh'-ee ahn-dah'-reh doh-mah'-nee*] I might go tomorrow
povero [*poh'-veh-roh*] poor
povertà *f. indecl.* [*poh-vehr-tah'*] poverty
pozzo [*pohts'-tsoh*] well [water]
pranzare *v.* [*prahn-tsah'-reh*] lunch
pranzo [*prahn'-tsoh*] lunch
Il pranzo è pronto! [*eel prahn'-tsoh eh' prohn'-toh*] Lunch is ready!
sala da pranzo [*sah'-lah dah prahn'-tsoh*] dining room
praticare *v.* [*prah-tee-kah'-reh*] practice
pratico [*prah'-tee-koh*] practical
prato [*prah'-toh*] lawn
precauzione *f.* [*preh-kah-oo-tsee-oh'-neh*] caution
precedente [*preh-cheh-dehn'-teh*] former, previous
precedentemente [*preh-cheh-dehn-teh-mehn'-teh*] formerly
precedere *v.* [*preh-cheh'-deh-reh*] precede
precisamente [*preh-chee-zah-mehn'-teh*] precisely
preciso [*preh-chee'-zoh*] precise
predica [*preh'-dee-kah*] sermon, preaching
prediletto [*preh-dee-leht'-toh*] pet

preferenza [*preh-feh-rehn'-tsah*] preference
preferibile [*preh-feh-ree'-bee-leh*] preferable
preferire *v.* [*preh-feh-ree'-reh*] prefer
preferito [*preh-feh-ree'-toh*] favorite
pregare *v.* [*preh-gah'-reh*] pray, beg
  Prego . . . [*preh'-goh*] (You are) welcome . . .
  Prego, entri! [*preh'-goh, ehn'-tree*] Please come in!
preghiera [*preh-gee-eh'-rah*] prayer
pregiudizio [*preh-jee-oo-dee'-tsee-oh*] prejudice
preliminare [*preh-lee-mee-nah'-reh*] preliminary
prematuro [*preh-mah-too'-roh*] premature
premere *v.* [*preh'-meh-reh*] press, squeeze
premio [*preh'-mee-oh*] award, prize
prendere *v. irreg.* [*prehn'-deh-reh*] take
  Prenda! [*prehn'-dah*] Take it!
prenotare *v.* [*preh-noh-tah'-reh*] reserve, book
prenotazione *f.* [*preh-noh-tah-tsee-oh'-neh*] reservation
preoccuparsi *v.* [*preh-ohk-koo-pahr'-see*] take care of, worry
  Non si preoccupi! [*nohn see preh-ohk'-koo-pee*] Don't worry!
preoccupato [*preh-ohk-koo-pah'-toh*] upset, worried
preoccupazione *f.* [*preh-ohk-koo-pah-tsee-oh'-neh*] worry
preparare *v.* [*preh-pah-rah'-reh*] prepare
preparazione *f.* [*preh-pah-rah-tsee-oh'-neh*] preparation
presa [*preh'-zah*] plug [electric]
presentabile [*preh-zehn-tah'-bee-leh*] presentable
presentare *v.* [*preh-zehn-tah'-reh*] present, introduce
  presentarsi [*preh-zehn-tahr'-see*] introduce oneself
presentazione *f.* [*preh-zehn-tah-tsee-oh'-neh*] introduction
presente [*preh-zehn'-teh*] present
presentemente [*preh-zehn-teh-mehn'-teh*] presently
presentimento [*preh-sehn-tee-mehn'-toh*] premonition
presenza [*preh-zehn'-tsah*] presence
preservare *v.* [*preh-sehr-vah'-reh*] preserve
presidente *m.* [*preh-zee-dehn'-teh*] president
  vice-presidente [*vee'-cheh preh-zee-dehn'-teh*] vice-president
preso [*preh'-zoh*] taken
pressare *v.* [*prehs-sah'-reh*] press
pressione *f.* [*prehs-see-oh'-neh*] pressure

prestare *v.* [*prehs-tah'-reh*] lend
prestigio [*prehs-tee'-jee-oh*] prestige
prestito [*prehs'-tee-toh*] loan
  chiedere *v.* **in prestito** [*kee-eh'-deh-reh een prehs'-tee-toh*] borrow
presto [*prehs'-toh*] soon, early
  il più presto possibile [*eel pee-oo' prehs'-toh pohs-see'-bee-leh*] as soon as possible
  Presto, presto! [*prehs'-toh, prehs'-toh*] Hurry up!
  più presto [*pee-oo' prehs'-toh*] sooner
  presto o tardi [*prehs'-toh oh tahr'-dee*] sooner or later
presupporre *v. irreg.* [*preh-zoop-pohr'-reh*] presume
presupposto [*preh-zoop-pohs'-toh*] assumption
prete *m.* [*preh'-teh*] priest
pretendere *v.* [*preh-tehn'-deh-reh*] pretend
pretenzioso [*preh-tehn-tsee-oh'-zoh*] pretentious
pretesa [*preh-teh'-zah*] pretense
prevalente [*preh-vah-lehn'-teh*] prevalent
prevenire *v.* [*preh-veh-nee'-reh*] prevent
prevenzione *f.* [*preh-vehn-tsee-oh'-neh*] prevention
prezioso [*preh-tsee-oh'-zoh*] precious
prezzo [*prehts'-tsoh*] price, rate
  al prezzo di [*ahl prehts'-tsoh dee*] at the rate of
  prezzo fisso [*prehts'-tsoh fees'-soh*] fixed price
  prezzo del viaggio [*prehts'-tsoh dehl vee-ahj'-jee-oh*] fare
prigione *f.* [*pree-jee-oh'-neh*] prison
prigioniero [*pree-jee-oh-nee-eh'-roh*] prisoner
prima (di) [*pree'-mah (dee)*] before
  prima che venga [*pree'-mah keh vehn'-gah*] before he (she) comes
  prima classe [*pree'-mah klahs'-seh*] first class
  prima di lei [*pree'-mah dee leh'-ee*] before you
primavera [*pree-mah-veh'-rah*] spring [season]
primitivo [*pree-mee-tee'-voh*] primitive
primo [*pree'-moh*] first
  primo nome [*pree'-moh noh'-meh*] first name
principale *m.* [*preen-chee-pah'-leh*] chief, principal, master
principale *adj.* [*preen-chee-pah'-leh*] main, leading
principalmente [*preen-chee-pahl-mehn'-teh*] mainly
principe *m.*, **principessa** *f.* [*preen'-chee-peh, preen-chee-*

pehs'-sah] prince, princess
principiante *m.* [*preen-chee-pee-ahn'-teh*] beginner
principio [*preen-chee'-pee-oh*] principle, beginning
al principio [*ahl preen-chee'-pee-oh*] at the beginning
privare *v.* [*pree-vah'-reh*] deprive
privato [*pree-vah'-toh*] private
privilegio [*pree-vee-lehj'-jee-oh*] privilege
privo di [*pree'-voh dee*] lacking in
probabile [*proh-bah'-bee-leh*] likely
probabilmente [*proh-bah-beel-mehn'-teh*] probably
problema *m.* [*proh-bleh'-mah*] problem
procedere *v.* [*proh-cheh'-deh-reh*] proceed
procedimento [*proh-cheh-dee-mehn'-toh*] procedure
processo [*proh-chehs'-soh*] process, trial
procurarsi *v.* [*proh-koo-rahr'-see*] obtain
prodotto [*proh-doht'-toh*] product
produrre *v. irreg.* [*proh-door'-reh*] produce
produzione *f.* [*proh-doo-tsee-oh'-neh*] production
produzione in serie [*proh-doo-tsee-oh'-neh een seh'-ree-eh*] mass production
professione *f.* [*proh-fehs-see-oh'-neh*] profession
professore *m.*, **professoressa** *f.* [*proh-fehs-soh'-reh*, *proh-fehs-soh-rehs'-sah*] professor
profezia [*proh-feh-tsee'-ah*] prophecy
profilo [*proh-fee'-loh*] profile
profittare *v.* [*proh-feet-tah'-reh*] profit
profitto [*proh-feet'-toh*] profit
profondità *f. indecl.* [*proh-fohn-dee-tah'*] depth
profondo [*proh-fohn'-doh*] deep
poco profondo [*poh'-koh proh-fohn'-doh*] shallow
profugo [*proh'-foo-goh*] refugee
profumo [*proh-foo'-moh*] perfume
progetto [*proh-jeht'-toh*] project, plan
programma *m.* [*proh-grahm'-mah*] program
progredire *v.* [*proh-greh-dee'-reh*] progress
progressivo [*proh-grehs-see'-voh*] progressive
progresso [*proh-grehs'-soh*] progress
proibire *v.* [*proh-ee-bee'-reh*] prohibit
proibito [*proh-ee-bee'-toh*] forbidden
promessa [*proh-mehs'-sah*] promise

promettente [*proh-meht-tehn'-teh*] promising
promettere *v.* [*proh-meht'-teh-reh*] promise
prominente [*proh-mee-nehn'-teh*] prominent
promozione *f.* [*proh-moh-tsee-oh'-neh*] promotion
pronome *m.* [*proh-noh'-meh*] pronoun
pronto [*prohn'-toh*] ready
  pronto soccorso [*prohn'-toh sohk-kohr'-soh*] first aid
pronuncia [*proh-noon'-chee-ah*] pronunciation
pronunciare *v.* [*proh-noon-chee-ah'-reh*] pronounce
  Come si pronuncia . . . ? [*koh'-meh see proh-noon'-chee-ah*] How do you pronounce . . . ?
propaganda [*proh-pah-gahn'-dah*] propaganda
proporre *v. irreg.* [*proh-pohr'-reh*] propose
proporzione *f.* [*proh-pohr-tsee-oh'-neh*] proportion
proposizione *f.* [*proh-poh-zee-tsee-oh'-neh*] proposition
proposito [*proh-poh'-zee-toh*] purpose, design
  a proposito [*ah proh-poh'-zee-toh*] by the way
  di proposito [*dee proh-poh'-zee-toh*] on purpose
proposta [*proh-pohs'-tah*] proposal
proprietà *f. indecl.* [*proh-pree-eh-tah'*] property
proprietario [*proh-pree-eh-tah'-ree-oh*] owner
proprio [*proh'-pree-oh*] just, exactly, own
  la mia propria casa [*lah mee'-ah proh'-pree-ah kah'-zah*] my own house
  proprio così [*proh'-pree-oh koh-zee'*] just so
  proprio un poco [*proh'-pree-oh oon poh'-koh*] a little bit
prosciutto [*proh-shee-oot'-toh*] ham
prosperità *f. indecl.* [*prohs-peh-ree-tah'*] prosperity
prospero [*prohs'-peh-roh*] prosperous
prossimo [*prohs'-see-moh*] next
  il prossimo anno [*eel prohs'-see-moh ahn'-noh*] next year
  il prossimo mese [*eel prohs'-see-moh meh'-zeh*] next month
  la prossima settimana [*lah prohs'-see-mah seht-tee-mah'-nah*] next week
  la prossima volta [*lah prohs'-see-mah vohl'-tah*] next time
proteggere *v. irreg.* [*proh-tehj'-jeh-reh*] protect
protesta [*proh-tehs'-tah*] protest, complain
protestante [*proh-tehs-tahn'-teh*] Protestant
protestare *v.* [*proh-tehs-tah'-reh*] protest
protezione *f.* [*proh-teh-tsee-oh'-neh*] protection

prova [*proh'-vah*] trial, test, proof
provare *v.* [*proh-vah'-reh*] prove, test, try
proverbio [*proh-vehr'-bee-oh*] proverb
provincia [*proh-veen'-chee-ah*] province
provinciale [*proh-veen-chee-ah'-leh*] provincial
provisorio [*proh-vee-zoh'-ree-oh*] temporary
provista [*proh-vees'-tah*] supply
provvedere *v.* [*prohv-veh-deh'-reh*] provide
prudente [*proo-dehn'-teh*] prudent, careful
prugna [*proo'-nyah*] plum
  prugna secca [*proo'-nyah sehk'-kah*] prune
psichiatra *m., f.* [*psee-kee-ah'-trah*] psychiatrist
psicoanalisi *f.* [*psee-koh-ah-nah'-lee-zee*] psychoanalysis
psicologico [*psee-koh-loh'-jee-koh*] psychological
pubblicare *v.* [*poob-blee-kah'-reh*] publish
pubblicazione *f.* [*poob-blee-kah-tsee-oh'-neh*] publication
pubblicità *f. indecl.* [*poob-blee-chee-tah'*] publicity, advertising
pubblico *n. & adj.* [*poob'-blee-koh*] public
pugilato [*poo-jee-lah'-toh*] boxing
pugno [*poo'-nyoh*] fist, punch
pulire *v.* [*poo-lee'-reh*] clean
  pulire a secco [*poo-lee'-reh ah sehk'-koh*] dry clean
pulito [*poo-lee'-toh*] clean
pulizia [*poo-lee-tsee'-ah*] cleaning
punire *v.* [*poo-nee'-reh*] punish
punizione *f.* [*poo-nee-tsee-oh'-neh*] punishment
punta [*poon'-tah*] point [form], tip
puntare *v.* [*poon-tah'-reh*] point
punto [*poon'-toh*] point, period [punctuation]
  punto di vista [*poon'-toh dee vees'-tah*] standpoint
  punto interrogativo [*poon'-toh een-tehr-roh-gah-tee'-voh*] question mark
puntuale [*poon-too-ah'-leh*] punctual
puntura [*poon-too'-rah*] sting, prick
pure [*poo'-reh*] also, as well
  Fate pure! [*fah'-teh poo'-reh*] Go ahead!, Certainly!
puro [*poo'-roh*] pure
purtroppo [*poor-trohp'-poh*] unfortunately

Q

qua [*koo-ah'*] here
quadrato [*koo-ah-drah'-toh*] square
quadro [*koo-ah'-droh*] picture
quaggiù [*koo-ahj-jee-oo'*] down here
qualche [*koo-ahl'-keh*] some, any
  in qualche luogo [*een koo-ahl'-keh loo-oh'-goh*] somewhere
  qualche volta [*koo-ahl'-keh vohl'-tah*] sometimes
qualcosa [*koo-ahl-koh'-zah*] something
qualcuno [*koo-ahl-koo'-noh*] somebody, someone
quale [*koo-ah'-leh*] what, which, who, whom
qualifica [*koo-ah-lee'-fee-kah*] qualification
qualificare *v.* [*koo-ah-lee-fee-kah'-reh*] qualify
qualificato [*koo-ah-lee-fee-kah'-toh*] qualified
qualità *f. indecl.* [*koo-ah-lee-tah'*] quality
qualora [*koo-ah-loh'-rah*] if, when
qualsiasi [*koo-ahl-see'-ah-see*] any, whatever
qualunque [*koo-ah-loon'-koo-eh*] whatever
  qualunque cosa [*koo-ah-loon'-koo-eh koh'-zah*] anything
quando [*koo-ahn'-doh*] when, how soon
  Da quando? [*dah koo-ahn'-doh*] Since when?
quanti *m. pl.*, **quante** *f. pl.* [*koo-ahn'-tee, koo-ahn'-teh*] how many
  Quanti anni ha? [*koo-ahn'-tee ahn'-nee ah*] How old are you?
quantità *f. indecl.* [*koo-ahn-tee-tah'*] quantity
quanto *m.*, **quanta** *f.* [*koo-ahn'-toh, koo-ahn'-tah*] how much?
  Quanto le devo? [*koo-ahn'-toh leh deh'-voh*] How much do I owe you?
  Quanto è lontano? [*koo-ahn'-toh eh' lohn-tah'-noh*] How far is it?
  Quanto tempo? [*koo-ahn'-toh tehm'-poh*] How long?
  Quanto vale questo? [*koo-ahn'-toh vah'-leh koo-ehs'-toh*] How much is this worth?
  in quanto a . . . [*een koo-ahn'-toh ah*] as for . . .

Per quanto tempo? [*pehr koo-ahn'-toh tehm'-poh*] For how long? [time]
quaranta [*koo-ah-rahn'-tah*] forty
quartiere *m.* [*koo-ahr-tee-eh'-reh*] neighborhood
quartiere generale [*koo-ahr-tee-eh'-reh jeh-neh-rah'-leh*] headquarters [army]
quarto [*koo-ahr'-toh*] quarter, fourth
quasi [*koo-ah'-zee*] nearly, almost
quasi mai [*koo-ah'-zee mah'-ee*] hardly ever
quattordici [*koo-aht-tohr'-dee-chee*] fourteen
quattrini *m. pl.* [*koo-aht-tree'-nee*] money
quattro [*koo-aht'-troh*] four
quattrocento [*koo-aht-troh-chehn'-toh*] four hundred
quelli *m. pl.*, **quelle** *f. pl.* [*koo-ehl'-lee, koo-ehl'-leh*] those
quello *m.* **quella** *f.* [*koo-ehl'-loh, koo-ehl'-lah*] that, that one
quello che [*koo-ehl'-loh keh*] that which
quello che desidera [*koo-ehl'-loh keh deh-zee'-deh-rah*] whatever you wish
questi *m. pl.*, **queste** *f. pl.* [*koo-ehs'-tee, koo-ehs'-teh*] these
questionario [*koo-ehs-tee-oh-nah'-ree-oh*] questionaire, form
questione *f.* [*koo-ehs-tee-oh'-neh*] question
questo *m.*, **questa** *f.* [*koo-ehs'-toh, koo-ehs'-tah*] this one
in questa maniera [*een koo-ehs'-tah mah-nee-eh'-rah*] in this way
Che cosa è questo? [*keh koh'-zah eh' koo-ehs'-toh*] What is this?
È questa la via giusta? [*eh' koo-ehs'-tah lah vee'-ah jee-oos'-tah*] Is this the right way?
qui [*koo-ee'*] here
Eccolo qui [*ehk'-koh-loh koo-ee'*] Here it is
proprio qui [*proh'-pree-oh koo-ee'*] right here
Venga qui! [*vehn'-gah koo-ee'*] Come here!
quieto [*koo-ee-eh'-toh*] quiet
quindi [*koo-een'-dee*] therefore
quindici [*koo-een'-dee-chee*] fifteen
quinto [*koo-een'-toh*] fifth
quotazione *f.* [*koo-oh-tah-tsee-oh'-neh*] quotation
quotidiano [*koo-oh-tee-dee-ah'-noh*] daily
quoziente *m.* [*koo-oh-tsee-ehn'-teh*] quotient

R

rabbia [*rahb'-bee-ah*] anger
rabbino [*rahb-bee'-noh*] rabbi
raccogliere *v.* [*rahk-koh'-lyeh-reh*] collect, pick up
raccolta [*rahk-kohl'-tah*] collection, harvest
raccolto [*rahk-kohl'-toh*] crop
raccomandare *v.* [*rahk-koh-mahn-dah'-reh*] recommend
raccomandazione *f.* [*rahk-koh-mahn-dah-tsee-oh'-neh*] recommendation
raccontare *v.* [*rahk-kohn-tah'-reh*] tell, relate
racconto [*rahk-kohn'-toh*] tale, story
radere *v. irreg.*, **radersi** [*rah-deh'-reh*, *rah-dehr'-see*] shave
radicale [*rah-dee-kah'-leh*] radical
radice *f.* [*rah-dee'-cheh*] root
radio *f.* [*rah'-dee-oh*] radio
radunarsi *v.* [*rah-doo-nahr'-see*] get together
raffinato [*rahf-fee-nah'-toh*] refined
raffineria [*rahf-fee-neh-ree'-ah*] refinery
raffreddare *v.* [*rahf-frehd-dah'-reh*] cool
  raffreddarsi [*rahf-frehd-dahr'-see*] catch cold
  Mi sono raffreddato [*mee soh'-noh rahf-frehd-dah'-toh*] I have caught a cold
raffreddore *m.* [*rahf-frehd-doh'-reh*] cold [illness]
ragazza [*rah-gahts'-tsah*] girl
ragazzo [*rah-gahts'-tsoh*] boy
raggiungere *v.* [*rahj-jee-oon'-jeh-reh*] reach, arrive
raggio [*rahj'-jee-oh*] ray
ragionare *v.* [*rah-jee-oh-nah'-reh*] reason
ragione *f.* [*rah-jee-oh'-neh*] reason
  avere *v.* **ragione** [*ah-veh'-reh rah-jee-oh'-neh*] be right
ragionevole [*rah-jee-oh-neh'-voh-leh*] reasonable
rallentare *v.* [*rahl-lehn-tah'-reh*] slow down
rame *m.* [*rah'-meh*] copper
ramo [*rah'-moh*] branch [of tree]
rana [*rah'-nah*] frog

rancore *m.* [*rahn-koh'-reh*] grudge
rapidamente [*rah-pee-dah-mehn'-teh*] quickly
rapido [*rah'-pee-doh*] rapid, fast
rapire *v.* [*rah-pee'-reh*] kidnap
rapporto [*rahp-pohr'-toh*] report
in rapporto a [*een rahp'-pohr-toh ah*] in reference to
rappresentante [*rahp-preh-zehn-tahn'-teh*] representative
rappresentare *v.* [*rahp-preh-zehn-tah'-reh*] represent
raramente [*rah-rah-mehn'-teh*] seldom
raro [*rah'-roh*] rare, unusual
rasoio [*rah-zoh'-ee-oh*] razor
rasoio di sicurezza [*rah-zoh'-ee-oh dee see-koo-rehts'-tsah*] safety razor
rasoio elettrico [*rah-zoh'-ee-oh eh-leht'-tree-koh*] electric razor
rassicurare *v.* [*rahs-see-koo-rah'-reh*] reassure
rassomiglianza [*rahs-soh-mee-lyahn'-tsah*] resemblance
rassomigliare *v.* [*rahs-soh-mee-lyah'-reh*] resemble
razza [*rahts'-tsah*] (human) race
re *m.* [*reh*] king
reale [*reh-ah'-leh*] royal, real
realizzare *v.* [*reh-ah-leedz-dzah'-reh*] realize
realmente [*reh-ahl-mehn'-teh*] really
reazione *f.* [*reh-ah-tsee-oh'-neh*] reaction
recente [*reh-chehn'-teh*] recent
recentemente [*reh-chehn-teh-mehn'-teh*] recently
recentissimo [*reh-chehn-tees'-see-moh*] latest
recipiente *m.* [*reh-chee-pee-ehn'-teh*] container
reciproco [*reh-chee'-proh-koh*] mutual
recitare *v.* [*reh-chee-tah'-reh*] recite
reclamare *v.* [*reh-klah-mah'-reh*] claim
reclame *f.* [*reh-klah'-meh*] advertising
record *m.* [*reh'-kohrd*] record [sports]
redattore *m.* [*reh-daht-toh'-reh*] editor
reddito [*rehd'-dee-toh*] income
imposta sul reddito [*eem-pohs'-tah sool rehd'-dee-toh*] income tax
redimere *v.* [*reh-dee'-meh-reh*] redeem
regalo [*reh-gah'-loh*] gift, present
reggimento [*rehj-jee-mehn'-toh*] regiment

reggipetto [*rehj-jee-peht'-toh*] bra, brassiere
regina [*reh-jee'-nah*] queen
regione *f.* [*reh-jee-oh'-neh*] region
registrare *v.* [*reh-jees-trah'-reh*] register
registro [*reh-jees'-troh*] register
regnare *v.* [*reh-nyah'-reh*] reign
regno [*reh'-nyoh*] kingdom
regola [*reh'-goh-lah*] rule
regolamento [*reh-goh-lah-mehn'-toh*] regulation
regolare *v.* [*reh-goh-lah'-reh*] settle, regulate
relativo [*reh-lah-tee'-voh*] relative
  relativo a [*reh-lah-tee'-voh ah*] pertaining to
religione *f.* [*reh-lee-jee-oh'-neh*] religion
religioso [*reh-lee-jee-oh'-zoh*] religious
remare *v.* [*reh-mah'-reh*] row
remo [*reh'-moh*] oar
remoto [*reh-moh'-toh*] remote
reparto [*reh-pahr'-toh*] department [of store]
republica [*reh-poob'-lee-kah*] republic
reputazione *f.* [*reh-poo-tah-tsee-oh'-neh*] reputation
requisito [*reh-koo-ee-zee'-toh*] requirement
residente [*reh-zee-dehn'-teh*] resident
residenza [*reh-zee-dehn'-tsah*] residence
residuo [*reh-zee'-doo-oh*] remainder
resoconto [*reh-zoh-kohn'-toh*] report
respingere *v.* [*rehs-peen'-jeh-reh*] repel
respirare *v.* [*rehs-pee-rah'-reh*] breathe
respirazione *f.* [*rehs-pee-rah-tsee-oh'-neh*] breathing
respiro [*rehs-pee'-roh*] breath
responsabile [*rehs-pohn-sah'-bee-leh*] responsible
responsabilità *f. indecl.* [*rehs-pohn-sah-bee-lee-tah'*] responsibility
resistenza [*reh-zees-tehn'-tsah*] resistance
resistere *v.* [*reh-zees'-teh-reh*] resist
restare *v.* [*rehs-tah'-reh*] remain, stay
restaurare *v.* [*rehs-tah-oo-rah'-reh*] restore
resto [*rehs'-toh*] change [money], rest, remainder
rete *f.* [*reh'-teh*] net
retina [*reh-tee'-nah*] (hair) net
rettangolo [*reht-tahn'-goh-loh*] rectangle

reumatismo [*reh-oo-mah-teez'-moh*] rheumatism
riacquistare *v.* [*ree-ahk-koo-ees-tah'-reh*] regain
ribellarsi *v.* [*ree-behl-lahr'-see*] rebel
ribelle *m., f.* [*ree-behl'-leh*] rebel
ricatto [*ree-kaht'-toh*] blackmail
ricchezza [*reek-kehts'-tsah*] wealth
ricciuto [*reech-chee-oo'-toh*] curly
ricco [*reek'-koh*] rich
ricerca [*ree-chehr'-kah*] search
  fare *v.* **ricerche** [*fah'-reh ree-chehr'-keh*] research
ricetta [*ree-cheht'-tah*] prescription
ricevere *v.* [*ree-cheh'-veh-reh*] receive
ricevimento [*ree-cheh-vee-mehn'-toh*] reception, party
ricevuta [*ree-cheh-voo'-tah*] receipt
richiamare (alla memoria) *v.* [*ree-kee-ah-mah'-reh (ahl'-lah meh-moh'-ree-ah)*] recall
richiedente [*ree-kee-eh-dehn'-teh*] applicant
richiedere *v.* [*ree-kee-eh'-deh-reh*] request
richiesta [*ree-kee-ehs'-tah*] request
  fare *v.* **la richiesta** [*fah'-reh lah ree-kee-ehs'-tah*] apply for
ricompensa [*ree-kohm-pehn'-sah*] reward
ricompensare *v.* [*ree-kohm-pehn-sah'-reh*] reward
riconoscente [*ree-koh-noh-shehn'-teh*] grateful
riconoscere *v.* [*ree-koh-noh'-sheh-reh*] recognize
ricordare a *v.* [*ree-kohr-dah'-reh ah*] remind
ricordarsi *v.* [*ree-kohr-dahr'-see*] remember
  Si ricorda di me? [*see ree-kohr'-dah dee meh*] Do you remember me?
ricordo [*ree-kohr'-doh*] souvenir
ricorrere a *v.* [*ree-kohr'-reh-reh ah*] resort to
ricorso [*ree-kohr'-soh*] appeal
ricreazione *f.* [*ree-kreh-ah-tsee-oh'-neh*] recreation
ricuperare *v.* [*ree-koo-peh-rah'-reh*] recover
ricupero [*ree-koo'-peh-roh*] recovery
ridere *v. irreg.* [*ree'-deh-reh*] laugh
ridicolo [*ree-dee'-koh-loh*] ridicule, ridiculous
ridurre *v. irreg.* [*ree-door'-reh*] reduce
riduzione *f.* [*ree-doo-tsee-oh'-neh*] reduction
riempire *v.* [*ree-ehm-pee'-reh*] fill
riesaminare *v.* [*ree-eh-zah-mee-nah'-reh*] review

riferire *v.* [*ree-feh-ree'-reh*] report
riferirsi [*ree-feh-reer'-see*] refer to
riferimento [*ree-feh-ree-mehn'-toh*] reference
punto di riferimento [*poon'-toh dee ree-feh-ree-mehn'-toh*] landmark
rifiutare *v.* [*ree-fee-oo-tah'-reh*] refuse
rifiuto [*ree-fee-oo'-toh*] refusal
riflessione *f.* [*ree-flehs-see-oh'-neh*] reflection, consideration
riflesso [*ree-flehs'-soh*] reflex
riflettere *v.* [*ree-fleht'-teh-reh*] reflect
riformare *v.* [*ree-fohr-mah'-reh*] reform
rifugio [*ree-foo'-jee-oh*] refuge, shelter
riga [*ree'-gah*] ruler [measure]
rigido [*ree'-jee-doh*] stiff
riguardo [*ree-goo-ahr'-doh*] regard
riguardo a [*ree-goo-ahr'-doh ah*] concerning
in riguardo a [*een ree-goo-ahr'-doh ah*] in regard to
rilassare *v.* [*ree-lahs-sah'-reh*] relax
rilievo [*ree-lee-eh'-voh*] projection
mettere *v.* **in rilievo** [*meht'-teh-reh een ree-lee-eh'-voh*] emphasize
rilluttante [*reel-loot-tahn'-teh*] reluctant
rima [*ree'-mah*] rhyme
rimandare *v.* [*ree-mahn-dah'-reh*] postpone
rimanere *v. irreg.* [*ree-mah-neh'-reh*] remain
rimborsare *v.* [*reem-bohr-sah'-reh*] repay
rimborso [*reem-bohr'-soh*] refund
rimedio [*ree-meh'-dee-oh*] remedy
rimessa [*ree-mehs'-sah*] remittance
rimorchiare *v.* [*ree-mohr-kee-ah'-reh*] tow
rimorso [*ree-mohr'-soh*] remorse
rimpiangere *v.* [*reem-pee-ahn'-jeh-reh*] regret
rimproverare *v.* [*reem-proh-veh-rah'-reh*] scold
rimuovere *v.* [*ree-moo-oh'-veh-reh*] remove
rinascimento [*ree-nah-shee-mehn'-toh*] renaissance
rinchiudere *v.* [*reen-kee-oo'-deh-reh*] enclose
rinfrescante [*reen-frehs-kahn'-teh*] refreshing
rinfrescare *v.* [*reen-frehs-kah'-reh*] refresh
rinfresco [*reen-frehs'-koh*] refreshment
ringraziare *v.* [*reen-grah-tsee-ah'-reh*] thank

rinnovare *v.* [*reen-noh-vah'-reh*] renew
rintracciare *v.* [*reen-trahch-chee-ah'-reh*] trace
riparare *v.* [*ree-pah-rah'-reh*] repair
riparazione *f.* [*ree-pah-rah-tsee-oh'-neh*] repair
ripetere *v.* [*ree-peh'-teh-reh*] repeat
Per favore ripeta! [*pehr fah-voh'-reh ree-peh'-tah*] Please repeat!
riposare *v.* [*ree-poh-zah'-reh*] rest
riposo [*ree-poh'-zoh*] rest
riprendere *v.* [*ree-prehn'-deh-reh*] resume
riproduzione *f.* [*ree-proh-doo-tsee-oh'-neh*] reproduction
risata [*ree-zah'-tah*] laughter
riscaldamento [*rees-kahl-dah-mehn'-toh*] heating
riscaldare *v.* [*rees-kahl-dah'-reh*] warm
rischiare *v.* [*rees-kee-ah'-reh*] take a chance, risk
rischio [*rees'-kee-oh*] risk
risentimento [*ree-sehn-tee-mehn'-toh*] resentment
riservare *v.* [*ree-zehr-vah'-reh*] reserve
riso [*ree'-zoh*] laugh
riso [*ree'-zoh*] rice
risoluzione *f.* [*ree-zoh-loo-tsee-oh'-neh*] resolution
risolvere *v.* [*ree-zohl'-veh-reh*] solve
risparmiare *v.* [*rees-pahr-mee-ah'-reh*] save, spare
risparmio [*rees-pahr'-mee-oh*] saving
libretto di risparmio [*lee-breht'-toh dee rees-pahr'-mee-oh*] savings account
rispettabile [*rees-peht-tah'-bee-leh*] respectable
rispettare *v.* [*rees-peht-tah'-reh*] respect
rispettivo [*rees-peht-tee'-voh*] respective
rispetto [*rees-peht'-toh*] respect
rispettoso [*rees-peht-toh'-zoh*] respectful
rispondere *v. irreg.* [*rees-pohn'-deh-reh*] answer, reply
risposta [*rees-pohs'-toh*] response
rissa [*rees'-sah*] row
ristorante *m.* [*rees-toh-rahn'-teh*] restaurant
vagone ristorante *m.* [*vah-goh'-neh rees-toh-rahn'-teh*] dining car
risultato [*ree-zool-tah'-toh*] result
risveglio [*ree-zveh'-lyoh*] awakening
ritardare *v.* [*ree-tahr-dah'-reh*] delay

essere *v.* **in ritardo** [*ehs'-seh-reh een ree-tahr'-doh*] be late
ritenere *v. irreg.* [*ree-teh-neh'-reh*] retain
ritirare *v.* [*ree-tee-rah'-reh*] withdraw
ritirarsi [*ree-tee-rahr'-see*] retire
ritmo [*reet'-moh*] rhythm
ritornare *v.* [*ree-tohr-nah'-reh*] return
Quando ritornerà? [*koo-ahn'-doh ree-tohr-neh-rah'*] When will you return?
ritorno [*ree-tohr'-noh*] return
andata e ritorno [*ahn-dah'-tah eh ree-tohr'-noh*] round trip
ritratto [*ree-traht'-toh*] portrait
rituale *m. & adj.* [*ree-too-ah'-leh*] ritual
riunione *f.* [*ree-oo-nee-oh'-neh*] meeting
riuscire *v.* [*ree-oo-shee'-reh*] succeed
riva [*ree'-vah*] shore
rivale *m. & adj.* [*ree-vah'-leh*] rival
rivelare *v.* [*ree-veh-lah'-reh*] reveal
rivelazione *f.* [*ree-veh-lah-tsee-oh'-neh*] revelation
riverenza [*ree-veh-rehn'-tsah*] reverence
rivista [*ree-vees'-tah*] magazine, review
rivolgere *v.* [*ree-vohl'-jeh-reh*] address
rivolta [*ree-vohl'-tah*] riot
rivoltarsi *v.* [*ree-vohl-tahr'-see*] turn around, rebel
rivoltato [*ree-vohl-tah'-toh*] inside out
rivoltella [*ree-vohl-tehl'-lah*] revolver
rivoluzione *f.* [*ree-voh-loo-tsee-oh'-neh*] revolution
roba [*roh'-bah*] goods, things, stuff
roccia [*rohch'-chee-ah*] rock
rognone *m.* [*roh-nyoh'-neh*] kidney
Romania [*roh-mah-nee'-ah*] Roumania
Roma [*roh'-mah*] Rome
romano [*roh-mah'-noh*] Roman
romantico [*roh-mahn'-tee-koh*] romantic
romanza [*roh-mahn'-tsah*] romance
romanziere *m.* [*roh-mahn-tsee-eh'-reh*] novelist
romanzo [*roh-mahn'-tsoh*] novel
Romeno [*roh-meh'-noh*] Roumanian
rompere *v. irreg.* [*rohm'-peh-reh*] break
rondine *f.* [*rohn'-dee-neh*] swallow

rosa [*roh'-zah*] rose
rossetto [*rohs-seht'-toh*] lipstick
rosso [*rohs'-soh*] red
rotondo [*roh-tohn'-doh*] round
rotta [*roht'-tah*] route
rotto [*roht'-toh*] broken
rottura [*roht-too'-rah*] fracture
rovesciare *v.* [*roh-veh-shee-ah'-reh*] reverse, overturn, upset
rovina [*roh-vee'-nah*] ruin
rovinare *v.* [*roh-vee-nah'-reh*] ruin
rovinato [*roh-vee-nah'-toh*] ruined
rubare *v.* [*roo-bah'-reh*] steal
rubato [*roo-bah'-toh*] stolen
rubinetto [*roo-bee-neht'-toh*] faucet
rude [*roo'-deh*] rude
ruga [*roo'-gah*] wrinkle
ruggine *f.* [*rooj'-jee-neh*] rust
rumore *m.* [*roo-moh'-reh*] rumor, noise
rumoroso [*roo-moh-roh'-zoh*] noisy
ruota [*roo-oh'-tah*] wheel
rurale [*roo-rah'-leh*] rural
ruscello [*roo-shehl'-loh*] brook
russare *v.* [*roos-sah'-reh*] snore
Russia [*roos'-see-ah*] Russia
russo [*roos'-soh*] Russian
rustico [*roos'-tee-koh*] rustic
ruvido [*roo'-vee-doh*] rough

S

sabato [*sah'-bah-toh*] Saturday
sabbia [*sahb'-bee-ah*] sand
sabbioso [*sahb-bee-oh'-zoh*] sandy
sabotaggio [*sah-boh-tahj'-jee-oh*] sabotage
sacco [*sahk'-koh*] sack
sacerdote *m.* [*sah-chehr-doh'-teh*] clergyman
sacrificare *v.* [*sah-kree-fee-kah'-reh*] sacrifice

sacrificio [*sah-kree-fee'-chee-oh*] sacrifice
sacro [*sah'-kroh*] sacred
saggezza [*sahj-jehts'-tsah*] wisdom
saggio [*sahj'-jee-oh*] wise
sala [*sah'-lah*] hall
  sala d'aspetto [*sah'-lah dahs-peht'-toh*] waiting room
salario [*sah-lah'-ree-oh*] salary
salato [*sah-lah'-toh*] salty
sale *m.* [*sah'-leh*] salt
salire *v. irreg.* [*sah-lee'-reh*] climb, go up
  salire su [*sah-lee'-reh soo*] board
salmone *m.* [*sahl-moh'-neh*] salmon
salone [*sah-loh'-neh*] room, hall
  salone di bellezza [*sah-loh'-neh dee behl-lehts'-tsah*] beauty parlor
salotto [*sah-loht'-toh*] parlor, living room
salsa [*sahl'-sah*] sauce
salsiccia [*sahl-seech'-chee-ah*] sausage
saltare *v.* [*sahl-tah'-reh*] jump
salto [*sahl'-toh*] jump
salutare *v.* [*sah-loo-tah'-reh*] greet, salute
salutare *adj.* [*sah-loo-tah'-reh*] healthy
salute *f.* [*sah-loo'-teh*] health
  Alla sua salute! [*ahl'-lah soo'-ah sah-loo'-teh*] To your health!
  in buona salute [*een boo-oh'-nah sah-loo'-teh*] in good health
saluti [*sah-loo'-tee*] greetings
saluto [*sah-loo'-toh*] salute
salvacondotta *m.* [*sahl-vah-kohn-doht'-tah*] safe conduct
salvagente *m.* [*sahl-vah-jehn'-teh*] life jacket
salvaggio [*sahl-vahj'-jee-oh*] rescue
salvare *v.* [*sahl-vah'-reh*] save, rescue
Salve! [*sahl'-veh*] Hello!
salvo *adj.* [*sahl'-voh*] safe
salvo *prep.* [*sahl'-voh*] except, excepting
sanatorio [*sah-nah-toh'-ree-oh*] sanatorium
sangue *m.* [*sahn'-goo-eh*] blood
sano [*sah'-noh*] sound, healthy
  sano di mente [*sah'-noh dee mehn'-teh*] sane

sano e salvo [*sah'-noh eh sahl'-voh*] safe and sound
santo [*sahn'-toh*] saint, holy
sanzione *f.* [*sahn-tsee-oh'-neh*] sanction
sapere *v. irreg.* [*sah-peh'-reh*] know [in general sense]
  Sa lei? [*sah leh'-ee*] Do you know?
  Non so [*nohn soh*] I don't know
  Chi sa? [*kee sah*] Who knows?
sapere *m.* [*sah-peh'-reh*] knowledge
sapienza [*sah-pee-ehn'-tsah*] knowledge
sapone *m.* [*sah-poh'-neh*] soap
sapore *m.* [*sah-poh'-reh*] flavor, taste
saporito [*sah-poh-ree'-toh*] tasty
sarà [*sah-rah'*] (he, she, it, you) will be
saranno [*sah-rahn'-noh*] (they, you [polite form]) will be
sarcastico [*sahr-kahs'-tee-koh*] sarcastic
Sardegna [*sahr-deh'-nyah*] Sardinia
sardina [*sahr-dee'-nah*] sardine
saremo [*sah-reh'-moh*] we will be
sarò [*sah-roh'*] I will be
sarta [*sahr'-tah*] dressmaker
sarto [*sahr'-toh*] tailor
sartoria [*sahr-toh-ree'-ah*] tailor shop
sasso [*sahs'-soh*] stone
satira [*sah'-tee-rah*] satire
satirico [*sah-tee'-ree-koh*] satirical
sbadigliare *v.* [*zbah-dee-lyah'-reh*] yawn
sbadiglio [*zbah-dee'-lyoh*] yawn
sbagliare *v.* [*zbah-lyah'-reh*] err, make an error
  sbagliarsi [*zbah-lyahr'-see*] be mistaken
sbagliato [*zbah-lyah'-toh*] mistaken, wrong
sbaglio [*zbah'-lyoh*] error, mistake
sbarazzarsi di *v.* [*zbah-rahts-tsahr'-see dee*] get rid of
sbarcare *v.* [*zbahr-kah'-reh*] land [ship]
sbarra [*zbahr'-rah*] bar [metal]
sbarrare *v.* [*zbahr-rah'-reh*] bar
sbucciare *v.* [*zbooch-chee-ah'-reh*] peel [food]
scacchi *m. pl.* [*skahk'-kee*] chess
scadenza [*skah-dehn'-tsah*] expiration
scadere *v.* [*skah-deh'-reh*] expire, fall due
scaduto [*skah-doo'-toh*] expired, due

scaffale *m.* [*skahf-fah'-leh*] shelf
scala [*skah'-lah*] ladder, stairs
scalzo [*skahl'-tsoh*] barefoot
scambiare *v.* [*skahm-bee-ah'-reh*] exchange
scandalo [*skahn'-dah-loh*] scandal
scapolo [*skah'-poh-loh*] bachelor
scappare *v.* [*skahp-pah'-reh*] escape
scaricare *v.* [*skah-ree-kah'-reh*] unload
scarico [*skah'-ree-koh*] discharge, unloading
scarlatto [*skahr-laht'-toh*] scarlet
scarpa [*skahr'-pah*] shoe
scarso [*skahr'-soh*] scarce, scanty
scatola [*skah'-toh-lah*] box, can
scattare *v.* [*skaht-tah'-reh*] spring up
scavare *v.* [*skah-vah'-reh*] dig
scegliere *v. irreg.* [*sheh'-lyeh-reh*] choose
scelta [*shehl'-tah*] choice
scelto [*shehl'-toh*] chosen
scena [*sheh'-nah*] scene
scenario [*sheh-nah'-ree-oh*] scenery
scendere *v. irreg.* [*shehn'-deh-reh*] descend, go down, get off
scheletro [*skeh'-leh-troh*] skeleton
schema *m.* [*skeh'-mah*] scheme
scherma [*skehr'-mah*] fencing
schermo [*skehr'-moh*] screen
scherzare *v.* [*skehr-tsah'-reh*] joke, kid
  Senza scherzi [*sehn'-tsah skehr'-tsee*] No kidding
scherzo [*skehr'-tsoh*] joke, trick
scherzoso[*skehr-tsoh'-zoh*] playful
schiacciare *v.* [*skee-ahch-chee-ah'-reh*] crush
schiaffeggiare *v.* [*skee-ahf-fehj-jee-ah'-reh*] slap
schiaffo [*skee-ahf'-foh*] slap
schiavitù *f. indecl.* [*skee-ah-vee-too'*] slavery
schiavo [*skee-ah'-voh*] slave
schiena [*skee-eh'-nah*] back [anat.]
schiuma [*skee-oo'-mah*] foam
sci *m.* [*shee*] ski
scialle *m.* [*shee-ahl'-leh*] shawl
scialuppa [*shee-ah-loo'-pah*] lifeboat
sciampagna [*shee-ahm-pah'-nyah*] champagne

sciacquare *v.* [*shee-ahk-koo-ah'-reh*] rinse
sciare *v.* [*shee-ah'-reh*] ski
sciarpa [*shee-ahr'-pah*] scarf
scienza [*shee-ehn'-tsah*] science
scienziato [*shee-ehn-tsee-ah'-toh*] scientist
scimmia [*sheem'-mee-ah*] monkey, ape
sciocchezza [*shee-ohk-kehts'-tsah*] nonsense
sciocco [*shee-ohk'-koh*] foolish
sciogliere *v. irreg.* [*shee-oh'-lyeh-reh*] melt, untie, dissolve
sciolto [*shee-ohl'-toh*] melted
sciopero [*shee-oh'-peh-roh*] strike
scintilla [*sheen-teel'-lah*] spark
sciupare *v.* [*shee-oo-pah'-reh*] waste
scivolare *v.* [*shee-voh-lah'-reh*] slip, slide
scivoloso [*shee-voh-loh'-zoh*] slippery
scodella [*skoh-dehl'-lah*] bowl
scolpire *v.* [*skohl-pee'-reh*] carve
scommessa [*skohm-mehs'-sah*] bet
scommettere *v.* [*skoh-meht'-teh-reh*] bet
scomodo [*skohm'-moh-doh*] uncomfortable
scomparire *v. irreg.* [*skohm-pah-ree'-reh*] disappear
scomparso [*skohm-pahr'-soh*] missing
scompartimento [*skohm-pahr-tee-mehn'-toh*] compartment
sconfiggere *v.* [*skohn-feej'-jeh-reh*] defeat
sconfitta [*skohn-feet'-tah*] defeat
sconosciuto [*skoh-noh-shee-oo'-toh*] unknown
sconto [*skohn'-toh*] discount
scontrino [*skohn-tree'-noh*] check, ticket, coupon
scontro [*skohn'-troh*] collision
sconvenienza [*skohn-veh-nee-ehn'-tsah*] inconvenience
scopa [*skoh'-pah*] broom
scopare *v.* [*skoh-pah'-reh*] sweep
scoperta [*skoh-pehr'-tah*] discovery
scopo [*skoh'-poh*] purpose, sake, aim
scoppio [*skohp'-pee-oh*] burst
scoprire *v. irreg.* [*skohp-pree'-reh*] discover
scoraggiare *v.* [*skoh-rahj-jee-ah'-reh*] discourage
scorciatoia [*skohr-chee-ah-toh'-ee-ah*] shortcut
scorrere *v.* [*skohr'-reh-reh*] flow
scorso [*skohr'-soh*] past

la notte scorsa [*lah noht'-teh skohr'-sah*] last night
scortese [*skohr-teh'-zeh*] unkind, impolite
scortesia [*skohr-teh-zee'-ah*] rudeness
scozzese [*skohts-tseh'-zeh*] Scotch
Scozia [*skoh'-tsee-ah*] Scotland
scritto [*skreet'-toh*] writing, written
scrittore *m.*, **scrittrice** *f.* [*skreet-toh'-reh, skreet-tree'-cheh*] writer
scrittura [*skreet-too'-rah*] writing
scrivania [*skree-vah-nee'-ah*] desk
scrivere *v. irreg.* [*skree'-veh-reh*] write
Come si scrive? [*koh'-meh see skree'-veh*] How do you spell it?
scrivere a macchina [*skree'-veh-reh ah mahk'-kee-nah*] type
scultura [*skool-too'-rah*] sculpture
scuola [*skoo-oh'-lah*] school
scuola elementare [*skoo-oh'-lah eh-leh-mehn-tah'-reh*] elementary school
scuola media [*skoo-oh'-lah meh'-dee-ah*] high school
scuotere *v.* [*skoo-oh'-teh-reh*] rock, shake
scusa [*skoo'-zah*] excuse, apology
scusare *v.* [*skoo-zah'-reh*] excuse
scusarsi [*skoo-zahr'-see*] apologize
Mi scusi! [*mee skoo'-zee*] Excuse me!
sdraiarsi *v.* [*zdrah-ee-ahr'-see*] lie down
se [*seh*] whether, if
se è possible [*seh eh' pohs-see'-bee-leh*] if it is possible
se no [*seh noh*] otherwise
sè [*seh'*] one's self, himself, herself, themselves
sebbene [*sehb-beh'-neh*] although
seccare *v.* [*sehk-kah'-reh*] vex, dry
secco [*sehk'-koh*] dry
secchio [*sehk'-kee-oh*] pail
secolo [*seh'-koh-loh*] century
secondario [*seh-kohn-dah'-ree-oh*] secondary
secondo *adj.* [*seh-kohn'-doh*] second
secondo a . . . [*seh-kohn'-doh ah*] according to . . .
secondo [*seh-kohn'-doh*] second [of a minute]
sede *f.* [*seh'-deh*] residence

sede centrale [*seh'-deh chehn-trah'-leh*] headquarters [business]
sedere *v. irreg.* [*seh-deh'-reh*] sit
sedersi [*seh-dehr'-see*] sit (down)
Si sieda, per favore! [*see see-eh'-dah, pehr fah-voh'-reh*] Have a seat, please!
sedia [*seh'-dee-ah*] chair
sedia a dondolo [*seh'-dee-ah ah dohn'-doh-loh*] rocking chair
sedici [*seh'-dee-chee*] sixteen
sedurre *v. irreg.* [*seh-door'-reh*] seduce
seduto [*seh-doo'-toh*] seated
segnalare *v.* [*seh-nyah-lah'-reh*] signal
segnale [*seh-nyah'-leh*] signal
segnare *v.* [*seh-nyah'-reh*] mark, point out
segno [*seh'-nyoh*] sign
segretario [*seh-greh-tah'-ree-oh*] secretary
segreto *n. & adj.* [*seh-greh'-toh*] secret
seguente [*seh-goo-ehn'-teh*] following
seguire *v.* [*seh-goo-ee'-reh*] follow
Mi segua! [*mee seh'-goo-ah*] Follow me!
seguito [*seh'-goo-ee-toh*] following
in seguito [*een seh'-goo-ee-toh*] afterwards
sei [*seh'-ee*] six
seicento [*seh-ee-chehn'-toh*] six hundred
sella [*sehl'-lah*] saddle
selvaggio [*sehl-vahj'-jee-oh*] savage
sembrare *v.* [*sehm-brah'-reh*] seem
Come le sembra? [*koh'-meh leh sehm'-brah*] How does it seem to you?
Mi sembra che . . . [*mee sehm'-brah keh*] It seems to me that . . .
seme *m.* [*seh'-meh*] seed
semiaperto [*seh-mee-ah-pehr'-toh*] half-open
seminare *v.* [*seh-mee-nah'-reh*] sow
semplice [*sehm'-plee-cheh*] simple
semplicemente [*sehm-plee-cheh-mehn'-teh*] simply
sempre [*sehm'-preh*] always
come sempre [*koh'-meh sehm'-preh*] as ever, like always
per sempre [*pehr sehm'-preh*] forever

senato [*seh-nah'-toh*] senate
senatore *m.* [*seh-nah-toh'-reh*] senator
seno [*seh'-noh*] bosom
sensible [*sehn-see'-bee-leh*] sensible
sensitivo [*sehn-see-tee'-voh*] sensitive
senso [*sehn'-soh*] sense
  buon senso [*boo-ohn' sehn'-soh*] common sense
  senso unico [*sehn'-soh oo'-nee-koh*] one-way street
sentiero [*sehn-tee-eh'-roh*] path
sentimentale [*sehn-tee-mehn-tah'-leh*] sentimental
sentimento [*sehn-tee-mehn'-toh*] feeling
sentire *v.* [*sehn-tee'-reh*] hear, listen
  Senta! [*sehn'-tah*] Listen!
sentirsi *v.* [*sehn-teer'-see*] feel
  Come si sente? [*koh'-meh see sehn'-teh*] How do you feel?
senza [*sehn'-tsah*] without
separare *v.* [*seh-pah-rah'-reh*] separate
separatamente [*seh-pah-rah-tah-mehn'-teh*] separately
separato [*seh-pah-rah'-toh*] separate
separazione *f.* [*seh-pah-rah-tsee-oh'-neh*] separation
sera [*seh'-rah*] evening
  Buona sera! [*boo-oh'-nah seh'-rah*] Good evening
  Domani sera [*doh-mah'-nee seh'-rah*] tomorrow evening
  durante la sera [*doo-rahn'-teh lah seh'-rah*] in the evening
  ieri sera [*ee-eh'-ree seh'-rah*] yesterday evening
serata [*seh-rah'-tah*] evening
serbatoio [*sehr-bah-toh'-ee-oh*] tank
serenata [*seh-reh-nah'-tah*] serenade
sereno [*seh-reh'-noh*] serene
seriamente [*seh-ree-ah-mehn'-teh*] seriously
serie *f. sing. & pl.* [*seh'-ree-eh*] series
serio [*seh'-ree-oh*] serious
serpente *m.* [*sehr-pehn'-teh*] snake
serratura [*sehr-rah-too'-rah*] lock
servire *v.* [*sehr-vee'-reh*] serve, wait on, be good for
  Che cosa serve questo? [*keh koh'-zah sehr'-veh koo-ehs'-toh*] What is this used for?
  In che posso servirla? [*een keh pohs'-soh sehr-veer'-lah*] What can I do for you?
  Non serve a nulla! [*nohn sehr'-veh ah nool'-lah*] It's not

good for anything!

Si serva! [*see sehr'-vah*] Help yourself!

servitore *m.*, **servitrice** *f.* [*sehr-vee-toh'-reh, sehr-vee-tree'-cheh*] servant

servizio [*sehr-vee'-tsee-oh*] service

di servizio [*dee sehr-vee'-tsee-oh*] on duty

essere *v.* **di servizio** [*ehs'-seh-reh dee sehr-vee'-tsee-oh*] be on duty

fuori servizio [*foo-oh'-ree sehr-vee'-tsee-oh*] out of order

servizio compreso [*sehr-vee'-tsee-oh kohm-preh'-zoh*] no tipping

servizio militare [*sehr-vee'-tsee-oh mee-lee-tah'-reh*] military service

sessanta [*sehs-sahn'-tah*] sixty

sessione *f.* [*sehs-see-oh'-neh*] session

sesso [*sehs'-soh*] sex

sesto [*sehs'-toh*] sixth

seta [*seh'-tah*] silk

seta artificiale [*seh'-tah ahr-tee-fee-chee-ah'-leh*] rayon

sete *f.* [*seh'-teh*] thirst

avere *v.* **sete** [*ah-veh'-reh seh'-teh*] be thirsty

setta [*seht'-tah*] sect

settanta [*seht-tahn'-tah*] seventy

sette [*seht'-teh*] seven

settembre *m.* [*seht-tehm'-breh*] September

settentrionale [*seht-tehn-tree-oh-nah'-leh*] northern

settimana [*seht-tee-mah'-nah*] week

la settimana scorsa [*lah seht-tee-mah'-nah skohr'-sah*] last week

la settimana prossima [*lah seht-tee-mah'-nah prohs'-see-mah*] next week

fine-settimana [*fee'-neh seht-tee-mah'-nah*] weekend

settimanale [*seht-tee-mah-nah'-leh*] weekly

settimo [*seht'-tee-moh*] seventh

severo [*seh-veh'-roh*] severe

sezione *f.* [*seh-tsee-oh'-neh*] section

sfavorevole [*sfah-voh-reh'-voh-leh*] unfavorable

sfida [*sfee'-dah*] challenge

sfidare *v.* [*sfee-dah'-reh*] challenge

sfiducia [*sfee-doo'-chee-ah*] distrust

sfigurare *v.* [*sfee-goo-rah'-reh*] mar
sfondo [*sfohn'-doh*] background
sfortuna [*sfohr-too'-nah*] hard luck
sfortunato [*sfohr-too-nah'-toh*] unlucky
sforzo [*sfohr'-tsoh*] effort
sgradevole [*zgrah-deh'-voh-leh*] unpleasant
sgradito [*zgrah-dee'-toh*] unwelcome
sgomberare *v.* [*zgohm-beh-rah'-reh*] vacate
sguardo [*zgoo-ahr'-doh*] look
si *refl. & impers. pron.* [*see*] oneself, himself, herself, etc; one, they, we; one another, each other
sì [*see'*] yes
sia . . . sia [*see'-ah . . . see'-ah*] both . . . and
siccome [*seek-koh'-meh*] as, inasmuch as
Sicilia [*see-chee'-lee-ah*] Sicily
siciliano [*see-chee-lee-ah'-noh*] Sicilian
sicuramente [*see-koo-rah-mehn'-teh*] surely
sicurezza [*see-koo-rehts'-tsah*] security
sicuro [*see-koo'-roh*] sure, secure
  È sicuro? [*eh' see-koo'-roh*] Are you sure?
siesta [*see-ehs'-tah*] afternoon nap
sigaretta [*see-gah-reht'-tah*] cigarette
sigaro [*see'-gah-roh*] cigar
sigillare *v.* [*see-jeel-lah'-reh*] seal
sigillo [*see-jeel'-loh*] seal [for document]
significato [*see-nyee-fee-kah'-toh*] meaning
significare *v.* [*see-nyee-fee-kah'-reh*] mean
signora [*see-nyoh'-rah*] madam, lady
  Sigra. Mrs.
  per signore [*pehr see-nyoh'-reh*] ladies' room
signore *m.* [*see-nyoh'-reh*] gentleman, sir, mister
  Sig. Mr.
  Gentile Signore: [*jehn-tee'-leh see-nyoh'-reh*] Dear Sir:
  Il signor tal dei tali [*eel see-nyohr' tahl deh'-ee tah'-lee*] Mr. So and So
signorina [*see-nyoh-ree'-nah*] miss, young girl
silenzio [*see-lehn'-tsee-oh*] silence
  Silenzio! [*see-lehn'-tsee-oh*] Quiet!, Shut up!
silenziosamente [*see-lehn-tsee-oh-zah-mehn'-teh*] silently
silenzioso [*see-lehn-tsee-oh'-zoh*] silent

sillaba [*seel'-lah-bah*] syllable
simile [*see'-mee-leh*] similar, alike, like
similmente [*see-meel-mehn'-teh*] likewise
simpatia [*seem-pah-tee'-ah*] sympathy
simpatico [*seem-pah'-tee-koh*] nice, pleasant, likable
simultaneo [*see-mool-tah'-neh-oh*] simultaneous
sinceramente [*seen-cheh-rah-mehn'-teh*] sincerely
sincero [*seen-cheh'-roh*] sincere
sindaco [*seen'-dah-koh*] mayor
sinfonia [*seen-foh-nee'-ah*] symphony
sinistro [*see-nees'-troh*] left
  a sinistra [*ah see-nees'-trah*] to the left
sinora [*seen-oh'-rah*] so far
sintetico [*seen-teh'-tee-koh*] synthetic
sintomo [*seen'-toh-moh*] symptom
sistema *m.* [*sees-teh'-mah*] system
sistemare *v.* [*sees-teh-mah'-reh*] arrange
sistematico [*sees-teh-mah'-tee-koh*] systematic
situato [*see-too-ah'-toh*] situated
situazione *f.* [*see-too-ah-tsee-oh'-neh*] situation
sleale [*sleh-ah'-leh*] disloyal
slittare *v.* [*zleet-tah'-reh*] slide
smacchiare *v.* [*zmahk-kee-ah'-reh*] clean [clothes]
smarrire *v.* [*zmahr-ree'-reh*] lose
  smarrirsi [*zmahr-reer'-see*] get lost
smentire *v.* [*zmehn-tee'-reh*] deny
smettere *v.* [*zmeht'-teh-reh*] stop [doing something]
  La smetta! [*lah zmeht'-tah*] Stop it!
smorfia [*zmohr'-fee-ah*] grin
snello [*znehl'-loh*] slender
soave [*soh-ah'-veh*] gentle, soft, mild
sobrio [*soh'-bree-oh*] sober
sobborgo [*sohb-bohr'-goh*] suburb
soccorso [*sohk-kohr'-soh*] help, aid
  pronto soccorso [*prohn'-toh sohk-kohr'-soh*] first aid
sociale [*soh-chee-ah'-leh*] social
socialista *m., f.* [*soh-chee-ah-lees'-tah*] socialist
società *f. indecl.* [*soh-chee-eh-tah'*] society
socio [*soh'-chee-oh*] associate, member
soda [*soh'-dah*] soda

soddisfacente [*sohd-dees-fah-chehn'-teh*] satisfactory
soddisfare *v.* [*sohd-dees-fah'-reh*] satisfy
soddisfatto [*sohd-dees-faht'-toh*] satisfied
soddisfazione *f.* [*sohd-dees-fah-tsee-oh'-neh*] satisfaction
soffiare *v.* [*sohf-fee-ah'-reh*] blow
soffitta [*sohf-feet'-tah*] attic
soffitto [*sohf-feet'-toh*] ceiling
soffocare *v.* [*sohf-foh-kah'-reh*] suffocate, choke
soffrire *v. irreg.* [*sohf-free'-reh*] suffer
soggetto [*sohj-jeht'-toh*] topic, subject
soggiorno [*sohj-jee-ohr'-noh*] stay, living room
sognare *v.* [*soh-nyah'-reh*] dream
sogno [*soh'-nyoh*] dream
solamente [*soh-lah-mehn'-teh*] only
soldato [*sohl-dah'-toh*] soldier
soldi *m. pl.* [*sohl'-dee*] money
soldo [*sohl'-doh*] penny
sole *m.* [*soh'-leh*] sun
  calar *m.* **del sole** [*kah-lahr' dehl soh'-leh*] sunset
  luce *f.* **del sole** [*loo'-cheh dehl soh'-leh*] sunshine
  levar *m.* **del sole** [*leh-vahr' dehl soh'-leh*] sunrise
  occhiali *m. pl.* **da sole** [*ohk-kee-ah'-lee dah soh'-leh*] sunglasses
solido [*soh'-lee-doh*] solid
solitario [*soh-lee-tah'-ree-oh*] lonely
solito [*soh'-lee-toh*] usual, customary
  di solito [*dee soh'-lee-toh*] usually
sollevamento [*sohl-leh-vah-mehn'-toh*] upheaval
sollevare *v.* [*sohl-leh-vah'-reh*] lift
sollievo [*sohl-lee-eh'-voh*] relief [from discomfort]
solo [*soh'-loh*] alone, single, only
  da solo [*dah soh'-loh*] all alone
soltanto [*sohl-tahn'-toh*] only
soluzione *f.* [*soh-loo-tsee-oh'-neh*] solution
somma [*sohm'-mah*] sum
sommare *v.* [*sohm-mah'-reh*] sum up
sommario [*sohm-mah'-ree-oh*] summary
sommità *f. indecl.* [*sohm-mee-tah'*] top, summit, peak
somministrare *v.* [*sohm-mee-nees-trah'-reh*] minister
sommo [*sohm'-moh*] very great

sonnecchiare *v.* [*sohn-nehk-kee-ah'-reh*] doze
sonnellino [*sohn-nehl-lee'-noh*] nap
sonno [*sohn'-noh*] sleep
  avere *v.* **sonno** [*ah-veh'-reh sohn'-noh*] be sleepy
sopportare *v.* [*sohp-pohr-tah'-reh*] support, bear
sopportabile [*sohp-pohr-tah'-bee-leh*] bearable
sopra [*soh'-prah*] above, on, over
sopracciglio, le sopracciglia *pl.* [*soh-prahch-chee'-lyoh, leh sohp-prahch-chee'-lyah*] eyebrow
soprano [*soh-prah'-noh*] soprano
soprattutto [*soh-praht-toot'-toh*] above all
sopravvivere *v.* [*soh-prahv-vee'-veh-reh*] survive
sopprimere *v.* [*sohp-pree'-meh-reh*] suppress, put down
sordo [*sohr'-doh*] deaf
sorella [*soh-rehl'-lah*] sister
sorgente *f.* [*sohr-jehn'-teh*] source, spring
sorgere *v.* [*sohr'-jeh-reh*] rise, arise
sorpassare [*sohr-pahs-sah'-reh*] overtake
sorprendente [*sohr-prehn-dehn'-teh*] surprising
sorprendere *v.* [*sohr-prehn'-deh-reh*] surprise
  sorprendersi di [*sohr-prehn'-dehr-see dee*] be surprised at
sorpresa [*sohr-preh'-zah*] surprise
sorridere *v. irreg.* [*sohr-ree'-deh-reh*] smile
sorriso [*sohr-ree'-zoh*] smile
sorvegliare *v.* [*sohr-veh-lyah'-reh*] guard
sospendere [*sohs-pehn'-deh-reh*] call off, suspend
sospettare *v.* [*sohs-peht-tah'-reh*] suspect
sospetto [*sohs-peht'-toh*] suspicion
sospettoso [*sohs-peht-too-oh'-zoh*] suspicious
sospirare *v.* [*sohs-pee-rah'-reh*] sigh
sospiro [*sohs-pee'-roh*] sigh
sosta [*sohs'-tah*] halt, rest, stop
  Sosta vietata [*sohs'-tah vee-eh-tah'-tah*] No parking
sostanziale [*sohs-tahn-tsee-ah'-leh*] substantial
sostare *v.* [*sohs-tah'-reh*] pause
sostegno [*sohs-teh'-nyoh*] support
sostenere *v.* [*sohs-teh-neh'-reh*] support
sostituire *v.* [*sohs-tee-too-ee'-reh*] replace
sostituto [*sohs-tee-too'-toh*] substitute
sostituzione *f.* [*sohs-tee-too-tsee-oh'-neh*] substitution

sottana [*soht-tah'-nah*] skirt
sotterranea [*soht-tehr-rah'-neh-ah*] subway
sotterraneo [*soht-tehr-rah'-neh-oh*] basement
sottile [*soht-tee'-leh*] thin, subtle
sotto [*soht'-toh*] below, under
sottomarino [*soht-toh-mah-ree'-noh*] submarine
sottomettere *v.* [*soht-toh-meht'-teh-reh*] submit
sottoporre *v.* [*soht-toh-pohr'-reh*] subject
sottoscritto [*soht-toh-skreet'-toh*] undersigned
sottosopra [*soht-toh-soh'-prah*] upside down
sottosuolo [*soht-toh-soo-oh'-loh*] underground
sottoveste *f.* [*soht-toh-vehs'-teh*] slip, underskirt
sottovoce [*soht-toh-voh'-cheh*] in a low voice
sottrazione *f.* [*soht-trah-tsee-oh'-neh*] subtraction
sovente [*soh-vehn'-teh*] often
spada [*spah'-dah*] sword
spaghetti *m. pl.* [*spah-geht'-tee*] spaghetti
  spaghetti alle vongole [*spah-geht'-tee ahl'-leh vohn'-goh-leh*] spaghetti in clam sauce
Spagna [*spah'-nyah*] Spain
spagnolo [*spah-nyoh'-loh*] Spanish, Spaniard
spago [*spah'-goh*] string
spalancato [*spah-lahn-kah'-toh*] wide-open
spalla [*spahl'-lah*] shoulder
spalliera [*spahl-lee-eh'-rah*] back of a seat
spalmare *v.* [*spahl-mah'-reh*] spread on
sparare *v.* [*spah-rah'-reh*] shoot
spargere *v. irreg.* [*spahr'-j-reh*] spread, scatter
sparire *v.* [*spah-ree'-reh*] disappear
sparo [*spah'-roh*] shot
spartire *v.* [*spahr-tee'-reh*] part, divide
spaventare *v.* [*spah-vehn-tah'-reh*] frighten
spavento [*spah-vehn'-toh*] fear, fright
spaventoso [*spah-vehn-toh'-zoh*] dreadful
spazio [*spah'-tsee-oh*] room, space
  Non c'è spazio [*nohn cheh' spah'-tsee-oh*] There is no room
spazioso [*spah-tsee-oh'-zoh*] spacious
spazzola [*spahts'-tsoh-lah*] brush
  spazzolino da denti [*spahts-tsoh-lee'-noh dah dehn'-tee*]

toothbrush
spazzolare *v.* [*spahts-tsoh-lah'-reh*] brush
specchio [*spehk'-kee-oh*] mirror
speciale [*speh-chee-ah'-leh*] special
specialmente [*speh-chee-ahl-mehn'-teh*] especially
specialista [*speh-chee-ah-lees'-tah*] specialist
specialità *f. indecl.* [*speh-chee-ah-lee-tah'*] specialty
specie [*speh'-chee-eh*] sort, kind
specificazione *f.* [*speh-chee-fee-kah-tsee-oh'-neh*] specification
spedire *v.* [*speh-dee'-reh*] send, forward, ship
spedizione *f.* [*speh-dee-tsee-oh'-neh*] expedition
spegnere *v. irreg.* [*speh'-nyeh-reh*] turn off, extinguish
spendere *v. irreg.* [*spehn'-deh-reh*] spend [money]
spensierato [*spehn-see-eh-rah'-toh*] carefree
speranza [*speh-rahn'-tsah*] hope
sperare *v.* [*speh-rah'-reh*] hope
spesa [*speh'-zah*] expense
fare *v.* **le spese** [*fah'-reh leh speh'-zeh*] go shopping
spesso *adv.* [*spehs'-soh*] often, frequently
spesso *adj.* [*spehs'-soh*] thick
spettacolo [*speht-tah'-koh-loh*] spectacle
spettatore *m.*, **spettatrice** *f.* [*speht-tah-toh'-reh, speht-tah-tree'-cheh*] spectator
spia [*spee'-ah*] spy
spiacente [*spee-ah-chehn'-teh*] sorry
essere *v.* **spiacente** [*ehs'-seh-reh spee-ah-chehn'-teh*] be sorry
spiaggia [*spee-ahj'-jee-ah*] beach
spiare *v.* [*spee-ah'-reh*] spy
spiccioli *m. pl.* [*speech'-chee-oh-lee*] small change
spiegare *v.* [*spee-eh-gah'-reh*] explain
Mi spieghi questo, per favore [*mee spee-eh'-gee koo-ehs'-toh, pehr fah-voh'-reh*] Explain this to me, please
spiegazione *f.* [*spee-eh-gah-tsee-oh'-neh*] explanation
spillo, spilla [*speel'-loh, speel'-lah*] pin
spina [*spee'-nah*] spine, thorn
spina dorsale [*spee'-nah dohr-sah'-leh*] spine, backbone
spina elettrica [*spee'-nah eh-leht'-tree-kah*] plug
spinaci *m. pl.* [*spee-nah'-chee*] spinach

spingere *v. irreg.* [*speen'-jeh-reh*] push, drive, shove
spirito [*spee'-ree-toh*] spirit
spirituale [*spee-ree-too-ah'-leh*] spiritual
splendido [*splehn'-dee-doh*] splendid
splendore *m.* [*splehn-doh'-reh*] glitter
spogliarsi *v.* [*spoh-lyahr'-see*] undress oneself
spontaneo [*spohn-tah'-neh-oh*] spontaneous
sporcizia [*spohr-chee'-tsee-ah*] dirt
sporco [*spohr'-koh*] dirty
sport *m.* [*spohrt*] sport
sportello [*spohr-tehl'-loh*] ticket window
sposa [*spoh'-zah*] bride
sposo [*spoh'-zoh*] bridegroom
sposare *v.* [*spoh-zah'-reh*] marry
sposarsi *v.* [*spoh-zahr'-see*] get married
sposato [*spoh-zah'-toh*] married
sprecare *v.* [*spreh-kah'-reh*] waste
spremere *v.* [*spreh'-meh-reh*] press, squeeze
spremuta di limone [*spreh-moo'-tah dee lee-moh'-neh*] lemon juice
spruzzare *v.* [*sproots-tsah'-reh*] spray
spugna [*spoo'-nyah*] sponge
sputare *v.* [*spoo-tah'-reh*] spit
squadra [*skoo-ah'-drah*] team, square
squisito [*skoo-ee-zee'-toh*] exquisite
stabile [*stah'-bee-leh*] stable
stabilire *v.* [*stah-bee-lee'-reh*] establish
staccare *v.* [*stahk-kah'-reh*] disconnect, detach
stadio [*stah'-dee-oh*] stadium
stagione *f.* [*stah-jee-oh'-neh*] season
stamane [*stah-mah'-neh*] this morning
stampa [*stahm'-pah*] press, print
stampare *v.* [*stahm-pah'-reh*] print
stampato [*stahm-pah'-toh*] printed matter
stancarsi *v.* [*stahn-kahr'-see*] get tired
stanco [*stahn'-koh*] tired
stanotte [*stah-noht'-teh*] tonight
stanza [*stahn'-tsah*] room
  stanza soggiorno [*stahn'-tsah sohj-jee-ohr'-noh*] living room
stare *v. irreg.* [*stah'-reh*] be, feel, stay, remain

Come sta? [*koh'-meh stah*] How are you?
Sto bene, grazie [*stoh beh'-neh, grah'-tsee-eh*] I am fine, thanks
Sono stanco [*soh'-noh stahn'-koh*] I am tired
stare in piedi [*stah'-reh een pee-eh'-dee*] stand up
starnutire *v.* [*stahr-noo-tee'-reh*] sneeze
starnuto [*stahr-noo'-toh*] sneeze
stasera [*stah-seh'-rah*] this evening
statista *m.* [*stah-tees'-tah*] statesman
stato [*stah'-toh*] state, condition
in buono stato [*een boo-oh'-noh stah'-toh*] in good condition
gli Stati Uniti [*lyee stah'-tee oo-nee'-tee*] United States
statua [*stah'-too-ah*] statue
stazione *f.* [*stah-tsee-oh'-neh*] station
stazione climatica [*stah-tsee-oh'-neh klee-mah'-tee-kah*] resort
stazione ferroviaria [*stah-tsee-oh'-neh fehr-roh-vee-ah'-ree-ah*] railway station
stazione di polizia [*stah-tsee-oh'-neh dee poh-lee-tsee'-ah*] police station
stazione radio [*stah-tsee-oh'-neh rah'-dee-oh*] radio station
stella [*stehl'-lah*] star
stendere *v.* [*stehn'-deh-reh*] stretch
stenografo [*steh-noh'-grah-foh*] stenographer
stesso [*stehs'-soh*] self, same
allo stesso tempo [*ahl'-loh stehs'-soh tehm'-poh*] at the same time
È la stessa cosa [*eh' lah stehs'-sah koh'-zah*] It does not make any difference
Per me è la stessa cosa [*pehr meh eh' lah stehs'-sah koh'-zah*] It's all the same to me
io stesso [*ee'-oh stehs'-soh*] I myself
Lei stesso [*leh'-ee stehs'-soh*] you [polite form], yourself
lei stessa [*leh'-ee stehs'-sah*] she herself
lui stesso [*loo'-ee stehs'-soh*] he himself
voi stessi [*voh'-ee stehs'-see*] you yourselves
loro stessi [*loh'-roh stehs'-see*] they themselves
sterilizzato [*steh-ree-leedz-dzah'-toh*] sterilized
stile *m.* [*stee'-leh*] style

stimare *v.* [*stee-mah'-reh*] esteem, value
stimolante [*stee-moh-lahn'-teh*] stimulant
stipendio [*stee-pehn'-dee-oh*] salary
stirare *v.* [*stee-rah'-reh*] press [clothes]
stivale *m.* [*stee-vah'-leh*] boot
stoffa [*stohf'-fah*] cloth
stomaco [*stoh'-mah-koh*] stomach
stordire *v.* [*stohr-dee'-reh*] stun
stordito [*stohr-dee'-toh*] dizzy
storia [*stoh'-ree-ah*] history, story
storta [*stohr'-tah*] sprain
storto [*stohr'-toh*] crooked
straccio [*strahch'-chee-oh*] rag
strada [*strah'-dah*] street, road
straniero [*strah-nee-eh'-roh*] foreign, foreigner
strano [*strah'-noh*] strange, odd
  Che strano! [*keh strah'-noh*] How queer!
straordinario [*strah-ohr-dee-nah'-ree-oh*] extraordinary
strappare *v.* [*strahp-pah'-reh*] tear, rip
stravagante [*strah-vah-gahn'-teh*] extravagant
strega [*streh'-gah*] witch
stretto [*streht'-toh*] tight, narrow
strillare *v.* [*streel-lah'-reh*] shout, scream
striscia [*stree'-shee-ah*] stripe
stringere *v. irreg.* [*streen'-jeh-reh*] tighten, grasp, bind fast
strofinare *v.* [*stroh-fee-nah'-reh*] rub
strumento [*stroo-mehn'-toh*] instrument
struttura [*stroot-too'-rah*] structure
studente *m.*, **studentessa** *f.* [*stoo-dehn'-teh, stoo-dehn-tehs'-sah*] student
studiare *v.* [*stoo-dee-ah'-reh*] study
studio [*stoo'-dee-oh*] study
studioso [*stoo-dee-oh'-zoh*] scholar
stufa [*stoo'-fah*] stove
stupido [*stoo'-pee-doh*] stupid
stuzzicadenti [*stoots-tsee-kah-dehn'-tee*] toothpick
su [*soo*] on, above, over, up
  su e giù [*soo eh jee-oo'*] up and down
subire *v.* [*soo-bee'-reh*] undergo, suffer
subito [*soo'-bee-toh*] at once, right away

succedere *v.* [*sooch-cheh'-deh-reh*] happen, occur
  Che succede? [*keh sooch-cheh'-deh*] What is the matter?
successivo [*sooch-chehs-see'-voh*] successive
successo [*sooch-chehs'-soh*] success
successore [*sooch-chehs-soh'-reh*] successor
succo [*sook'-koh*] juice
  succo di frutta [*sook'-koh dee froot'-tah*] fruit juice
succursale *f.* [*sook-koor-sah'-leh*] branch [business]
sud *m.* [*sood*] south
sudamericano [*sood-ah-meh-ree-kah'-noh*] South American
sudare *v.* [*soo-dah'-reh*] perspire
suddetto [*sood-deht'-toh*] abovementioned
sudore *m.* [*soo-doh'-reh*] sweat
sudicio [*soo-dee'-chee-oh*] filth
sufficiente [*soof-fee-chee-ehn'-teh*] sufficient
suggerimento [*sooj-jeh-ree-mehn'-toh*] suggestion, advice
sugo [*soo'-goh*] gravy, sauce
suicidio [*soo-ee-chee'-dee-oh*] suicide
suo, sua, suoi *m. pl.* **sue** *f. pl.* [*soo'-oh, soo'-ah, soo-oh'-ee, soo'-eh*] yours [polite form], his, hers
suocera [*soo-oh'-cheh-rah*] mother-in-law
suocero [*soo-oh'-cheh-roh*] father-in-law
suolo [*soo-oh'-loh*] soil, ground
suonare *v.* [*soo-oh-nah'-reh*] sound, ring, play
  suonare il companello [*soo-oh-nah'-reh eel kahm-pah-nehl'-loh*] ring the bell
  suonare il pianoforte [*soo-oh-nah'-reh eel pee-ah-noh-fohr'-teh*] play the piano
  Non suona bene [*nohn soo-oh'-nah beh'-neh*] It doesn't sound good
suonata [*soo-oh-nah'-tah*] ringing
suono [*soo-oh'-noh*] sound
suora [*soo-oh'-rah*] nun
superbo [*soo-pehr'-boh*] superb
superficiale [*soo-pehr-fee-chee-ah'-leh*] superficial
superficie *f.* [*soo-pehr-fee'-chee-eh*] surface
superfluo [*soo-pehr'-floo-oh*] superfluous
superiore [*soo-peh-ree-oh'-reh*] superior, upper
superiorità *f. indecl.* [*soo-peh-ree-oh-ree-tah'*] superiority
superstizioso [*soo-pehr-stee-tsee-oh'-zoh*] superstitious

supplementare [*soop-pleh-mehn-tah'-reh*] extra
supporre *v. irreg.* [*soop-pohr'-reh*] suppose
supposizione *f.* [*soop-poh-zee-tsee-oh'-neh*] supposition, guess
supremo [*soo-preh'-moh*] supreme
sussurrare *v.* [*soos-soor-rah'-reh*] whisper
svanire *v.* [*zvah-nee'-reh*] vanish
svantaggio [*zvahn-tahj'-jee-oh*] disadvantage
svedese [*zveh-deh'-zeh*] Swedish
sveglia [*zveh'-lyah*] alarm clock
svegliare *v.* [*zveh-lyah'-reh*] awake
  svegliarsi [*zveh-lyahr'-see*] wake up
sveglio [*zveh'-lyoh*] alert
sveltezza [*zvehl-tehts'-tsah*] quickness
svelto [*zvehl'-toh*] quick
svenimento [*zveh-nee-mehn'-toh*] faint
svenire *v. irreg.* [*zveh-nee'-reh*] faint
svestire *v.* [*zvehs-tee'-reh*] undress
  svestirsi [*zvehs-teer'-see*] undress oneself
Svezia [*zveh'-tsee-ah*] Sweden
sviare *v.* [*zvee-ah'-reh*] mislead
sviluppare *v.* [*zvee-loop-pah'-reh*] develop
sviluppo [*zvee-loop'-poh*] development
Svizzera [*zveets'-tseh-rah*] Switzerland
svizzero [*zveets'-tseh-roh*] Swiss
svolgere *v.* [*zvohl'-jeh-reh*] develop, unroll
svolta [*zvohl'-tah*] turn, turning point

T

tabacco [*tah-bahk'-koh*] tobacco
  sale *m.* **e tabacchi** [*sah'-leh eh tah-bahk'-kee*] tobacco shop
tacco [*tahk'-koh*] heel [of shoe]
tacchino [*tahk-kee'-noh*] turkey
taccuino [*tahk-koo-ee'-noh*] notebook
tacere *v. irreg.* [*tah-cheh'-reh*] be silent
taglia [*tah'-lyah*] size [of clothes]
tagliare *v.* [*tah-lyah'-reh*] cut

tagliatelle [*tah-lyah-tehl'-leh*] noodles
taglio [*tah'-lyoh*] cut [of dress]
taglio di capelli [*tah'-lyoh dee kah-pehl'-lee*] haircut
tale [*tah'-leh*] such
talento [*tah-lehn'-toh*] talent
talvolta [*tahl-vohl'-tah*] sometimes
tamburo [*tahm-boo'-roh*] drum
tanto [*tahn'-toh*] so, so much, so long
tanto quanto [*tahn'-toh koo-ahn'-toh*] as much as
di tanto in tanto [*dee tahn'-toh een tahn'-toh*] occasionally
tanto . . . quanto [*tahn'-toh . . . koo-ahn'-toh*] as . . . as
tappeto [*tahp-peh'-toh*] carpet
tappezzeria [*tahp-pehts-tseh-ree'-ah*] tapestry
tappo [*tahp'-poh*] cork
tardi [*tahr'-dee*] late
più tardi [*pee-oo' tahr'-dee*] later
Noi siamo tardi [*noh'-ee see-ah'-moh tahr'-dee*] We are late
tariffa [*tah-reef'-fah*] rate, tariff
tartaruga [*tahr-tah-roo'-gah*] turtle
tasca, tasche *pl.* [*tahs'-kah, tahs'-keh*] pocket
tassa [*tahs'-sah*] tax
esente da tassa [*eh-zehn'-teh dah tahs'-sah*] duty-free
tassare *v.* [*tahs-sah'-reh*] tax
tassì *m.* [*tahs-see'*] taxi
tastiera [*tahs-tee-eh'-rah*] keyboard
tasto [*tahs'-toh*] key [of piano]
tatto [*taht'-toh*] tact
taverna [*tah-vehr'-nah*] tavern, inn
tavola [*tah'-voh-lah*] table
preparare *v.* **la tavola** [*preh-pah-rah'-reh lah tah'-voh-lah*] set the table
tazza [*tahts'-tsah*] cup
tazza di tè [*tahts'-tsah dee teh'*] teacup
tè *m.* [*teh'*] tea
teatro [*teh-ah'-troh*] theater
tecnico [*tehk'-nee-koh*] technical
tedesco [*teh-dehs'-koh*] German
teiera [*teh-ee-eh'-rah*] teapot
telefonare *v.* [*teh-leh-foh-nah'-reh*] telephone
chiamata telefonica [*kee-ah-mah'-tah teh-leh-foh'-nee-kah*]

telephone call
elenco telefonico [*eh-lehn'-koh teh-leh-foh'-nee-koh*] telephone book
telefonista [*teh-leh-foh-nees'-tah*] telephone operator
telefono [*teh-leh'-foh-noh*] telephone
per telefono [*pehr teh-leh'-foh-noh*] by phone
telegrafare *v.* [*teh-leh-grah-fah'-reh*] cable
telegramma *m.* [*teh-leh-grahm'-mah*] telegram
telescopo [*teh-lehs'-koh-poh*] telescope
televisione *f.* [*teh-leh-vee-zee-oh'-neh*] television
televisore *m.* [*teh-leh-vee-zoh'-reh*] television set
tema *m.* [*teh'-mah*] theme, subject
temere *v.* [*teh-meh'-reh*] fear
temperatura [*tehm-peh-rah-too'-rah*] temperature
temperino [*tehm-peh-ree'-noh*] penknife
tempesta [*tehm-pehs'-tah*] storm
tempio [*tehm'-pee-oh*] temple
tempo [*tehm'-poh*] time [extent], weather
a tempo [*ah tehm'-poh*] on time
allo stesso tempo [*ahl'-loh stehs'-soh tehm'-poh*] at the same time
Come e il tempo? [*koh'-meh eh' eel tehm'-poh*] How is the weather?
poco tempo fa [*poh'-koh tehm'-poh fah*] a while ago
temporale *m.* [*tehm-poh-rah'-leh*] thunderstorm
temporaneo [*tehm-poh-rah'-neh-oh*] temporary
tenda [*tehn'-dah*] curtain
tendenza [*tehn-dehn'-tsah*] tendency
tenere *v. irreg.* [*teh-neh'-reh*] keep
tenero [*teh'-neh-roh*] tender, soft
tenore *m.* [*teh-noh'-reh*] tenor
tensione *f.* [*tehn-see-oh'-neh*] stress, tension
tentare *v.* [*tehn-tah'-reh*] try
tentativo [*tehn-tah-tee'-voh*] attempt, try
tentazione *f.* [*tehn-tah-tsee-oh'-neh*] temptation
teoria [*teh-oh-ree'-ah*] theory
terminare *v.* [*tehr-mee-nah'-reh*] finish, end
termine *m.* [*tehr'-mee-neh*] term, limit, end
termometro [*tehr-moh'-meh-troh*] thermometer
termosifone *m.* [*tehr-moh-see-foh'-neh*] radiator [heating]

terra [*tehr'-rah*] ground, land
a terra [*ah tehr'-rah*] ashore
terrazza [*tehr-rahts'-tsah*] terrace
terreno di gioco [*tehr-reh'-noh dee jee-oh'-koh*] playground
terremoto [*tehr-reh-moh'-toh*] earthquake
terribile [*tehr-ree'-bee-leh*] terrible
terribilmente [*tehr-ree-beel-mehn'-teh*] terribly
territorio [*tehr-ree-toh'-ree-oh*] territory
terrore [*tehr-roh'-reh*] terror
terzo [*tehr'-tsoh*] third
tesoreria [*teh-zoh-reh-ree'-ah*] treasury
tesoriere *m.* [*teh-zoh-ree-eh'-reh*] treasurer
tesoro [*teh-zoh'-roh*] treasure
buono del tesoro [*boo-oh'-noh dehl teh-zoh'-roh*] bond
tessere *v.* [*tehs'-seh-reh*] weave
tessile [*tehs'-see-leh*] textile
tessitore *m.*, **tessitrice** *f.* [*tehs-see-toh'-reh, tehs-see-tree'-cheh*] weaver
tessuto [*tehs-soo'-toh*] fabric, cloth, tissue
testa [*tehs'-tah*] head
a testa [*ah tehs'-tah*] apiece
teste, testimone *m., f.* [*tehs'-teh, tehs-tee-moh'-neh*] witness
testimone oculare *m.* [*tehs-tee-moh'-neh oh-koo-lah'-reh*] eye witness
testimoniare *v.* [*tehs-tee-moh-nee-ah'-reh*] testify
testo [*tehs'-toh*] text
tetto [*teht'-toh*] roof
Tevere *m.* [*teh'-veh-reh*] Tiber
ti [*tee*] you, to you, yourself
tifoso [*tee-foh'-zoh*] fan [sports]
tigre *f.* [*tee'-greh*] tiger
timido [*tee'-mee-doh*] timid
timbrare *v.* [*teem-brah'-reh*] stamp
tingere *v.* [*teen'-jeh-reh*] dye
tintura [*teen-too'-rah*] dye
tipico [*tee'-pee-koh*] typical
tipo [*tee'-poh*] type
tipografo [*tee-poh'-grah-foh*] printer
tirannia [*tee-rahn-nee'-ah*] tyranny
tiranno [*tee-rahn'-noh*] tyrant

tirare *v.* [*tee-rah'-reh*] pull
  tirar calci [*tee-rahr' kahl'-chee*] kick
titolo [*tee'-toh-loh*] title
toccare *v.* [*tohk-kah'-reh*] touch
tocco [*tohk'-koh*] touch
togliere *v. irreg.* [*toh'-lyeh-reh*] take away, remove
toletta [*toh-leht'-tah*] toilet, dressing table
tollerare *v.* [*tohl-leh-rah'-reh*] tolerate
tomba [*tohm'-bah*] tomb, grave
tonnellata [*tohn-nehl-lah'-tah*] ton
tonno [*tohn'-noh*] tuna
tono [*toh'-noh*] tone
tonsille *f. pl.* [*tohn-seel'-leh*] tonsils
topo [*toh'-poh*] rat
torace [*toh-rah'-cheh*] chest
torbido [*tohr'-bee-doh*] turbid, muddy
torcere *v.* [*tohr'-cheh-reh*] twist
Torino [*toh-ree'-noh*] Turin
tormento [*tohr-mehn'-toh*] anguish
tornare *v.* [*tohr-nah'-reh*] return, come back
toro [*toh'-roh*] bull
torpedone *m.* [*tohr-peh-doh'-neh*] bus, motor coach
torre *f.* [*tohr'-reh*] tower
torta [*tohr'-tah*] pie, cake
torto [*tohr'-toh*] wrong
  avere *v.* **torto** [*ah-veh'-reh tohr'-toh*] be wrong
tortura [*tohr-too'-rah*] torture
torturare *v.* [*tohr-too-rah'-reh*] torture
tosse *f.* [*tohs'-seh*] cough
tossire *v.* [*tohs-see'-reh*] cough
tostapane *m.* [*tohs-tah-pah'-neh*] toaster
totale [*toh-tah'-leh*] total
tovaglia [*toh-vah'-lyah*] tablecloth
tovagliolo [*toh-vah-lyoh'-loh*] napkin
tra [*trah*] among, between
traccia [*trahch'-chee-ah*] trace
tradimento [*trah-dee-mehn'-toh*] betrayal
tradire *v.* [*trah-dee'-reh*] betray
traditore *m.*, **traditrice** *f.* [*trah-dee-toh'-reh, trah-dee-tree'-cheh*] traitor

tradizionale [*trah-dee-tsee-oh-nah'-leh*] traditional
tradizione *f.* [*trah-dee-tsee-oh'-neh*] tradition
tradurre *v. irreg.* [*trah-door'-reh*] translate
traduttore *m.*, **traduttrice** *f.* [*trah-doot-toh'-reh*, *trah-doot-tree'-cheh*] translator
traduzione *f.* [*trah-doo-tsee-oh'-neh*] translation
traffico [*trahf'-fee-koh*] traffic
tragedia [*trah-jeh'-dee-ah*] tragedy
tragico [*trah'-jee-koh*] tragic
tram *m.* [*trahm*] streetcar
tramite [*trah'-mee-teh*] through
tramonto [*trah-mohn'-toh*] sunset
tranne [*trahn'-neh*] except, save
tranquillo [*trahn-koo-eel'-loh*] quiet
transito [*trahn'-zee-toh*] transit
transitorio [*trahn-zee-toh'-ree-oh*] transient
trappola [*trahp'-poh-lah*] trap
trarre *v. irreg.* [*trahr'-reh*] draw, get
trascinare *v.* [*trah-shee-nah'-reh*] drag
trascurare *v.* [*trahs-koo-rah'-reh*] neglect
trasferimento [*trahs-feh-ree-mehn'-toh*] transfer
trasferire *v.* [*trahs-feh-ree'-reh*] transfer
trasformare *v.* [*trahs-fohr-mah'-reh*] transform
trasgredire *v.* [*trahz-greh-dee'-reh*] trespass
trasmettere *v.* [*trahz-meht'-teh-reh*] broadcast, transmit
trasmissione *f.* [*trahz-mees-see-oh'-neh*] broadcast, transmission
trasparente [*trahs-pah-rehn'-teh*] transparent
trasportare *v.* [*trahs-pohr-tah'-reh*] transport
trasporto [*trahs-pohr'-toh*] transportation
trattamento [*traht-tah-mehn'-toh*] treatment
trattare [*traht-tah'-reh*] treat, deal
trattative [*traht-tah-tee'-veh*] negotiations
trattato [*traht-tah'-toh*] treaty
trattenimento [*traht-teh-nee-mehn'-toh*] entertainment, party
trattenere *v. irreg.* [*traht-teh-neh'-reh*] withhold
trattoria [*traht-toh-ree'-ah*] restaurant
traversata [*trah-vehr-sah'-tah*] crossing
travestimento [*trah-vehs-tee-mehn'-toh*] disguise
tre [*treh*] three

trecento [*treh-chehn'-toh*] three hundred
tredici [*treh'-dee-chee*] thirteen
tregua [*treh'-goo-ah*] truce
tremare *v.* [*treh-mah'-reh*] tremble, shake
tremendo [*treh-mehn'-doh*] tremendous
tremulo [*treh'-moo-loh*] quivering
treno [*treh'-noh*] train
trenta [*trehn'-tah*] thirty
triangolo [*tree-ahn'-goh-loh*] triangle
tribunale *m.* [*tree-boo-nah'-leh*] tribunal, court
tributo [*tree-boo'-toh*] tribute
trimestre *m.* [*tree-mehs'-treh*] quarter [three months]
trionfante [*tree-ohn-fahn'-teh*] triumphant
trionfo [*tree-ohn'-foh*] triumph
trippa [*treep'-pah*] tripe
triste [*trees'-teh*] sad
tristezza [*trees-tehts'-tsah*] sadness
triviale [*tree-vee-ah'-leh*] trivial
tromba [*trohm'-bah*] horn [musical instrument]
troncare *v.* [*trohn-kah'-reh*] cut off, break off
trono [*troh'-noh*] throne
tropicale [*troh-pee-kah'-leh*] tropical
troppi [*trohp'-pee*] too many
troppo [*trohp'-poh*] too much, too many
trovare *v.* [*troh-vah'-reh*] find
trovato [*troh-vah'-toh*] found
truccarsi *v.* [*trook-kahr'-see*] make up [oneself]
trucco [*trook'-koh*] trick
truffare *v.* [*troof-fah'-reh*] cheat
truppa [*troop'-pah*] troop
tu *pron., 2d pers. sing.*, **voi** *pl.* [*too, voh'-ee*] you [informal address]
tubercolosi [*too-behr-koh-loh'-zee*] tuberculosis
tubo [*too'-boh*] tube
tuffarsi *v.* [*toof-fahr'-see*] dive
tumulto [*too-mool'-toh*] uproar
tuo *m.*, **tua** *f.*; **tuoi** *m. pl.*, **tue** *f. pl.* [*too'-oh, too'-ah, too-oh'-ee, too'-eh*] your
tuonare *v.* [*too-oh-nah'-reh*] thunder, roar
tuono [*too-oh'-noh*] thunder

turbare *v.* [*toor-bah'-reh*] upset
Turchia [*toor-kee'-ah*] Turkey
turco [*toor'-koh*] Turkish, Turk
turismo [*too-reez'-moh*] tourism
turista [*too-rees'-tah*] tourist
turno [*toor'-noh*] turn [order]
tuttavia [*toot-tah-vee'-ah*] nevertheless, yet, still
tutto [*toot'-toh*] all, whole
  Ecco tutto [*ehk'-koh toot'-toh*] That's all
  dopo tutto [*doh'-poh toot'-toh*] after all

U

ubbidiente [*oob-bee-dee-ehn'-teh*] obedient
ubbidire *v.* [*oob-bee-dee'-reh*] obey
ubriaco [*oo-bree-ah'-koh*] drunk
uccello [*ooch-chehl'-loh*] bird
uccidere *v. irreg.* [*ooch-chee'-deh-reh*] kill, slay
ucciso [*ooch-chee'-zoh*] killed
udienza [*oo-dee-ehn'-tsah*] audience
udire *v. irreg.* [*oo-dee'-reh*] hear
udito [*oo-dee'-toh*] hearing
ufficiale *m. & adj.* [*oof-fee-chee-ah'-leh*] officer, official
ufficio [*oof-fee'-chee-oh*] office
  ufficio postale [*oof-fee'-chee-oh pohs-tah'-leh*] post office
uguale [*oo-goo-ah'-leh*] equal
ulteriore [*ool-teh-ree-oh'-reh*] further
ultimo [*ool'-tee-moh*] last
umanità *f. indecl.* [*oo-mah-nee-tah'*] humanity
umano [*oo-mah'-noh*] human
umidità *f. indecl.* [*oo-mee-dee-tah'*] humidity, moisture
umido [*oo'-mee-doh*] humid
umile [*oo'-mee-leh*] humble
umiltà *f. indecl.* [*oo-meel-tah'*] humility
umore *m.* [*oo-moh'-reh*] mood, humor
  essere *v.* **di buonumore** [*ehs'-seh-reh dee boo-ohn-oo-moh'-reh*] be in a good mood

essere *v.* **di malumore** [*ehs'-seh-reh dee mahl-oo-moh'-reh*] be in a bad mood
umoristico [*oo-moh-rees'-tee-koh*] humorous
un, uno, una, un' [*oon, oo'-noh, oo'-nah, oon*] a, an, one
unanime [*oo-nah'-nee-meh*] unanimous
undici [*oon'-dee-chee*] eleven
ungherese [*oon-geh-reh'-zeh*] Hungarian
Ungheria [*oon-geh-ree'-ah*] Hungary
unghia [*oon'-gee-ah*] (finger)nail
unico [*oo'-nee-koh*] only, unique
uniforme *f. & adj.* [*oo-nee-fohr'-meh*] uniform
unione *f.* [*oo-nee-oh'-neh*] union
unire *v.* [*oo-nee'-reh*] join, unite
unirsi *v.* [*oo-neer'-see*] unite together
unità *f. indecl.* [*oo-nee-tah'*] unity
unitamente [*oo-nee-tah-mehn'-teh*] jointly
unito [*oo-nee'-toh*] united
universale [*oo-nee-vehr-sah'-leh*] universal
università *f. indecl.* [*oo-nee-vehr-see-tah'*] university, college
universo [*oo-nee-vehr'-soh*] universe
uomo, uomini *pl.* [*oo-oh'-moh, oo-oh'-mee-nee*] man
uovo, le uova *pl.* [*oo-oh'-voh, leh oo-oh'-vah*] egg
  uova a la coque [*oo-oh'-vah ah lah kohk*] soft-boiled eggs
  uova fritte [*oo-oh'-vah freet'-teh*] fried eggs
  uova sode [*oo-oh'-vah soh'-deh*] hard-boiled eggs
  uova strapazzate [*oo-oh'-vah strah-pahts-tsah'-teh*] scrambled eggs
(L')Urbe [*(l)oor'-beh*] Rome, the Eternal City
uragano [*oo-rah-gah'-noh*] hurricane
urbano [*oor-bah'-noh*] urban
urgente [*oor-jehn'-teh*] urgent
urgenza [*oor-jehn'-tsah*] urgency
urtare *v.* [*oor-tah'-reh*] collide
urto [*oor'-toh*] shock
usanza [*oo-zahn'-tsah*] custom
usare *v.* [*oo-zah'-reh*] use
usato [*oo-zah'-toh*] used
usciere *m.* [*oo-shee-eh'-reh*] usher
uscire *v. irreg.* [*oo-shee'-reh*] go out, come out
uscita [*oo-shee'-tah*] exit

uso [*oo'-zoh*] use
  fuori uso [*foo-oh'-ree oo'-zoh*] out of order
usuale [*oo-zoo-ah'-leh*] usual
utensile *m.* [*oo-tehn-see'-leh*] tool
utile [*oo'-tee-leh*] useful
utilizzare *v.* [*oo-tee-leedz-dzah'-reh*] utilize
uva [*oo'-vah*] grape
  uva secca [*oo'-vah sehk'-kah*] raisin

V

vacante [*vah-kahn'-teh*] vacant
  posto vacante [*pohs'-toh vah-kahn'-teh*] vacancy
vacca [*vahk'-kah*] cow
vacanza [*vah-kahn'-tsah*] vacation
vaccinazione *f.* [*vahch-chee-nah-tsee-oh'-neh*] vaccination
vagabondo [*vah-gah-bohn'-doh*] vagabond
vagamente [*vah-gah-mehn'-teh*] vaguely
vago [*vah'-goh*] vague
vagone *m.* [*vah-goh'-neh*] wagon
  vagone ferroviario [*vah-goh'-neh fehr-roh-vee-ah'-ree-oh*] railroad car
  vagone letto [*vah-goh'-neh leht'-toh*] sleeping car
valere *v. irreg.* [*vah-leh'-reh*] be worth
  Non ne vale la pena [*nohn neh vah'-leh lah peh'-nah*] It is not worthwhile
  vale a dire [*vah'-leh ah dee'-reh*] that is to say
valido [*vah'-lee-doh*] valid
valigia [*vah-lee'-jee-ah*] suitcase
valle *f.* [*vahl'-leh*] valley
valore *m.* [*vah-loh'-reh*] value
valorosamente [*vah-loh-roh-zah-mehn'-teh*] bravely
valuta [*vah-loo'-tah*] value, currency
  valuta estera [*vah-loo'-tah ehs'-teh-rah*] foreign currency
valutare *v.* [*vah-loo-tah'-reh*] value, estimate
valutazione *f.* [*vah-loo-tah-tsee-oh'-neh*] estimate
valvola [*vahl'-voh-lah*] valve

vaniglia [*vah-nee'-lyah*] vanilla
vanità *f. indecl.* [*vah-nee-tah'*] vanity
vanitoso [*vah-nee-toh'-zoh*] vain
vano [*vah'-noh*] vain
  in vano [*een vah'-noh*] vainly, in vain
vantaggio [*vahn-tahj'-jee-oh*] advantage
vantarsi *v.* [*vahn-tahr'-see*] boast, brag
vapore *m.* [*vah-poh'-reh*] steam
vari [*vah'-ree*] various
variabile [*vah-ree-ah'-bee-leh*] variable, changeable
variare *v.* [*vah-ree-ah'-reh*] vary
varicella [*vah-ree-chel'-lah*] smallpox
varietà *f. indecl.* [*vah-ree-eh-tah'*] variety
vasca [*vahs'-kah*] tub
  vasca da bagno [*vahs'-kah dah bah'-nyoh*] bathtub
vasellame *m.* [*vah-zehl-lah'-meh*] pottery
vaso [*vah'-zoh*] vase
vassoio [*vahs-soh'-ee-oh*] tray
vasto [*vahs'-toh*] vast
Vaticano [*vah-tee-kah'-noh*] Vatican
vecchiaia [*vehk-kee-ah'-ee-ah*] old age
vecchio [*vehk'-kee-oh*] old
vedere *v. irreg.* [*veh-deh'-reh*] see
  Mi faccia vedere [*mee fahch'-chee-ah veh-deh'-reh*] Let me see
  Vede la luna? [*veh'-deh lah loo'-nah*] Do you see the moon?
  Sì, la vedo [*see, lah veh'-doh*] Yes, I see it
  Vede il libro? [*veh'-deh eel lee'-broh*] Do you see the book?
  Sì, lo vedo [*see, loh veh'-doh*] Yes, I see it
  Vediamo un po [*veh-dee-ah'-moh oon poh*] Let's see
vedova, vedovo [*veh'-doh-vah, veh'-doh-voh*] widow, widower
veduta [*veh-doo'-tah*] view
veicolo [*veh-ee'-koh-loh*] vehicle
vela [*veh'-lah*] sail
veleno [*veh-leh'-noh*] poison
velenoso [*veh-leh-noh'-zoh*] poisonous
velluto [*vehl-loo'-toh*] velvet
velo [*veh'-loh*] veil
veloce [*veh-loh'-cheh*] fast
velocità *f. indecl.* [*veh-loh-chee-tah'*] speed

a tutta velocità [*ah toot'-tah veh-loh-chee-tah'*] at full speed
velocità massima [*veh-loh-chee-tah' mahs'-see-mah*] speed limit
vena [*veh'-nah*] vein
vendere *v.* [*vehn'-deh-reh*] sell
vendetta [*vehn-deht'-tah*] vengeance
vendicare *v.* [*vehn-dee-kah'-reh*] avenge
vendita [*vehn'-dee-tah*] sale
in vendita [*een vehn'-dee-tah*] for sale
vendita all'ingrosso [*vehn'-dee-tah ahl-leen-grohs'-soh*] wholesale
vendita al minuto [*vehn'-dee-tah ahl mee-noo'-toh*] retail
vendita all'asta [*vehn'-dee-tah ahl-lahs'-tah*] auction sale
venditore *m.* [*vehn-dee-toh'-reh*] seller
venditore ambulante [*vehn-dee-toh'-reh ahm-boo-lahn'-teh*] peddler
venduto [*vehn-doo'-toh*] sold
venerdì *m.* [*veh-nehr-dee'*] Friday
Venezia [*veh-neh'-tsee-ah*] Venice
venire *v. irreg.* [*veh-nee'-reh*] come
ventaglio [*vehn-tah'-lyoh*] fan
venti [*vehn'-tee*] twenty
ventilatore *m.* [*vehn-tee-lah-toh'-reh*] ventilator
vento [*vehn'-toh*] wind
verbo [*vehr'-boh*] verb
verde [*vehr'-deh*] green
verdetto [*vehr-deht'-toh*] verdict
verdura [*vehr-doo'-rah*] vegetables
vergine *f. & adj.* [*vehr'-jee-neh*] virgin
vergogna [*vehr-goh'-nyah*] shame
vergognoso [*vehr-goh-nyoh'-zoh*] shameful
verificare *v.* [*veh-ree-fee-kah'-reh*] verify
verità *f. indecl.* [*veh-ree-tah'*] truth
in verità [*een veh-ree-tah'*] indeed
verme *m.* [*vehr'-meh*] worm
vernice *f.* [*vehr-nee'-cheh*] paint [house]
vero [*veh'-roh*] true
È vero [*eh' veh'-roh*] It is true
Non è vero [*nohn eh' veh'-roh*] It isn't true
versare *v.* [*vehr-sah'-reh*] pour, spill

versatile [*vehr-sah'-tee-leh*] versatile
versione *f.* [*vehr-see-oh'-neh*] version
verso *n.* [*vehr'-soh*] verse
verso *prep.* [*vehr'-soh*] toward, about
verticale [*vehr-tee-kah'-leh*] veritcal
vertigine *f.* [*vehr-tee'-jee-nee*] dizziness
  avere *v.* **le vertigini** [*ah-veh'-reh leh vehr-tee'-jee-nee*] feel dizzy
vescovo [*vehs'-koh-voh*] bishop
vestibolo [*vehs-tee'-boh-loh*] lobby
vestire *v.* [*vehs-tee'-reh*] dress
  vestirsi [*vehs-teer'-see*] get dressed
Vesuvio [*veh-zoo'-vee-oh*] Vesuvius
veterano [*veh-teh-rah'-noh*] veteran
veterinario [*veh-teh-ree-nah'-ree-oh*] veterinary
vetrina [*veh-tree'-nah*] shopwindow
vetro [*veh'-troh*] glass [material]
vi *adv.* [*vee*] there
vi *pron.* [*vee*] you, to you
via *n.* [*vee'-ah*] street, road, way
via *adv.* [*vee'-ah*] away, off
  Via! [*vee'-ah*] Come on!
via aerea [*vee'-ah ah-eh'-reh-ah*] air mail
viaggiare *v.* [*vee-ahj-jee-ah'-reh*] travel
viaggiatore *m.*, **viaggiatrice** *f.* [*vee-ahj-jee-ah-toh'-reh, vee-ahj-jee-ah-tree'-cheh*] traveller
viaggio [*vee-ahj'-jee-oh*] travel, trip
  agenzia di viaggi [*ah-jehn-tsee'-ah dee vee-ahj'-jee*] travel agency
viale *m.* [*vee-ah'-leh*] avenue
vibrare *v.* [*vee-brah'-reh*] vibrate
viceversa [*vee-cheh-vehr'-sah*] vice versa
vicinanza [*vee-chee-nahn'-tsah*] vicinity
vicino [*vee-chee'-noh*] near, neighbor
  vicino a [*vee-chee'-noh ah*] next to
vicolo [*vee'-koh-loh*] alley
vietare *v.* [*vee-eh-tah'-reh*] forbid
  vietato fumare [*vee-eh-tah'-toh foo-mah'-reh*] no smoking
  vietato l'ingresso [*vee-eh-tah'-toh leen-grehs'-soh*] no admittance

vigile *m. & adj.* [*vee'-jee-leh*] city policeman, alert
vigilia [*vee-jee'-lee-ah*] eve
  vigilia di Natale [*vee-jee'-lee-ah dee nah-tah'-leh*] Christmas Eve
vigliacco [*vee-lyahk'-koh*] coward
vigneto [*vee-nyeh'-toh*] vineyard
vigoroso [*vee-goh-roh'-zoh*] vigorous
villa [*veel'-lah*] villa
villaggio [*veel-lahj'-jee-oh*] village
villeggiatura [*veel-lehj-jee-ah-too'-rah*] vacation [in the country]
vincere *v. irreg.* [*veen'-cheh-reh*] win
vincita [*veen'-chee-tah*] victory, winning
vincitore *m.*, **vincitrice** *f.* [*veen-chee-toh'-reh, veen-chee-tree'-cheh*] winner
vincolo [*veen'-koh-loh*] tie, bond
vino [*vee'-noh*] wine
  vino bianco [*vee'-noh bee-ahn'-koh*] white wine
  vino rosso [*vee'-noh rohs'-soh*] red wine
vinto [*veen'-toh*] conquered
viola [*vee-oh'-lah*] violet [color]
violare *v.* [*vee-oh-lah'-reh*] violate
violazione *f.* [*vee-oh-lah-tsee-oh'-neh*] violation
violetta [*vee-oh-leht'-tah*] violet [flower]
violenza [*vee-oh-lehn'-tsah*] violence
violino [*vee-oh-lee'-noh*] violin
virgola [*veer'-goh-lah*] comma
virtù *f. indecl.* [*veer-too'*] virtue
virtuoso [*veer-too-oh'-zoh*] virtuous
visibile [*vee-zee'-bee-leh*] visible
visionario [*vee-zee-oh-nah'-ree-oh*] visionary
visione *f.* [*vee-zee-oh'-neh*] vision
visita [*vee'-zee-tah*] visit
  biglietto da visita [*bee-lyeht'-toh dah vee'-zee-tah*] visiting card
  fare *v.* **una visita** [*fah'-reh oo'-nah vee'-zee-tah*] pay a visit to
visitare *v.* [*vee-zee-tah'-reh*] visit
visitatore *m.*, **visitatrice** *f.* [*vee-zee-tah-toh'-reh, vee-zee-tah-tree'-cheh*] visitor

viso [*vee'-zoh*] face
visone *m.* [*vee-zoh'-neh*] mink
vista [*vees'-tah*] eyesight, view
  punto di vista [*poon'-toh dee vees'-tah*] point of view
visto [*vees'-toh*] visa
vita [*vee'-tah*] life, waist
  assicurazione *f.* **sulla vita** [*ahs-see-koo-rah-tsee-oh'-neh sool'-lah vee'-tah*] life insurance
vitale [*vee-tah'-leh*] vital
vitamina [*vee-tah-mee'-nah*] vitamin
vite *f.* [*vee'-teh*] screw, vineyard
vitello [*vee-tehl'-loh*] calf
  carne *f.* **di vitello** [*kahr'-neh dee vee-tehl'-loh*] veal
vittima [*veet'-tee-mah*] victim
vitto [*veet'-toh*] food, board
vittoria [*veet-toh'-ree-ah*] victory
vivace [*vee-vah'-cheh*] lively
vivere *v. irreg.* [*vee'-veh-reh*] live
viveri *m. pl.* [*vee'-veh-ree*] food supplies
vivido [*vee'-vee-doh*] vivid
vivo [*vee'-voh*] alive
viziare *v.* [*vee-tsee-ah'-reh*] spoil
vizio [*vee'-tsee-oh*] vice
vizioso [*vee-tsee-oh'-zoh*] vicious
vocabolario [*voh-kah-boh-lah'-ree-oh*] vocabulary
vocale *f.* [*voh-kah'-leh*] vowel, vocal
vocazione *f.* [*voh-kah-tsee-oh'-neh*] vocation
voce *f.* [*voh'-cheh*] voice
  ad alta voce [*ahd ahl'-tah voh'-cheh*] loud
voglia [*voh'-lyah*] desire, wish
voi [*voh'-ee*] you [informal]
volante *m.* [*voh-lahn'-teh*] steering wheel
volare *v.* [*voh-lah'-reh*] fly
volentieri [*voh-lehn-tee-eh'-ree*] willingly
volere *v. irreg.* [*voh-leh'-reh*] want
volgare [*vohl-gah'-reh*] vulgar
volgere *v. irreg.* [*vohl'-jeh-reh*] turn, revolve
volo [*voh'-loh*] flight
volontà *f. indecl.* [*voh-lohn-tah'*] will
  forza di volontà [*fohr'-tsah dee voh-lohn-tah'*] willpower

volontario [*voh-lohn-tah'-ree-oh*] voluntary, volunteer
volta [*vohl'-tah*] time [occasion], vault
ancora una volta [*ahn-koh'-rah oo'-nah vohl'-tah*] once again
ogni volta [*oh'-nyee vohl'-tah*] each time
una volta [*oo'-nah vohl'-tah*] once
a volte [*ah vohl'-teh*] at times
voltare *v.* [*vohl-tah'-reh*] turn
volto [*vohl'-toh*] face
volume *m.* [*voh-loo'-meh*] volume
voluminoso [*voo-loo-mee-noh'-zoh*] bulky
vomitare *v.* [*voh-mee-tah'-reh*] vomit
vostro, vostra [*vohs'-troh, vohs'-trah*] your
il vostro, la vostra [*eel vohs'-troh, lah vohs'-trah*] yours
votare *v.* [*voh-tah'-reh*] vote
voto [*voh'-toh*] vote, vow
vulcano [*vool-kah'-noh*] volcano
vulnerabile [*vool-neh-rah'-bee-leh*] vulnerable
vuoto [*voo-oh'-toh*] empty

Z

zaffiro [*dzahf-fee'-roh*] sapphire
zaino [*dzah'-ee-noh*] knapsack
zampa [*dzahm'-pah*] paw
zanzara [*dzahn-dzah'-rah*] mosquito
zebra [*dzeh'-brah*] zebra
zelante [*dzeh-lahn'-teh*] zealous
zelo [*dzeh'-loh*] zeal
zero [*dzeh'-roh*] zero
zia [*dzee'-ah*] aunt
zinco [*dzeen'-koh*] zinc
zingaro [*dzeen'-gah-roh*] gypsy
zio, zii *pl.* [*dzee'-oh, dzee'-ee*] uncle
Zitto! [*dzeet'-toh*] Be quiet! [to several persons]
zona [*dzoh'-nah*] zone
zoo [*zoh'-oh*] zoo

zoppo [*dzohp'-poh*] lame
zucca [*dzook'-kah*] pumpkin
zucchero [*dzook'-keh-roh*] sugar
zucchino [*dzook-kee'-noh*] squash
zuppa [*dzoop'-pah*] soup

Phrases for Use Abroad

Helpful Expressions

Good morning./Good evening.
Buon giorno./Buona sera.
Boo-ohn' jee-ohr'-noh./Boo-oh'-nah seh'-rah.

How do you do?/How are you?
Come sta?
Koh'-meh stah?

This is Mr./Mrs./Miss. . . .
Le presento il signor/la signora/la signorina. . . .
Leh preh-zehn'-toh eel see-nyohr'/lah see-nyoh'-rah/lah see-nyoh-ree'-nah. . . .

What is your name?
Lei, come si chiama?
Leh'-ee, koh'-meh see kee-ah'-mah?

My name is. . . .
Mi chiamo . . . .
Mee kee-ah'-moh . . . .

I am pleased to meet you.
Piacere di conoscerla.
Pee-ah-cheh'-reh dee koh-noh'-shehr-lah.

I don't understand.
Non capisco.
Nohn kah-pees'-koh.

Could you speak more slowly, please?
Può parlare più lentamente, per favore?
Poo-oh' pahr-lah'-reh pee-oo' lehn-tah-mehn'-teh, pehr fah-voh'-reh?

Could you repeat, please?
Può ripetere, per favore?
Poo-oh' ree-peh'-teh-reh, pehr fah-voh'-reh?

Goodbye./See you later.
Arrivederla.
Ahr-ree-veh-dehr'-lah.

Thank you.
Grazie.
Grah'-tsee-eh.

You're welcome.
Prego.
Preh'-goh.

Excuse me.
Mi scusi.
Mee skoo'-zee.

Do you speak English?
Scusi, lei parla inglese?
Skoo'-zee, leh'-ee pahr'-lah een-gleh'-zeh?

How do you say . . . in Italian?
Come si dice . . . in italiano?
Koh'-meh see dee'-cheh . . . een ee-tah-lee-ah'-noh?

What does . . . mean?
Cosa vuol dire . . . ?
Koh'-zah voo-ohl' dee'-reh . . . ?

Customs

May I see your passport/visa, please?
Mi fa vedere il suo passaporto/visto, per favore?
Mee fah veh-deh'-reh eel soo'-oh pahs'-sah-pohr-toh/vees'-toh, pehr fah-voh'-reh?

Do you have anything to declare?
Ha qualcosa da dichiarare?
Ah koo-ahl-koh'-zah dah dee-kee-ah-rah'-reh?

It is for my personal use.
È per mio uso personale.
Eh pehr mee'-oh oo'-zoh pehr-soh-nah'-leh.

How long are you staying?
Quanto tempo si ferma?
Koo-ahn'-toh tehm'-poh see fehr'-mah?

I will be here for . . . days/weeks/months.
Ci starò per . . . giorni/settimane/mesi.
Chee stah-roh' pehr . . . jee-ohr'-nee/seht-tee-mah'-neh/meh'-zee.

Money

Where can I cash this traveler's check?
Dove posso cambiare questo assegno turistico?
Doh'-veh pohs'-soh kahm-bee-ah'-reh koo-ehs'-toh ahs-seh'-nyoh too-rees'-tee-koh?

Please give me some small change.
Per favore, mi dia della moneta spicciola.
Pehr fah-voh'-reh, mee dee'-ah dehl'-lah moh-neh'-tah speech'-chee-oh-lah.

What is the rate of exchange for dollars?
Quant'è il cambio del dollaro?
Koo-ahn-teh' eel kahm'-bee-oh dehl dohl'-lah-roh?

At the Hotel

I want a room with/without bath.
Vorrei una camera con/senza bagno.
Vohr-reh'-ee oo'-nah kah'-meh-rah kohn/sehn'-tsah bah'-nyoh.

How much is the room?
Quant'è la camera?
Koo-ahn-teh' lah kah'-meh-rah?

Are meals included?
Sono inclusi i pasti?
Soh'-noh een-kloo'-zee ee pahs'-tee?

I would like something cheaper.
Vorrei qualcosa meno caro.
Vohr-reh'-ee koo-ahl-koh'-zah meh'-noh kah'-roh.

Where is the manager?
Dove è il direttore?
Doh'-veh eh eel dee-reht-toh'-reh?

Laundry/Dry Cleaning

Where is a laundry/dry cleaner?
Dove c'è una lavanderia/tintoria?
Doh'-veh cheh oo'-nah lah-vahn-deh-ree'-ah/teen-toh-ree'-ah?

When will my clothes be ready?
Quando saranno pronti i miei vestiti?
Koo-ahn'-doh sah-rahn'-noh prohn'-tee ee mee-eh'-ee vehs-tee'-tee?

Please wash these clothes.
Vorrei far lavare questa biancheria.
Vohr-reh'-ee fahr lah-vah'-reh koo-ehs'-tah bee-ahn-keh-ree'-ah

I want these clothes dry cleaned.
Vorrei questi vestiti lavati a secco.
Vohr-reh'-ee koo-ehs'-tee vehs-tee'-tee lah-vah'-tee ah sehk'-koh.

Please press these trousers.
Per favore, vorrei far stirare questi pantaloni.
Pehr fah-voh'-reh, vohr-reh'-ee fahr stee-rah'-reh koo-ehs'-tee pahn-tah-loh'-nee.

Barber/Hairdresser

I would like a haircut/trim.
Vorrei farmi tagliare/aggiustare i capelli.
Vohr-reh'-ee fahr'-mee tah-lyah'-reh/aj-jee-oos-tah'-reh ee kah-pehl'-lee.

Make it shorter, please.
Li tagli un pò più corti, per favore.
Lee tah'-lyee oon poh pee-oo' kohr'-tee, pehr fah-voh'-reh.

I would like a shampoo and set.
Vorrei uno shampoo e la messa in piega.
Vohr-reh'-ee oo'-noh shahm'-poo eh lah mehs'-sah een pee-eh'-gah.

Getting Around

When is the next flight to . . . ?
Quand è il prossimo volo per . . . ?
Koo-ahn-deh' eel prohs'-see-moh voh'-loh pehr . . . ?

I want a ticket to . . . .
Vorrei un biglietto per . . . .
Vohr-reh'-ee oon bee-lyeht'-toh pehr . . . .

Is lunch/dinner served on this flight?
Servono il pranzo/la cena sull'aereo?
Sehr'-voh-noh eel prahn'-tsoh/lah cheh'-nah sool-lah-eh'-reh-oh?

I want to confirm my flight.
Vorrei riconfermare il mio volo.
Vohr-reh'-ee ree-kohn-fehr-mah'-reh eel mee'-oh voh'-loh.

Take my bags to my cabin, please.
Porti le valigie nella mia cabina, per favore.
Pohr'-tee leh vah-lee'-jee-eh nehl'-lah mee'-ah kah-bee'-nah, pehr fah-voh'-reh.

At what time does the boat dock?
A che ora arriva la nave al molo?
Ah keh oh'-rah ahr-ree'-vah lah nah'-veh ahl moh'-loh?

Where is the ticket window?
Dove è la biglietteria?
Doh'-veh eh lah bee-lyeht-teh-ree'-ah?

May I have a timetable?
Posso avere un orario?
Pohs'-soh ah-veh'-reh oon oh-rah'-ree-oh?

How much is a one-way/round-trip first-class/second-class ticket to . . . ?
Quanto costa un biglietto di andata/andata e ritorno di prima classe/seconda classe per . . . ?
Koo-ahn'-toh kohs'-tah oon bee-lyeht'-toh dee ahn-dah'-tah/ ahn-dah'-tah eh ree-tohr'-noh dee pree'-mah klahs'-seh/seh-kohn'-dah klahs'-seh pehr . . . ?

From which track does the train for . . . leave?
Su che binario parte il treno per . . . ?
Soo keh bee-nah'-ree-oh pahr'-teh eel treh'-noh pehr . . . ?

At what time does this train leave?
A che ora parte questo treno?
Ah keh oh'-rah pahr'-teh koo-ehs'-toh treh'-noh?

Is this seat taken?
È occupato questo posto?
Eh ohk-koo-pah'-toh koo-ehs'-toh pohs'-toh?

When is the dining car open?
Quando è aperto il vagone ristorante?
Koo-ahn'-doh eh ah-pehr'-toh eel vah-goh'-neh rees-toh-rahn'-teh?

Where is the bus station?
Dove è la stazione degli autobus?
Doh'-veh eh lah stah-tsee-oh'-neh deh'-lyee ah'-oo-toh-boos?

When is the next bus to . . . ?
Quando parte il prossimo autobus per . . . ?
Koo-ahn'-doh pahr'-teh eel prohs'-see-moh ah-oo'-toh-boos pehr . . . ?

Where do I get off to go to . . . ?
Dove devo scendere per andare a . . . ?
Doh'-veh deh'-voh shehn'-deh-reh pehr ahn-dah'-reh ah . . . ?

Take me to . . . .
Mi porti a . . . .
Mee pohr'-tee ah . . .

Where can I rent a car?
Dove posso prendere in affito un'automobile?
Doh'-veh pohs'-soh prehn'-deh-reh een ahf-feet'-toh oon-ah-oo-toh-moh'-bee-leh?

Do you charge by the day or by the mile?
Come si paga, per giorni o per chilometraggio?
Koh'-meh see pah'-gah, pehr jee-ohr'-nee oh pehr kee-loh-meh-trahj'-jee-oh?

Where is the nearest gas station?
Dove è la stazione di servizio più vicina?
Doh'-veh eh lah stah-tsee-oh'-neh dee sehr-vee'-tsee-oh pee-oo' vee-chee'-nah?

Fill it up with regular/premium.
Mi faccia il pieno con benzina normale/super.
Mee fahch'-chee-ah eel pee-eh'-noh kohn behn-dzee'-nah nohr-mah'-leh/soo'-pehr.

Please check the oil/the tires.
Verifichi l'olio/le gomme, per favore.
Veh-ree'-fee-kee loh'-lee-oh/leh gohm'-meh, pehr fah-voh'-reh.

Shopping

Where is there a bookstore?
Dove c'è una libreria?
Doh'-veh cheh oo'-nah lee-breh-ree'-ah?

How much does this cost?
Quanto costa questo?
Koo-ahn'-toh kohs'-tah koo-ehs'-toh?

Have you anything better/cheaper?
Ha qualcosa di meglio/meno costoso?
Ah koo-ahl-koh'-zah dee meh'-lyoh/meh'-noh kohs-toh'-soh?

This is too large/small.
Questo è troppo grande/piccolo.
Koo-ehs'-toh eh trohp'-poh grahn'-deh/peek'-koh-loh.

Do you accept checks/traveler's checks?
Accettate assegni/assegni turistici?
Ahch-cheht-tah'-teh ahs-seh'-nyee/ahs-seh'-nyee too-rees'-tee-chee?

I would like a roll of color/black and white film.
Vorrei un film a colori/in bianco e nero.
Vohr-reh'-ee oon feelm ah koh-loh'-ree/een bee-ahn'-koh eh neh'-roh.

Here are some films to develop.
Vorrei far sviluppare questi film.
Vohr-reh'-ee fahr svee-loop-pah'-reh koo-ehs'-tee feelm.

Sightseeing

Where is the museum/zoo?
Dove è il museo/lo zoo?
Doh'-veh eh eel moo-zeh'-oh/loh dzoh'-oh?

Do we have to pay to go in?
Dobbiamo pagare per entrare?
Dohb-bee-ah'-moh pah-gah'-reh pehr ehn-trah'-reh?

What hours are the museums open?
Quando sono aperti i musei?
Koo-ahn'-doh soh'-noh ah-pehr'-tee ee moo-zeh'-ee?

Entertainment

I would like to see an opera.
Vorrei vedere un'opera.
Vohr-reh'-ee veh-deh'-reh oon-oh'-peh-rah.

We would like a table for two, please.
Un tavolo per due, per favore.
Oon tah'-voh-loh pehr doo'-eh, pehr fah-voh'-reh.

May we have a menu/wine list, please?
Vuol darci il menù/la lista dei vini, per favore?
Voo-ohl' dahr'-chee eel meh-noo'/lah lees'-tah deh'-ee vee'-nee, pehr fah-voh'-reh?

What do you recommend?
Lei, che cosa raccomanda?
Leh'-ee, keh koh'-zah rahk-koh-mahn'-dah?

Please bring the check.
Il conto, per favore.
Eel kohn'-toh, pehr fah-voh'-reh.

Is the tip included?
È incluso il servizio?
Eh een-kloo'-zoh eel sehr-vee'-tsee-oh?

Where do I pay?
Dove pago?
Doh'-veh pah'-goh?

There is a mistake in the bill.
C'è un errore nel conto.
Cheh oon ehr-roh'-reh nehl kohn'-toh.

Health

I don't feel well.
Non mi sento bene.
Nohn mee sehn'-toh beh'-neh.

I need a doctor/dentist.
Ho bisogno di un medico/dentista.
Oh bee-zoh'-nyoh dee oon meh'-dee-koh/dehn-tees'-tah.

I have a headache/stomachache/toothache.
Ho mal di testa/stomaco/denti.
Oh mahl dee tehs'-tah/stoh'-mah-koh/dehn'-tee.

I have a bad cold/fever.
Ho un brutto raffreddore/ho la febbre.
Oh oon broot'-toh rahf-frehd-doh'-reh/oh lah fehb'-breh.

I have burned myself.
Mi sono bruciato.
Mee soh'-noh broo-chee-ah'-toh.

My . . . hurts.
Mi fa male il/la . . . .
Mee fah mah'-leh eel/lah . . . .

My . . . is bleeding.
Mi sanguina il/la . . . .
Mee sahn-goo-ee'-nah eel/lah . . . .

Please fill this prescription.
Vorrei questa medicina.
Vohr-reh'-ee koo-ehs'-tah meh-dee-chee'-nah

Emergencies

Help!
Aiuto!
Ah-ee-oo'-toh.

Police!
Polizia!
Poh-lee-tsee'-ah.

Please call a policeman/an ambulance.
Chiami la polizia/l'ambulanza, per favore.
Kee-ah'-mee lah poh-lee-tsee'-ah/lahm-boo-lahn'-tsah, pehr fah-voh'-reh.

I need a lawyer.
Ho bisogno di un avvocato.
Oh bee-zoh'-nyoh dee oon ahv-voh-kah'-toh.

I have been robbed.
Mi hanno derubato.
Mee ahn'-noh deh-roo-bah'-toh.

Is there anyone here who speaks English?
C'è qualcuno qui che parli inglese?
Cheh koo-ahl-koo'-noh koo-ee' keh pahr'-lee een-gleh'-zeh?

I am lost.
Ho perso la giusta direzione.
Oh pehr'-soh lah jee-oos'-tah dee-reh-tsee-oh'-neh.

Someone is injured.
Qualcuno si è fatto male
Koo-ahl-koo'-noh see eh faht'-toh mah'-leh.

Menu Reader

Beverages

acqua [*ah'-koo-ah*] water
  fresca [*frehs'-kah*] cold water
  minerale [*mee-neh-rah'-leh*] mineral water
acquavite [*ahk-koo-ah-vee'-teh*] liquor, brandy
aperitivo [*ah-peh-ree-tee'-voh*] aperitif (drink before meals)
aranciata [*ah-rahn-chee-ah'-tah*] orangeade
bibite [*bee'-bee-teh*] soft drinks
birra [*beer'-rah*] beer
caffè [*kahf-feh'*] coffee
  espresso [*ehs-prehs'-soh*] strong black coffee (Italian style)
  americano [*ah-meh-ree-kah'-noh*] American-style coffee
  freddo [*frehd'-doh*] iced coffee
  latte [*laht'-teh*] coffee with milk (sugar)
  macchiato [*mahk-kee-ah'-toh*] light coffee
  cappuccino [*kahp-poo-chee'-noh*] coffee with cream
  nero [*neh'-roh*] black coffee
cioccolata [*chee-ohk-koh-lah'-tah*] chocolate
  con latte [*kohn laht'-teh*] hot chocolate
ghiacciata [*gee-ahch-chee-ah'-tah*] fruit drink over ice
grappa [*grahp'-pah*] grape brandy
latte [*laht'-teh*] milk
limonata [*lee-moh-nah'-tah*] lemonade
succo [*sook'-koh*] juice
  d'arancia [*dah-rahn'-chee-ah*] orange
  di pomodoro [*dee poh-moh-doh'-roh*] tomato
  di frutta [*dee froot'-tah*] fruit
tè [*teh*] tea
vino [*vee'-noh*] wine
  bianco [*bee-ahn'-koh*] white wine
  da tavola [*dah tah'-voh-lah*] table wine
  Marsala [*mahr-sah'-lah*] renowned Sicilian red dessert wine

rosato, rosatello [*roh-zah'-toh, roh-zah-tehl'-loh*] rosé wine
rosso [*rohs'-soh*] red wine
spumante [*spoo-mahn'-teh*] sparkling wine

The Menu

acciughe [*ahch-chee-oo'-geh*] anchovies
aceto [*ah-cheh'-toh*] vinegar
aglio [*ah'-lyoh*] garlic
agnello [*ah-nyehl'-loh*] lamb
abbacchio alla cacciatora [*ahb-bahk'-kee-oh ahl'-lah kahch-chee-ah-toh'-rah*] lamb with garlic and white wine
agnolotti [*ah-nyoh-loht'-tee*] small filled envelopes of dough
alla casalinga [*ahl'-lah kah-zah-leen'-gah*] homemade
alla francese [*ahl'-lah frahn-cheh'-zeh*] cooked in butter
all'inglese [*ahl-leen-gleh'-zeh*] boiled
all'italiana [*ahl-lee-tah-lee-ah'-nah*] with pasta
alla napoletana [*ahl'-lah nah-poh-leh-tah'-nah*] breaded
alla romana [*ahl'-lah roh-mah'-nah*] sautéed
alla spagnola [*ahl'-lah spah-nyoh'-lah*] with tomatoes
al sangue/poco cotto [*ahl sahn'-goo-eh/poh'-koh koht'-toh*] rare
antipasto [*ahn-tee-pahs'-toh*] hors d'oeuvres
arancia [*ah-rahn'-chee-ah*] orange
arrosto di vitello [*ahr-rohs'-toh dee vee-tehl'-loh*] roast veal
asparagi [*ahs-pah'-rah-jee*] asparagus
ben cotto [*behn koht'-toh*] well done
biscotti [*bees-koht'-tee*] cookies, crackers
bistecca [*bees-tehk'-kah*] steak
all'inglese [*ahl-leen-gleh'-zeh*] rare
ben cotto [*behn koht'-toh*] well done
bollito [*bohl-lee'-toh*] boiled
braciola [*brah-chee-oh'-lah*] rib steak
di maiale [*dee mah-ee-ah'-lee*] pork chop
di manzo [*dee mahn'-tsoh*] rolled beef
spezzatino di manzo [*spehts-tsah-tee'-noh dee mahn'-tsoh*] beef stew
broccoli [*brohk'-koh-lee*] broccoli
brodo di pesce [*broh'-doh dee peh'-sheh*] seafood chowder
burro [*boor'-roh*] butter

cannelloni [*kahn-nehl-loh'-nee*] meat-filled pasta
carciofi [*kahr-chee-oh'-fee*] artichokes
carne [*kahr'-neh*] meat
carote [*kah-roh'-teh*] carrots
cavolfiore [*kah-vohl-fee-oh'-reh*] cauliflower
cavoli [*kah'-voh-lee*] cabbages
cervello [*chehr-vehl'-loh*] brains
cetriolo [*cheh-tree-oh'-loh*] cucumber
ciliege [*chee-lee-eh'-jeh*] cherries
cipolle [*chee-pohl'-leh*] onions
composta di frutta [*kohm-pohs'-tah dee froot'-tah*] stewed fruit
coscia di montone [*koh'-shee-ah dee mohn-toh'-neh*] leg of lamb
costoletta [*kohs-toh-leht'-tah*] chop, cutlet
  alla bolognese [*ahl'-lah boh-loh-nyeh'-zeh*] with melted cheese
  alla milanese [*ahl'-lah mee-lah-neh'-zeh*] breaded
cotto [*koht'-toh*] cooked, stewed
crudo [*kroo'-doh*] raw
dolce [*dohl'-cheh*] dessert
dolci [*dohl'-chee*] pastries, cakes
fagioli [*fah-jee-oh'-lee*] beans
fagiolini [*fah-jee-oh-lee'-nee*] stringbeans
fave [*fah'-veh*] broad beans
fegato [*feh'-gah-toh*] liver
fettuccine [*feht-too-chee'-neh*] noodles
fichi [*fee'-kee*] figs
filetto [*fee-leht'-toh*] fillet
  di bue [*dee boo'-eh*] fillet of beef
  di sogliola [*dee soh-lyoh'-lah*] fillet of sole
formaggio [*fohr-mahj'-jee-oh*] cheese
fragole [*frah'-goh-leh*] strawberries
frittata [*freet-tah'-tah*] omelet
fritelle [*free-tehl'-leh*] pancakes
fritto [*freet'-toh*] fried
fritto misto [*freet'-toh mees'-toh*] assorted tiny fried fish
frutta [*froot'-tah*] fruit
gamberi [*gahm'-beh-ree*] shrimp
gelato [*jeh-lah'-toh*] ice cream
gnocchi [*nyohk'-kee*] dumplings

granchio [*grahn'-kee-oh*] crab, crabmeat
insalata [*een-sah-lah'-tah*] salad
mista [*mees'-tah*] mixed
russa [*roos'-sah*] potato
verde [*vehr'-deh*] lettuce
lasagne [*lah-zah'-nyeh*] a kind of large, flat spaghetti
lattuga [*laht-too'-gah*] lettuce
legumi [*leh-goo'-mee*] vegetables
maccheroni [*mahk-keh-roh'-nee*] macaroni
maiale [*mah-ee-ah'-leh*] pork
manicotti [*mah-nee-koht'-tee*] pasta with a filling of chopped ham and ricotta cheese
manzo [*mahn'-tsoh*] beef
arrosto ripieno [*ahr-rohs'-toh ree-pee-eh'-noh*] stuffed roast
lesso [*lehs'-soh*] boiled
marinata [*mah-ree-nah'-tah*] marinated, pickled
marmellata [*mahr-mehl-lah'-tah*] jam
mela [*meh'-lah*] apple
melanzana [*meh-lahn-dzah'-nah*] eggplant
melone [*meh-loh'-neh*] melon
minestra [*mee-nehs'-trah*] soup
in brodo [*een broh'-doh*] bouillon with noodles or rice
di funghi [*dee foon'-gee*] cream of mushroom soup
minestrone [*mee-nehs-troh'-neh*] thick vegetable soup
mostarda [*mohs-tahr'-dah*] mustard
olio [*oh'-lee-oh*] oil
d'oliva [*doh-lee'-vah*] olive oil
olive [*oh-lee'-veh*] olives
osso buco [*ohs'-soh boo'-koh*] veal shank stewed in wine and tomatoes
ostriche [*ohs'-tree-keh*] oysters
pan di Genova [*pahn dee jeh'-noh-vah*] almond cake
pan di spagna [*pahn dee spah'-nyah*] sponge cake
pancetta [*pahn-cheht'-tah*] bacon
pagnotta [*pah-nyoht'-tah*] long loaf of bread
pane [*pah'-neh*] bread
tostato [*tohs-tah'-toh*] toasted bread
panettone [*pah-neht-toh'-neh*] raisin cake (Milan)
panino [*pah-nee'-noh*] roll, bun

imbottito [*eem-boht-tee'-toh*] sandwich
pasta (asciutta) [*pahs'-tah* (*ah-shee-oot'-tah*)] the traditional Italian first course (macaroni)
al burro [*ahl boor'-roh*] with butter
al sugo [*ahl soo'-goh*] with tomato sauce
al sugo di carne/al ragù [*ahl soo'-goh dee kahr'-neh/ahl rah-goo'*] with meat sauce
pasticceria [*pahs-teech-cheh-ree'-ah*] pastry
patate [*pah-tah'-teh*] potatoes
al forno [*ahl fohr'-noh*] baked
fritte [*freet'-teh*] French fried
lesse [*lehs'-seh*] boiled
in padella [*een pah-dehl'-lah*] home fried
purèe di patate [*poo-reh' dee pah-tah'-teh*] mashed
pepe [*peh'-peh*] black pepper
peperoni [*peh-peh-roh'-nee*] green peppers
pera [*peh'-rah*] pear
pesca [*pehs'-kah*] peach
pesce [*peh'-sheh*] fish
piselli [*pee-zehl'-lee*] peas
pollo [*pohl'-loh*] chicken
alla diavola [*ahl'-lah dee-ah'-voh-lah*] grilled with pepper, pimiento, mustard
alla cacciattora [*ahl'-lah kahch-chee-ah-toh'-rah*] chicken with tomato and vegetable sauce
polpette [*pohl-peht'-teh*] meat balls
polpettone [*pohl-peht-toh'-neh*] meat loaf
pomodori [*poh-moh-doh'ree*] tomatoes
pompelmo [*pohm-pehl'-moh*] grapefruit
prosciutto [*proh-shee-oot'-toh*] ham
ravioli [*rah-vee-oh'-lee*] pasta stuffed with meat, cheese, etc.
alla fiorentina [*ahl'-lah fee-oh-rehn-tee'-nah*] with cheese
alla vegetariana [*ahl'-lah veh-jeh-tah-ree-ah'-nah*] with tomato sauce
fatti in casa [*faht'-tee een kah'-zah*] homemade
ripieno con carne [*ree-pee-eh'-noh kohn kahr'-neh*] stuffed with meat
riso [*ree'-zoh*] rice
risotto [*ree-zoht'-toh*] rice with butter, white wine, etc.

alla milanese [*ahl'-lah mee-lah-neh'-zeh*] with white wine, parmesan cheese, and saffron
rosbif [*rohz-beef'*] roast beef
salame [*sah-lah'-meh*] salami
sale [*sah'-leh*] salt
salmone affumicato [*sahl-moh'-neh ahf-foo-mee-kah'-toh*] smoked salmon
salsiccia [*sahl-seech'-chee-ah*] sausage
saltimbocca [*sahl-teem-bohk'-kah*] veal and ham dish
scaloppine al Marsala [*skah-lohp-pee'-neh ahl mahr-sah'-lah*] thin sautéed slices of veal with Marsala wine sauce
sedano [*seh'-dah-noh*] celery
spaghetti [*spah-geht'-tee*] spaghetti
alla bolognese [*ahl'-lah boh-loh-nyeh'-zeh*] with meat sauce
alla bosaiola [*ahl'-lah boh-zah-ee-oh'-lah*] with tuna, mushrooms and cheese
alla carbonara [*ahl'-lah kahr-boh-nah'-rah*] cooked with eggs and bacon
al sugo di carne [*ahl soo'-goh dee kahr'-neh*] with meat sauce
spinaci [*spee-nah'-chee*] spinach
tagliatelle [*tah-lyah-tehl'-leh*] long, narrow noodles
tonno [*tohn'-noh*] tuna
torta [*tohr'-tah*] cake, open pie
uova [*oo-oh'-vah*] eggs
a la coque [*ah lah kohk*] soft-boiled
fritte [*freet'-teh*] fried
sode [*soh'-deh*] hard-boiled
strapazzate [*strah-pahts-tsah'-teh*] scrambled
uva [*oo'-vah*] grapes
verdura [*vehr-doo'-rah*] vegetables
vermicelli [*vehr-mee-chehl'-lee*] thin noodles
vitello al forno [*vee-tehl'-loh ahl fohr'-noh*] roast veal
vongole [*vohn'-goh-leh*] small clams
zabaglione [*dzah-bah-lyoh'-neh*] dessert of beaten egg yolks, sugar and Marsala wine, usually served warm
zucchero [*dzook'-keh-roh*] sugar
zucchini [*dzook-kee'-nee*] squash
zuppa [*dzoop'-pah*] soup
alla pavese [*ahl'-lah pah-veh'-zeh*] consommé

A Concise Italian Grammar

Nouns

1. Italian nouns have grammatical gender. Nouns ending in *-o* are usually masculine, and those ending in *-a* feminine. Singular nouns ending in *-e* may be masculine or feminine, and they are marked *m.* or *f.* in the Dictionary. To form the plural, the *-o* and *-e* endings regularly become *-i*; the *-a* ending becomes *-e*.

2. Some nouns do not change in the plural, such as masculine nouns ending in *-a*, *il cinema*, *i cinema*, and those nouns ending in an accented vowel, *la città*, *le città*. The plurals of nouns (and adjectives) ending in *-co* and *-go* are *-ci* and *-gi* in some cases, but in others *-chi* and *-ghi*.

lago	lake	**laghi**	**amico**	friend	**amici**
fuoco	fire	**fuochi**	**fico**	fig	**fichi**

Irregular plurals and other exceptions to these rules are shown in the Dictionary.

Articles

1. An article agrees with the noun it precedes, and is sometimes the best clue to the gender and number of the noun. In the masculine, the form of the article depends on the first letter of the word which follows it, whether noun or adjective.

2. The forms of the *definite article*, the, are:

	Masculine		*Feminine*	
	Sing.	*Pl.*	*Sing.*	*Pl.*
Before most consonants	**il**	**i**	**la**	**le**
Before impure s, z, gn, ps	**lo**	**gli**	**la**	**le**
Before vowels	**l'**	**gli (gl')**	**l'**	**le (l')**

lo stato **gli stati** **il grande stato**

3. When *a*, *di*, *da*, *in*, and *su* precede a definite article, the two words contract:

	il	**lo**	**i**	**gli**	**la**	**le**	**l'**
a	al	allo	ai	agli	alla	alle	all'
di	del	dello	dei	degli	della	delle	dell'
da	dal	dallo	dai	dagli	dalla	dalle	dall'
in	nel	nello	nei	negli	nella	nelle	nell'
su	sul	sullo	sui	sugli	sulla	sulle	sull'

4. The forms of the *indefinite article*, a, an, are:

	Masculine		*Feminine*	
	Sing.	*Pl.*	*Sing.*	*Pl.*
Before most consonants	**un**	**dei**	**una**	**delle**
Before impure s, z, gn, ps	**uno**	**degli**	**una**	**delle**
Before vowels	**un**	**degli**	**un'**	**delle**

uno specchio **degli specchii** **un grande specchio**

5. The *partitive article* (*dei*, *delle*, etc.) is used when speaking of an indefinite quantity. The nearest English equivalent is "some" or "any," but often English does not express the idea at all. The partitive is formed by the contraction of the preposition *di* and the definite article, as shown above.

Qualifying Adjectives

1. There are two classes of adjectives: (*a*) gender adjectives ending in *-o* in the masculine and having four forms: *-o*, *-a* in the singular, *-i*, *-e* in the plural; (*b*) neuter adjectives having two forms: *-e* in the singular, *-i* in the plural, the masculine and feminine being identical. Adjectives agree in number and gender with the nouns they modify. An adjective which modifies two or more nouns is always masculine plural if at least one noun is masculine.

2. The adjective normally follows the noun, but certain adjectives usually precede it — demonstratives, numerals, possessives, and the following (unless they are modified by an adverb or unless special emphasis is desired): *molto*, *tutto*,

giovane, *vecchio*, *buono*, *cattivo*, *bello*, *brutto*, *lungo*, *largo*, *breve*, *grande*, *piccolo*, *nuovo*, *antico*, *altro*.

3. The comparative of adjectives is formed by using *più*, more, or *meno*, less, before the adjective. The equivalent of "than" in comparisons is *di* before nouns, pronouns, and numbers, and *che* before adjectives, adverbs, prepositions, participles, and infinitives.

Pietro è più intelligente di Marco.
Peter is more intelligent than Mark.

Dino è meno forte che intelligente.
Dino is less strong than intelligent.

The relative superlative is formed by the definite article and *più* or *meno*.

The absolute superlative is formed either by adding *-issimo*, which changes according to gender and number, or by using modifying adverbs *molto*, *assai*, etc., with the adjective.

Certain adjectives have irregular as well as regular forms of comparison, for example, *grande*, big, great, *maggiore*, bigger, greater; *cattivo*, bad, *peggiore*, worse.

Personal Pronouns

1. Italian has different pronoun forms for subject, object, and indirect object, plus a special category called disjunctives.

			Singular	
	Subj.	*Dir. Obj.*	*Indir. Obj.*	*Disjunctive*
I	io	mi	mi	me
you (*familiar*)	tu	ti	ti	te
he, *she*, *it*	lui	lo	gli	lui
	lei	la	le	lei
you (*polite*)	lei	la	le	lei, sè
			Plural	
we	noi	ci	ci	noi
you (*familiar*)	voi	vi	vi	voi
they	loro	li, le	loro (gli)	loro
you (*polite*)	loro	li, le	loro	loro, sè

2. Subject pronouns are often omitted when the verb ending clearly indicates the subject.

3. The second person singular form *tu* and its corresponding verb forms are used familiarly, with relatives and close friends. The polite or formal form of address is *lei*, *loro*.

4. All pronouns except disjunctives and the plural indirect object *loro* precede the verb. If both direct and indirect objects occur in the same clause, the indirect object precedes the direct object. When *gli* or *le* precedes a direct object pronoun, it is written *glie* and combined with the direct object.

Glielo do. I give it to him.

5. Personal pronouns contract with words beginning with a vowel. Exceptions are *li*, *le*, and *loro*; and *ci* does not contract with the letters *u*, *o*, *a*.

T'aspetto. I wait for you.
Ci amano. They love us.

6. The word *stesso*, self, is used with a personal pronoun for emphasis, as in English.

È venuto lui stesso. He himself came.

7. The disjunctive form, so called because it is independent of the verb, is used after prepositions, in exclamations and for emphasis, after *come* and *quanto*, after comparisons, and after *essere*.

Parlava con me. He was talking to me.

Other Pronouns and Adjectives

An adjective is used with a noun; a pronoun is used instead of a noun. In Italian, the two are often the same for the possessives, demonstratives, and interrogatives.

1. *Possessive adjectives and pronouns.* Possessives are usually preceded by the definite article. The adjectives usually precede the noun, but may follow it for emphasis.

	Masculine		*Feminine*	
	Sing.	*Pl.*	*Sing.*	*Pl.*
my	**il mio**	**i miei**	**la mia**	**le mie**
your	**il tuo**	**i tuoi**	**la tua**	**le tue**
his, her, its, your	**il suo**	**i suoi**	**la sua**	**le sue**
our	**il nostro**	**i nostri**	**la nostra**	**le nostre**
your	**il vostro**	**i vostri**	**la vostra**	**le vostre**
their, your	**il loro**	**i loro**	**la loro**	**le loro**

Since possessives agree in gender and number with the object possessed, not the possessor, the phrase *il suo libro* can mean either "his book" or "her book," depending on the context. To avoid ambiguity you may rephrase the sentence. Instead of saying *la sua casa*, you may say *la casa di Carlo* if you mean "Charles's house."

2. *Demonstrative adjectives and pronouns.* The demonstratives have the following forms:

	THIS, THIS ONE THE LATTER		THESE	
	m. sing.	*f. sing.*	*m. pl.*	*f. pl.*
	questo	**questa**	**questi**	**queste**
	THAT, THAT ONE THE FORMER		THOSE	
Before most consonants	**quel**	**quella**	**quei**	**quelle**
Before impure s, z, gn, ps	**quello**	**quella**	**quegli**	**quelle**

When the singular adjective precedes words beginning with a vowel, the final vowel of the adjective is dropped.

3. *Interrogative adjectives and pronouns.* (*a*) The interrogative *what?* is expressed by *che* as an adjective, *che cosa* (or simply *che* or *cosa*) as a pronoun. The pronoun is always singular, and the adjective has the same form with nouns of any gender and number.

Che libri hai letto? What books have you read?
Che cosa/Che/Cosa vuoi? What do you want?

(*b*) *Who*, *whom*, *whose*, is expressed by *chi* for both genders, and as a pronoun it is followed by a singular verb, unless the verb is a form of *essere*, to be. *Chi* is used with the preposition *di* to mean *whose.*

Chi va prima? Who goes first?
Con chi parlavi? Whom were you talking to?
Chi sono quelle donne? Who are those women?
Di chi è questo libro? Whose book is this?

(*c*) *Quale* and *quali* are the singular and plural forms, respectively, for *which?*, *which one?* They are used with both masculine and feminine.

Quale di quelle case e la sua?
Which one of those houses is yours?
Di quali ragazzi parli?
Which boys are you talking about?

(*d*) The adjective *quanto* has four regular endings, *-o* and *-a* in the singular, meaning *how much*, and *-i* and *-e* in the plural, meaning *how many*.

4. *Relative pronouns.* (*a*) The most common relative pronoun is *che*, who, whom, that, which. It is used as the subject or direct object of a verb, but not after a preposition.

La ragazza che parlava è mia sorella.
The girl who was speaking is my sister.
Mi piaciono i libri che mi hai dato.
I like the books (that) you gave me.

Note in the second sentence that the word for "that" may not be omitted in Italian, though it often is in English.

(*b*) *Cui* means *whom* or *which* as the object of a preposition, the one form functioning for persons and things of all genders and numbers. When preceded by a noun and the definite article, *cui* means *whose.*

i ragazzi di cui parlo
the boys of whom I am talking
la signora la cui madre è morta
the lady whose mother is dead

(*c*) *Quale* (plural *quali*) is used sparingly in place of *che* and *cui* when there is a possibility of ambiguity. It is used with the article agreeing in gender and number with its reference noun.

La figlia del professore, della quale parlavamo, è qui.
The daughter of the professor, of whom (f.) we were speaking, is here.

Quel libro e la penna con la quale scrivo sono miei.
That book and the pen with which I am writing are mine.

(*d*) *Quel che*, *ciò che*, and *quello* are different ways of saying *what*. They are singular and refer to things.

Io so quel che lui vuole.
I know what he wants.
Ciò che egli dice non è vero.
What he says is not true.

(*e*) *Chi*, meaning he who, she who, the one who, those who, is always singular, even though the English translation may be plural. It may be replaced by *colui che* (m.), *colei che* (f.), or *coloro che* (plural, using plural verb).

Chi visita l'Italia è colpito dalla sua bellezza.
He who visits (One who visits/Those who visit) Italy is (are) struck by its beauty.

Chi is at times used as a correlative pronoun, repeated before each verb.

Chi giocava, chi ballava.
Some were playing, some were dancing.

Adverbs

In Italian, adverbs are formed from adjectives in two ways. The usual form is by adding *-mente* to the feminine form, unless the ending is *-le* or *-re*, in which case the *-e* is dropped before *-mente*. Some adverbs can be formed from an adjective preceded by a preposition.

rapido **rapidamente** rapidly
felice **felicemente** happily
abile **abilmente** ably
recente **recentemente** *or* **di recente** recently
breve **brevemente** *or* **in breve** briefly

Some words function as both adjective and adverb: *basso*, *caro*, *certo*, *lontano*, *molto*, *piano*, *poco*, *proprio*, *sicuro*, *vero*, *vicino*.

Some adverbs, like adjectives, have irregular comparative and superlative forms:

Positive	*Comparative*	*Relative Superlative*	*Absolute Superlative*
bene, well	**meglio**	**il meglio**	**ottimamente**
male, badly	**peggio**	**il peggio**	**pessimamente**
molto, much	**più**	**il più**	**massimamente**
poco, little	**meno**	**il meno**	**minimamente**

Prepositions

Preposition usage is idiomatic in any language and it must be learned by exposure. The dictionary gives most equivalences. Prepositions contract with the definite article, as shown in the chart on page 344. The following prepositions, when used with a personal pronoun, must be followed by *di*:

contro against	**dopo** after	**sopra** on, upon
dentro inside	**fra** between	**sotto** under
dietro behind	**senza** without	**su** on, over

Verbs

Italian verbs have different forms for the different persons and numbers, as well as for the different tenses. The infinitive form of the verb is given in the dictionary. For a special category of verbs in Italian, the reflexive, the subject and object are the same. The infinitive form of a reflexive verb is formed by the regular infinitive without the final vowel and with an added *-si* (*lavare*, to wash; *lavarsi*, to wash oneself). These verbs are conjugated like any active verb, but they take the reflexive pronoun (*mi*, *ti*, *si*, *ci*, *vi*, *si*) that agrees in person and number with the subject. The plural form of the reflexive can express reciprocity: *Si amano*. They love each other.

Infinitives are regularly of three classes, ending in *-are*, *-ere*, or *-ire*. Conjugation tables for these regular verbs, as well as for the auxiliaries *avere* and *essere* and for many irregular verbs, are given at the end of this section.

1. Principle parts. (*a*) The *infinitive* itself is often used as a noun, (*i*) with the article as a subject of a clause, just as English uses the gerund:

Il mangiare troppo fa male.
Eating too much is harmful.

(*ii*) without the article, just as in English:

È importante dire la verità.
It is important to tell the truth.

(*iii*) as object of another verb or of a preposition:

una casa da affitare a house for rent
preferire dormire prefer to sleep

(*iv*) as an imperative:

Non fumare! Don't smoke! *or* No smoking!

(*b*) The *present gerund*, formed by dropping the infinitive ending and adding to the verb stem *-ando* for the first conjugation verbs or *-endo* for the second and third, translates the English present participle, whether or not preceded by a preposition.

Leggendo si imparano molte cose.
By reading one learns many things.
Vedendo che non c'era, andai via.
Seeing that he wasn't there, I went away.

(*c*) The *past gerund*, formed by the present gerund of the auxiliary verb and the past participle of the desired verb, is used as in English.

Essendo arrivato prima del tempo, dovetti aspettare.
Having arrived before time, I had to wait.

The gerund is also used with the present or past imperfect of the verb *stare*, stay, be, feel, to form a progressive tense.

Sto scrivendo una lettera.
I am writing a letter.

Stavo scrivendo una lettera.
I was writing a letter.

(*d*) The *present participle* of a verb is formed by adding the following endings to the verb stem: *-ante* for the first conjugation, *-ente* for the second or third. The present participle is rarely used, and some verbs do not have this form. When used it has the function of an adjective or noun: *cane dormente*, sleeping dog; *acqua corrente*, running water.

(*e*) The *past participle* of regular verbs is formed by adding to the stem *-ato*, *-uto*, or *-ito*, respectively, for the three conjugations. Many verbs, especially *-ere* verbs, have irregular past participles. The past participle is mainly used in the formation of compound tenses. In such compounds it agrees with a preceding direct object, whether noun or pronoun.

la signorina che ho invitata
the young lady I invited

The past participle is often used in an absolute construction, without the auxiliary verb.

Tornato dal lavoro è andato a dormire.
Having returned from work, he went (has gone) to sleep.

2. Verb tenses. (*a*) The *present tense* translates the English present: *parlo*, I speak, I do speak, I am speaking. Unlike English, Italian also uses the present to indicate an action that began in the past and continues in the present.

È all'ospedale da due settimane.
He (she) has been in the hospital for two weeks.

(*b*) The *imperfect* corresponds to the past progressive or to expressions showing habitual action: *piangevo*, I was crying, I used to cry, I would cry (for hours).

(*c*) The *past definite* or remote past or past absolute expresses a state of action definitely completed in the past with no relation to the present.

Prima finì gli studi e poi si sposò.
First he completed his studies and then got married.

(*d*) The *future tense* corresponds to the English future: *canterò*, I will sing. It may also be used to express probability.

Chi fischia cosi? Sarà Giuseppe.
Who is whistling so? It must be Joe.

(*e*) The *present conditional* is similar in form to the future tense and is used in expressing probability.

Io uscirei volentieri con quella signorina.
I would willingly go out with that young lady.
Egli non farebbe mai una cosa simile.
He would never do such a thing.

(*f*) The *imperative* is used as it is in English: the first person plural *Andiamo*! means Let's go! For the negative, the affirmative form is preceded by *non*: *Non parlate*! Don't speak! (plural you).

(*g*) The *subjunctive* in all its tenses is always used in a subordinate clause. Its use is determined by the verb in the main clause. The subjunctive is used primarily: (*i*) when the verb in the main clause is one of emotion, opinion, desire, command or wishes:

Speriamo che sia venuto.
We hope that he has come.
Crede lei che ella sia qui?
Do you think she is here?

(*ii*) after verbs referring to indefinite subjects and after impersonal expressions which do not express certainty:

Qui non c'è nessuno che capisca l'Italiano.
There is no one here who understands Italian.
È probabile che vengano anch'essi.
It is probable that they too will come.

BUT: **È evidente che ella non capisce questa lingua.**
It is evident that she does not understand this language.

(*iii*) after a relative superlative:

Questo è il libro più vecchio che io abbia.
This is the oldest book I have.

(*iv*) after adverbial expressions of time, purpose, condition;
(*v*) in the imperfect or pluperfect tense in *if*-clauses ex-

pressing a condition contrary to fact, with the verb of the main clause in the conditional:

Se io avessi denaro farei quel viaggio.
If I had money, I would take that trip.

(*h*) All *compound tenses* of verbs are a combination of a form of an auxiliary verb *avere*, have, or *essere*, be, and the past participle of the main verb. Most Italian verbs are conjugated with *avere*; *essere* is used with reflexive verbs, verbs used in the passive voice, impersonal verbs, and verbs of motion, the most common of which are:

andare go	**ritornare** return
venire come	**diventare** become
entrare enter	**nascere** be born
uscire go out	**morire** die
cadere fall	**essere** be
partire leave	**salire** climb
arrivare arrive	**scendere** descend
giungere arrive	**rimanere** remain

restare stay, remain

The past participle of verbs conjugated with *essere* agrees with the subject in gender and number, unless the verb is reflexive and followed by a direct object. In that case, the participle agrees with the object.

The past participle of verbs conjugated with *avere* agrees with the subject unless the verb is preceded by a direct object, in which case the participle agrees with the object.

3. Conjugating verbs. An Italian verb has two parts: the stem, which is different for each verb, and the ending, which varies according to person, number, and tense. Conjugating a verb is a matter of finding the right stem and adding the proper ending: *parl-o*, *parl-avo*, etc. A regular verb has one stem for all tenses, while an irregular verb's stem may change. The endings remain basically the same.

There are three groups of regular verbs which you will recognize by the ending of the infinitive: verbs in *-are* (*parlare*, to speak); verbs in *-ere* (*credere*, to believe); and verbs in *-ire* (*partire*, to leave; *capire*, to understand). Within the third group are two subgroups, those adding *-isc-* to the stem in some tenses and those not. In general, *-ire* verbs having a single consonant before the infinitive ending (*cap-ire*) do add *-isc-*, and those having a double consonant (*part-ire*) do not. The list which follows give three basic forms for each conjugation: infinitive, present participle, and past participle. The stem precedes the hyphen. The endings which follow it must be added to the stem of the verb you are using.

4. Model Conjugation.

1st Group	*2nd Group*	*3rd Group*	
INFINITIVE			
parl-are	**cred-ere**	**part-ire**	**cap-ire**
to speak	*to believe, think*	*to leave*	*to understand*
PAST PART.:			
parl-ato	cred-uto	part-ito	cap-ito
PRESENT PART.:			
parl-ante	cred-ente	part-ente	——

INDICATIVE

PRESENT:			
parl-o	cred-o	part-o	cap-isco
parl-i	cred-i	part-i	cap-isci
parl-a	cred-e	part-e	cap-isce
parl-iamo	cred-iamo	part-iamo	cap-iamo
parl-ate	cred-ete	part-ite	cap-ite
parl-ano	cred-ono	part-ono	cap-iscono
IMPERFECT:			
parl-avo	cred-evo	part-ivo	cap-ivo
parl-avi	cred-evi	part-ivi	cap-ivi
parl-ava	cred-eva	part-iva	cap-iva
parl-avamo	cred-evamo	part-ivamo	cap-ivamo
parl-avate	cred-evate	part-ivate	cap-ivate
parl-avano	cred-evano	part-ivano	cap-ivano
PAST DEFINITE:			
parl-ai	cred-ei	part-ii	cap-ii
parl-asti	cred-esti	part-isti	cap-isti
parl-ò	cred-è	part-ì	cap-ì
parl-ammo	cred-emmo	part-immo	cap-immo

parl-aste	cred-este	part-iste	cap-iste
parl-arono	cred-erono	part-irono	cap-irono

FUTURE:

parl-erò	cred-erò	part-irò	cap-irò
parl-erai	cred-erai	part-irai	cap-irai
parl-erà	cred-erà	part-irà	cap-irà
parl-eremo	cred-eremo	part-iremo	cap-iremo
parl-erete	cred-erete	part-irete	cap-irete
parl-eranno	cred-eranno	part-iranno	cap-ranno

CONDITIONAL:

parl-erei	cred-erei	part-irei	cap-irei
parl-eresti	cred-eresti	part-iresti	cap-iresti
parl-erebbe	cred-erebbe	part-irebbe	cap-irebbe
parl-eremmo	cred-emmo	part-iremmo	cap-iremmo
parl-ereste	cred-este	part-ireste	cap-ireste
parl-erebbero	cred-erebbero	part-irebbero	cap-irebbero

IMPERATIVE:

——	——	——	——
parl-a	cred-i	part-i	cap-isci
parl-i	cred-a	part-a	cap-isca
parl-iamo	cred-iamo	part-iamo	cap-iamo
parl-ate	cred-ete	part-ite	cap-ite
parl-ino	cred-ano	part-ano	cap-iscano

SUBJUNCTIVE

PRESENT:

parl-i	cred-a	part-a	cap-isca
parl-i	cred-a	part-a	cap-isca
parl-i	cred-a	part-a	cap-isca
parl-iamo	cred-iamo	part-iamo	cap-iamo
parl-iate	cred-iate	part-iate	cap-iate
parl-ino	cred-ano	part-ano	cap-iscano

IMPERFECT:

parl-assi	cred-essi	part-issi	cap-issi
parl-assi	cred-essi	part-issi	cap-issi
parl-asse	cred-esse	part-isse	cap-isse
parl-assimo	cred-essimo	part-issimo	cap-issimo

parl-aste	cred-este	part-iste	cap-iste
parl-assero	cred-essero	part-issero	cap-issero

PERFECT:
ho parlato, creduto, capito, etc.; sono partito, -a, etc.

PAST PERFECT:
avevo parlato, creduto, capito, etc.; ero partito, -a, etc.

FUTURE PERFECT:
avrò parlato, creduto, capito, etc.; sarò partito, -a, etc.

CONDITIONAL PERFECT:
avrei parlato, creduto, capito, etc.; sarei partito, -a, etc.

PERFECT SUBJUNCTIVE:
abbia parlato, creduto, capito, etc.; sia partito, -a, etc.

5. Auxiliary Verbs.

INF.: **avere,** to have
PAST PART.: avuto

INDICATIVE

PRESENT:

ho	abbiamo
hai	avete
ha	hanno

IMPERFECT:

avevo	avevamo
avevi	avevate
aveva	avevano

PAST DEFINITE:

ebbi	avemmo
avesti	aveste
ebbe	ebbero

FUTURE:

avrò	avremo
avrai	avrete
avrà	avranno

CONDITIONAL:

avrei	avremmo
avresti	avreste
avrebbe	avrebbero

PERFECT:

ho avuto, etc.

PAST PERFECT:

avevo avuto, etc.

FUTURE PERFECT:

avrò avuto, etc.

CONDITIONAL PERFECT:

avrei avuto, etc.

IMPERATIVE:

——	abbiamo
abbi	abbiate
abbia	abbiano

SUBJUNCTIVE

PRESENT:

abbia	abbiamo
abbia	abbiate
abbia	abbiano

IMPERFECT:

avessi	avessimo
avessi	aveste
avesse	avessere

PERFECT:

abbia avuto, etc.

INF.: **essere,** to be
PAST PART.: stato

INDICATIVE

PRESENT:

sono	siamo
sei	siete
è	sono

IMPERFECT:

ero	eravamo
eri	eravate
era	erano

PAST DEFINITE:

fui	fummo
fosti	foste

fu	furono

FUTURE:

sarò	saremo
sarai	sarete
sarà	saranno

CONDITIONAL:

sarei	saremmo
saresti	sareste
sarebbe	sarebbero

PERFECT:
sono stato, etc.

PAST PERFECT:
ero stato, etc.

FUTURE PERFECT:
sarò stato, etc.

CONDITIONAL PERFECT:
sarei stato, etc.

IMPERATIVE:

——	siamo
sii	siate
sia	siano

SUBJUNCTIVE

PRESENT:

sia	siamo
sia	siate
sia	siano

IMPERFECT:

fossi	fossimo
fossi	foste
fosse	fossero

PERFECT:
sia stato, etc.

6. Irregular verbs. This list shows the conjugations of those tenses containing irregular forms; that is, the tenses shown here cannot be derived from the "Model Conjugations." Tenses not shown are regularly formed.

accendere light PAST PART. acceso

PAST DEFINITE accesi, accendesti, accese, accendemmo, accendeste, accesero

accogliere receive, welcome PAST PART. accolto
PRESENT accolgo, accogli, accoglie, accogliamo, accogliete, accolgono
PAST DEFINITE accolsi, accogliesti, accolse, accogliemmo, accoglieste, accolsero

andare go (*Aux.*: ESSERE)
PRESENT vado, vai, va, andiamo, andate, vanno
FUTURE andrò, andrai, andrà, andremo, andrete, andranno
CONDITIONAL andrei, andresti, andrebbe, andremmo, andreste, andrebbero
IMPERATIVE và, vada, andiamo, andate, vadano
PRESENT SUBJUNCTIVE vada, vada, vada, andiamo, andiate, vadano

appartenere belong *See* TENERE

aprire open PAST PART. aperto
PAST DEFINITE aprii *or* apersi, apristi, aprì *or* aperse, aprimmo, apriste, aprirono *or* apersero

assumere assume, take, hire PAST PART. assunto
PAST DEFINITE assunsi, assumesti, assunse, assunemmo, assumeste, assunsero

bere drink (Conjugated from the old infinitive *bevere*)
PAST PART. bevuto
PAST DEFINITE bevvi, bevesti, bevve, bevemmo, beveste, bevvero
FUTURE berrò, berrai, berrà, berremo, berrete, berranno
CONDITIONAL berrei, berresti, berrebbe, berremmo, berreste, berrebbero

cadere fall (*Aux.*: ESSERE)
PAST DEFINITE caddi, cadesti, cadde, cademmo, cadeste, caddero
FUTURE cadrò, cadrai, cadrà, cadremo, cadrete, cadranno
CONDITIONAL cadrei, cadresti, cadrebbe, cadremmo, cadreste, cadrebbero

chiedere ask PAST PART. chiesto
PAST DEFINITE chiesi, chiedesti, chiese, chiedemmo, chiedeste, chiesero

chiudere close PAST PART. chiuso
PAST DEFINITE chiusi, chiudesti, chiuse, chiudemmo, chiudeste, chiusero

concedere grant, concede PAST PART. concesso
PAST DEFINITE concessi, concedesti, concesse, concedemmo, concedeste, concessero

conoscere know PAST PART. conosciuto
PAST DEFINITE conobbi, conoscesti, conobbe, conoscemmo, conosceste, conobbero

coprire cover PAST PART. coperto

correggere correct PAST PART. corretto
PAST DEFINITE corressi, correggesti, corresse, correggemmo. correggeste, corressero

correre run (*Aux.*: ESSERE when it means from one place to another; otherwise AVERE) PAST PART. corso
PAST DEFINITE corsi, corresti, corse, corremmo, correste, corsero

crescere grow (*Aux.*: ESSERE except when it has a direct object) PAST PART. cresciuto
PAST DEFINITE crebbi, crescesti, crebbe, crescemmo, cresceste, crebbero

cuocere cook PAST PART. cotto
PRESENT cuocio, cuoci, cuoce, cuociamo *or* cociamo, cuocete *or* cocete, cuociono
PAST DEFINITE cossi, cocesti, cosse, cuocemmo, cuoceste, cossero
PRESENT SUBJUNCTIVE cuocia, cuocia, cuocia, cuociamo, cuociate, cuociano

dare give PAST PART. dato
PRESENT do, dai, dà, diamo, date, danno
PAST DEFINITE diedi, desti, diede, demmo, deste, diedero

IMPERFECT davo, davi, dava, davamo, davate, davano
FUTURE darò, darai, darà, daremo, darete, daranno
CONDITIONAL darei, daresti, darebbe, daremmo, dareste, darebbero
IMPERATIVE dà, dia, daimo, date, diano
PRESENT SUBJUNCTIVE dia, dia, dia, diamo, diate, diano
IMPERFECT SUBJUNCTIVE dessi, dessi, desse, dessimo, deste, dessero

decidere decide PAST PART. deciso
PAST DEFINITE decisi, decidesti, decise, decidemmo, decideste, decisero

difendere defend PAST PART. difeso
PAST DEFINITE difesi, difendesti, difese, difendemmo, difendeste, difesero

dire say, tell (Conjugated from old infinitive *dicere*) PAST PART. detto
PRESENT GERUND dicendo
PRESENT dico, dici, dice, diciamo, dite, dicono
PAST DEFINITE dissi, dicesti, disse, dicemmo, diceste, dissero
IMPERFECT dicevo, dicevi, diceva, dicevamo, dicevate, dicevano
FUTURE dirò, dirai, dirà, diremo, direte, diranno
CONDITIONAL direi, diresti, direbbe, diremmo, direste, direbbero
IMPERATIVE di' *or* dici, dica, diciamo, dite, dicano
PRESENT SUBJUNCTIVE dica, dica, dica, diciamo, diciate, dicano
IMPERFECT SUBJUNCTIVE dicessi, dicessi, dicesse, dicessimo, diceste, dicessero

discutere discuss PAST PART. discusso
PAST DEFINITE discussi, discutesti, discusse, discutemmo, discuteste, discussero

dividere divide PAST PART. diviso
PAST DEFINITE divisi, dividesti, divise, dividemmo, divideste, divisero

dovere have, must PAST PART. dovuto

PRESENT devo *or* debbo, devi, deve, dobbiamo, dovete, devono *or* debbono

PAST DEFINITE dovei *or* dovetti, dovesti, dovè *or* dovette, dovemmo, doveste, doverono *or* dovettero

FUTURE dovrò, dovrai, dovrà, dovremo, dovrete, dovranno

CONDITIONAL dovrei, dovresti, dovrebbe, dovremmo, dovreste, dovrebbero

PRESENT SUBJUNCTIVE deva, deva, deva (*or* debba, debba, debba), dobbiamo, dobbiate, devano *or* debbano

fare do, make (Conjugated from the old infinitive *facere*) PAST PART. fatto

PRESENT GERUND facendo

PRESENT faccio, fai, fa, facciamo, fate, fanno

PAST DEFINITE feci, facesti, fece, facemmo, faceste, fecero

IMPERFECT facevo, facevi, faceva, facevamo, facevate, facevano

FUTURE farò, farai, farà, faremo, farete, faranno

CONDITIONAL farei, faresti, farebbe, faremmo, fareste, farebbero

IMPERATIVE fà, faccia, facciamo, fate, facciano

PRESENT SUBJUNCTIVE faccia, faccia, faccia, facciamo, facciate, facciano

IMPERFECT SUBJUNCTIVE facessi, facessi, facesse, facessimo, faceste, facessero

giungere arrive, reach (*Aux.*: ESSERE) PAST PART. giunto

PAST DEFINITE giunsi, giungesti, giunse, giungemmo, giungeste, giunsero

leggere read PAST PART. letto

PAST DEFINITE lessi, leggesti, lesse, leggemmo, leggeste, lessero

mantenere maintain, keep, support *See* TENERE

mettere put PAST PART. messo

PAST DEFINITE misi, mettesti, mise, mettemmo, metteste, misero

mordere bite PAST PART. morso

PAST DEFINITE morsi, mordesti, morse, mordemmo, mordeste, morsero

morire die (*Aux.*: ESSERE) PAST PART. morto
PRESENT muoio, muori, muore, moriamo, morite, muoiono
FUTURE morrò, morrai, morrà, morremo, morrete, morranno
CONDITIONAL morrei, morresti, morrebbe, morremmo, morreste, morrebbero
IMPERATIVE muori, muoia, moriamo, morite, muoiano
PRESENT SUBJUNCTIVE muoia, muoia, muoia, moriamo, moriate, muoiano
NOTE: The regular forms for the future and conditional are also used.

muovere move (*Not* to change residence) PAST PART. mosso
PRESENT muovo, muovi, muove, moviamo, movete, muovono
PAST DEFINITE mossi, movesti, mosse, movemmo, moveste, mossero
IMPERATIVE muovi, muova, muoviamo, movete, muovano
PRESENT SUBJUNCTIVE muova, muova, muova, moviamo, moviate, muovano

nascere be born (*Aux.*: ESSERE) PAST PART. nato
PAST DEFINITE egli nacque, essi nacquero

nascondere hide, conceal PAST PART. nascosto
PAST DEFINITE nascosi, nascondesti, nascose, nascondemmo, nascondeste, nascosero

offendere offend PAST PART. offeso
PAST DEFINITE offesi, offendesti, offese, offendemmo, offendeste, offesero

offrire offer PAST PART. offerto
PAST DEFINITE offrii *or* offersi, offristi, offrì *or* offerse, offrimmo, offriste, offrirono *or* offersero

perdere lose PAST PART. perduto *or* perso
PAST DEFINITE persi *or* perdei *or* perdetti, perdesti, perse *or*

perdè *or* perdette, perdemmo, perdeste, persero *or* perderono *or* perdettero

persuadere persuade PAST PART. persuaso
PAST DEFINITE persuasi, persuadesti, persuase, persuademmo, persuadeste, persuasero

piacere like, please (*Aux.*: ESSERE) PAST PART. piaciuto
PRESENT piaccio, piaci, piace, piacciamo, piacete, piacciono
PAST DEFINITE piacqui, piacesti, piacque, piacemmo, piaceste, piacquero
PRESENT SUBJUNCTIVE piaccia, piaccia, piaccia, piacciamo, piacciate, piacciano
NOTE: This verb is used mostly in the third person singular and plural.

piangere cry, weep PAST PART. pianto
PAST DEFINITE piansi, piangesti, pianse, piangemmo, piangeste, piansero

porre (ponere) put, place PAST PART. posto
PRESENT GERUND ponendo
PRESENT pongo, poni, pone, poniamo, ponete, pongono
PAST DEFINITE posi, ponesti, pose, ponemmo, poneste, posero
FUTURE porrò, porrai, porrà, porremo, porrete, porranno
CONDITIONAL porrei, porresti, porrebbe, porremmo, porreste, porrebbero
IMPERFECT ponevo, ponevi, poneva, ponevamo, ponevate, ponevano
IMPERATIVE poni, ponga, poniamo, ponete, pongano
PRESENT SUBJUNCTIVE ponga, ponga, ponga, poniamo, poniate, pongano
IMPERFECT SUBJUNCTIVE ponessi, ponessi, ponesse, ponessimo, poneste, ponessero

potere be able to, can, may
PRESENT posso, puoi, può, possiamo, potete, possono
FUTURE potrò, potrai, potrà, potremo, potrete, potranno
CONDITIONAL potrei, potresti, potrebbe, potremmo, potreste, potrebbero

IMPERATIVE possa, possa, possiamo, possiate, possano
PRESENT SUBJUNCTIVE possa, possa, possa, possiamo, possiate, possano

prendere take PAST PART. preso
PAST DEFINITE presi, prendesti, prese, prendemmo, prendeste, presero

produrre produce *See* CONDURRE

radere shave PAST PART. raso
PAST DEFINITE rasi, radesti, rase, rademmo, radeste, rasero

rendere render, give back PAST PART. reso
PAST DEFINITE resi, rendesti, rese, rendemmo, rendeste, resero

ridere laugh PAST PART. riso
PAST DEFINITE risi, ridesti, rise, ridemmo, rideste, risero

rimanere remain (*Aux.*: ESSERE) PAST PART. rimasto
PRESENT rimango, rimani, rimane, rimaniano, rimanete, rimangono
PAST DEFINITE rimasi, rimanesti, rimase, rimanemmo, rimaneste, rimasero
FUTURE rimarrò, rimarrai, rimarrà, rimarremo, rimarrete, rimarranno
CONDITIONAL rimarrei, rimarresti, rimarrebbe, rimarremmo, rimarreste, rimarrebbero
IMPERATIVE rimani, rimanga, rimaniamo, rimanete, rimangano
PRESENT SUBJUNCTIVE rimanga, rimanga, rimanga, rimaniamo, rimaniate, rimangano

rispondere answer, reply PAST PART. risposto
PAST DEFINITE risposi, rispondesti, rispose, rispondemmo, rispondeste, risposero

ritenere retain *See* TENERE

rompere break PAST PART. rotto
PAST DEFINITE ruppi, rompesti, ruppe, rompemmo, rompeste, ruppero

salire go up, climb, ascend, get on (*Aux.*: ESSERE)
PRESENT salgo, sali, sale, saliamo, salite, salgono
IMPERATIVE sali, salga, saliamo, salite, salgano
PRESENT SUBJUNCTIVE salga, salga, salga, saliamo, saliate, salgano

sapere know, know how
PRESENT so, sai, sa, sappiamo, sapete, sanno
PAST DEFINITE seppi, sapesti, seppe, sapemmo, sapeste, seppero
FUTURE saprò, saprai, saprà, sapremo, saprete, sapranno
CONDITIONAL saprei, sapresti, saprebbe, sapremmo, sapreste, saprebbero
IMPERATIVE sappi, sappia, sappiamo, sappiate, sappiano
PRESENT SUBJUNCTIVE sappia, sappia, sappia, sappiamo, sappiate, sappiano

scendere descend, go down, get off (*Aux.*: ESSERE)
PAST PART. sceso
PAST DEFINITE scesi, scendesti, scese, scendemmo, scendeste, scesero

sciogliere untie, dissolve, melt PAST PART. sciolto
PAST DEFINITE sciolsi, sciogliesti, sciolse, sciogliemmo, scioglieste, sciolsero
IMPERATIVE sciogli, sciolga, sciogliamo, sciogliete, sciolgano
PRESENT SUBJUNCTIVE sciolga, sciolga, sciolga, sciogliamo, sciogliate, sciolgano

scoprire discover PAST PART. scoperto
PAST DEFINITIVE scoprii *or* scopersi, scopristi, scoprì *or* scoperse, scoprimmo, scopriste, scoprirono *or* scopersero

scrivere write PAST PART. scritto
PAST DEFINITIVE scrissi, scrivesti, scrisse, scrivemmo, scriveste, scrissero

sedere sit (*Aux.*: ESSERE, except with a direct object)
PRESENT siedo *or* seggo, siedi, siede, sediamo, sedete, siedono *or* seggano
IMPERATIVE siedi, segga, sediamo, sedete, seggano

PRESENT SUBJUNCTIVE segga, segga, segga (*or* sieda, sieda, sieda), sediamo, sediate, seggano *or* siedano

sorgere arise, rise PAST PART. sorto

PAST DEFINITE sorsi, sorgesti, sorse, sorgemmo, sorgeste, sorsero

spendere spend PAST PART. speso

PAST DEFINITE spesi, spendesti, spese, spendemmo, spendeste, spesero

stare stay, be, stand, feel (*Aux.*: ESSERE) PAST PART. stato

PRESENT sto, stai, sta, stiamo, state, stanno

PAST DEFINITE stetti, stesti, stette, stemmo, steste, stettero

IMPERFECT stavo, stavi, stava, stavamo, stavate, stavano

FUTURE starò, starai, starà, staremo, starete, staranno

CONDITIONAL starei, staresti, starebbe, staremmo, stareste, starebbero

IMPERATIVE stà, stia, stiamo, state, stiano

PRESENT SUBJUNCTIVE stia, stia, stia, stiamo, stiate, stiano

IMPERFECT SUBJUNCTIVE stessi, stessi, stesse, stessimo, steste, stessero

supporre suppose *See* PORRE

tacere be silent, keep quiet PAST PART. taciuto

PRESENT taccio, taci, tace, taciamo, tacete, tacciono

PAST DEFINITE tacqui, tacesti, tacque, tacemmo, tacete, tacquero

IMPERATIVE taci, taccia, taciamo, tacete, tacciano

PRESENT SUBJUNCTIVE taccia, taccia, taccia, tacciamo, tacciate, tacciano (May also be written with one *c*.)

tenere hold, have, keep

PRESENT tengo, tieni, tiene, teniamo, tenete, tengono

PAST DEFINITE tenni, tenesti, tenne, tenemmo, teneste, tennero

FUTURE terrò, terrai, terrà, terremo, terrete, terranno

CONDITIONAL terrei, terresti, terrebbe, terremmo, terreste, terrebbero

IMPERATIVE tieni, tenga, teniamo, tenete, tengano

PRESENT SUBJUNCTIVE tenga, tenga, tenga, teniamo, teniate, tengano

trarre draw out; drag, haul, derive PAST PART. tratto
PRESENT GERUND traendo
PRESENT traggo, trai, trae, traiamo, traete, traggono
PAST DEFINITE trassi, traesti, trasse, traemmo, traeste, trassero
IMPERFECT traevo, traevi, traeva, traevamo, traevate, traevano
FUTURE trarrò, trarrai, trarrà, trarremo, trarrete, trarranno
CONDITIONAL trarrei, trarresti, trarrebbe, trarremmo, trarreste, trarrebbero
IMPERATIVE trai, tragga, traiamo, traete, traggano
PRESENT SUBJUNCTIVE tragga, tragga, tragga, traiamo, traiate, traggano
IMPERFECT SUBJUNCTIVE traessi, traessi, traesse, traessimo, traeste, traessero

uccidere kill PAST PART. ucciso
PAST DEFINITE uccisi, uccidesti, uccise, uccidemmo, uccideste, uccisero

udire hear
PRESENT odo, odi, ode, udiamo, udite, odono
IMPERATIVE odi, oda, udiamo, udite, odano
PRESENT SUBJUNCTIVE oda, oda, oda, udiamo, udiate, odano

uscire go out (*Aux.*: ESSERE)
PRESENT esco, esci, esce, usciamo, uscite, escono
IMPERATIVE esci, esca, usciamo, uscite, escano

valere be worth (*Aux.*: ESSERE) PAST PART. valso
PRESENT valgo, vali, vale, valiamo, valete, valgono
PAST DEFINITE valsi, valesti, valse, valemmo, valeste, valsero
FUTURE varrò, varrai, varrà, varremo, varrete, varranno
CONDITIONAL varrei, varresti, varrebbe, varremmo, varreste, varrebbero
IMPERATIVE vali, valga, valiamo, valete, valgano
PRESENT SUBJUNCTIVE valga, valga, valga, valiamo, valiate, valgano

NOTE: Usually only the third person singular and plural of this verb are used.

vedere see PAST PART. visto *or* veduto
PAST DEFINITE vidi, vedesti, vide, vedemmo, vedeste, videro
FUTURE vedrò, vedrai, vedrà, vedremo, vedrete, vedranno
CONDITIONAL vedrei, vedresti, vedrebbe, vedremmo, vedreste, vedrebbero

venire come (*Aux.*: ESSERE) PAST PART. venuto
PRESENT vengo, vieni, viene, veniamo, venite, vengono
PAST DEFINITE venni, venisti, venne, venimmo, veniste, vennero
FUTURE verrò, verrai, verrà, verremo, verrete, verranno
CONDITIONAL verrei, verresti, verrebbe, verremmo, verreste, verrebbero
IMPERATIVE vieni, venga, veniamo, venite, vengano
PRESENT SUBJUNCTIVE venga, venga, venga, veniamo, veniate, vengano

vincere win PAST PART. vinto
PAST DEFINITE vinsi, vincesti, vinse, vincemmo, vinceste, vinsero

vivere live (*Aux.*: AVERE if followed by a direct object; otherwise ESSERE.) PAST PART. vissuto
PAST DEFINITE vissi, vivesti, visse, vivemmo, viveste, vissero
FUTURE vivrò, vivrai, vivrà, vivremo, vivrete, vivranno
CONDITIONAL vivrei, vivresti, vivrebbe, vivremmo, vivreste, vivrebbero

volere want, be willing, desire, wish
PRESENT voglio, vuoi, vuole, vogliamo, volete, vogliono
PAST DEFINITE volli, volesti, volle, volemmo, voleste, vollero
FUTURE vorrò, vorrai, vorrà, vorremo, vorrete, vorranno
CONDITIONAL vorrei, vorresti, vorrebbe, vorremmo, vorreste, vorrebbero
IMPERATIVE (rarely used) vogli, voglia, vogliamo, vogliate, vogliano
PRESENT SUBJUNCTIVE voglia, voglia, voglia, vogliamo, vogliate, vogliano